The Republic Reborn

New Studies in American Intellectual and Cultural History
THOMAS BENDER, CONSULTING EDITOR

The Republic Reborn

War and the Making of Liberal America,
1790–1820

Steven Watts

The Johns Hopkins University Press
Baltimore and London

This book has been brought to
publication with the generous
assistance of the National Endowment
for the Humanities.

The Johns Hopkins University Press
701 West 40th Street
Baltimore, Maryland 21211
The Johns Hopkins Press Ltd., London

Originally published, 1987
Johns Hopkins Paperbacks edition, 1989

Library of Congress Cataloging-in-Publication Data
Watts, Steven, 1952–
The republic reborn.
(New studies in American intellectual and cultural history)
Bibliography: p.
Includes index.
1. United States—Politics and government—
1789–1815. 2. Liberalism—United States—History.
3. United States—History—War of 1812—Influence.
4. United States—Civilization—1783–1865. I. Title.
II. Series.
E310.W37   1987   973.5   87-4147
ISBN 0-8018-3420-1 (alk. paper)
ISBN 0-8018-3941-6 (pbk.)

For a remarkable trio among twelve siblings,
two generations in my family past:
Clare Kunz McLaughlin, an inspiring and demanding
late-Victorian schoolteacher;
Clarence "Bud" Kunz, a shrewd and cantankerous
old dirt farmer;
and Gladys Kunz Watts, an enduring matron
devoted to church and community.
In their own special way,
each has taught me more about the human meanings
of historical change than any book ever could.

Contents

Acknowledgments

Acknowledgments in first books, like acceptance speeches for Academy Awards, often inspire homocidal fantasies in audiences by dint of gushing displays of sentiment and self-indulgence. This one will be no different.

To begin with, I owe a large debt of gratitude to all those in my family who have supported my studying and writing over the years. This includes a great many people, but especially my parents, Kenneth and Mary Watts, whose warm and steady encouragement has been nourishing, Daniel P. C. Watts, whose equestrian showmanship has been inspiring, Julie Watts Brown, whose friendship and irreverent sense of humor have been a delight, and "Nick" Watts, whose recumbent, detached sense of life has provided a useful perspective on academic endeavor. My thanks also go to a number of individuals for their friendship and interest: Loren and Anita Nikolai, Mitchell Guthrie, Kathleen Wells-Morgan, Arthur and Kathryn Messier, Virginia Thompson, and Mark Thomas. The motley group at Rothwell Gym on MWF did nothing for this book, but they got me away from it and helped sharpen something more important: my jump shot.

A host of people at the University of Missouri can never be adequately repaid for all of their assistance. Among the many graduate students in the Department of History who read and commented on parts of the manuscript at various stages, three stand out. Kenneth Plax taught me what it meant to be an intellectual, in the best sense of that term. Besides being one of a small group of people who make me feel lazy, Robert Hunt was a caring and imaginative critic. Susan Curtis Mernitz, in countless conversations over coffee, shared generously of her knowledge and sensitivity to keep me focused on the big social and cultural issues in nineteenth-century America. She also helped me referee a recurring intellectual tag-team wrestling match between Marx, Freud, Weber, and Calvin. In addition, Susan Yarbro and Patty Eggleston skillfully reproduced the manuscript on a word processor as it was pounded into shape, while Anne Edwards and Patsy Hahn at Ellis Library helped secure many important research materials. The University of Missouri Faculty Research Council generously provided funds to help defray the costs of typing.

Numerous faculty colleagues in the Missouri History Department have provided various kinds of friendship and support: N. Gerald Barrier, Richard Bienvenu, John L. Bullion, Gerard H. Clarfield, Robert Collins, John Lankford, Kerby Miller, and the late Fordyce Mitchel. Special thanks go to Thomas B. Alexander, whose radically different approach to history has not kept him from helping me professionally in every way possible, and to Noble E. Cunningham, Jr., who tolerated with good humor my sometimes soaring interpretations while offering his unsurpassed knowledge of Jeffersonian America. More recently, a new group of comrades and colleagues— Tani Barlow, Susan Benson, Dina Copelman, Robbie Lieberman, David Roediger, Jonathan Sperber, and Eli Zaretsky—have not only read and criticized portions of the manuscript, but also created a congenial and exciting intellectual community in which to work.

Several people at the Johns Hopkins University Press have resolutely seen this project through to completion. Peggy Hoover served as a careful and discerning copy editor and saved me from numerous infelicities in my writing. Both Henry Y. K. Tom and Thomas Bender steered me through the long process of revision and publication. Their calm efficiency, good-natured guidance, and perceptive recommendations have made them everything editors should be.

A number of scholars interested in early American liberalism have kindly read all or part of the book and offered a wealth of insights and suggestions. These include Drew R. McCoy, Cathy N. Davidson, Daniel Walker Howe, Gordon S. Wood, Christopher Lasch, and especially Alfred Young, Linda K. Kerber, and James A. Henretta. Joyce Appleby has been in a class by herself. Her willingness to take the project seriously at a very early stage, her keen criticism, and her unfailing encouragement have inspired me as a model of scholarly generosity.

Two people have earned my greatest gratitude. T. J. Jackson Lears saw this manuscript struggle to life in its earliest form and my debt to him is enormous. He opened doors to many new intellectual worlds, his advice forced me both to tighten my conceptualizations and to expand my imagination, and his own work provided an example of intellectual power and moral commitment. And he's not a bad tennis player. Very special thanks go to Barbara Brockman. She endured this undertaking for a long time, helped with the expenses incurred, and offered love and emotional support at home. She often has reminded me, unintentionally, that there are things more important than history.

Introduction

The liberal tradition in America used to be taken for granted. Like cheap land, large breakfasts, and sin, it has been an American article of faith for two centuries. Most citizens of the New World's largest republic have traditionally found comfort in viewing themselves as fundamentally different from their European progenitors, as members of a liberal society happily devoid of feudal traditions and class distinctions and devoted to individual expression, social mobility, pragmatic self-interest, and protection of property rights. A dizzying variety of cultural spokesmen and critics have proclaimed this "exceptionalism": Benjamin Franklin and Alexis de Tocqueville, Horatio Alger and Theodore Roosevelt, Ralph Waldo Emerson and Dale Carnegie, Mark Twain and Edmund Wilson. Moreover, the nation's most eminent historians have often moved to the forefront in confirming or confronting this American presumption. From George Bancroft, who apotheosized it, to Frederick Jackson Turner, who charted its westward movement, to Charles Beard, who challenged its verities, to Louis Hartz, who delineated it, to Richard Hofstadter, who disparaged it, the sovereignty of the republic's liberal heritage has seemed unassailable. By mid-twentieth century, doubts had all but vanished. America had been born free with the first brave settlements in the early 1600s, and the rest of its history consisted of a fulfillment of destiny, of variations on a theme.[1]

Yet things have changed. Cheap land has given way to suburban sprawl and agribusiness, sausage and eggs to fruit juice and bran flakes, and human depravity to "inappropriate behavior." And the liberal reading of the American experience has become less persuasive, its plot less compelling, its subject less monolithic in recent decades. For many citizens certain public problems—civil rights controversy, divisive foreign war, political corruption—have tainted the image of a pristine liberal society dedicated to social striving, material prosperity, and personal achievement. For historians, however, doubts also have crept in through two scholarly, serpentine passageways.

First, beginning in the 1960s practitioners of the "new" social and labor history discovered not universal acclamation of opportunity, competition, and individualism in America's past, but rather a heritage of ethnic and racial division, frequent episodes of class-based dissent from liberal authority, and strong "premodern" loyalties to clan and community dating back to the earliest colonial settlements. Moreover, in linking ideas to material and social interests many have suggested that the development of American liberalism cannot be divorced from the evolution of its capitalism. Thus power, resistance, and accommodation—*not* consensus—flavor this fresh telling of our history.[2]

Second, intellectual historians focusing on American "republicanism"—this trend also gathered stream in the 1960s—have concluded that John Locke, contractualism, and natural rights did not form the mainspring of American Revolutionary ideology. Instead, they demonstrated convincingly that republican values of "virtue" (devotion to the public good over self-interest), "civic humanism" (participation in a republic promotes the full flowering of human potential), and "independence" (the social and political integrity of the small producer) not only pervaded the political culture of late eighteenth-century America, but also extended its influence well into the nineteenth century. Here citizenship and public-mindedness, not private enterprise and social mobility, color a retouched portrait of the nation's founding.[3]

So while virtually no one disputes that liberal values had become the official ideology of dominant social groups in the United States by the mid-1800s—the facts of galloping industrialization, leaping westward growth, and a powerful Victorian culture make the conclusion difficult to avoid[4]—the sweep of the liberal tradition has been called into question. Socially, its pervasiveness among, and attractiveness to, all classes and ethnic groups appears far less certain than it once did. Historically, its appearance in American life seems equally shadowy. Exactly when, why, and how did a liberal creed of self-made success and competitive materialism come to overshadow the republican canon of America's revolutionary age? Thus the modern historian of early American liberalism faces an imposing twofold task. First, the association of liberal values and liberal consciousness with the social relations and culture òf capitalism demands extended exploration and explanation. Second, the long-buried historical process that shaped the dynamic liberal society evident in Jacksonian America, but missing earlier, needs to be unearthed and analyzed.

In *The Republic Reborn*, I address these difficulties and attempt to resolve them, at least in part, by advancing three broad and interrelated contentions. First, a preponderance of evidence suggests that the decades from 1790 to 1820 encompassed a massive, multifaceted transformation away from republican traditions and toward modern liberal capitalism in America. This sea change involved the consolidation of a market economy and society, a liberal political structure and ideology, and a bourgeois culture of self-controlled individualism. Second, this study proposes that the War of 1812—both as fantasy and reality—played a crucial role in this crystallizing process by energizing and validating larger liberalizing impulses in early nineteenth-century America. Serving as a vehicle for the forces of change *and* offering an outlet for the anxieties of a changing society, the war ultimately intensified and sanctioned the imperatives of a developing world-view. Third, I contend that a particular social group—middle- and upper-class elites, most of them articulate writers and speakers, who were important members of the post-1800 Jeffersonian Republican majority—took the lead both in advancing liberal ideals and in sanctifying them in war. The nature, thrust, and implications of this three-pronged argument require a few additional words of explanation.

Taken as a whole, this book suggests a new interpretive synthesis for understanding the decades of the early American republic. The political founding of the nation has long preoccupied scholars, of course, and the historiography of the years from 1790 to 1820 traditionally has been the domain of political historians. Only in the last twenty years has this body of work been broadened extensively by the rediscovery of Revolutionary republicanism and forays into social, cultural, and economic history. While recent work remains rather diffuse conceptually, taken together it points to a fundamental reshaping of American life in the three decades after the ratification of the Constitution. Monographs by such scholars as Gordon Wood, Joyce Appleby, Joseph Ellis, and Michael Rogin have illuminated different dimensions of the late-eighteenth-century breakup of republican categories and their realignment into new patterns.[5] I build on this scholarship, yet to try to go beyond it by weaving together social, cultural, psychological, and political trends that have heretofore been treated in isolation. By proposing an interconnected shift toward liberal capitalism as the crucial fact of early national life, this study offers an overarching theoretical framework that reintegrates fragments of experience from this age of profound change. It shows that a liberal revolution in the early republic, and the important role played by war in that process, comprised a long first step in the creation of modern, industrial America.

Yet this fundamental shift in the early republic, though broad and far-reaching, did not appear as stormy or even dramatic. To the contrary, a complex subtlety defined its nature and often befuddled participants. While republican society and liberal society represented different stages in the historical development of the postfeudal West, they did not stand diametrically opposed in America, as some scholars would have it, with defenders of civic virtue angrily arrayed against the minions of self-regarding individualism. Instead, as I show in the following pages, republican traditions served as a seedbed for the growth of liberal commitments. The eighteenth-century notion of "independence," for instance, at once maintained a significantly different social meaning from nineteenth-century "self-interest" while also providing a conceptual foundation for the latter's growth. Moreover, impulses toward individual gain and status-seeking certainly existed in colonial America, but they circulated as nascent, half-formed conceptions lacking the intellectual and economic framework to provide true legitimacy. Only in the period of the early republic did they gain solidity and widespread approval and cohere into a social creed. Thus the story unfolded here is not an epic of heroic confrontation or sinister purpose, but rather a tangled tale of discovery: of half-conscious motives, unintended consequences, frequent self-deception, and new meanings for old words.

The Republic Reborn also attempts to contribute to a more comprehensive and nuanced understanding of war and its role in the development of modern Western society. Perhaps influenced by a boyhood in Springfield, Illinois, where the currents of the Civil War still run strong, or by coming of age in a period of intense agitation over the Vietnam conflict, I always have suspected that war involves far more than foreign affairs, strategic maneuver, or power politics. Several trenchant studies encountered over the years—Richard Slotkin's *Regeneration Through Violence*, George Frederickson's *The Inner Civil War*, and Richard Hofstadter's "Cuba, the Philippines, and Manifest Destiny,"[6] among others—reinforced this suspicion by suggesting that the attraction that war holds for Americans has sprung less from calculating assessments of policy and power and more from some fundamental national dynamic of social psychology, cultural aspiration, and sense of collective experience. Indeed, as the sources began to speak from the American early republic, it became apparent that what was projected onto the looming conflict of 1812—fantasies and nightmares, visceral emotions and lofty ideals—often influenced people's views and actions more than a detached analysis of policy and instrumentality. For many citizens, the British confrontation appeared as an immense blank slate on which they wrote their hopes and fears. It also appeared evident that the stuff of this projection emerged from wrenching historical change in the early-nineteenth-century republic.

The "critical theorists" associated with the German-American Frankfurt School proved especially useful for trying to make sense of this situation. Bringing together the theoretical work of Karl Marx and Sigmund Freud, thinkers like Max Horkheimer and Herbert Marcuse focused on the dialectical development of modern capitalism and modern personality structure in the West. Along with a number of other scholars—Michael Walzer, Richard Sennett, Erik Erikson, Richard Slotkin, Michael Rogin, for instance—they suggest that socioeconomic structures, private states of mind, and the seductions of war are inextricably linked for modern man. Drawing on such efforts, this study attempts to sustain a sensitivity to the personal nuances of changing modes of authority and experience in the early American republic and to examine how they partially surfaced in an early-nineteenth-century war crisis. In other words, the argument attempts to relocate the military confrontation of 1812 in the larger historical logic of consolidating liberal capitalism. By viewing this conflict as emerging from a complex historical matrix of social change, cultural tension, and attenuating personality structure, we may gain fresh insights into the nature of modern war.[7]

In the broadest sense, the notion of "cultural hegemony" provides the interpretive framework for this study. First offered by Antonio Gramsci and later developed by a number of English and American historical theorists, this concept refers to the way by which dominant class values, organization, and definitions of reality seem to attract "spontaneous" loyalty rather than simply being imposed on society through brute force. Its proponents contend that ruling groups achieve and maintain social power not so much through economic intimidation or police strength—although this is indeed part of the picture—but rather through successfully prescribing the conventional wisdom of a society, defining its criteria of success, and establishing the acceptable boundaries of discourse. The great danger of this scheme lies in a tendency to oversimplify—to use cultural hegemony, first, as a limp, intellectualist version of "social control" with ideas taking the place of guns and institutions or, second, to use it as a theory describing a static situation of authority relationships, a frozen social landscape where the ideology of the powerful, like those horrifying blobs that regularly level the world's cities in B-grade science fiction movies, has descended to crush everything before it. Raymond Williams mapped a way around such crude formulations by explaining that cultural hegemony results from the interaction of "dominant," "residual," and "emergent" cultures in any society. Dominant ideologies do not appear alone on historical center stage, he rightly insists, but interact with a background chorus of dissent that mingles both older traditions and avant-garde values. Jackson Lears added that hegemonists should avoid envisioning a "closed system of ruling class domination" and instead cultivate a greater sensitivity to "the creation of counter hegemonies." They should recognize the "complex interaction of relatively autonomous spheres (public and private; political, cultural, and economic) within a totality of attitudes and practices." In Lears' felicitous phrase, the historian of cultural hegemony must "take a banal question—'who has power'—and deepen it at both ends."[8]

Thus, what follows is an attempt to understand and explain cultural hegemony as a *process*, as something that not simply is, but continually *becomes*. In my examination of the immensely complicated shift of liberal capitalist values from an "emergent" to a "dominant" position in early national America, two factors—an influential social-political group, and the specter of war—moved steadily to the explanatory forefront. First, the crucial role of articulate Jeffersonian Republicans became obvious. In reading practically everything written and printed by Jeffersonians between 1810 and 1815, and a large sample of that produced between 1790 and 1820—speeches, sermons, essays, newspapers, pamphlets, and novels from all over the nation—I began to grasp their importance as shapers and popularizers of a liberal creed in the transforming young republic. These men enthusiastically embraced, or just as frequently they stumbled half-consciously toward, the notion of self-made man, or the ethos of self-control, or the vision of a productive entrepreneurial economy based on the home market. Not themselves a majority of the American citizenry or typical "common" men, young Jeffersonian leaders proved significant beyond their numbers. These moralists, ministers, and politicians set the tone and defined the issues of public discussion in the early nineteenth century. Quite simply, men like Henry Clay, "Parson" Mason Weems, and Mathew Carey became important spokesmen for an emerging new dominant culture. As their history reveals, however, the process of cultural hegemony moves only infrequently according to purposive action and clear intent. A volatile compound of ambivalence and struggling redefinition propelled most influential Jeffersonians into a liberal future.

Their psychological states proved as important as their ideological inclinations, their cultural anxieties as critical as their concern with social power. Indeed, these factors emerged from historical shadows as completely inseparable. In addition, the role of war in making this hegemonic process "work" seemed equally evident, if not always easily fathomed. Endorsing conflict with Great Britain in 1812 for complicated reasons—social, cultural, psychological, political—an articulate Republican elite illustrated how war expressed congealing liberal values, but as well vented frustrations accruing to historical change. Here too the growing cultural hegemony of liberal capitalism resulted quite as much from private need and unforeseen consequences as from intentionality.

A special methodological procedure requires brief mention. The following pages contain some two dozen short biographies of significant Jeffersonians, presented either as free-standing essays in the first four chapters or woven into the narrative, as in the last two chapters. Presented partly for dramatic effect as a way to animate lifeless historical abstractions, the stories of these *dramatis personae* serve other purposes as well. In one sense they are a contribution to what Gore Vidal has called "the art of the biographical sketch." These treatments of the single life do not emulate the recent multivolume tradition in early national biography, but instead modestly try to follow in the giant footsteps of writers like Richard Hofstadter in *The American Political Tradition* and Edmund Wilson in *Patriotic Gore*. With a few broad strokes they attempt to capture the man in the historical moment, using each to illuminate hidden characteristics in the other. The results may be idiosyncratic; they are intended to be suggestive. But in another sense these biographical sketches focus on a larger interpretive issue: exploration of the individual experience is essential for understanding the process of cultural hegemony. As David Brion Davis noted, "By showing how cultural tensions and contradictions may be internalized, struggled with, and resolved within actual individuals, biography offers the most promising key to the synthesis of culture and history." The lives of certain early-nineteenth-century Americans—some old and skeptical, others young and innovative, many confused and anxious—suggest the truth of this observation. While their outspoken, sometimes eccentric qualities made them more than typical, it was precisely those attributes that often reflected a heightened sensitivity to the transformational age in which they lived. The intellectual and emotional ordeals of this book's *dramatis personae* unfold some of the texture and variety of experience common to articulate Americans straining under historical pressures. They verify that the consolidation of liberal values prompted divisions and antagonisms not only among people, but also within people.[9]

In the end some readers may be troubled less by what is included in this story than by what is *not* here. The list of those missing-in-action from the narrative is substantial, and it is bound to raise some scholarly eyebrows. How can one examine the birth of American liberal society in the era of the early republic without treating the Federalists, those well-known purveyors of economic growth and profit-gathering? In addition, isn't it just a bit peculiar to present an analysis of emerging capitalist values in which no practicing capitalists *per se* are encountered? And what about the working class, women, Indians, and black slaves? They do not appear in the text, yet surely they played important roles in the consolidation of liberal America as proponents, opponents, or foils. Such skeptical questions raise legitimate concerns, but they also miss the point of this study. This demands one final clarification.

The Republic Reborn examines the emergence not so much of capitalism itself as of the "culture of capitalism": those complex and ambivalent ways in which impulses toward self-interest entered public discourse to be challenged, modified, and eventually legitimated as the moral basis for marketplace practice. Moreover, the analysis focuses on—again to put forward Raymond Williams' schema—the shaping of a "dominant" mode of cultural hegemony from 1790 to 1820. This is not to say that the opinions, reactions, and formulations of certain subsidiary groups in the early republic were unimportant. It is merely to state that many social groups hovered on the periphery of this cultural process, and hence beckon as the subjects of other kinds of books.[10] The Federalists are absent here because their advocacy of commercial profit, while it partly reflected the spirit of the age, also was leavened with heavy doses of paternalist social theory and mercantilist economic theory that sought to prop up existing elites rather than to encourage the ascendancy of self-made men. Early-nineteenth-century capitalists themselves linger in the wings because, with few exceptions, they were more concerned with gaining material success than with justifying it. These hard-nosed figures sought profit and left to others the difficult task of building a moral foundation that such pursuit required if it was to endure in American society. Finally, various ethnic, gender, and class subgroups stay in the shadows here simply because they stood outside the public arena of cultural power and influence in the early republic. To Jeffersonian ideologues fell the self-appointed task of justifying economic self-ishness, validating self-control, and translating social and psychological impulses into political language. By their struggles with values, perceptions, and ideas, they mapped the way from America's republican past to her liberal future.

So as a "social history of ideas"[11] that explores historical change and war in Jeffersonian America, this book approaches an old-fashioned subject with some newfangled interpretive concepts. It ultimately casts a wide net, one of rather large mesh, perhaps, through which small-fry historical issues may escape. But the argument's basic knot-strength, it is to be hoped, snares and holds some of the leviathan interpretive problems at large in early national America. My concern is with deepening our understanding of cultural hegemony by gauging the complexity, ambivalence, and tangled connections accruing to the consolidation of liberal capitalism around the dawn of the nineteenth century. My intent is to bring to light the hidden history of a social and cultural elite, since understanding the powerful—especially for critics of America's dominant culture—is at least as useful as admiring the dissenters. My hope is that, by analyzing the complicated function of war in American society, the disturbing role of violent conflict in the forging of larger social and cultural commitments will become clearer. This study's significance, then, lies in offering a new view of the making of liberal America. By trying to tell the story well, it is an exercise in doing history both as art and as criticism.

The Republic Reborn

tennis player. Very special thanks go to Barbara Brockman. She endured this undertaking for a long time, helped with the expenses incurred, and offered love and emotional support at home. She often has reminded me, unintentionally, that there are things more important than history.

The Birth of the Liberal Republic, 1790–1820

*Look about you and you will see adventurers uppermost
everywhere; in the government, in the towns, in your villages,
in the country, even. We are a nation of changes. . . .
The constant recurrences of the election accustom men to changes
in their public functionaries; the great increase
in population brings new faces; and the sudden accumulation
of property places new men in conspicuous stations.*

JAMES FENIMORE COOPER
Home as Found

*Each citizen of a democracy generally spends his time
considering the interests of a very insignificant person, namely,
himself. If he ever does raise his eyes higher, he sees nothing
but the huge apparition of society or the even larger form of the
human race. He has nothing between very limited and clear ideas
and very general and very vague conceptions;
the space between is empty.*

ALEXIS DE TOCQUEVILLE
Democracy in America

*In this republican society, amid the fluctuating waves
of our social life, somebody is always at the drowning point.*

NATHANIEL HAWTHORNE
House of the Seven Gables

"A New Era Has Commenced in the United States"

In the spring of 1806 a matter-of-fact Scottish merchant disembarked at the American port of New York City. Heavily involved in the transatlantic carrying trade and worried about the tense commercial situation caused by the Napoleonic Wars, John Melish had come to the young republic to monitor his monetary interests. Detained at first in New York, Melish journeyed to Boston before slowly working his way down the eastern seaboard. He stopped at Philadelphia and Baltimore on the way to Charleston, South Carolina, where his mercantile firm had its southernmost trade facility. A man of utilitarian bent and stern Protestant values and with a deep interest in economic development, Melish gradually found his attention wandering from the commercial ledger to the American social landscape. He marveled at the dynamic, bustling republic through which he was moving. The fascination became so great that he decided to renew and extend his travels and to record his impressions systematically. Thus Melish returned on a second excursion in 1810 that led southward to the Georgia frontier, westward down the Ohio River to Louisville, and northward through New York into the southern provinces of British Canada. The result of these wide-ranging forays was *Travels in the United States, 1806–1811*, a massive two-volume collection of observations on life in the young nation. And Melish offered there an enthusiastic and emphatic conclusion: "A new era has commenced in the United States."[1]

This proclamation of a "new era" emerged in part from the Scotsman's own sensibility. Unlike many European travelers, he did not disdain the raw provincialism of American life. In fact, he admitted a certain fondness for the forthright manners and industrious values of these New World republicans. Having little of the aristocrat about him, he focused on the practical configurations of American life that seemed to be swelling and changing shape all around him. Melish traversed the length and breadth of the young republic and fastidiously compiled long catalogs of the kinds and extent of agriculture, the varieties of professional and craft skills, the profusion of commercial exchanges, and the progress of domestic manufactures. From these dry statistic and unadorned lists emerged a striking portrait of social expansion, economic growth, and individual opportunity. Melish seemed continually amazed by it, even overwhelmed at times, but the constant whirl of productive activity always warmed the heart of this profit-minded merchant in the end. So with all pretensions set aside, *Travels in America* opened a plainly constructed window on the panorama of a dynamic society in flux. Through it wafted the sensations of change that seemed to be in the very air of the early-nineteenth-century American republic.

From the outset, Melish was struck by the flourishing growth of American agriculture and commerce. Journeying initially through the major commercial ports on the Atlantic, he became profoundly impressed both with the volume of their foreign commerce and their market connections radiating into the interior. He recognized that the Napoleonic Wars had prompted this explosion in the American export and carrying trade after 1793, as well as fostering increased European demand for American foodstuffs. Melish also was affected by the abundant state of agriculture throughout the United States. He continually made note of the "prosperous farms" of New England, western farmers who were making "the wilderness to blossom as the rose," the "ease and affluence" of agriculturalists in Pennsylvania, and the surging cotton production in the southern states.[2]

It was the newly settled areas over the Appalachians, however, that particularly excited Melish with their vast geographic scope and already thriving river commerce. Waves of immigrants had begun washing westward over the mountains in the early 1790s, and the Scottish traveler noted the rapid development of western New York, western Pennsylvania, and the fledgling states of Ohio and Kentucky. In such places the atmosphere remained decidedly rustic, and the accoutrements of civilization were often absent. Even Melish, determined as he was to avoid snobbery, frequently blanched at frontier inns that served food that "looked like train oil thickened with salt" and was accompanied by "violent retching in the adjoining room." He persevered, however, to discover western towns like Cincinnati and Louisville, Kentucky, that launched "a considerable commerce in the produce of the country on the river." Arriving in Pittsburgh in 1810, Melish wrote, "In the course of my walks through the streets, I heard everywhere the sound of the hammer and the anvil; all was alive; everything indicated the greatest industry, and attention to business." Even smaller villages like Zanesville, Ohio, seemed like beehives of activity with "building going rapidly on," the neighboring countryside "getting into a state of cultivation," while "bridges, banks, and manufactures were projected. The situation . . . for all these projects appeared favorable."[3]

Yet Melish recorded more than mere quantitative facts of economic growth and geographic expansion. He also trained a perceptive eye on the qualitative transformation of American social and economic affairs in the early republic. First in 1807, and even more strongly in 1810, the Scotch traveler discerned that American entrepreneurial energy was turning steadily inward, away from foreign horizons. Noting both the push of English and French restrictions on America's overseas commerce, and the pull of domestic market expansion, he shrewdly judged that "*the foreign trade is gone, never to be recalled to its former state,*" while "the seeds of manufactures are sown throughout the country, never to be rooted out." The evidence for this shift, Melish argued, could be seen quite as much west of the Appalachian Mountains as along the Atlantic Coast. While domestic manufactures—both of a "household" type and a more "extensive" type—were mushrooming in the east, western towns like Frankfort, Kentucky, prompted this report: "Two manufactories of cotton bagging have been recently established, and are doing well; and two rope-walks, a tobacco factory, and several carding machines are also in operation." In Melish's assessment this process was already establishing in the young republic a home market with "internal consumpt for produce and raw materials." He prudently calculated, "Internal manufactures and commerce would, in all probability, be substituted for foreign commerce," and he "resolved to shape my course accordingly."[4]

Although not by nature a speculative man, Melish sporadically ventured deeper to explore the sources of the social fluidity he described. As he frequently recounted in *Travels in America*, early-nineteenth-century Americans seemed to be motivated in part by a strong sense of opportunity. Traveling through upstate New York, he reflected that the hard-working farmers "are sure to succeed" while the mechanic, through diligent habits and judicious investment, "may accumulate money as fast as the farmer." Both groups, he wrote, should thank God for living in "a land where they have advantages so far transcending what the same classes have in any other." But once more, the western areas of the republic added evidence even more convincing. In Lexington, Kentucky, for example, "workmen are almost always in demand, the more so as industrious journeymen soon become masters," while an Ohio farmer told Melish, "Those who are industrious . . . could not fail to lay up a comfortable stock for old age, and for posterity." As one Westerner summed up in 1810, the original settlers of the previous decade "already were selling their improvements, and moving off, while men of capital were coming in and making elegant improvements."[5]

This pervasive atmosphere of opportunity, however, reflected not just external social and economic circumstances, but also internal cultural values. Almost in spite of himself, Melish perceived that "the American character" loomed large in the social flux of the early republic. A work ethic of "industry" and "productivity" immediately attracted his attention, and he habitually described Americans as "civil, discreet, and industrious." This practical-minded man noticed that even public documents urged citizens to productive endeavor, with state constitutions proclaiming "industry and economy, honesty and punctuality" and encouraging "the promotion of agriculture, arts, sciences, commerce, trade, manufactures." The fact that many mechanical trades were practiced, even though farmland was abundant and cheap, also drew Melish's eye. Confused at first, he finally attributed it to the American penchant for hard work and material gain, recording that these "branches are organized and practiced with persevering industry, because the profits resulting from them are equal to those resulting from agriculture."[6]

Yet *Travels in America* eventually settled on a "spirit of independence" as the defining characteristic of restless Americans in the early nineteenth century. Somewhat surprised to discover that the typical individual "will brook no superiority" and "will suffer none to treat him with disrespect," Melish noticed further that this disposition was not "confined to one rank; it pervades the whole." At times this rough-hewn self-reliance seemed but a cover for crude self-indulgence. At a tavern in Geneva, New York, for instance, the Scotsman encountered with considerable shock a gathering of American gentlemen who chewed and smoked tobacco and were "nasty in the highest degree, and seemed to pay no attention to where they spat, in the fire, on the hearth, on the floor; the face, the neck, or the pocket; it was all *one*." But more important, the merchant chronicler discovered that the concern with social equality and personal autonomy had an economic dimension. Americans seemed determined to avoid pecuniary dependence on others. The great majority of American farmers were "proprietors" of their own land, yet urban mechanics also relished the notion that "independence is easily attained by labour." After months of reflection, Melish offered an evaluation of the common citizen of the rapidly growing republic:

> There is a noble trait in the character of the mass of the American people, that of *independence*. They place themselves on an equal footing with whoever they come in contact. If they do anything for you, they will have their price, and a good price too; but they will take nothing in a sneaking way: they will never leave it to the honour or the generosity of the employer.[7]

What John Melish sensed with his finger on the pulse of the American republic was a vast, multifaceted transformation gaining momentum in the early nineteenth century. The features captured by *Travels in America*—social and geographic mobility, the emergence of domestic manufactures and a home market, the growing sense of individual autonomy—were important dimensions of a larger process that had accelerated after the Revolution and would remake American society by the Age of Jackson. From a vantage point of nearly two centuries later, the nature of that massive shift in the early republic of 1790–1820 seems clear: in a heated atmosphere of opportunity and ambition where many colonial traditions and commitments were evaporating, "liberal capitalism" took shape as a new, dominant system of values, organization, and authority for nineteenth-century Americans.[8] This process cemented several interconnected elements: an economy of entrepreneurial capitalism, a social structure rooted in free labor and achieved status, a politics of liberalism, and a bourgeois culture of possessive individualism and self-control. Thus, as Melish perceived, dynamic forces of change were highly active in early national America. But the "new era" he shrewdly proclaimed proved more complex and far-reaching than he realized.

THE history of the American republic from 1790 to 1820 ushered the young nation into a new age. While the War for Independence had secured dramatic results—political independence for the former colonies, the heroic establishment of republican governments—events of the next three decades brought changes that were more impalpable but probably more fundamental: a transformation of social perception, political judgment, economic endeavor, and private sensibility. This new world could be glimpsed in ways both striking and subtle. It appeared in gentlemen's abandonment of knee breeches for pantaloons and the cravat, and the disappearance of the powdered tiewig before romantic curls and the "Brutus" haircut. Or in Independence Day parades where urban artisans marched under the banner of their respective crafts and proclaimed the dignity of their labor. Or in the streams of wagons winding westward through the Cumberland Gap, the great commercial ships lining the docks at Baltimore or Charleston waiting to convey wheat and cotton to Europe, or the whirring of mechanical looms in New England's first primitive textile mills. To contemporaries such shifting scenes often seemed so incongruous, sudden, and fluid that their overall meaning easily evaded grasp. But beneath the complex

and tangled developments of the early republic emerged underlying
trends that provided a larger pattern of significance. Not least
among them was the consolidation of the market in the economy and
society of America.

Social and economic change in the early republic expressed a
larger evolutionary current pulsing throughout the early modern
West: a centuries-long transition from seigneurialism to capitalism.
While feudal structures and values had begun disintegrating in most
parts of western Europe by the early sixteenth century, capitalism,
with its strikingly different economic and social relations, did not
emerge full-blown until the early nineteenth century. Thus the
intervening epoch saw a long and tangled remaking of material life
and human values. It is significant that it also saw the settlement and
early development of England's North American colonies. As historians have come to discover, American settlements before the Revolution thus existed neither as an "ideal type" of traditional, ascrip-
tive society nor as an "ideal type" of competitive, individualist
capitalism. Instead, they took shape amid a slow historical movement from one to the other, as an amalgam of varied elements even
as the migration to the New World had involved both an escape
from restrictions and a recreation of community. Although characterized by a certain social and geographic mobility, frontier individualism, and economic self-reliance—especially in contrast to
more rigid European structures—colonial America was not "born
free" as a pure liberal, Lockean society. To the contrary, recent
historical work demonstrates that Americans stubbornly retained
many premodern economic and social traditions until late in the
eighteenth century. These included a "household system" of economic production, commodity exchange often revolving around
"use-value" rather than cash, and a "moral economy" based on task-
oriented work and a social valuation of economic endeavor. Moreover, social relations for the most part remained in the mold of
"paternalism." This deferential system of authority ordered both the
structure of the household and the larger society in a hierarchical
form. Overall, the colonial experience defined, in the words of
historian James Henretta, a "distinct precapitalist period."[9]

By the late eighteenth century, however, tremors had begun to
shake and crumble the social and economic foundation of colonial
America. The commercial growth, geographic expansion, and challenges to traditional authority that had begun to appear in the
mid-1700s gained unstoppable force after the War for Independence. From 1790 to 1820 several revolutionary developments re-

shaped social and economic life. In agriculture, as new historical research has made us aware, significant commercialization began to occur. A large commodity-producing region took shape in a great arc from Virginia through the mid-Atlantic states to New York in response to European demand for foodstuffs. Beginning in the early 1800s, rapidly growing cotton production in the South also entangled that region increasingly in the web of international trade. In terms of commerce, equally drastic changes occurred. As a result of European preoccupation with the Napoleonic Wars, in the fifteen years after 1793 the American portion of the carrying and reexport trade became the largest in the Atlantic world. The three decades after 1790 also encompassed rapid expansion of both "household" and "extensive" manufactures, especially in the mills of New England and the Delaware Valley. This virtual explosion of economic activity took place against the backdrop of a massive geographical expansion beginning in the early 1790s. Heading westward over the Appalachians to the frontiers of the Old Northwest and Southwest, restless Americans by 1820 had brought into statehood nearly all the territory east of the Mississippi River.[10]

Yet more was involved than mere growth. The *nature* of social and economic experience also changed fundamentally in America's early national decades. With rapid commercial expansion, the pervasive "household economy" began to lose its grip under pressure from "intraregional markets" spreading into the countryside from growing urban areas. The export of grain, meat, timber, and cotton further encouraged the market motive of production for profit. According to Thomas Cochran, commercialization in the 1790s also ignited a "business revolution" of systemization: incorporation, sophisticated bookkeeping procedures, and the creation of wholesale commission houses, banks, insurance companies. But even more important, this expansive economic growth between 1790 and 1820 brought significant alterations in the social relations of production. While dynamic commercial development placed a disproportionate "concentration of wealth" in the hands of merchant businessmen, a general aura of opportunity spurred an ethos of entrepreneurialism and self-made success. This held true for those eastern farmers making market connections to urban centers, western farmers seeking independence and social advancement on the frontier, and urban master craftsmen engaging in capitalist-oriented production. As social and labor historians have discovered, the early republic marked the first emergence of a "new dichotomy between Labor and Capital" in areas where urban growth and manufacturing development began to flourish. So Americans not only overturned the moral economy and household system of colonial tradition, but also began to replace the social notion of paternalism with a new sense of competitive individualism. [11]

In other words, the development of America after the Revolution involved the consolidation of a market economy *and* a market society. Both are necessary for the existence of liberal capitalism. While mere trade had existed for some time in the colonies, extensive markets and a social system based on individual competition did not congeal until the early nineteenth century. And nothing better illustrates this early national ascendancy of commodity production, cash-value exchange, and achieved status than the Panic of 1819. The appearance of this first modern depression in American history revealed the dominance of a capitalist market economy with its internal rhythm of prosperity and contraction. The confused and frustrated reaction of Americans to this depression also disclosed the existence of a liberal society with an ethos of individual striving and pervasive expectations of success. [12]

Since consciousness stands inseparable from material life, it is not surprising that American thought and feeling also became transformed fundamentally in the decades after independence. Enmeshed with the social distentions and creeping commercialization of the Revolutionary era, American cultural values and attitudes became strained and uncertain by the late 1700s. This fragmentation, however, eventually led to a new consolidation in the early nineteenth century as the cultural traditions of colonial America gradually gave way before the emergence of what would eventually be called a "Victorian" sensibility. By 1820 a distinctly bourgeois culture had crystallized in the young republic.

American colonial culture had rested on the bedrock of several integrated premodern and precapitalist conceptions. Emanating from a number of sources—Puritan theology, republican ideology, paternal tradition—attachments to community, family, hierarchy, and deference largely dominated colonial perceptions until late in the eighteenth century. The moral ideal of "virtue"—in public a sacrifice to the commonweal, in private an ethic of hard work and middling prosperity—encouraged independence but mitigated against the greed and self-interest of economic man. A gentry culture, utilizing symbols of Church and Courthouse, nourished networks of paternal and family authority. A widespread traditional work culture, with its rituals of task-oriented work and conviviality, further buttressed the precapitalist framework of colonial values. Overall, as historians

have begun to discern, colonial America tended not to separate values
and ideas from their social context. Instead, they largely viewed
culture as only one dimension of an organic whole. [13]

After the middle of the eighteenth century, nascent liberal values
began surfacing everywhere in the American colonies. While the first
Great Awakening raised challenges to standing religious authority, a
few prophetic figures like Benjamin Franklin began formulating a
message of secular striving and success. Proponents of commercial
expansion lauded its potential for liberation, and the revolt against
Great Britain subtly subverted paternal relations and raised political
expectations for the common citizen. These cultural waves slowly
gathered tremendous force during the years 1790–1820 and crashed
over the walls of traditional restraint. Amid this immense liberalizing onslaught, several trends appeared especially powerful.

The Second Great Awakening of 1800–1830 proved central to the
shaping of a self-conscious Protestant consensus—an "organizing
process," as one historian aptly described it—that idealized "moral
free agency" and "benevolence." This religious upheaval not only
established a new sense of middle-class orthodoxy, but also encouraged a larger commitment to American "civil religion," or the special destiny of God's Republic. A transforming valuation of work also
fed the surge toward a liberal, bourgeois culture. By the late 1700s a
narrow economic assessment of labor had begun replacing older
social and moral perceptions. Opportunity, worldly success, and
prosperity superseded the community demands of an older "moral
economy." Moreover, as labor and cultural historians have begun to
uncover, around the year 1800 entrepreneurial Americans started to
combine new notions of punctuality and work discipline with older
Protestant misgivings about drinking and gambling to forge a bourgeois ethic of "self-control." In the more formal world of educational
and moral theory, Scottish "common-sense philosophers" achieved
new prominence with their insistence on the validity of the "moral
sense" and practical experience. By 1815, as Henry May concluded,
the Scottish-inspired "Didactic Enlightenment" had permeated the
culture of early-nineteenth-century America. Finally, a flurry of
organization-making for charity, religious instruction, cultural up-
lift, "useful knowledge," and vocational fellowship established "vol-
untarism" as a cultural article of faith in the young republic. [14]

As this cultural tidal wave largely spent its destructive force by
1820 and receded, a coherent cluster of values and attitudes appeared
out of the wreckage of colonial tradition. It connected Protestant
moralism, capitalist acquisitiveness, and possessive individualism to
establish common-sense boundaries of discourse for nineteenth-cen-

tury official culture. The compelling power of these integrated beliefs became evident in a pair of broad cultural commitments grown highly visible by the 1820s. First, the "domestic ideal" of middle-class family life—it pictured the home as a private haven under the moral guidance of the wife and mother—provided a temporary refuge from the public world of liberal capitalist competition and thereby indirectly reinforced it. Even more clearly, the popular cult of the "self-made man" revealed the sense of individual opportunity and self-contained achievement that had transformed the early-nineteenth-century republic. Both pressured by and encouraging liberal change in social, political, and economic life, a bourgeois culture became dominant in the United States between the Revolution and the Age of Jackson.[15]

With society, economy, and culture in a state of flux during the early national decades, it was no coincidence that American political life also underwent a sea change in its ideology and structure. Political culture in eighteenth-century America, as historians have come to understand, was dominated by the imperatives and expectations of "republicanism." This way of doing politics had rested on two broad beams of support. First, the notion of "civic humanism"—a conviction that citizenship in a republic allowed for the fullest flowering of man's humanity—provided a moral context for political action. Second, an economy of household production and a society ordered by relationships of paternal hierarchy sustained a supportive social milieu. But a whole series of interlocking ideological principles gave concrete substance to the republican world-view: "virtue," or the subordination of private interests to the general good of the commonwealth; an "organic" vision of society cohering by mutual obligations and deference; a singular understanding of "independence" as the self-reliance and economic capacity flowing from property ownership; and finally, a cyclical view of history as recurring development and decay to which fragile republics seemed particularly susceptible. This is not to say, however, that republicanism held sway in pure and unadulterated form. To the contrary, especially by the late 1700s, American republican ideology was wracked by division. Divergent tendencies within a common creed—should one emphasize individual independence or corporate welfare, achievement or hierarchy, political rights or deference?—generated internal pressures. So too did ethnic, regional, and social-class versions of republican notions like freedom. Market growth and commercial development also created external pressures as champions joined battle over the question of "virtue and commerce." Terrified of decay and corruption, American republicans in the decades after the Revolution ultimately split over the best means to keep the young republic at a "middle stage of development" between barbarism and decadence. Thus while the American Revolution apotheosized republican ideals, its transforming force also fed a "contagion of liberty" that ultimately proved subversive. Over the next few decades, the republican world of the late colonial age changed radically, if almost imperceptibly.[16]

Although the rhetoric of republicanism remained prominent well into the nineteenth century, by 1820 meanings and contexts had altered in significant ways. Building on yet departing from republican traditions—and intimately connected as well with the social and economic embrace of the market—a liberal political culture of pluralist consensus and capitalist political economy became dominant during the decades of the early republic. Several indicators marked this gradual process of transition. As numerous historians have pointed out, the ideological momentum of Revolutionary "popular sovereignty" carried politics after 1780 from a "deferential" to a "participant" mode and slowly pushed into prominence the notion of public opinion as arbiter of public affairs. In addition, the Constitution of 1787—its authors having recognized the decline of republican self-sacrifice—institutionalized a governmental structure that checked and balanced economic interests and social factions.[17]

Perhaps the key to this slowly shifting political sensibility was the complex evolution of political disputation in the early national decades. In the 1790s both Federalists and Republicans claimed the mantle of republicanism, but they divided passionately over questions of economic development, popular control of government, and sympathy for the French Revolution. As historians are coming to grasp, however, these angry skirmishes did not just reflect one of several clear-cut dichotomies: agricultural/industrial, rural/urban, socially mobile/stagnant, democratic/aristocratic, or even the Country/Court division of Anglo-American republican tradition. Instead, in their own way each ideological coalition strove to maintain republican imperatives while melding them with liberating social and economic impulses. Each divided internally into a traditional wing devoted to deference, paternalism, and organic stability, and an entrepreneurial wing favoring various kinds of social and economic opportunity. By 1800 a generational split also became evident as younger political figures increasingly abandoned the shelter of republican verities for a politics of participation, organization, economic development, and geographic expansion. In other words, the political factions of the early republic struggled not only with older republican issues but also with an inchoate politics of liberalism. In light of this volatile and ambiguous political atmosphere, Jefferson's famous dictum of 1801—"We are all Federalists; we are all Republicans"—probably carried a deeper meaning than he knew.[18]

Yet however much Federalists and Jeffersonians shared the task of making political sense out of complex social and cultural changes in the early republic, they ultimately diverged in terms of their basic historical roles. The Federalists assumed a largely negative posture. For all their boosting of overseas commerce and a national bank in the 1790s, they could only view with skepticism the emergence of a liberal society and a culture of self-controlled ambition. They clung to paternal traditions of elitism and obligation in their social thinking and expressed fear of, or disdain for, the self-made man. Federalist advocacy of commercial growth also tended to flow in older channels. Federalists did indeed play a leading role in the Atlantic commercial boom that began to transform the American economy beginning in the early 1790s, but they tended to justify this development in traditional and restricted mercantilist terms: the growth of profits among merchant groups would sustain and strengthen the existing social structure, thereby increasing the republic's strength for survival in the international struggle. Moreover, even younger Federalists who eventually tried to organize themselves into an efficient party structure—parties had always been anathema in the republican politics of virtue—did so from a cynical desire for elite manipulation rather than popular involvement. Thus the Federalists, although venturous conservatives for whom material gain and individualism held a certain allure, persisted largely as the party of republican memory.[19]

The Jeffersonian Republicans, on the other hand, by the early nineteenth century gradually staked out positions as designers and shapers of a new order. In the beginning this had not been their explicit goal. Coming together in the mid-1790s, followers of Thomas Jefferson and James Madison summoned the Revolutionary spirit of American republicanism to defend against several perceived dangers in Federalist politics: the corruptions of English-style "Court" politics, the social inequalities of a mercantilist political economy, the restraints of an elitist paternal society. Against this specter of decay and decline Jeffersonians posed the vision of an expanding republic of independent producers, a society where hard-working farmers, mechanics, craftsmen, and entrepreneurs would sustain themselves economically and thus maintain the capacity for virtuous republican politics. Yet by the turn of the century the energy and momentum of the Republican movement was carrying it beyond original destinations. The famous "revolution of 1800" swept Jefferson into the Presidency, sent the Federalists into a tailspin from which they never recovered, and marked the political triumph of the Republican coalition that would dominate American life for the next quarter-century. In the very process of victory, however, their ideology gradually took on a new cast. Under pressure from changing social conditions and cultural values, the idealized figure of the independent republican producer almost imperceptibly changed shape into the striving self-made man. Especially with the ascendancy of a young, post-Revolutionary generation of leaders, the Jeffersonians captured the ambitious spirit of a growing market society and translated it into a political agenda. The process was always complex, often confused, and frequently given to unintended consequences, but its ultimate results were profound. In the early nineteenth century, Republicans forged a social, cultural, and political mind-set that established liberalism—a creed fusing public good with private interest and offering a pluralist civic life of individualism, public opinion, and organized faction—as the framework for modern American development. Thus the Jeffersonians, although guilty innovators for whom memories of virtue still lingered, emerged as the party of liberal desire in the early 1800s.[20]

Ultimately the complex shaping of the American liberal republic from 1790 to 1820 offered several common denominators that spread across categories of society, economy, politics, and culture. First, a powerful dynamic of countervailing fragmentation and reordering infused all dimensions of change in the early republic. John Higham and others have seen "boundlessness," or a dissolving sense of limits, as characteristic of nineteenth-century liberal society. This seems only half-correct. To be sure, the liberating promise of free labor, moral free-agency, and political participation was often exhilarating. Yet just as frequently it created desperate feelings of isolation and insecurity. So while many Americans sought the freedom of a liberal ethos after the Revolution, they searched simultaneously for new means to stabilize its centrifugal momentum and avoid chaos. Examples abound. The cultural imperative to self-control, for instance, blunted the dangerous desire for self-assertion. Protestant benevolence and the formulation of a new liberal dictum—the public good results from the convergence of many private goods—made reasonable the market drive for profit and advancement. Americans directed a politics of public opinion and popular sovereignty into channels of organized party activity and diffused it even more in a governmental structure of checks and balances. Thus liberal capitalism attained a hegemonic position by a double-edged process in the early nineteenth century: Americans promoted competition, fragmentation, and individualism in practically all realms of life, while at the same time making them palatable with new strategies of reassurance, security, and order.[21]

An impulse toward social-class formation and dissent formed a second characteristic of the emerging liberal republic. To note the ascending hegemony of American liberal capitalism is not to assert the complete acceptance of its values and practices. On the contrary, it is evident that significant groups resisted the advancement of liberal values and market structures. Urban merchants and commercial farmers, master craftsmen and entrepreneurs—with intellectual and emotional assistance from ministers, mothers, and moral philosophers—certainly shaped a bourgeois creed in the early nineteenth century. And their commitments to free labor, achieved status, pragmatic politics, and self-control certainly became hallmarks of a new mode of cultural hegemony in nineteenth-century America. Yet tradition did not die completely, nor did new forms of opposition fail to arise. As Raymond Williams has pointed out, the hegemonic process always involves an interplay of "dominant," "residual," and "emergent" configurations. While the dominant culture embodies the interests and perceptions of ruling social groups, a residual opposition takes shape in defense of prior social formations and values. And an emergent culture arises to challenge dominant pieties and assumptions with avant-garde visions. Thus notions of republican "virtue" and "independence," of moral economy and premodern work habits, of family loyalty and organic attachment persisted among significant numbers of Americans—small subsistence farmers, common urban laborers, gentry defenders of a deferential social order. Moreover, unfamiliar kinds of dissent gradually emerged in reaction to the unexpected harshness of market competition, the degradations of the workplace, and the evasions of a pluralist politics. So if liberal individualism and market competition assumed the hegemonic throne during the early republic, they did not reign unchallenged.[22]

Finally, and most important, a common thread of ambiguity connected the vast and complex changes occurring in early nineteenth-century America. It seems clear that the consolidation of a liberal society brought a sharp break with the past and established crucial preconditions for the development of later industrial capitalism. The process, however, involved real human beings who did not have the advantage of hindsight. They did not perceive a clear choice between premodern tradition and liberal capitalism. They did not walk a steady linear progression from one to the other, nor did they simply refuse to walk. They saw no such clear path. Instead, they acted out a multi-act drama of complicated motives and responses, confusion, rejected alternatives, and unintended consequences. Rather than marching confidently into the future—or, at the other extreme, standing to battle against the forces of change—Americans of the early republic presented another, less tidy image. They backed into the future, prompting or resisting innovation, or sometimes doing both at once, for a variety of complex rational and emotional reasons.[23]

Yet this ambiguity is not easily seen or grasped. Seemingly unabashed Jeffersonian boosters of a liberalizing society—for instance, Henry Clay, the politician, or Mathew Carey, the political economist—painted misleading pictures of rosy progress and bright achievement. Other nostalgic or reactionary figures—landowner John Randolph of Virginia, or minister Timothy Dwight of Connecticut—offered moving, sometimes bitter laments on the world they had lost. A few observers, however, came closer to the truth. Among them were three aging, curmudgeonly men—all of them would end up in the Jeffersonian fold—who reflected the powerfully ambivalent experience of the mass of their countrymen in the first decades of nationhood. Perceptive and judgmental, respectful of tradition yet responsive to change, with one foot in a republican past and the other in a liberal future, they stood astride an upheaval and struggled to understand and direct it. John Taylor of Virginia, John Adams of Massachusetts, and Hugh Henry Brackenridge of Pennsylvania were wide-ranging writers, politicians, and social critics. And they held profoundly divided allegiances that they sought to resolve with great cascades of words, sharing a compulsion to write out their personal struggles with historical change. Their explorations and unconscious revelations of the dialectical stress between ambition and fear, desire and guilt, bring to light hidden dimensions of the liberalizing transformation of early-nineteenth-century America. They reveal an early republic seldom seen: a society painfully swollen with tension, where anxious citizens in pursuit of the "main chance" glanced frantically around for new guidelines of authority and cohesion.

John Taylor: "The Family of the Earth"

John Taylor of Caroline County, Virginia, gazes out at us across a century-and-three-quarters with an expression of impeccable calm. His features appear serene in his early-nineteenth-century portrait, his eyes benign and confident, his whole countenance exuding steadiness and contentment. If Taylor's rhetoric offers any indication, that studied firmness stemmed from a myopic attachment to the past. Taylor was clearly an agrarian enthusiast—many have said an agrarian reactionary—in a commercializing age. Much of his historical reputation rests on the *Arator*, a series of paeans to the virtues of agricultural life composed for newspapers in the early years of the nineteenth century and collectively published in 1818. Perhaps his most famous work, *An Inquiry into the Principles and Policy of the Government of the United States*, seemed a relic of the past even as it appeared. Some twenty years in the writing, this long and rambling exposition of republican principles of government was intended as a reply to John Adams' *Defense of the Constitutions of Government of the United States*, which Taylor considered to be outdated in formulation and aristocratic in sentiment. But while Adams' volume was published in 1787, Taylor's did not appear until 1814, and by that time the polemical ardor of the debate had cooled. As Taylor himself noted early in the text, his comments likely would seem as "almost letters from the dead." Taylor's extensive ruminations on social and political issues thus were dismissed by many contemporaries—and by most historians since—as being irrelevant or at best anachronistic.

Such an impression misleads. For one thing, the olympian tone of Taylor's prose barely masked a deeply felt passion about civic principles and the moral nature of human life in a republic. Far more than many of his so-called "realistic" colleagues, he perceived the dawning of a new age in the era of the early republic. His major writings embodied intense struggles to criticize the development of liberal capitalism, or "finance capitalism" as he usually called it. Far from being merely an agrarian conservative out of touch with nineteenth-century forces of change, Taylor was actually a more penetrating observer of the emerging liberal world than many of its hard-nosed advocates and visionary boosters. He cut through to the ethical and moral issues that lay at its heart. Moreover, Taylor was not so reactionary as he seems at first glance. In fact, his social thinking rested on an idealistic vision of an agrarian market society. In many ways he represented an American agricultural version of Adam Smith and foreshadowed later critics of monopoly capitalism. But the abiding irony is that Taylor's obsession with hard work and industrious endeavor ultimately supported the emerging system for which he held such deep reservations. In short, John Taylor personified many of the tensions of his age. Although one of America's most profound early critics of liberal capitalism, he nevertheless could not totally escape the web of its logic. The fervor that seeped through the calm facade of his prose betrayed the complexity, emotions, and contradictions within.[24]

Taylor lived and died a Virginian. Born in 1753, he suffered the death of his father at age six and was sent to live with his uncle, the prominent lawyer Edmund Pendleton. Growing up in the Pendleton household, Taylor entered the gentry network of local power and influence in Caroline County. He attended private academies and the College of William and Mary before entering the bar in 1774. Taylor played an active role in the Revolution. He fought as an officer both in the Virginia theater of action and with George Washington's army in the middle states. Frustrated with army life and in poor health, Taylor returned to Virginia in 1779 to practice law and pursue a political career in the state legislature. He emerged as a lukewarm Antifederalist in 1788, most likely because of his intense attachment to Virginia's state interests and fear of a strong national government. But one year later he retired from his extensive law practice to become a full-time farmer. After 1790 he answered the call of his state's legislature twice and consented to serve in the U.S. Senate both in 1792 and 1822. Over the last three decades of his life, however, Taylor dedicated himself largely to farming and social and political philosophy. He died in 1824.[25]

In his major writings Taylor concerned himself with the dynamics of a complex new society coming to life in the post-Revolutionary decades. In the first chapter of *Inquiry*, he explained his belief that England had fallen completely under the sway of a modern aristocracy of "paper and patronage" and that the United States was on the verge of doing so. This perception of the rise of a new civic and social system—"finance capitalism" he termed it—lay as the bedrock of his subsequent commentary on American life. It triggered two critical responses. First, it forced Taylor to examine the nature and implications of finance capitalism, then it pressured him to conceive a contrary model of an ideal republic.

Particular conceptions of work and property lay near the heart of Taylor's social and political analysis as it took form after 1790. He came to believe that hard work was the lifeblood of a healthy republic. The practice of productive habits, he contended, nurtured not only personal integrity and morality but also the well-being of society in general. As he asserted in the *Inquiry*, the "charming goddess" of industry created prosperity, increased virtue and health, and enhanced "our happiness by enabling us to blend it with the happiness of others." Taylor even went so far as to identify "industry, talents, and labour" as the only "genuine republican" mode of distributing property and material goods.[26]

However important industrious labor may have been for Taylor's ideal republic, he enclosed this imperative in a sturdy moral and social casing. Industry remained desirable only insofar as it operated within a larger commitment to the public good. The appropriate goal of hard work was modest wealth, socially useful productivity, and a wide distribution of property. Taylor argued that since "natural" property consisted only of land or of the finite products of one's own labor, a pervasive social ethic of productive labor would help preclude the danger of a society polarized between the propertyless poor and a wealthy aristocracy. Pride in property ownership, if unencumbered by pecuniary greed, would shape a felicitous republican society. Taylor stated simply, "He who dissipates his property, dissipates also his virtue and honour." He envisioned an ideal republic consisting of a mass of hard-working, moderately wealthy, independent and virtuous citizenry. This median conception of gain lay between the twin excesses of ambition and avarice, on the one hand, and paternal dependence and social polarization, on the other hand.[27]

Such general concepts translated into a concrete system of political economy in Taylor's early nineteenth-century theorizing. A disciple of Adam Smith, Taylor eagerly grafted an idealized vision of a market economy onto the stock of republican principles. The "natural" and unrestrained exchange of goods—both domestically and in channels of "free trade" abroad—would bring prosperity and social harmony to the American republic, he argued. "The products of agriculture and manufacturing, unshackled by law, would seek each for themselves, the best markets through commercial channels." This view of the market, like Smith's associated with the Enlightenment critique of feudal economic regulation, inculcated an ethos of liberation. For Taylor, the enemy of republican political economy was not market capitalism as such, or even manufacturing. It was English-style mercantilism with its system of regulation and taxation. He argued that government should shy away from involvement in economic matters and expressed instead a minimalist view: "The utmost boon with which government can endow it [the interest of general labor], is the enjoyment of that portion of its own earning which the public good can spare." Taylor generally approved of the policies of America's republican governments in this regard. He noted in the 1814 *Inquiry*, that American governments prudently had avoided taxation and other economic regulation, thereby exciting "an industrious spirit to improve, and a commercial spirit to enrich our country."[28]

Free trade was crucial to Taylor's republican political economy, but even more crucial was his conception of "useful" labor. Historians traditionally have cast disagreements over political economy in the early republic in these terms: the initiatives of Federalist proto-industrialists and capitalist merchants were opposed by Jeffersonians committed to an agrarianism of independent, self-sufficient yeoman farmers. And Taylor has been labeled among the most reactionary of the Jeffersonian agrarians. But Taylor's reflections on political economy tell a somewhat different story. The critical distinction he articulated consisted not of a rural/urban or farming/industrial split, but a separation between productive and nonproductive labor. Productive endeavor, he argued, encompassed both agriculture and manufacturers. Such activities were legitimate because they involved the production of tangible, useful goods and bolstered the general prosperity of society. But unproductive labor, which Taylor found abhorrent to republican principles, was located in "excessive commerce." While Taylor recognized that merchants were necessary to republican free trade, he believed their enterprise to be inherently unproductive and unsteady. Early in his writing career, Taylor revealed the grounds of his suspicions of mercantile activity. In 1794 the Hamiltonian programs favoring commercial creditors and investors triggered this rejoinder. In the language of the Protestant ethic, Taylor wrote:

> Merchants are brokers, honourable and useful, whilst adhering to a steady line of commerce, and supplying the wants of a nation; but pernicious and dangerous, whilst speculating indiscriminately on foes and friends for the acquisition of wealth, and aspiring to exclusive privileges and prerogatives.

"They are a class unproductive," he concluded. So while Taylor believed that the practice of commerce should be tolerated to lubricate the flow of goods in a market society, its position in a republican political economy should remain strictly secondary to the "real labour" and "lasting improvements" of agriculture and manufacturing.[29]

Taylor's political precepts flowed naturally from his social ideals and fundamental principles of political economy. Throughout the *Inquiry*, but especially in the sixth section, he explained "The Good Moral Principles of the Government of the United States." The traditional republican commitment to the commonwealth, or public good, headed the ideological list. For Taylor, the preeminence of the common interest over selfish considerations defined the citizen's obligation to the republic. Deference to the public good, he believed, certainly involved a measure of self-sacrifice. But Taylor also saw the commonwealth as a "natural" coalition of the majority forces of "industry, effort and talents" in a republic. Taylor best expressed this notion in the *Arator* essays, noting that republican government favored those who subsist by "useful talents in every form, such as those employed in agriculture, manufacturing, tuition, physic, and all trades and scientific professions." From this Taylor logically deduced a distrust of factions and political parties. In a viable republic, he maintained, "knaves or fools only, surrender their duties and rights to party despotism. . . . Can an honest man of sound understanding think himself bound by wisdom or duty, to give or sell himself to one of two parties, prompted by interest and ambition to impair the publick good?"[30]

John Taylor's faithfulness to the traditional commonwealth, however, did not prompt traditional thinking about republican constitutions. The classical theory of republican government—rooted in ancient political discourse, it had reappeared in the Renaissance Atlantic world in the guise of "civic humanism"—held that a republic should balance monarchy, aristocracy, and democracy. This formulation beheld a "mixed government" of social orders: of "the one, the few, and the many," as it was usually expressed. For most American republicans, the English constitutional arrangement of King, Lords, and Commons expressed this vision best until the Revolution. John Adams gave the fullest American voice to traditional republican thought in his *Defense of the Constitutions of Government of the United States*. But Taylor found Adams' dissertation deeply disturbing and spent twenty-odd years framing a reply in his *Inquiry*. Like many other Americans, Taylor had come to embrace a new theory of republicanism shaped in the Revolutionary era and embodied in the Constitution.[31]

Prodded by the social and political disturbances of the 1780s and encouraged by the belief that republican industry would vitiate the very existence of social orders in favor of a rough equality of condition, the framers of the Constitution and their supporters abandoned the notion of mixed government toward the end of the eighteenth century. They fashioned instead a uniquely American political theory based on a modified set of republican principles. Taylor delineated them in the *Inquiry*. First, the homogeneous body of the people retained sovereignty for the whole government, instead of separate social orders reserving sovereignty for separate organs of government. This notion of "popular sovereignty," Taylor continued, made possible a "political equality of rights" in the American republic. Second, rather than embodying a balance of social orders, American republicanism instead rested on a "functional" division of powers both within the national government and between the state and national levels. This arrangement, Taylor argued, would remain vital if animated by "actual representation"—the practice of representing the "actual" interests of one's constituents. Finally, a nascent pluralist

vision of society informed this new arrangement of republican government. Aware of growing social ambition yet committed to industrious habits and a regard for the public good, Taylor and others
believed that America's new constitutional arrangement would remove any danger. The pursuit of self-gain, if done in moderation,
would vitalize the republic by promoting prosperity and economic
independence among its citizens. Moreover, the functional counter-
balance of checks and balances within government would ensure that
no faction would gain an upper hand. America's social kaleidoscope
of shifting interests and groups, Taylor contended, would be strained
through a "natural" government of "reason." There, much like in
his vision of an economic market, the gentle friction of hard-working
groups would balance each other and support the public good. As
Taylor stated flatly in the *Inquiry*, American republicanism showed
that "an avaricious society can form a government able to defend
itself against the avarice of its members."[32]

Taylor's discussion of republican government and political economy proved notable for its length and thoroughness of explanation,
but less so for its originality. His defense of hard work and the felicity
of the marketplace, his promotion of a republican government of
functional checks and balances, and his attempts to meld personal
initiative with the public good were common to much public discourse in the early republic. So too was his support for the farmer and
the mechanic and his distrust of the merchant, especially among
Jeffersonian Republicans of the middle and southern states. But Taylor's acute perception of change in the decades after 1790 set him
apart in a striking manner. Sooner than most contemporary observers
he became aware of vast waves of change engulfing the republican
world of the late eighteenth century. His critique seems extraordinary even now, both for its passionate sense of urgency and for its
incisive predictions of unfamiliar social, cultural, and political
problems.

Early in the *Inquiry*, Taylor identified what he saw as the central
feature of American life in the early republic: the emergence of
"finance capitalism." He denigrated it as a "modern aristocracy" of
"paper," "patronage," "commerce," and "alienation." The focus of
his ire was the whole cluster of institutions, mechanisms, careers, and
power relationships that accompanied the development of an advancing market structure after 1790: banks, insurance companies, paper
money, wealthy merchants and financiers, stock companies, speculators, alliances between commercial interests and governmental
bodies. American ascendancy over the Atlantic carrying trade during
the Napoleonic Wars had played the largest part in shaping these new

structures, but so too had booming American exports of foodstuffs to a demanding Europe and the post-Revolutionary development of more extensive domestic market networks. Banks, paper speculation, and powerful economic figures may seem normal accessories to modern capitalism, but for Taylor they seriously threatened his idealized vision of a smooth-working, rational, and even-handed market society of hard-working republican producers.[33]

In addressing the emergence of "finance capitalism," Taylor zeroed in on its moral dimension. He believed that too many writers on government and society—and here he included John Adams and the authors of *The Federalist* essays—concentrated on "political skeletons" of sovereignty and constitutional arrangements of power. While not unimportant, such considerations were for Taylor strictly secondary to "the ethereal moral principles, alone able to bind governments to the interest of nations." And above all else, it was the quality of those principles under the emerging system which so disturbed him. Any system, he noted, "is merely a moral being," and "finance capitalism" was "suggested by, or founded in, the evil moral qualities of avarice and ambition." Rather than the rational interchanges of a productive society, Taylor saw a frightening system of manipulative social relations permeating American private and civic intercourse. Not an ethos of production but one of gain seemed to be gaining ground. Not a spirit of industriousness but one of pecuniary competition appeared to be permeating American values. This moral distinction was pronounced for Taylor, and he eloquently warned of the dangers of "finance capitalism" in the *Inquiry:*

> Avarice and ambition being its whole soul, what private morals will it infuse and what national character will it create? It subsists by usurpation, deceit, and oppression. A consciousness of fraud, impels it toward perpetration. By ever affecting, and never practicing sincerity, it teaches a perpetual fear of treachery, and a perpetual effort to insnare. Its end is distrust and fraud, which convert the earth into a scene of ambuscade, man against man.[34]

This passionate moral condemnation arose from several sources. The permeation of banks, paper money, and stock companies, Taylor began, fundamentally undermined industrious work habits. The activities of finance capitalism consisted of manipulation pure and simple, not the productive endeavor vital to a republican society. He contrasted the "real labour" of agriculture and manufacturers with "mercantile or speculating people" who pursue "sudden strokes at good bargains only." The returns made by lasting improvements, he said, "bear no similitude to those of speculating rogueries. Who

will lend for the purpose of encouraging industry, or aid lasting
improvements at five per centum, when by investing his money in
bank stock, he will certainly gain above eight per centum?" Moreover, such paper manipulation actually discouraged hard work. Taylor observed:

> Wealth in both cases is supposed to be the spur to exertion. By a laborious
> cultivation of my talents and persevering industry, I acquire a moderate
> degree of wealth; by banking, I acquire infinitely more, without labour
> or talents. Why should I subject myself to the fatigue of becoming
> learned and useful, to become the scoff of a rich, idle, and voluptuous
> order?

Finance capitalism, with its paper speculations, he concluded, destroyed moral imperatives to productive labor and hence undermined
a key support of republican society.[35]

Taylor also fervently believed that the manipulations of financiers
and bankers blurred the critical moral distinction between "natural"
and "fictitious" property. "Paper stock" tried to legitimate itself by
claiming to be genuine private property. But natural property, Taylor insisted, could consist only of "the earning of labour, the reward
of merit." He angrily inquired, "If the acquisitions of useful
qualities are genuine private property, can the crafty pilferings from
useful qualities under fraudulent laws, to gratify bad qualities, be
genuine private property also?" Even more than eroding republican
respect for hard-won and independence-granting property, however,
proponents of finance capitalism threatened to manipulate property
away from its rightful owners. Taylor saw a tangible target here:
government support for banks and paper currency. Paper money, he
insisted, did not comprise "real capital" but only *represented* it. Only
the "value of labour" constituted genuine capital. However, when
bank paper became legitimated, encouraged, and supported by law, it
became the master instead of the servant of property. Not work but
manipulation of credit and speculation in stock became the shaper of
property-holding. Taylor characterized "artificial currency" manip-
ulated by financiers as "employed, not for the useful purpose of
exchanging, but for the fraudulent one of transferring property,"
converting paper currency into "a thief and a traitor." And the paper
credit web, Taylor believed, had become even more entangling for
Americans by the early nineteenth century. In the *Inquiry*, he denounced its creeping hegemony:

> It is asked whether the borrowing class, may not forbear to borrow, and
> whether this power of forbearance, is not an evidence, that the profit or
> income collected by banking, proceeds from the voluntary act of indi-

viduals. Should bread and water be placed in abundance before a hungry and thirsty multitude, could their eating and drinking be fairly said to be merely voluntary? Currency is the medium for exchanging necessaries. If gold and silver, the universal medium, are legislated out of sight, all human wants unite to compel men to receive the tax collecting substitute. This is banking. By the help of law it creates a necessity for its own currency; and this extreme hunger is misnamed volition.

This remarkably prescient analysis foreshadowed the later experiences of many Americans. The complaints throughout the nineteenth century of Jacksonian Locofocos, midwestern farmers enamored of "free labor," immigrant urban workers, and Populist dissenters would reflect Taylor's prediction of the property-diluting tendencies of "finance capitalism." They would echo his angry rhetorical question of 1814: "If the fruit of labour is private property, can stealing this fruit from labour also make private property?"[36]

The final source of Taylor's fervent condemnation of the republic's emerging economic system lay in the deeply disturbing prospect of social polarization. Whereas the contamination of work habits disrupted American values, and the erosion of property patterns upended republican political economy, the social impact of "finance capitalism" actually turned Americans against one another. Taylor believed that "while a paper system pretends to make a nation rich and potent, it only makes a minority of that nation rich and potent, at the expense of the majority, which it makes poor and impotent." He went on to sketch a farsighted analysis of class conflict in a capitalist society. If allowed to develop unchecked, he argued, finance capitalism would reap a grim social harvest in America:

> It divides a nation into two groups, creditors and debtors; the first supplying its want of physical strength, by alliances with fleets and armies, and practicing the most unblushing corruption. A consciousness of inflicting or suffering injuries, fills each with malignity towards the other. This malignity first begets a multitude of penalties, punishment and executions, and then vengeance.

Taylor clearly foresaw a concentration of wealth and power in the hands of a "monied aristocracy." This situation, he believed most firmly, would destroy the social basis of republicanism, because "without a very considerable division of property, a free government cannot exist." This class conflict would only be exacerbated by ties of "patronage" between powerful financial interests and government, even though proponents of such an alliance offered enticements of wealth and prosperity to citizens of all classes. Taylor exploded at this contention in the *Arator* essays, insisting that the actual social consequences would be far different. "What! Secure our independence by impoverishing, discouraging, and annihilating nine-tenths of our social yeomanry? By turning them into swindlers, and dependents on a master capitalist for daily bread?" If the body of productive, honest farmers and mechanics fell for the promises of a "combination of capitalists," Taylor concluded, the results would prove disastrous for the republic. "From its dreams of wealth," he prophesied, "it is awakened under the fetters of a monied aristocracy, and unfortunate as Prometheus, it is destined to eternal and bitter toil to feed this political harpy, and to suffer excruciating anguish from its insatiable voraciousness."[37]

This passionate critique of finance capitalism, in combination with an equally fierce loyalty to a virtuous and productive American republic, molded John Taylor's reaction to the specific political disputes of the early republic. The issue of "protective legislation" most consistently aroused his concern. He opposed Hamilton's programs in the 1790s as granting special privileges to the financial interests of bankers and speculators. He dreaded the appearance of an unholy alliance in which "members, both of the government and of the corporation, will prefer the interests of the corporation to the interests of the nation . . . and bend government into a subserviency to their designs." Taylor retained this sentiment over some two decades and even eventually opposed the post-1812 policies of the Jeffersonian Republicans. James Madison's 1815 proposals for a new national bank, federally financed internal improvements, and a protective tariff for infant American manufacturing—a program vigorously endorsed by young Republicans like Henry Clay and John C. Calhoun—roused Taylor's opposition. He insisted that protective bounties for any branch of industry, be it agricultural or manufacturing, merely "enslaved" honest labor at the power of "their masters, the capitalists." "The project of creating a race of capitalists, as an engine to endow the government with more power," Taylor argued in 1818, "seems to me to be unfavorable to all the callings and interests of society, save to the calling of the governing, and the calling of capitalists." He insisted that "protecting duties" operated unfairly because "monied capital drives industry without money out of the market and forces it into its service." Taylor instead upheld the original Jeffersonian plan of political economy: westward expansion, proliferation of commercial farming, free trade for American foodstuffs abroad, and the avoidance of commercial decadence. In his 1804 tract *A Defense of the Measures of the Administration of Thomas Jefferson*, he supported the Louisiana Purchase for precisely those reasons. This vast grant of rich agricultural land, Taylor argued, would induce "solid prosperity," "habits of industry and hard-ihood," "plain and regular manners," and a "love of virtue and independence," and would function as "the surest preservative of equality of possessions."[38]

Although a staunch Jeffersonian Republican, Taylor remained skeptical enough to be an astute observer of developing party politics. According to traditional republican ideology, parties were to be avoided because they represented the interests of a faction instead of the common good. Taylor largely agreed in principle, although he tended to see the Republicans as genuine representatives of the public interest while the Federalists reflected only "monarchical" sentiment. But in a larger sense Taylor was ahead of his time in noting the peculiarly disembodied quality of American party disputes. By 1814 he was already perceiving that minions of "finance capitalism" had crept into the inner chamber of *both* party structures. The forces of "stock and patronage," he wrote, had already been "accepted on both sides as recruits, by an ardour for victory." This economic system, he concluded, was "not yet able to stand alone; but whilst it is fondling first one and then the other of its muses, it is sucking both into consumption, and itself towards maturity." Taylor thus came to see elections as little more than contests between manipulators allied to financial interests, or between "the inns [*sic*] and the outs," neither of whom belonged to "the general interest class." Hence, in the *Inquiry*, Taylor fundamentally challenged the integrity of emerging popular politics. American elections between mere "clans" or "factions"—each allied with financial interests—simply "expose it [the republic] to sale, as in England." To be meaningful, he insisted, elections must drag deeper and focus "moral principles" to "produce good effects." In penetrating the vapid functionalism of "popular opinion" to assess the "moral principles" beneath it, he flew in the face of crystallizing common wisdom. The optimistic rhetoric of disembodied democracy held no appeal for this wary old Virginian.[39]

Taylor summed up much of his thinking in a revealing metaphor in the *Inquiry*. The drama of American life during the early republic, he suggested, ultimately consisted of an enormous clash of two groups. The "family of the earth," whose members were hard-work-ing farmers and mechanics, had become locked in a fatal struggle with the "family of cunning," composed of paper stock-jobbers and capitalist financiers. "These two families," he proclaimed, "in all their branches, are natural enemies." This imagery tells much about Taylor. It accented his affinity for a society of organically connected, honest productive laborers, and his distaste for the manipulative, pecuniary characteristics of emerging modern capitalism. As such it prefigured later radical critiques of vicious social relations in a society of aspiring, self-made men. [40]

But Taylor's vision of "family" discord in the young republic also masked a deep personal dilemma. In the end, Taylor reflected his times in the peculiar awkwardness of his intellectual position. He unrelentingly revealed the compulsions of infant economic man, but remained blind to the implications of his own faith in a simple market of hard-working producers. He stood caught between attachment to a republicanized Protestant Ethic and resistance to the Spirit of Capitalism. Thus Taylor accepted the economic market, but became resentful when its invisible hand crushed some while allowing others to scramble successfully for advantage. He believed in the conception of politics set out in *Federalist Paper* No. 10, but lashed out in anger when the pluralist struggle actually began to occur. He yearned both for organic ties and for freedom, like many of his fellow citizens. For all his insight, Taylor never quite understood that the two families of "cunning" and "the earth" gradually were merging into one great clan in the early republic. By the early nineteenth century, numerous Americans had begun proclaiming loyalty to the new, larger "family of opportunity."

John Adams: "Our Country Is in Masquerade!"

John Adams remains a curious anomaly from an age dominated by demigods. George Washington's wooden dignity, Thomas Jefferson's austere elegance, Alexander Hamilton's consuming lust for power, and James Madison's methodical brilliance traditionally have colored the historical portrait of the early republic. Adams, by contrast, never quite fit the larger-than-life mold of the Founding Fathers. He was nothing if not exasperatingly human. The short, rotund New Englander was unpredictable, sometimes stuffy and pretentious, independent, and possessed both an acerbic wit and a moody temperament. His unbounded intellectual curiosity seemed matched only by his relentless and often brutal self-examination. Many Americans of his time—and many historians since—have been put off by the rolling torrents of verbiage and emotion that so characterized his life. Benjamin Franklin's famous comment on the volatile Adams—he "is always an honest man, often a wise one, but sometimes, and in some things, absolutely out of his senses"—seems uncomfortably close to the mark. Yet in many ways Adams' impetuous character, contentious intellect, and long-winded fulminations offer a breath of fresh air. They provide a highly informative digest of one man's tenacious encounter with the emerging new society of post-Revolutionary America.

Adam's long career was both distinguished and erratic. Probably no American except Thomas Jefferson served his country so long, so well, or in such a variety of positions in the last quarter of the eighteenth century. Adams first gained notice as a radical lawyer in Boston in the years before the Revolution. A leader of the city's Whig resistance to British regulatory legislation, he actively participated as a speaker, organizer, and pamphleteer on English constitutional history and theory. Elected to the First Continental Congress, Adams soon emerged as an outspoken and respected advocate of American independence. In fact, his leadership earned for him from contemporaries the title "Atlas of Independence." He continued as a leading figure in the Continental Congresses of the late 1770s and drafted the Massachusetts state constitution in 1779. The New Englander then did yeoman service in Europe for the young republic over the next decade. Adams proved instrumental in securing much-needed loans from Dutch bankers, helped negotiate the 1783 peace treaty with Great Britain, and became America's first ambassador to the Court of St. James. He returned to the United States to serve as the nation's first Vice-President, and then was elected President in 1796. Turned out of office by the Jeffersonian "revolution of 1800," Adams returned to his farm considerably embittered and retired from active political life.[41]

Amid this flurry of public activity, Adams maintained a steady flow of writings through the decades. Several series of early essays helped crystallize New England opinion on behalf of the Revolution: the 1765 *Dissertation on the Canon and Feudal Law*, the 1775 *Novanglus* essays, and the 1776 *Thoughts on Government*. In 1787–88 Adams published the three-volume *Defense of the Constitutions of Government of the United States of America*, an explanation of America's republican principles of government. The *Discourses on Davila*, a defense of "balanced" constitutions, followed in 1790. But the bulk of Adams' published works shrank before his mountainous private correspondence, especially over the last three decades of his life. Adams wrote hundreds of letters to his sons, his wife, political associates like Elbridge Gerry and Josiah Quincy, and fellow intellectuals like John Taylor and Benjamin Rush. His most famous exchange of letters followed his reconciliation with Thomas Jefferson in 1812. Over the next decade, the two elderly men compared views on every topic imaginable—history, science, philosophy, religion, economics, literature, politics, and the prospects for the young American republic. The correspondence makes for fascinating and sometimes moving reading. So too the picture of the exchange: the two aged giants of the Revolution betrayed by their bodies but not by their minds; the playful, passionate, effusive New Englander pouring forth three letters to every one from the incisive, elegant Virginian. The public and private lives of Adams and Jefferson finally merged in their nearly simultaneous deaths on July 4, 1826, the fiftieth anniversary of the Declaration of Independence.[42]

Much has been written about Adams over the last twenty years, with two aspects of his life attracting particular attention. Adams' notoriously intense personal struggle with ambition, popularity, and motivation has provided one source of persistent interest. His diary, private letters, and public utterances were characterized by constant agonizing over virtuous conduct, the temptations of fame, and a simultaneous craving for and contempt of popular approval. Adams' checkered career of accomplishment and rejection only heightened this obsession with self-scrutiny. Moments of achievement and public praise—such as in the halcyon early days of the Revolution, or in 1798–99, when as President he almost single-handedly kept the United States from war with France—propelled Adams to heights of self-satisfaction. But episodes of rejection—like his Presidential defeat in 1800 or his Vice-Presidential campaign for government titles, which earned him the derisive epithet "His Rotundity"—prompted extended bouts of bitter self-pity. One recent student of Adams' character noted of this inner tension: "Adams found irresistible the opportunities in eighteenth-century America for attaining worldly fame, while at the same time retaining a vision of the Puritans' striving for a perfect soul. As with the Puritans, purity of motive continued to be essential to his sense of personal integrity."[43]

In addition to his private character, Adams' oft-noted evolution in the 1780s and 1790s from an outspoken republican revolutionary to a cautious Federalist also has roused curiosity. Historians have offered several explanations for Adams' post-Revolutionary movement toward a cranky conservatism. It has been argued that social unrest and political factionalism in America during the 1780s moved him toward a new concern with social control and order. Incidents like the 1786 Shays' Rebellion in western Massachusetts prompted fears of violent chaos for Adams and raised serious doubts about the capacity of Americans for virtue. Other scholars have pointed to his experience in Europe, especially in France, during the 1780s as shaping episodes. The debate in France between "egalitarians," who supported the notion of a national will expressed through a single representative body, and "Anglomanes," who favored a government of balanced orders and passions, drew the ever-combative Adams into support of the latter group. At the same time, the first tremors of the gigantic revolutionary upheaval in France intensified his nervous distrust of wild schemes of reform. Finally, Adams' conservatism has been explained as a casualty of changing American ideology in the young nation. Gordon Wood has argued that while Adams clung to the classical republican formulation of government as a negating balance of constituted social orders, most Americans had moved by the 1790s to a conception of homogeneous "popular sovereignty" and functional checks and balances as the best expression of republican government. In Wood's words, by the 1790s "it was as if Adams were speaking a language different from that of other Americans."[44]

These treatments of Adams' political thought and personality illuminate different dimensions of the man. Yet if viewed from a broader perspective, these interpretations appear as but parts of a whole. They each examine a portion of the great, if only dimly perceived, problem for Adams in the post-Revolutionary decades: coming to terms with an emerging liberal society and expanding market economy. His voluminous writings, his torrent of observations on everything imaginable in public and private life, were largely attempts to define, understand, and criticize this unfamiliar world. Adams' attempts to deal with a new ideological politics, a kaleidoscopic society of clashing groups, the challenge of the French Revolution, and the problem of personal ambition represented facets of the larger struggle. The New Englander's life was above all a life of the mind, and his reflections—and passionate outbursts—on American society merged in an intense intellectual confrontation with the transforming American republic of the early nineteenth century.

Adams' relationship with John Taylor offered one glimpse of Adams' role as a searching critic of emerging liberal capitalism. Several ironies attract notice. Ostensibly Adams and Taylor were great ideological opponents, with Taylor's massive 1814 *Inquiry* appearing as a tardy response to Adams' even more massive *Defense* of 1788. The public exchange triggered a years-long private exchange of letters between the two. Moreover, both were ultimately dismissed by popular opinion as living in the past intellectually—Adams for his antiquated notions of republicanism, Taylor for his romantic agrarianism. By the 1810s they seemed merely interesting but dispensable unrealists, two eccentric old men fighting battles of bygone days. But Adams, like Taylor, was actually a complicated and insightful figure with one foot in the past and another in the future. Like Taylor, he served as a skeptical and penetrating analyst of the pretensions of a new American society. Like Taylor, Adams also committed himself to certain values and tendencies that brought about that society in unintended fashion. In other words, the New Englander, like the Virginian, was an eighteenth-century man uncomfortable in a new age, yet he proved to be a revealing critic of the great era of change in which he grew old.

Adams' passion for politics and government—"the divine science" he often called it—was the touchstone of his intellectual life, the centerpiece of an incredibly wide-ranging regimen of reading, observation, and study. Although political theory intrigued him and the intricacies of government structure delighted him "like poetry delights other men," Adams was no airy political philosopher. A long and stormy career had blown the grit of reality into his theoretical speculations. Overall, his meditations on government appeared unremarkable in the context of eighteenth-century men of the Enlightenment. Throughout his life Adams defended a constitutional arrangement involving a system of balanced orders. Following in the best tradition of English republican thinkers like James Harrington, he held forth in behalf of a mixture of "the one, the few, and the many." And like other American republicans of the late 1700s, Adams modified the structure slightly by replacing the king with an executive and making "the few" a selected instead of a hereditary body (although his angry outbursts and reckless speculations of the 1790s led to accusations that he favored monarchy and hereditary aristocracy). On the surface at least, his theory of government seems notable mostly for the wide reading on which it was based, the great length at which he expounded it, and the fact that much of his texts consisted of near-verbatim transcriptions from European political writers.[45]

The real import of Adams' social and political thought, however, lay concealed in the interstices of his constitutional maxims. His letters, marginalia, and the introductory sections of works like the 1790 *Discourses on Davila* indicate greater originality than his more formal efforts. These passages bespeak a subtle and substantive mind at work, a speculative and penetrating intelligence. They also show that the shell of his governmental edifice did not ring hollow, but rather reverberated from elements within: an unsystematic but brilliant body of social, psychological, and economic insights into the new polity consolidating in America by the 1790s. Adams' public and private writings further disclose two primary concerns in his attempts to formulate viable governments for a changing American society. A deep curiosity about the psychology of human motivation constituted the first concern. The second was Adams' lifelong preoccupation with the social basis of government. From these flowed subsidiary conclusions about political economy, the philosophy of human "progress," and the appropriate framework of republican government. The random and diffuse quality of Adams' observations keep him from the first rank of Enlightment political philosophers, but fortunately for the study of history they throw a good deal of light on the crystallization of American liberal capitalism in the first years of nationhood.

The problem of human motivation always fascinated the New Englander. It led him, like many other Enlightenment thinkers, to a search for the "laws of Nature." With his concern for political theory, that meant an unceasing examination of the wellspring of man's impulse for association and action. From the earliest adolescent entries in his diary to the last years of his life, Adams probed the psychological sources of human conduct. This voyage in search of a universal impulse departed from the harbor of Puritan sensibility. Adams' Calvinist upbringing—like most promising young men in colonial Massachusetts he had been pushed by his parents toward the ministry—survived in disguised fashion his later rejection of the formal church and embrace of deism. It crept into his speculations on human nature to shape a darkly complex view of man. As he admitted to Jefferson in 1817, he could not deny that "men are rational and consciencious [sic] Creatures." But, he continued, "I say at the same time that their passions and Interests generally prevail over their Reason and their consciences: and if Society does not continue some means of controuling [sic] and restraining the former the World will go on as it has done."[46]

Although suspicious of man's benevolent nature, Adams did not harp on human viciousness or greed. Instead he focused on a more complex mental dynamic: man's desire for esteem. As he succinctly stated in the *Discourses on Davila*, "There is none among them [human propensities] more essential or remarkable, than the *passion for distinction*. A desire to be observed, considered, esteemed, praised, beloved, and admired by his fellows, is one of the earliest, as well as keenest dispositions in the heart of man." This individual desire for distinction, Adams continued, traveled different routes in the human psyche. The consequences were profound, as he noted in this piquant passage:

> This passion, while it is simply a desire to excel another, by fair industry in the search of truth, and the practice of virtue, is properly called *Emulation*. When it aims at power, as a means of distinction, it is *Ambition*. When it is in a situation to suggest the sentiments of fear and apprehension, that another, who is not inferior, will become superior, it is denominated *Jealousy*. When it is a state of mortification, at the superiority of another, and desires to bring him down to our level, or to depress him below us, it is properly called *Envy*. When it deceives a man into a

belief of false professions of esteem or admiration, or into a false opinion of his importance in the judgement of the world, it is *Vanity*.[47]

Several manifestations of the search for distinction particularly aroused Adams' interest. One was pure "ambition," or men's effort at "distinguishing themselves and growing considerable among those with whom they converse." "This ambition," Adams believed, "is natural to the human soul." He was struck that ambition often translated into a yearning for social status, a fact that appeared to be as prevalent among the poor as the rich. Even the most common of men, Adams noted, sought to climb to a prominent position among their fellows. Scrutinizing the people around him, he observed that even the most insignificant men tried to procure "a kind of little grandeur or respect . . . in the small circle of their acquaintances."[48]

Man's obsessive pursuit of riches also fascinated Adams. He remarked of the curious psychology of avarice, "The labor and anxiety, the enterprises and adventures, that are voluntarily undertaken in pursuit of gain, are out of all proportion to the utility, convenience, or pleasure of riches." Satisfying the wants of nature—food, clothing, and shelter—could be done with minimal activity, but Adams saw that men "tempt the seas and encompass the globe" to "accumulate wealth, which will be forever useless to them." As to why men "affront heaven and earth" to accumulate gain, Adams could only conclude that it was because "riches attract the attention, consideration, and congratulations of mankind; it is not because the rich have really more of ease or pleasure than the poor . . . [but] there is more respectability, in the eyes of the greater part of mankind, in the gaudy trappings of wealth, than there is in genius or learning, wisdom and virtue."[49]

In Adams' final analysis, this multifaceted passion for distinction comprised the germ of human motivation. As he summed up in the 1790 *Davila* essays, "avarice and ambition, vanity and pride, jealousy and envy, hatred and revenge, as well as love of knowledge and desire of fame," were simply variations of the search for distinction, that "great spring of social activity." This complex craving for esteem seemingly prompted *both* the good and the evil in mankind, a critical conclusion for Adams' social theory. The passion for distinction was universal, but the consequences could be either useful or destructive, or both. The individual's desire for favorable "comparison" might excite "rivalries" and "jealousies, envy, enmity, hatred, revenge, quarrels, factions, seditions, and wars." But on the other hand, Adams continued, the impulse to "emulation" could also arouse "the most heroic actions in war, the sublimest virtues in peace, and the most useful industry in agriculture, arts, manufacturers, and commerce." He believed that this ambiguous "constitution of things" was universal—"Nature has ordained it," he said—and provided "a constant incentive to activity and industry." The need for the "esteem and admiration of others," Adams contended, softened greedy instincts and tempered self-interest. The complex mixture of selfishness and altruism embodied in the quest for distinction offered the key to human nature and to human social relations. For Adams, a viable polity must strive to balance the various manifestations of this central passion or, in his words, "direct it to right objects."[50]

Adams believed that the search for distinction had been a constant human impulse since time began. Examples drawn from ancient Greece and Rome, medieval Europe, and contemporary Atlantic affairs littered his explication of this theme. Here Adams appeared the good Enlightenment thinker in tracking down the universal, the timeless, the laws of nature that regulate the affairs of man. And there was a ring of truth in Adams' assessment. Certain traits and qualities undoubtedly lay embedded in human nature and resist the corrosive pressures of time. Yet just as surely, the process of historical evolution transforms and molds traits of personality and character. The shape of a historical epoch causes demands to be placed on certain characteristics of human endeavor, while others lie fallow. Thus it seems no accident that Adams' ruminations on the individual's craving for distinction—and his own intense struggle with ambition and fame—appeared at a time when a liberal society of self-made men was beginning to overwhelm traditional constraints of deference and community in America. Adams was himself a captive of time, a historical actor whose perceptions and understanding were shaped by the nature of his experience. What he saw as timeless seems in hindsight far more time-bound, a reflection of historical change in the early republic.

The myriad cultural and social realignments of post-Revolutionary America—the converging streams of liberal capitalism—lent hidden power and import to Adams' analysis. Like an intellectual weathervane, his investigation of the individual's struggle to be placed high in the esteem of his fellows indicated the direction of the winds of change. As C. B. MacPherson suggested, beginning in the seventeenth century the social relations and political discourse of English society began to be permeated by a new conception of the individual. He termed this notion, an accompaniment of extending market society, "possessive individualism." By the nineteenth century, MacPherson argues, the solitary person came to be seen "neither as a moral whole, nor as part of a larger social whole, but as an owner of himself." "The human essence is freedom from dependence on the wills of others," he further notes of this emerging liberal mentality, "and freedom is a function of possession. Society becomes a lot of free equal individuals related to each other as proprietors of their own capacities and what they have acquired by their exercise."[51]

This attachment to "possessive individualism" formed the cultural linchpin of the liberal society consolidating in America after 1790. In many ways it defined precisely the broad object of John Adams' concern. His portrait of the distinction-hungry individual revealed many contours of the type, and the particular virtue of his analysis lay in its psychological dimension. He grasped instinctively many of the quandaries facing the possessive individual cut loose in a competitive society. Adams dug beneath the obvious but superficial desire for material gain to uncover its deeper roots. The yearning for distinction, he argued persuasively, not only tinted pecuniary impulses but also colored the whole range of human social relations in a variety of complex ways. His observation about the manipulative search for "distinction" illuminated not only the anxious individual thrown back on his own resources, but also the liberalizing society in which he strove in the early decades of nationhood. As a social psychologist of possessive individualism, the brilliant but erratic Adams was unsurpassed in his own time.[52]

Adams' insights into the motivations of liberal man shaped his social analysis. In the scramble for distinction, he began, some inevitably emerged more successful than others. Antagonistic social groups were a fact of life for Adams, and he believed that the question of labor lay at the bottom of such divisions. He noted in 1790, "The great question will forever remain, *who shall work?* Our species cannot be idle. Leisure for study must ever be the portion of a few." Those "who labor little will always be envied by those who labor much," he asserted, and such divisions "will continue, and rivalries will spring out of them." This analysis prefigured later theories of class conflict, but Adams preferred to rely on the past for lessons in human conduct rather than peer into the future. He knew only that social inequality and antagonism would exist forever, and he believed that the best hope was to mute their effects.[53]

With the centrifugal, liberalizing American society evident to John Adams by the 1790s, two problems appeared paramount. The specter of unrestrained faction and social anarchy was the first. The social structure of the infant republic, he contended in the *Davila* essays, seemed increasingly wracked by fragmentation of every kind. "The great division of our country into a northern and southern interest," he wrote, "will be a perpetual source of Parties and Struggles." Moreover, "We have the great divisions of the rich and poor, Creditors and Debtors." The yearning for distinction seemed to possess not only individuals but also every sort of human association. Looking about him, Adams saw everywhere rivalries between families, trades, professions, congregations, schools, villages, and states, and he grew deeply disturbed. Adams observed to Josiah Quincy in 1811, "There is no people on earth so ambitious as the people of America. The reason is, because the lowest can aspire as freely as the highest." And this restless pursuit of opportunity especially infected the young. Writing to William B. Giles of Virginia in 1812, Adams noted with concern:

> This country and our forms of government which must have their course, opens vast views of ambition to every eye and fascinating temptations to every passion. The aged & experienced & the middle-aged too, find younger generations rising after them ardently coveting their places and not very delicate in the choice of measures to supplant them and shove them off the stage.[54]

Adams posed the second great dilemma of American society as how best to recognize, reward, and control achievers of distinction. He argued that in every polity, including a republic, all seek the gratifications of esteem but few have real merit. Many seek it by false means of ostentatious displays of wealth, magnificence, and family lineage. Others seek distinction by even less savory tactics like "artifice, dissimulation, hypocrisy, flattery, imposture, empiricism, quackery, and bribery." To complicate the issue even further, Adams believed, "the increase and dissemination of knowledge" in the European world of the Enlightenment had made "titles," "ranks," "orders," and "parade and ceremony" unfashionable. So Americans, he contended, not only had to distinguish real merit from false, but also had to find a way to honor it when it was discovered—and, more critical, to segregate and restrain the dominion of the talented. It mattered little to Adams whether this "aristocracy"—his term for the meritorious in any society—was "artificial" and hereditary as in traditional Europe, or the "natural" product of success as in Jeffersonian America. The impulse would be the same: a coveting of power and profit.[55]

Adams evinced rather decided opinions on the political economy of the early republic after 1790, opinions that also stemmed from his understanding of a liberalizing society of distinction-seeking individuals. He perceptively grasped a subtle shift in attitude among not only Americans but also Western Europeans in the late eighteenth century. The "pursuit of gain," he feared, seemed to be sweeping all before it, including attachments to "honor" and "family." This shift in attitude, which historians have since explained as part of a massive change from a feudal to a modern sensibility, disturbed Adams in several ways. He could not condemn it outright. The virtues of "temperance and industry" and expanding "commerce and manufactures" were crucial both to the vitality of a republic and the "morals" of its citizens. In the typical fashion of American republicanism in the late eighteenth century, Adams believed an ethic of hard work to be the moral lifeblood of a republican society of independent producers. But more than most, he saw the inevitable, if unintended, consequences of such values. He burst out to Jefferson in 1819, "Will you tell me how to prevent riches from becoming the effects of temperance and industry? Will you tell me how to prevent riches from producing luxury? Will you tell me how to prevent luxury from producing effeminacy, intoxication, extravagance, Vice and folly?" Thus for Adams the transmutation of hard work into grasping materialism boded ill for the American republic.[56]

The growth of "paper wealth" seemed to be a particularly insidious manifestation of this trend in American political economy. Adams' commentary after 1790 abounded with vehement condemnations of banks, speculation, and stock-jobbing. He approved of "a national bank of deposit" and pronounced himself "not an enemy to funding systems," justifying both as "indispensably necessary in the present state of the world." But, he burst out in an 1811 letter to Benjamin Rush, "Our whole banking system I ever abhorred, I continue to abhor, and shall die abhorring." What bothered Adams was that "every bank of discount, every bank by which interest is to be paid on profit of any kind made by the deponent, is downright corruption. It is taxing the public for the benefit and profit of individuals." The manipulation of paper money and stocks, he insisted, undermined legitimate hard work and honestly-gained private property. It also "swindled so much out of the pockets of the poor and the Middle Class of People" and put it into the hands of a "few Aristocratical Friends and Favourites." Banks and corporations promised to monopolize wealth into fewer and fewer hands. Adams was astounded that Americans of all classes seemed enamored of such financial institutions in the early-nineteenth-century scramble for gain. He gloomily confided to John Taylor in 1814 that "paper wealth" was "a swindler, a pickpocket, a pirate, a thief, or a robber." But solution seemed impossible "when the few are craving and the many mad for the same thing."[57]

Thus habits of industry and commerce appeared to be a double-edged sword in Adams' republican political economy. While they fostered material prosperity, the changing socioeconomic milieu of post-Revolutionary America indicated also the "universal gangrene of avarice in commercial countries." Adams hoped that this "coming in like a flood" could be abated by hard work, hard money composed of a "circulating medium of gold and silver," and values of economic regularity and modest gain. But such barricades seemed to totter before the onslaught of profit and paper-money schemes. Adams caustically observed in 1812, "The Republicans are as deep in this absurdity and this guilt as the Federalists." "Our bedollared country," he wrote, "has become a miser and a spendthrift," "covetous of others possessions, lavish of his own." The political economy of an emerging market society gnawed at Adams. He paused in the reading of one optimistic tract on social and economic liberation and angrily scribbled in the margin, "Are riches to be the only distinction? Is there any distinction more degrading than riches?" The passion for material gain seemed everywhere in the early-nineteenth-century republic, and public discontent with Jefferson's Embargo of 1807–8 seemed but one indicator of declining public virtue. He complained to one correspondent about this: "Of all the people in the Universe, those of the U.S. are the worst qualified to bear privations. . . . I know not what Power could compel this Nation to live upon Oatmeal and Potatoes and Cold Water." Adams contended to Benjamin Rush in 1808 that "commerce, luxury, and avarice have destroyed every republican government." Such a prospect, surmised the worried New Englander, seemed not unlikely for the United States in the early years of the new century.[58]

Adams' critique of liberal society, market economy, and the psychology of the possessive individual finally led him to excoriate contemporary doctrines of human "progress." Fashionable currents of Enlightenment thought in the late eighteenth century swept forward notions of the human capacity for reason, liberty, and perfectibility. Most Enlightenment thinkers tied such hope to two developments in the postfeudal West: the freeing of human knowledge from the shackles of medieval Christianity, and the peaceful growth of commercial intercourse. Adams, however, swam vigorously against this intellectual tide, especially after 1790. He shared some of the *philosophes'* enthusiasm for the growth of modern knowledge and entertained modest hopes for advances in the human condition. But what he perceived as an excessive faith in human nature drew his ire. "Bad men increase in knowledge as fast as good men," Adams wrote acidly in the *Davila* essays, "and science, arts, taste, sense, and letters, are employed for the purpose of injustice and tyranny, as well as those of law and liberty; for corruptions, as well as for virtue." Moreover, the expansion of commercial activity brought not only prosperity and the peaceful exchange of material goods, but also the dangers of avarice and ambition. So Adams came down hard on what he described as impractical and bookish philosophers of "progress." Having read Condorcet's *Outlines of an Historical View of the Progress of the Human Mind* at least twice, for example, Adams characterized its optimistic pronouncements as "memorable examples of the profoundest science, most extensive literature united with total ignorance and palpable darkness in the science of government." Mary Wollstonecraft's laudatory *The French Revolution* prompted this exasperated comment: "The improvement, the exaltation of the human character, the perfectibility of man, and the perfection of the human faculties are the divine objects which her enthusiasm beholds in beatific vision. Alas, how airy and baseless a fabric!"[59]

If such philosophical optimism appeared naive to Adams' Puritan sensibility, when put into practice it became profoundly dangerous. The French and the Americans needed to be particularly cautious, Adams had concluded by 1790, because of the innocent hopes and "wild schemes of reform" raised by their revolutions. As he soberly warned, even amid revolutionary exultation, "Cold will still freeze and fire will never cease to burn; disease and vice will continue to disorder." The French Revolution particularly showed the effects of precipitous and ambitious schemes of progress. The "philosophers" of France had been too rash and hasty, Adams insisted in 1811, and they had not understood what they were about. "The public mind was improving in knowledge and the public heart in humanity, equity, and benevolence," he continued. "But the philosophers must arrive at perfection per saltum. Ten times more furious than Jack in the Tale of the Tub, they rent and tore the whole garment to pieces and left not one whole thread in it." Napoleon and two decades of bloody war resulted from such temerity. The Corsican also illustrated for Adams the ultimate degradation of the modern craving for distinction if allowed free play. He wrote angrily, "Genius is now deified and substituted for Heathen gods and Roman Catholic saints. Genius is now the mythology of French philosophies. Because men of genius want to be worshipped." The brooding New Englander could only view darkly in France the twisted vision of a liberal society of unfettered, achieving, harmonious individuals.[60]

Because John Adams was a thoroughly political man the challenge of a swelling liberal society in America drove him in the end to seek stability in the structures of government. The emergence of a commercializing economy of "paper wealth," of pervasive ambition and avarice, of a scurrying body of citizens eager for distinction and advancement, only ossified his support of a traditional republican constitution. An arrangement of balanced republican government linked to social orders seemed more necessary than ever. Adams lectured in 1790, "The great act of lawgiving consists in balancing the poor against the rich in the legislature, and in constituting the legislative a perfect balance against the executive power, at the same time that no individual or party can become its rival."[61]

This notion of branches of government as representative of certain social constituencies flew in the face of consolidating liberal ideology in the early republic. But the Madisonian structure of American government seemed dangerously unrealistic to Adams. By advancing the doctrine of "popular sovereignty" as the support for *all* of government, emerging pluralist theory attempted to meld the "aristocracy" into the body of the people. To Adams, this denied the inevitability of social class and only furthered the prospect of oligarchy. He asserted in a letter of 1794, "Let the Laws and conventions of Society be what they will, the natural Inequalities, intellectual, moral and corporeal will produce other inequalities of Wealth and Power." Those who fulfilled the passion for distinction, Adams believed, needed to be both rewarded and controlled. And "the many"—those seeking but not finding distinction—needed to be represented and defended. He concluded that this could best be accomplished by representing each in "an independent branch of the legislature" and setting up "an independent executive authority" to mediate between them.[62]

Adams did not delude himself about the enormity of the task. While a balanced government of social orders promised stability, the impulses of ambition and avarice in the young republic's liberalizing society seemed particularly powerful and resistant to control. As he darkly admitted to Jefferson in 1813, every class of American was suspect to Adams:

> When I consider the weakness, the folly, the Pride, the Vanity, the Selfishness, the Artifice, the low craft and mean cunning, the want of Principle, the Avarice, the unbounded Ambition, the unfeeling cruelty of a majority of those . . . who are allowed an aristocratical influence; and on the other hand, the Stupidity with which the more numerous multitude, not only become their Dupes, but even love to be taken in by their Tricks: I feel a stronger disposition to weep at their destiny, than to laugh at their Folly.

American expansion westward by the 1790s seemingly made matters even worse. Adams saw the frontier as an ungoverned wilderness where "desperate Debtors and unthinking Plebians" would clash with speculating "Proprietors" and "great fortunes" seeking to "lay the foundation for great estates for their Posterity." Envy, hatred, violence, fly-by-night "Paper Money," "Banks," and "Corporations" seemed the likely result. Moreover, the entire scramble for distinction and success entailed several psychological problems. Adams noted of his countrymen in 1790 that the individual "feels a keener affliction when he sees that one or more of them, are more respected than himself." He added, "The higher a man rises, if he has any sense of duty, the more anxious he must be."[63]

John Adams moved far ahead of most contemporaries in sensing the moral void at the center of the kinetic liberal society. In the mad dash for success in the society of early-nineteenth-century America, artifice and manipulation seemed distressingly ascendant in human relations. In a remarkable prescient expression of what later generations of Americans would call the problem of the "confidence man," Adams declared to Benjamin Rush in 1808,

> My friend! Our country is in masquerade! No party, no man, dares to avow his real sentiments. All is disguise, visard, cloak. The people are totally puzzled and confounded. They cannot penetrate the views, designs, or objects of any party, or any individual.[64]

Adams' stance, however, was ultimately one of irony. For all his telling criticisms of the transforming American of the early republic, he endorsed certain values and beliefs that helped create the very society he was fearfully obsessed with controlling. Adams' support for a productive ethos of hard work, his belief in the efficacy of enlightened commerce, and his acceptance of an embroidery on Adam Smith's "theory of moral sentiments" helped to germinate a liberal society of possessive individualism in America. So, like John Taylor, the New Englander personified the dilemma of his age. Although viewing more lucidly than most both where distinction-seeking Americans had been and where they were going as a society, he finally could not disentangle himself from the complicated process by which they were doing so.

Hugh Henry Brackenridge: Modern Chivalry *and the Search for Self*

Novels can be an interesting and richly rewarding source for the study of history. Compared to conventional documents such as speeches, diaries, and tax records, literature often speaks with more imagination and less restraint to the cultural and social sensibility of an age. Although one should not deny the independent integrity of the creative writer, neither can it be forgotten that the novelist is partly a product and a reflection of his time. He often deliberately explores important cultural tendencies and social pressures in the world around him. Moreover, the novelist can bring to light less tangible but equally critical tensions and impulses buried deep in human consciousness. In other words, the imaginative author can open for the historian windows on the past too often left shuttered by the politician, the minister, or the census-taker.

Such is the case with Hugh Henry Brackenridge, a writer of the early republic. This Scottish immigrant led a varied career—journalist, newspaper publisher, lawyer, state representative, judge, man of letters—but he is best remembered as the author of *Modern Chivalry*, one of the first American novels. A massive and ungainly book of some eight hundred pages, it is hardly a novel at all, but rather a series of loosely connected sketches written between 1792 and 1815. Inspired by Cervantes' *Don Quixote* and the English novels of Jonathan Swift and Henry Fielding, Brackenridge conceived *Modern Chivalry* as a picaresque-style social satire of the young American republic. It chronicles the travels and adventures of Captain Farrago, a genial republican of the American gentry, and his manservant Teague O'Regan, an Irishman with an eye for both trouble and the main chance.

On the surface, the novel is an obvious and often quite humorous treatment of expanding political participation and social mobility in post-1790 America. Its modus operandi has Teague seeking and usually achieving some political office or prestigious job for which he is totally unqualified. The distressed Captain then rescues him from the brink of disaster while bemoaning the nature of a society that would even think of fostering such capricious ambitions. Frequently interspersed between such comical episodes are chapters entitled "Observations," in which Brackenridge directly addresses the reader with solemn, sometimes playful, pronouncements on social and political issues. Thus the book has usually been presented as a social commentary and caricature of a transitory America "somewhere between the classical eighteenth-century America of the founding fathers and the modern nineteenth-century America of the Jacksonian Democrats," with Brackenridge appearing as a "reluctant democrat."[65]

These characteristics alone make *Modern Chivalry* a worthwhile study of change in the early American republic. But several deeper and unsounded layers of meaning in the novel reveal it to be a far richer and more complex source of understanding. It has customarily been assumed that Captain Farrago serves as Brackenridge's mouthpiece in the book, and hence that the author was concerned above all with criticizing the excesses of democracy and the overreaching aspirations of the common man as embodied in the unscrupulous Teague. This view appears well grounded, since Brackenridge throws about many broad hints to this effect. As D. H. Lawrence once said, however, "Never trust the artist. Trust the tale." And indeed the tale of *Modern Chivalry* tells a different and more elaborate story.[66]

First, the dynamics of the plot concern not just political "democracy" but a wide variety of social, cultural, economic, and religious concerns that reflected the liberal society of self-made men consolidating in post-1790 America. Second, Brackenridge's imaginative mapping of the uncertain territory of a liberalizing society concealed a deeper exploration in the novel: a journey into the troubled inner world of the liberal self. The Captain certainly reflects Brackenridge's mature—and conscious—opinions to a great degree. Yet Teague also mirrors, albeit less explicitly and directly, much of the author's own career, ambitions, and impulses. In fact, this interplay between the two characters adds a broad resonance to the novel and takes it beyond mere social satire. The clashes of the staid republican Captain and the irascibly ambitious Teague portray not only confusion over acceptable social roles in the early republic, but also a fundamental inner confusion over identity and control of the self in the fluidity of a burgeoning market society. A brief look at Brackenridge's life begins to shed some light on these valuable, if probably unconscious, dimensions of *Modern Chivalry*.

Brackenridge was himself the epitome of the self-made man in the early republic. Born in Scotland in 1748 as the son of a poor farmer, he migrated to America at age five with his family. They settled in a Scotch-Irish frontier settlement just west of the Susquehanna River in colonial Pennsylvania. Hugh Henry apparently demonstrated an early proclivity for books and learning, and by age fifteen he was teaching school at a village in Maryland. After five years Brackenridge used his savings to enter the College of New Jersey at Princeton. He excelled in most areas of study, although "the narrowness of his pecuniary circumstances often depressed him." He graduated in 1771 as the salutatorian of his class. At the commencement ceremony, Brackenridge read from a poem that he and fellow student Philip Freneau had written, "The Rising Glory of America," which has since become quite famous.

The young Pennsylvanian began his mature career as a teacher on the Eastern Shore of Maryland, but migrated to Philadelphia in 1776 with the beginning of the Revolution. In that year he became the editor of *The United States Magazine*, and the following year a chaplain to a regiment of the Continental Army. However, wartime inflation stripped Brackenridge of his savings and salary, and he decided against entering the ministry because of a growing skepticism about religion and a love of "the active life." *The United States Magazine* suffered financial failure in 1779, an event that apparently embittered its young editor, so Brackenridge took up the study of law in the Annapolis, Maryland, office of Samuel Chase. He began legal practice in Philadelphia in 1780, but limited financial success pushed him westward. In 1781 Brackenridge headed inland to Pittsburgh. He recalled some time later:

> When I left Philadelphia, almost twenty years ago, I saw no chance of being anything in that city, there were such great men before me. . . . I pushed my way to these woods where I thought I might emerge one day, and get forward myself in a congress or some other public body.[67]

Once in the booming western city, the ambitious Brackenridge quickly became one of its leading citizens. Aside from successfully practicing law and becoming the head of the bar in Western Pennsylvania, he both encouraged and wrote himself numerous political and satirical pieces for the *Pittsburgh Gazette*. Elected to the state legislature in 1786, he found himself rejected by his constituents after one term in favor of a common weaver. Brackenridge actively supported the new federal Constitution in western areas of the state and played a moderating role in the abortive Whiskey Rebellion by frontier farmers in 1793. In 1799 his legal success led to a judgeship in Pittsburgh, and he culminated his career by an appointment as a justice of Pennsylvania's Supreme Court in 1801.[68]

Several aspects of Brackenridge's life appear particularly prominent in shaping the essence of *Modern Chivalry*. The author's protracted search for an acceptable career and financial success was the first. Like increasing numbers of men of his era, Brackenridge moved through a variety of jobs in an attempt to find a secure niche in a whirling society of expanding opportunity. Considering one vocation before moving to the next—teaching, the ministry, law, journalism, the writing of fiction—and drifting about geographically, he embodied many instincts of early republican society. His position as an individual eager for advancement and dependent on his own devices for gaining it became even more pronounced because of his immigrant status. But as *Modern Chivalry*'s critique of the aspirations of the common man indicated, Brackenridge's journey to success was socially and psychologically problematic. Like many parvenues in a liberalizing society, he overtly rejected much of his own past while becoming a steadfast defender of social stability.

Brackenridge also evinced a good deal of personal tension over the meaning of "vocation" itself. For the talented Scotsman, this particularly took shape as the dilemma of an artist in a society devoted to material pursuits. As he noted in an 1804 aside in his novel, the cultivation of art involved "a neglect of riches" as "the main chance is overlooked." Yet the practice of "an art for its own sake," he continued wistfully, could be "useful and pleasing to the world." This friction between the "main chance" and love of "art for its own sake" did not resolve itself smoothly in Brackenridge's mind. Rather, the ambivalence seems to have characterized and fueled his dualistic career as lawyer and journalist, politician and satirical essayist, judge and novelist. The ambivalence also manifested itself in Brackenridge's extremely equivocal treatment of material success in *Modern Chivalry*.[69]

His traumatic experience in the short-lived Whiskey Rebellion proved to be the final definitive influence on Brackenridge's sensibility. Although he was sympathetic to the complaints of Western Pennsylvania's farmers—they bitterly opposed the new federal excise tax on liquor, which they believed annihilated their already thin profits—he did not join the rebellion as an active participant. Instead, he merely accompanied the rebels as an adviser and "moderate citizen." In Brackenridge's own words, he mixed with the angry farmers to "correct the fury on both sides until an accommodation can be brought about." By "seeming to be one of the insurgents," he explained, he hoped to "soften all their measures and finally prevent a civil war." Brackenridge's role, however, brought only a stream of abuse from all sides. Eastern Federalists, aware of his prominence in the area, insisted on branding him as the chief insurgent. And the western Republican farmers, slowly becoming aware of the lawyer's strategy, began to accuse him of betrayal. As the revolt began to fizzle on the outskirts of Pittsburgh and the vigilante "army" crumbled, Brackenridge began writing a defense of his conduct entitled *Incidents of the Insurrection in Western Pennsylvania in the Year 1794*. Probably the most complete firsthand account of the episode, the tract helped exonerate Brackenridge with the federal authorities. Personally interrogated by Alexander Hamilton, who had been left in command of the expeditionary force sent to quell the disturbance, he was cleared of any wrongdoing. But the whole episode proved to be extremely frustrating and draining.[70]

More important, the experience left Brackenridge with deep emotional scars. The Whiskey Rebellion provided a severe ideological and psychological jolt. In the *Insurrection*, Brackenridge recalled his deep apprehension as he lay encamped with the rebel force outside

Pittsburgh. Fear would overcome "anyone who has seen a large and enraged body of men under the command of one as mad as themselves or under no command at all." Wild talk of killing and burning reflected "the human mind in a state of anarchy." Recoiling in horror from this mob psychology, Brackenridge denounced it as "impregnated with the Jacobin principles of France" and noted that "during the whole period of the insurrection, I could scarcely bear to cast my eye upon a paragraph of French news."[71]

Brackenridge grew even more disturbed as he observed the character of many of the revolt's leaders. Their motivating impulse seemed to come from frustrated ambition. As he remarked early in the rebellion upon observing a meeting of the instigating "Mingo Creek Society," some of their leaders were frustrated office-seekers, while others acted "from a desire natural to men, of being conspicuous." Brackenridge had already begun *Modern Chivalry* in 1792, of course, an act probably inspired by his removal from the state legislature in favor of an untutored craftsman. But the Whiskey Rebellion seems to have hardened the author's disillusionment with a liberalizing society of self-made men. It undercut Brackenridge's faith in public opinion as the arbiter of political and social life and intensified his distrust of an ethos of ambition.[72]

Brackenridge's climb to success, his struggle with vocation, and his distress over the Whiskey Rebellion informed the most overt and conspicuous messages of *Modern Chivalry*. Among them was an ideological defense of traditional republicanism, a defense usually presented by the sincere Captain Farrago. Early in the book, Brackenridge laid out his conception of a felicitous republic: a "democracy" of popular sovereignty and equal protection under the law directed by a "natural aristocracy" of talent and virtue. "The people are a sovereign," he believed, "and greatly despotic, but in the main, just." But Brackenridge queried, "Is it necessary that every man should become a statesman?" "Genius and virtue are independent of rank and fortune," he insisted, "and it is neither the opulent, nor the indigent, but the man of ability and integrity that ought to be called forth to serve his country." Unrestrained clamor for political office and influence seemed a dangerous trend in post-Revolutionary America, and it was the most consistent object of satire in the novel. As Brackenridge confessed, "The great moral of this book is the evil of men seeking office for which they are not qualified." Furthermore, the author's ideal republic demanded loyalty to the common good over private interest. In addressing a member of the Society of Cincinnati, Captain Farrago condemned the organization as one of those "partial institutions" that "cut men off from the common mass, and alienate their affections from the whole, concentrating their attachments to a particular point and interest." Thus commitments to deference, education, virtue, and reason were the ultimate supports of Brackenridge's polity. And he used *Modern Chivalry* to skewer its assailants: men of "preposterous ambition," "blackguard journalists," fomenters of "popular phrenzy," and agents of a divisive politics of "party."[73]

A cluster of attitudes toward work further animated Brackenridge's conception of the ideal republic. Like many other late-eighteenth-century Americans, the Pennsylvanian believed that hard work and steady productivity sustained a virtuous republic. As he lectured his fellow citizens in a 1793 installment of *Modern Chivalry*,

> The attainments of men are made to depend usually upon their industry. As ye sow, so shall ye reap. In well regulated societies this economy is imitated, and where one estate comes by accident, five hundred are acquired by common means. Such an institution of things constitutes the health of any people.

"Happiness depends on a gradual accession of attainment," Brackenridge continued. "There can be nothing more hurtful to a people than sudden losses and sudden gains to individuals."[74]

This emphasis on an ethic of hard work—the citizen's capacity for being "content to labour in his vocation" with "common industry"—led Brackenridge to oppose an ethic of pecuniary gain. He particularly opposed speculators, since they attempted to profit by manipulation and chance rather than by productive endeavor. As Hugh Henry's son later recalled in 1856, "No one despised money, and the lovers and getters of money, more heartily than he did. He was, in fact, continually inveighing against speculators, misers, and avaricious people, and was a perfect example of the philosophy he taught." The willful pursuit of money would not only warp the regard given to talent and virtue, but also cause common people "dissatisfaction with their state in life." Brackenridge even carried his argument to the point of opposing a property requirement for voting. "A government of liberty is the most delicate of all structures," he contended, "and there is no preserving it, if the love of money is encouraged, and made the sole evidence of patriotism."[75]

Brackenridge appreciated nonetheless the tension between his advocacy of hard labor, on the one hand, and his condemnation of materialism, ambition, and avarice, on the other. The problem was that the one often led quite naturally to the other. The novelist pondered this complex republican dilemma at one point in *Modern Chivalry*. Disparaging "ambition" as "the poison of public virtue," he paused to reflect, "but take away the spring of ambition . . . and you relax industry; you increase indolence. I grant it. But it saves the heart. There may be less eminence; but there will be more goodness." The problem ultimately called forth a moral appeal from Bracken-ridge. Hard work and productivity were good insofar as they shaped virtue in private and public life. Material gain was a secondary by-product—acceptable, perhaps even salutary, in moderation—but it required restraint if corruption was to be avoided. A character in *Modern Chivalry* explained the necessity of this moral forbearance: "Self-denial is the virtue of a republic. It is the opposite of ambition. Self-denial looks only at justice. It looks at the public good." In this investigation of the social consequences of work and advancement, Brackenridge showed himself to be poised uneasily between the re-publican and liberal worlds, midway in the larger American journey from the Protestant Ethic to the Spirit of Capitalism. While casting a skeptical and satirical eye on the tendencies of the emerging new social code of early-nineteenth-century America, he also knew of its origins in older American traditions.[76]

Thus *Modern Chivalry* clearly manifested several of Hugh Henry Brackenridge's social and political concerns: the imperatives neces-sary to a virtuous republic, the need for hard work but material restraint, the distrust of ambition and avarice as social principles. But as the "tale" of the book unfolds, more complex and interesting themes bob to the surface. Probably raised in unconscious fashion by the author as devices to provide structure and detail for the narrative, certain incidents nonetheless reflect the author's dim perception of deeper and more intense difficulties in the process of social change during the early republic.

The novel's very first episode, for instance, presented a disturbed portrait of "con men," unscrupulous profit-seeking, and violence, all coated with but a thin veneer of humor. Leaving home at the outset of their journey through the states, Captain Farrago and Teague quickly came across a gathering of rural youngbloods at a country village. They had organized a horse race and tried to persuade the Captain to pay a fee, enter the old plow-horse he was riding, and win the purse. They assured him that the animal had "some hidden quality of swiftness" and that "there is no trusting appearances." "For they could have no idea," Brackenridge wrote, "that a man could come there in so singular a manner, with a groom at his foot, unless he had some great object of making money by the adventure." The Captain, having at least some good sense, indignantly refused their invitation but dismounted to observe the race. It was hotly contested, and a close and inconclusive finish set several of the owners clamoring for the winner's share. Tempers flaring, the crowd erupted into a full-fledged brawl. The Captain rose to his feet amid the mayhem of fist-fighting and then climbed atop his horse to lecture the combatants on their scurrilous behavior. He sternly announced the need for "principles of decorum, and good breeding" and appealed to the honorable standards of ancient chivalry. The Captain was first ignored, of course, and then knocked from his horse in the melee and punched in the head. Dazed and bleeding from the skull wound, he was pulled from amid the swirling crowd by the quick-witted Teague.[77]

This initial episode, although funny in its slapstick quality, established an underlying tone of disquietude that persisted throughout the novel. The "race" of life in a liberalizing society—as the horse race episode quickly indicated—could be a thoroughly nasty affair. A sense of social disarray, vicious competitive wrangling, and emotional unsteadiness pervaded Brackenridge's narrative. The theme of fragmentation and violent conflict, for example, also appeared in an ethnic and religious guise. When Teague temporarily left the service of the Captain, he was replaced as servant by the self-righteous Presbyterian Scotsman, Duncan Ferguson. When Teague returned, the "Papist" and the "Presby" took an instant dislike to one another. The two immigrants hurled ethnic and religious slurs at one another until the Captain narrowly headed off a bout of fighting. In satirizing the revivals of the Second Great Awakening, Brackenridge further suggested the agitation of social fragmentation in the early republic. In an 1805 installment he sarcastically described the character of a religious camp meeting. "Convulsive gestures and gesticulations are symptoms of a mind conceiving new ideas," he wrote. "Shouting, falling down, and tumbling are concomitants of a reform, and an evidence of a right conception of things. The more extravagant the actions, the surer signs of being in the true faith." Teague involved himself in the action by "participating in this tumult." By shrieking, standing on his head, walking on his hands, and curling into a ball to roll down the hills, the Irishman became the center of attention and was pronounced one of the "converted" by the preachers present. The Captain could only express his astonishment and disapproval of this "phrenzy" and "fanaticism," while the shrewd Teague was smothered by the kisses of young evangelical women.[78]

But in the end, *Modern Chivalry*'s accounts of fraud, dissembling, and dishonest manipulation comprised the darkest theme in Brackenridge's underlying social commentary. Several incidents in the narrative reveal a persistent anxiety over "con men" and their profit-making deceits. The case of the "Indian treaty-maker" is one of the more humorous and indicative. Early in the novel, a stranger from the frontier asked the Captain to borrow Teague for a few days in return for a sum of money. When the Captain inquired about his purposes, the gentleman explained that he often utilized immigrants—"because some unknown gibberish is necessary"—and dressed them up in costume to impersonate Indian chiefs. Approaching public officials, he then swindled the government out of several thousands of dollars designated for treaty negotiation and distribution of goods to frontier tribes. The scam was an easy one, explained the stranger, because the government "knows no more of Indians than a cow does of Greek." When the Captain expressed his outrage at such bald deception—Teague, of course, was happy to participate—the stranger only shrugged and said, "It is a very common thing for men to speculate now a-days. If you will not, another will. An 100 dollars might as well be in your pocket as another man's." Confidence men and their "masks of duplicity," as the Indian treaty-maker pointed out to the innocent Captain, "are now reduced to a system."[79]

Brackenridge's depictions of social turmoil and distrust also colored his observations about politics in the early republic. Certain incidents in the novel indicate an uncertainty about American civic life that went beyond a concern with the excesses of "democracy." *Modern Chivalry* portrays a politics in which increased popular participation was sullied by growing class friction and resentment. In the novel's second incident, a group of rural electors explained to the Captain their preference for a "common weaver" over a well-to-do "man of education." They informed him, "It is better to trust a plain man like him, than one of the high flyers, that will make laws to suit their own purposes." And later in their travels, Captain Farrago and Teague arrived in a large city—more than likely Philadelphia—where they found that the leading candidates for election "were all remarkably pot-bellied" and "lived in large brick buildings." A local resident explained to them that local politics provided success only to someone who had "his scores o' shares in the bank; and was in league with the brokers, and had . . . a ship or two on the docks." Political life, the townsman concluded, "is now lost in substantial interest, and the funds command everything." Another character put the matter differently. Every government, he asserted, saw a "perpetual war" between "a patrician class" and "the multitide." Brackenridge, through the use of such incident and detail, demonstrated a grasp of emerging liberal politics. His sketches of elite manipulation, resentment by commoners, and class friction went beyond a critique of "democracy." They also made for a gloomy assessment.[80]

Thus the "tale" of *Modern Chivalry* involved a hidden report on agitated public life in the early republic. As it unfolded, however, a

complex and subliminal story of profound private agitation also came
into focus. The geographical journey of Captain Farrago and Teague
was in many ways only a cover for the novel's real journey: the pair's
exploration of personality and character, a psychic adventure that
instigated much of the novel's implicit drama. The running clashes
between the restrained Captain and the impulsive Teague reproduced
the dialectical pressures descending on the individual in a liberalizing
society. Brackenridge's handling of their relationship—especially
when considered in light of his own career—imparts much about the
liberal individual's problems of character formation and identity
achievement.

Recovering this psychological dimension of *Modern Chivalry*
must begin with the author's characterization of the primary protagonists. Teague, the ebullient Irishman, provided the novel's
spark. Full of mischief and cheerfully anarchic, he is one of the most
compelling figures in early American fiction. As created by Brackenridge, he leaps through the pages as an aspiring self-made man run
amok in the society of the early republic. A good part of Teague's
personality consisted of his well-known ambition. As the author described him early in the novel, "Teague insisted that he had a right to
make the best of his fortune: and as there was a door open to his
advancement he did not see why he might not make use of it."
Moreover, this eagerness to push ahead involved him in a variety of
vocations. Through the course of the narrative, Teague attempted to
become successively a statesman, philosopher, minister, actor, government official, military officer, lawyer, judge, doctor, and professor of literature. And near the novel's end he became a professional
"con man" in his capacity as assistant to a "conjurer," a particularly
fitting endeavor since all his earlier vocations had been but mere
impersonations and scams.[81]

A consistent craving for sexual adventure also seasoned Teague's
unrestrained scramble for advancement. Early in *Modern Chivalry*,
he assaulted a chambermaid at a rural village inn by sneaking into her
bed in the middle of the night. When her howls of protest brought
fellow roomers running, Teague characteristically blamed the incident on a minister in the adjoining room and claimed only to be
rescuing the virtue of the poor girl. Just as characteristically, he also
demanded and received "hush money" from the poor minister, who
had been completely unnerved by the incident. At later points in the
story, the Irishman engaged in similar sexual shenanigans. He
feigned religious conversion to gain the caresses of emotionally over-
wrought women at a revival. He pretended to be "Major O'Regan,"
a military hero, and became the pet of high-society women of an

eastern city. It thus seems no accident that Brackenridge meta-
phorically associated not only Teague, but also most aspiring common men of his ilk, with animals in the novel. For example, shortly
after his appointment as a government excise officer, Teague was
tarred and feathered by angry farmers. Found lying in the woods by
several rural entrepreneurs, he was subsequently hauled around the
territory and exhibited as an "uncommon creature" of possibly the
"Ouran Outang" family or the "bird family" or maybe a link between "the brutal and the human species." Brackenridge continued
the leitmotif in his satirization of popular politics. He contrived a
serious public debate over the merits of "bestial suffrage," the question being whether "any mere quadruped" could vote, or only particularly valuable animals. Thus Teague materialized in the novel as an
amalgam of intense sexual, social, and pecuniary appetites.[82]

Brackenridge presented Captain John Farrago as a stark contrast.
An old bachelor of cordial disposition, the Captain maintained a
respectable farm of moderate income and stood esteemed in his community. He was possessed of "good natural sense, and considerable
reading; but in some things whimsical, owing perhaps to his greater
knowledge of books than of the world." According to the author, the
ideas of the old republican gentleman "were drawn chiefly from what
may be called the old school; the Greek and Roman notions of
things." His politics followed traditional republican guidelines: an
abiding concern for the public good, a commitment to virtue, a belief
in deference to leadership by the talented, and support for a balanced
government of "near equipoise of the legislative, judicial, and executive powers." Highly suspicious of ambition and avarice as social
values, the Captain instead held forth in favor of hard work, restraint, and modest advancement. He once lectured to Teague, "It
must be a bad nature that has generated this proposterous aiming and
stretching at promotion. . . . You [are] a republican, and yet destitute of republican virtue, the basis of which I take to be *humility*
and *self-denial*."[83]

Brackenridge so constructed *Modern Chivalry* as to focus on the
inevitable clash of the wild, unscrupulous Irishman and the slightly
befuddled but earnest gentleman farmer. The personality of each
character functioned as a foil for the other. The novel unfolds by
virtue of scenarios in which Teague's endless schemes to achieve
success—usually conducted by dubious means and ending in a tangle
of difficulty—are opposed, thwarted, or disembarrassed by the Captain. Such incidents suggest the historical friction of an older republican and newer liberal society at the turn of the eighteenth century. As such they provided the grist for Brackenridge's satirical

mill. He poked fun both at the naive, stuffy traditionalism of the Captain and at the social-climbing irresponsibility of Teague.

But the *way* in which the protagonists' relationship developed also suggested the strain of character formation in the society of the early republic. Their friction followed a persistent and significant pattern. First, Teague's indulgence of instinctual appetites and his slovenly appearance consistently triggered the Captain's sense of restraint, propriety, and self-control. At one point, for example, the Captain decided to aid Teague by making him more presentable. He forcibly subjected the Irishman to a bath, purchased new clothes for him, and tried to compel him to weed out "vulgarities" and "indecencies" from his manners. Second, while Teague constantly engaged in manipulation and scheming to get ahead, the Captain insisted that hard work was the only acceptable path. When Teague proposed to become a fly-by-night lawyer to gain a quick buck, for instance, the Captain reacted by having him committed to an urban "workhouse" where "hard labour" would cure his unseemly ambition. As the final strand of the pattern, Teague persistently practiced dishonesty, fraud, and the deceptive use of "masks" in his social dealings. The Captain, on the other hand, countered with a code of truth, honesty, and reason. To choose but one example, early in the novel the irascible servant attempted to become a candidate for "holy orders" by dispensing a long line of religious "blarney" to a group of ministers. The Captain consequently exposed the Irishman as a "hypocrit" and "ragamuffin" and declared that he had "no more religion than my horse."[84]

This whole cluster of contrary traits duplicated the process by which a liberal temperament took shape in the early republic. Brackenridge, not wholly committed to either Teague or Captain Farrago, unconsciously sketched a key historical drama of the era: the slow emergence of a character ethic of individual freedom, mobility, and ambition tempered with a substantial dose of hard work and moral restraint. This cultural commitment to "self-control" became a hallmark of nineteenth-century American Victorian culture and an animating feature of its capitalist society. *Modern Chivalry*, through its handling of Teague and Captain Farrago, opens a window on the dialectical cultural process that produced this ethos in the early years of nationhood.

Brackenridge's imaginative deployment of the two protagonists also indicated—at an even deeper and more inchoate psychological level—the individual's problematic striving for identity in a liberalizing society. The oppositional arrangement of Teague and the Captain, with the author posed somewhat uneasily between them, duplicates Freud's model of personality. Teague, with his libidinous instincts constantly seeking gratification, seems to be a near-perfect representation of the Id. His employer, with his strict moral code and bent for punishment, likewise appears to be a token for the Superego. The author—always looming behind and frequently intruding directly into the text of *Modern Chivalry*—symbolically bounces between and mediates the demands of each. Operating according to an uncertain "reality principle" in the transforming early republic, Brackenridge signifies a frail Ego struggling to stabilize the personality. Erik Erikson insightfully describes this functioning of the Ego in a historical context. "Between the id and superego," he writes, "the ego dwells. Consistently balancing and warding off the extreme ways of the other two, the ego keeps tuned to the reality of the historical day, testing perceptions, selecting memories, governing action, and otherwise integrating the individual's capacities of orientation and planning." Erikson notes further the correlation between the nature of "ego qualities, social institutions, and historical eras." It seems not unreasonable to conclude, then, that the centrifugal tendencies in the decades from 1790 to 1820 made the Ego's tasks that much more difficult. In a society where flux seemed increasingly the only rule, the obstacles impeding the liberal individual's achievement of ego identity and personal stability must have been enormous. *Modern Chivalry* certainly indicated this. The tension between the two protagonists never resolved itself in the narrative. Teague never achieved legitimate success. Captain Farrago never overcame his befuddlement and resentment. And Brackenridge never finalized in the novel any psychological integration of these clashing instincts within the personality. Indeed, as the author noted of Teague's character at one point, "I have not been able to do it justice, being but half an Irishman myself."[85]

Furthermore, Brackenridge's own life indicated this process of identity diffusion at work in the early republic. This self-made man's long struggle to find a satisfying vocation offered one symptom. His lifelong ambivalence over art and the demands of a pecuniary society suggested another. But Brackenridge's own personality put forward the most conclusive evidence. By almost all accounts the Pennsylvanian was decidedly eccentric, and many thought him downright mad. Brackenridge admitted in 1795, "I am subject to a delinquency or failing of nerves, especially when anything affects my mind." Stories of his weird behavior abounded. He often appeared in court, even after becoming a judge of the Pennsylvania Supreme Court, in severe disrepair. One observer commented that he once charged a jury "standing in his bare feet, with his boots beside him, for he had no stockings at that time.". Another expressed amazement at his appearance on the bench. "In the coldest weather he sat with his breast entirely open," he wrote of Brackenridge, "his small clothes without suspenders, and neither exactly on or off; his beard unshaven, and his hair undressed . . . and feet propped up against the desk." Another witness reported even stranger behavior while out riding in a coach during a rainstorm. While heading for shelter, the passengers came across a figure "what might be conceived of Don Quixote, in one of his wildest moods: a man with nothing on but his hat and boots." With the shocked observers staring, the nude Brackenridge reportedly explained, "Although I am a judge, I have but one suit, and the storm, you know, would spoil the clothes; but it wouldn't spoil me."[86]

Brackenridge's family life offered further hints of a personality somewhat loosely wrapped. In that arena, however, harshness and caprice seemed to replace inappropriateness. When the author's wife died in 1787, he practically abandoned his infant son, Henry Marie. Placed with a local cobbler and ignored by his father, the child was harshly treated and had to be rescued by a landlady named "Madam Marie." Brackenridge continued to neglect the child until an interest in religion appeared at age two, at which time the father purchased a slim volume on religion and tried to force the child to learn to read by beating him. The youngster's screams brought "Madam Marie" to the rescue once more. Then in 1790 Brackenridge remarried under rather bizarre circumstances. Traveling through the countryside, he happened to observe Sabina Wolfe, the beautiful daughter of a poor Dutch farmer, at work and became infatuated with her. After slipping the father some money and conducting a two-day courtship, he married the untutored girl and promptly hustled her off to Philadelphia for grooming and polishing. A short time later, young Henry picked up some German phrases from his new step-grandfather. His father decided that a talent for languages had surfaced and promptly shipped his son several hundred miles into the interior of the continent with a near stranger. The boy was placed with a French family, unknown to the elder Brackenridge, in Ste. Genevieve in the Missouri Territory. When young Henry returned to Pittsburgh in 1795, the judge coldly noted their years-long separation with the question "Well, boy, can you read French?"[87]

Brackenridge's persistent use of humor as a means of social communication tendered a final suggestion of personal turbulence. *Modern Chivalry* itself comprised nearly a quarter-century of sustained satirical writing. But an observer noted Brackenridge's compulsion to humor even in everyday life, saying, "In the most of his discussions even of the gravest subjects, [he] intermingled some facetious story, or a quotation from ancient or modern poets, either in the way of merriment or ridicule." Brackenridge apparently reveled in his capacity for making witticisms, boasting to one visitor, "I enjoy a truly inexhaustible richness of mind." But the significance of this humor lies in its deeper meaning. Freud argued that such a tendency to joke-making emerges from impulses in the unconscious. One possibility is that sexual urges, blocked by the repressions of civilization, find indirect expression through "obscene wit"—the sexual innuendo or dirty joke. In similar fashion, aggressive instincts can also seek a circuitous outlet through the "hostile wit"—the satire, the put-down, the joke of ridicule. This latter variety of humor seems most evident in *Modern Chivalry*. In many ways Brackenridge was an angry and violent man, and the intersection of wit and rage in his expression deserves brief mention.[88]

The Pennsylvanian had something of a reputation for outbursts of physical violence. While practicing as an attorney, he would occasionally and inexplicably chase clients out of his office and into the street while they were trying to discuss their legal problems. His son Henry Marie later recalled his father's not infrequent bouts of fighting, relating with relish one particular incident where a gentleman followed Hugh Henry into the back room of a tavern and drew a sword over some perceived insult. Brackenridge leveled the assailant with a nearby wooden chair and threw him into the fireplace. The author's affinity for violence and anger seems to have found expression also in the novel, where it surfaced in the attire of humor. One incident that reflected this wit-rage dichotomy occurred when Brackenridge had the Captain reply to a duel challenge:

> Sir, I have two objections to this duel matter. The one is, lest I should hurt you; the other is, lest you should hurt me. . . . If you want to try your pistols, take some object, a tree or barn door about my dimensions. If you hit that, send me word, and I shall acknowledge that if I had been in the same place, you might also have hit me.

This use of wit either to vent the steam of anger or to express it indirectly also cropped up in real life. According to Brackenridge's account of the Whiskey Rebellion, he continually tried to defuse the anger of the insurgents by making them laugh. The night before the proposed rebel attack on Pittsburgh, the lawyer passed from group to group answering questions and trying to head off the coming assault. When asked if attacking the garrison would mean a great loss, Brackenridge replied with pointed humor, "Not at all; not above a thousand killed and five hundred mortally wounded." When one also considers the mountains of ridicule heaped on offending character

types and social groups in *Modern Chivalry*, it is evident that Brackenridge's "hostile wit" reflected a personality at odds both with itself
and with a radically changing society.[89]

Brackenridge's private struggles—with identity diffusion, with
the rage of an unintegrated personality, with the isolation engendered
by a social ethic of self-made success—illuminated personal tensions.
But they also pointed to a broad psychological predicament in the
wider culture of the early American republic. The emergence of a
liberal society in the decades from 1790 to 1820 placed uniquely
intense pressures on the individual psyche. Drifting ever farther
from traditional anchors of family, community, and hierarchy, the
"self" was forced to search anxiously for new sources of moral authority and personal cohesion. Some found stability relatively quickly, but many Americans apparently experienced the crucial process of
meshing social system with personality integration as a long, arduous,
and often only partially successful one. *Modern Chivalry* indicated
rather convincingly, if unconsciously, the subsequent appearances of
the "personae" in antebellum America. This distinctly modern
psyche—described by theorists as the "fractured self" or technically
defined as a "pluralist personality structure"—is characterized by
personal incoherence and anxiety-ridden anger. Of frail ego strength
and adopting sundry "masks" to achieve social success, the "personae" struggles for stability and identity. Like an impressionist paint-
ing, Brackenridge's novel provides a brilliantly blurred image of the
"personae's" painful adjustments to the commercializing market society that had produced it. The author, through his personal fusion of
hostility and wit and his juxtaposition of Captain Farrago and Teague
O'Regan, stood forth as the "personae" personified in the early
republic.[90]

In the manner of Taylor and Adams, Brackenridge emerged ultimately as a trenchant if paradoxical social critic of early national
America. He typified a profound cultural dichotomy in Jeffersonian
America. On the one hand, his career and many of his values suggested an instinct for ambition and self-made success. But on the
other hand the personal guilt and uncertainty accruing to such a social
ethic manifested itself in subsequent demands for self-control and
angry outbursts against social disorder. Thus Brackenridge's novel,
by exploring this dichotomy, supplies a wealth of insights into the
deeper complexities and tensions of life in the early stages of American capitalist culture. In the end, however, it is ironic that Brackenridge's embodiment of social mobility and advancement and his es-
pousal of hard work and self-denial helped create the "modern
chivalry" he found so troubling.

War and the Wages of Change

John Taylor, John Adams, and Hugh Henry Brackenridge pene-
trated the optimistic facade of early-nineteenth-century America and
caught glimpses of the complex, disquieting ambiance beneath. Yet
their analyses of the transforming early republic ultimately converged in another way. Each man perceived, although vaguely and in
a different fashion, that historical change and war somehow became
intertwined in the spring of 1812 in the looming confrontation with
Great Britain. They sensed that the issues that preoccupied them—
capitalism and confusion, ambition and humbug, virtue and self-
interest, public and private cohesion—were feeding the spreading
flames of war in a variety of complex ways. These three aging critics
saw the War of 1812 as a crucial event for the young republic—
fraught with danger and opportunity alike, and bound up with the
forces of change encircling them.

Typical of most Westerners, Brackenridge fully supported the
war effort, noting, "It was always a matter of astonishment to me to
hear it suggested that this war in which we are engaged with Great
Britain was unjust." As a frontier inhabitant, he expressed particular
anger over the British supply of "implements not of agriculture, but
of hatcheting and scalping" to western Indian tribes. But Brackenridge's endorsement was not without reservation. He grew deeply
troubled over two underlying issues. First, the association between
commercial pursuits and war left him very uneasy. He attributed to
commercial greed "the greater part of the bloodshed that we have had
in the eastern and western world for half a century. Commercial
avidity, and love of gain, have been at the bottom of all our wars."
Second, he grew suspicious that war opened numerous opportunities
for the unscrupulous and the ambitious. In one of the later installments of *Modern Chivalry,* for example, he satirized Americans who
seemed eager to use violent conflict for cheap glory and advancement.
Teague, stumbling into the midst of an Indian war on the frontier,
successfully persuaded a group of townspeople that he had van-
quished an entire tribe of savages in a heroic battle. The facts told a
different story. While Teague indeed had fallen into an Indian am-
bush, the frightful volume of his screaming—not his heroism—
convinced his assailants that an entire army was at hand. When the
Indians melted into the woods, Teague happily accepted the credit
and became a "major general" in the local militia. So war with
England, while eminently justifiable for Brackenridge, also raised
his fears that it would construct a stage on which "con men" and
money-grubbers could act out their ambitions.[91]

Like the Pennsylvania novelist, John Taylor of Caroline saw the 1812 conflict as linked to the wide-ranging changes that had been so unsettling to him since 1790. But in contrast to Brackenridge, he fervently opposed the confrontation with Great Britain. Taylor was convinced that war posed extreme dangers for the young American republic, primarily because it would raise taxes and dramatically increase executive prerogatives. As he observed to James Monroe shortly before the declaration of hostilities, the United States would only "gain taxes and tyranny by conquest." Taylor also believed that war would intensify the distressing factionalism of post-1790 American politics. Perceiving that patriotism would become the tool of partisan political interests, he denounced saber-rattling as a childish "habit of blowing up a mob as boys blow up bladders which by heating are made to burst with a great noise." Or as he put it more calmly in the 1814 *Inquiry*, "War is the keenest carving knife for cutting up nations into delicious morsels for parties and their leaders. It swells a few people to monstrous moral size. . . . It breeds a race of men, nominally heroes, mistaken for patriots, and really tyrants."[92]

Yet for Taylor, war's ultimate threat to republican institutions lay elsewhere. He condemned the War of 1812 longest and loudest for its service to the interests of "finance capitalists." Whereas in medieval Europe wars had enriched "titled orders" by pillage and the seizing of land, now "paper orders acquire wealth in modern wars by loaning, although nothing is obtained by conquest." Ironically, continued the Virginian, it was in England where the forces of "paper and patronage" had been most successful in fomenting war as a boon to their own advancement. The example of Great Britain demonstrated that war "put arms into the hands of ambition, avarice, pride, and self-love." Thus, by fighting England the younger nation merely imitated the older nation's depravity. So for John Taylor, even if England suffered military defeat, a victorious America would lose its republican soul to a more dangerous internal enemy: the spirit of "finance capitalism."[93]

While John Adams also saw the War of 1812 as part and parcel of the social transformation of the early American republic, he offered a more ambivalent and nuanced assessment than either Brackenridge or Taylor did. Skeptical of war with any European power since the 1790s, he gradually became an enthusiastic backer of the English conflict. The New Englander's process of rationalization proved very revealing. In one way, he viewed war as an especially dangerous undertaking for republics. It threatened to involve them in "monstrous Debt," "Taxes," and "Corruption." In addition to posing these overt hazards to republican virtue, war in Adams' eyes also

excited the passion for "distinction." Foreseeing the wartime temptations for personal aggrandizement, he warned as early as 1790 that
"every man in an army is constantly aspiring to be something higher,
as every citizen in the commonwealth is constantly struggling for a
better rank, that he may draw the observation of more eyes." So for
this troubled old man, the War of 1812 seemed to embody the restless
ambition of post-Revolutionary social change.[94]

Yet the voice of Adams' somber, cold-eyed Puritan ancestors whis-
pered to him another message of realism. War, as he frequently noted
to himself and others, unfortunately appeared to be an inevitable and
perhaps necessary part of human affairs. He scribbled in the margin
of a tract on political rights: "Nations in every stage of society from
savages to the most civilized are too much addicted to war, and the
freer they are, the greater their pride, the stronger their resentment,
and the more prone to war." Not only were wars unavoidable, Adams
continued, but they held potential for purging and strengthening the
national spirit. He remarked to his close friend Dr. Benjamin Rush
in July 1812:

> I believe . . . that wars, at times, are as necessary for the preservation
> and perfection, the prosperity, liberty, happiness, virtue, and indepen-
> dence of nations as gales of wind to the salubrity of the atmosphere, or the
> agitations of the ocean to prevent its stagnation and putrefecation [sic].[95]

By the summer of 1812, Adams concluded that the United States
must go to war with the English "aggressor" and allied himself with
the Jeffersonian Republicans. Yet he endorsed the military struggle
for reasons that ultimately transcended any strategic quarrel with
Great Britain. He interpreted the conflict as a trial of American
virtue, as a test of her republican citizens' capacity for disinterested
support of the common good. Adams had been rather traumatized by
the liberalizing changes in American society following the Revolution, and the war seemed to him a barometer of whether that transformation had brought ascendancy or decay. He remained uncertain,
declaring to President Madison in late 1814, "It is the decree of
Providence, as I believe, that this nation must be purified in the
furnace of affliction." The temptations of ambition and avarice had
unraveled the American social fabric, but the war seemed to be
teaching the folly of such unrestrained selfishness. Even during the
war's darkest hours, when American arms had been consistently
crushed by the British, Adams found a certain solace. Writing to
Benjamin Rush once more in 1813, he declared, "Alas! Defeat after
defeat. I hope these defeats will teach us the necessity of system,

subordination, discipline, and obedience!" Adams eventually came to appreciate the war as melding several felicitous impulses—a vigorous public spirit, a virtuous and nonmaterialist ethos, an assertive sense of American independence—under the rubric of nationalism. He had announced early in the nineteenth century, "My principle has been to support a National government; national Honour; national Union and national Independence." By 1812 Adams believed that war with Great Britain advanced those principles. He predicted of the military successes he hoped would be forthcoming, "They will ferment in the Minds of this People till they generate a national self-respect, a Spirit of Independence and a national Pride which has never before been felt in America."[96]

THE commentary of Adams, Taylor, and Brackenridge on the War of 1812 suggests much about its American origins. Each man knew that the reasons for war transcended mere politics, or foreign affairs, or national resentment. They sensed that the conflict was intertwined with the manifold forces overturning American society in the era of the early republic. Each saw, however dimly, some of the tangled ties between various pressures of liberalizing social change—commercial growth, individual ambition, nervous concern for the public good, ambivalence over profit-seeking, the survival of republicanism, problematic social cohesion—and war. They tried to articulate the broad reverberations they felt between the impulse to war and the massive transformation of early nineteenth-century America. Yet issues of war and social change raised by these aging critics proved even more complex than they realized. An elaborate mosaic of tension, aspiration, and violence existed in the summer of 1812. As Jeffersonian Republicans nudged the republic toward confrontation with Great Britain, various pieces in this pattern—social, cultural, psychological, political—grew brighter before merging into a luminous whole. Each piece had a fascinating history and, inter-locking in 1812, linked war with the consolidating authority of American liberal capitalism. To this motivational mosaic we now turn.

II

Ambition and Civism:
War and Social Regeneration

Thus not only does democracy make every man forget his ancestors,
but it hides his descendents and separates his contemporaries from him;
it throws him back forever upon himself alone
and threatens in the end
to confine him entirely within the solitude of his own heart.

ALEXIS DE TOCQUEVILLE
Democracy in America

Man is not a farmer, or a professor, or an engineer, but he is all.
Man is priest, and scholar, and statesman, and producer, and soldier.
In the divided or social state these functions are parcelled out
to individuals. . . . The state of society is one in which
the members have suffered amputation from the trunk, and strut about
as so many walking monsters—a good finger, a neck, a stomach,
an elbow, but never a man.

RALPH WALDO EMERSON
The American Scholar

In 1793 Enos Hitchcock published *The Farmer's Friend; or, The History of Mr. Charles Worthy*, a didactic tale of aspiration and success. The piece enthusiastically described its protagonist as a youth "who, from being a poor orphan, rose through various scenes of distress and misfortune to wealth and eminence by industry, economy, and good conduct." Praising young Charles' reliance on "his own character" after the early death of his parents, Hitchcock pictured the subsequent "glow of manly pride excited by rising wealth and independence." The orphan began his climb to prosperity by entering the household of Mr. Smith, a well-to-do farmer, as a hired hand. Working hard for several years, he finally glimpsed his chance to buy a small tract of land. To do so, he secured credit from his employer, an action by which, in the author's words, "Charles felt the benefit of a good character." The rest of the story detailed the young farmer's growing abundance and attributed it to his "steady industry and frugality," "strict attention to his affairs," and diligence as "an economist of time."[1]

Yet perhaps the most significant portion of *The History of Charles Worthy* came near the end of the story. In drawing the narrative to a close, Hitchcock paused to reflect on the larger context of social mobility in the early American republic. He carefully built on, yet went beyond, eighteenth-century idealogues of success like Benjamin Franklin. Relishing the commercial spirit of the age, Hitchcock affirmed that it was *better* to "save" than to "earn" a penny, because "the same economy that teaches how to save a penny, will teach us also how to make the best and most advantageous use of it." This primitive sense of thrift and investment as a key to individual success led the author to a final directive. Ambitious Americans, he instructed, should steer a middle course between "Liberality," or giving material goods away, and "Avarice," or hoarding them. The appropriate goal was "Economy," the lovely "mistress of the golden mean." Thus this story suggested that the wise use of money, combined with hard work and upstanding moral conduct, would hoist upward through society the aspiring individual.[2]

Hitchcock's allegorical tale expressed clearly a new American social *mentalité* consolidating in the era of the early republic. In the decades after the Revolution, scores of like-minded polemicists—most of them ambitious, energetic Jeffersonians—busily began to shape a full-fledged success ethic for restless American republicans. Cropping up in all sections of the republic and in a variety of modes—newspaper editorials, political speeches, moral pamphlets, almanacs, holiday orations, sermons, and essays—this Jeffersonian social ideology gradually gathered momentum, cohesion, and force by the early nineteenth century. They did not quite roll off the presses "like water over Niagara," as one historian described the advice pieces issuing forth in post-1830 Victorian America, but the modest endeavors of Hitchcock and others did provide the basic text for subsequent "apostles of the self-made man" like Horatio Alger. Admittedly, respect for hard work had flourished in both the Puritan and republican traditions of colonial America, while a sense of social opportunity had prompted in part even the first migrations to English North America in the early 1600s. Yet recent scholarship has shown that colonial Americans also had faced their environment armed with significant and resilient premodern and precapitalist values: overriding loyalty to the lineal family, a predominant moral valuation of work, an ethos of paternalism, and a social and political regard for the common good.[3] So if discourse like Hitchcock's did not represent a total revolution in American social values, it did suggest a significant shift. It indicated that earlier restraints were crumbling after 1790 before a new creed promoting individual ambition, upward mobility, commercial activity, and profit. *The History of Charles Worthy* and similar tales pulsated with a visionary energy and sense of opportunity generated by liberalizing change in the young nation.[4]

In predictable fashion, early national success literature usually began by insisting on the necessity of industrious habits. Reaching out to a popular audience, *The Youth's Guide to Wisdom for the Rising Generation* (1812), for instance, admonished in time-worn fashion, "He that hath not energy to work, is but little respected, and is in general clothed in rags." Yet paeans to energetic labor also contained subtle nuances and departures in the decades after 1790. Almanacs, for example, often urged reliance on autonomous effort and deemphasized social attachment, directing, "He who will not help himself shan't have help from no one." Other essays stressed productivity as the primary value of hard work. Like the pamphlet *Moral and Prudential Maxims and Savings* (1810), they enthusiastically announced, "He that in the same time can produce more than others, has *rigour;* that can produce more and better, has *talents;* that can produce what none else can, has *genius.*"[5]

As a means of focusing habits of productive work and individual autonomy, many didactic writers began to urge a strengthening of the individual "will." John Foster, an English Baptist preacher whose essays were widely reprinted in America, argued in 1807 that the young man entering the world should cultivate a "decisive character" combining health, observation, energy, and "complete confidence in his own judgement." "A strenuous *will* must accompany the conclusions of thought," the minister wrote, "and constantly urge the utmost efforts for their practical accomplishment." Foster also assured his readers that "*success* tends considerably to reinforce this character" after the individual "has measured his force with various persons, when he has braved and conquered difficulty, and partly seized the prize." Other tracts warned readers that, without strong willpower, talent and intelligence would mean nothing in the social arena. To gain advantage the individual must strive to be "uniform" in all actions, "distinguish with exactness" between "*wishes* and *will*," and "act with vigour and decision." One anonymous pamphleteer summed up: "The more independent of accidents, the more self-subsistent, the more fraught with internal resources—the greater the character." In a liberalizing society where opportunity beckoned but failure always threatened, inner strength as well as work became critical to individual accomplishment.[6]

From this moral matrix of industrious habits and the strenuous will emerged social guidelines of behavior for the individual success-seeker. Moralists grounded their advice partly in traditional republican and Protestant appeals to "improvement" and "emulation." The virtuous individual, according to these older traditions, was duty-bound to improve himself by education, hard work, and piety in order to become a good citizen and a godly being. Thus tracts like *True Stories to Inculcate Principles of Virtue and Piety* (1811) would continue teaching in part that "virtuous youth" was necessary for "accomplished and flourishing manhood." Didactic literature of the early republic, however, began to depict "emulation" as only a first step toward success. Americans began grafting almost imperceptibly values of energy and accomplishment onto time-worn moral imperatives. *True Stories* further suggested that excellent characters and actions "stimulate our endeavors . . . animate our exertions. They beget a chastened confidence in the powers of the mind." Other moralists put the matter more bluntly and explicitly connected emulation to an ethos of competition. One writer typically enthused, "By a virtuous emulation the spirit of man is exalted within him; he panteth after fame, and rejoiceth as a racer to run his course."[7]

The multiplying literature of success in the early republic also promoted an unprecedented attentiveness to money and profit as the standard of achievement. Washington Irving lampooned this tendency in an 1807 number of *Salmagundi*. "Mustapha," a fictitious Turkish traveler stranded in the United States, wrote to a correspondent in his homeland of "a great maxim, which in this country comprehends all the rules of prudence, and all the duties a man owes to himself—namely, *getting the worth of their money*." Other commentaries followed a less satirical vein. In the *New England Almanack for 1811*, for example, there appeared an intriguing forty-two-line poem entitled simply "Cash." It began by noting, "Wise moralists in vain have told, how sordid is the love of gold, Which they call filthy trash; Thou stranger to these of mine, Ten thousand virtues still are thine, Thou all sufficient *Cash!*" The poem went on extolling the power and influence of money—"The earth is at thy sole command, It gravitates to *Cash*"—and urged Americans to pursue it as a means of avoiding poverty, gaining respect, and remaining independent. Another popular poem, written by George Beverstoc and published in 1811, had the imposing title *The Silver Key; or, A Fancy to Truth and a Warning to Youth, Shewing the Benefit of Money, and the Contempt of the Poor*. From the opening stanza, the author (significantly calling himself "Time") urged his audience to pursue "the silver key," or profit. One reward, of course, would be prosperity and respect. But in the final stanza, Beverstoc implied ominously that gaining money had become a matter of personal survival: "The silver key keep while you may, Whatever care it cost. For you will find few will be kind, If you have lost this Key."[8]

By the early nineteenth century, Jeffersonian social ideologues were building on such simple moral instruction and spinning exemplary tales of the self-made man in America. Tracts like the juvenile essay *The Pullet; or, A Good Foundation for Riches and Honour* (1810) crudely expressed an ideal of social-climbing and monetary gain. The story promoted "honest industry, and civility of conduct" as the road to wealth and respect. Its unsophisticated plot, however, disclosed additional aids to success. The protagonist, an impoverished but industrious young man, raised a beautiful young chicken to present to the daughter of the local squire. The squire was so touched that he made the young man a frequent guest at his house. When the youthful laborer grew enamored of the daughter, they married, with the squire's encouragement, and the young man became heir to "an estate in connection with a well-stocked farm." The moral, it appeared, was that social manipulation as well as hard work propelled one up the ladder of success.[9]

Other pieces unfolded variations on the rags-to-riches motif. *The Way to Grow Rich; or, Historical Memories of the Life of Tom Gardner* (1811), for instance, breathlessly told the story of a man's rise to property valued "at ONE MILLION OF DOLLARS IN CASH!!!"

The details followed what was to become a classic formula for the American success story: a young man rises from stock boy to apprentice tailor to shopkeeper to wealthy merchant and businessman. Yet a strangely amoral tone permeated the narration, especially concerning Gardner's unsavory personal characteristics. The pamphlet noted that he displayed the rudiments of a money-making character even as a child by selling Bibles and stockings. As Gardner's career accelerated, it was fueled by equal parts of admirable ambition and unsavory greed. His character, the tract explained, was a mixture of "the most laudable industry, with the most contemptible selfishness and sordid avarice." The author ultimately struck a pose of tense moral distance, dispassionately praising Gardner's "great qualities of decision, activity, and dispatch," while condemning his "cunning," "overreaching," "niggardly" instincts, and "master-passion" for "the love and acquisition of money." The point, according to this memoir, was not that the pursuit of status and money was bad, but rather that excesses in pursuing them should be avoided. After all, as the author concluded ambiguously, Gardner "died one of the richest, but not one of the most respected of men."[10]

Such endorsements of the pursuit of self-interest were echoed in many early-nineteenth-century social tracts and gradually formed the conceptual centerpiece of an emerging liberal social ideology. It became an article of faith in much popular discourse that individual ambition was commensurate with the public good. No longer must the individual be prepared to sacrifice private gain to the commonweal, as the republican ideal of virtue had demanded. Instead, according to growing numbers of social observers in the post-Revolutionary decades, personal enterprise engaged the gears of productivity and prosperity and thus propelled forward the collective good. David Humphreys, for example, noted in the preface to his 1804 "Poem on the Industry of the United States of America" that citizens' productive work "will advance at the same moment, their own interest and that of the commonwealth." *Houghton's Genuine Almanac for 1811* reinforced this notion to its readers, noting that productive agriculture and manufactures would "be the means of benefitting the nation and enriching ourselves." Thus the old republican ideal of individual "independence"—the imperative to work hard to sustain one's economic and political integrity—was subtly being transformed into the liberal notion of "self-interest."[11]

Jeffersonian social commentators in the early nineteenth century slowly began to formulate systematically this concept of a society of liberal individuals. Condemnations of monopoly and tributes to unbridled enterprise often prefaced such efforts. Lemuel Sawyer, a Kentucky Republican, presenting a July 4, 1810 oration in Lexington, Kentucky, praised his country as a land where "each person is left to follow what occupation he pleases; industry is perfectly free. . . . Here no monopolies and exclusive privileges. Hence our progress . . . has extended through every part of the globe." Jeffersonian newspapers like the *Richmond Enquirer* and the *National Intelligencer* often amplified this theme. They acclaimed "the untrammeled action of the free and virtuous will" in America and concluded, "Whilst every man is free to promote his own interest by the dictates of his judgement, be assured that capital and labor will be appropriated to the most productive purposes, and that every description of the community will actually benefit."[12]

A series of letters by "Solon" in the 1811 *National Intelligencer* painted this liberal vision in especially striking colors. Surveying the United States, the author found little or no evidence to dispute that the nation was growing every day in wealth and numbers as a result of "honest industry and enterprise." "Cast your eyes around you, my fellow-citizens," he wrote, "and describe, if you can, any man . . . that fails in accomplishing the virtuous objects of his *ambition*. None are to be found." "Solon" waxed rapturous in describing a newborn American society that combined private enterprise and public virtue:

> While the physical and intellectual powers of man are left free to employ themselves as the judgement of their possessor may direct, everything valuable finds its proper level and its due value. . . . An active industry and lively competition constantly tend to equalize, and consequently to distribute among the greatest numbers the good things of this life. . . . The condition of every individual as well as that of the nation is in a progressive state.[13]

While early-nineteenth-century moralists expressed liberal social hopes, an array of observers confirmed that such hopes were becoming reality. John Melish offered much persuasive testimony, but hosts of newspapers and speeches brimmed over with convincing corroborations. In January 1812, Congressman Samuel Mitchell of New York told Congress that his constituents were "bred to commerce." "They are devoted to navigation; barter and sale are their delight. The spirit of business warms them." Henry Clay replied only to expand the assertion. The spirit of commercial enterprise "is diffused throughout the country," he noted, and "it exhibits itself as well on the waters of the Western country." Republican newspapers like Cincinnati's *Western Spy* also bubbled with news about the advances of liberal enterprise. It praised the "spirit of enterprise which has, at length, been roused in this town and its vicinity" and approvingly reported the entrepreneurial projects mushrooming in the area: manufactories for hempen and cotton fabrics, exporting companies, the import and raising of Merino sheep for high-grade wool. Other papers, like the *National Intelligencer,* praised the commercial potential promised by the first steamboats—"These ingenious vessels"—that were beginning to appear on America's rivers. Or they surveyed, as did the *Richmond Enquirer* in 1811, the swarms of enterprising citizens heading westward in search of opportunity: "From the 6th day of October last, to the 6th day of November, 236 wagons & other wheeled carriages passed through this place to Ohio with families—with four of the small waggons were sixty persons—within the same time 600 Merino sheep passed in the same direction."[14]

George Fowler's three-hundred-page *Wandering Philanthropist; or, Lettres from a Chinese* (1810) accurately summarized the social situation of the young American republic. Cast in the popular mode of letters from a foreign visitor, Fowler's account featured a "Chinese" traveler assessing the United States since the American Revolution. Farming and commerce flourished everywhere, he reported, while "domestic manufactures" gathered growing attention. "New towns are daily founded, and the old ones [are] rapidly increasing." Such growth, and the ambitious social energy motivating it, led the Chinese visitor to a prediction: "The period is not far distant when America . . . will shew the world that she can live on her own national resources."[15]

Tracing the contours of early national didactic literature and social discourse, one is struck by its visionary enthusiasm for the prospects of the young American republic. Liberalizing social change and economic growth seemed to promise material prosperity, enhanced status, and independent happiness for the greatest number of citizens. But these vivid portrayals of a society of purposeful self-made men also contained a dark dynamic of doubt. Less easily discernible than the confident rhetoric of success were underlying fears about social chaos and dissipation. These seeds of disquietude quietly germinated within the bustling society of the early republic and sporadically sprang to life in the nation's early decades. Thus the burgeoning ideal of self-made success generated ardor, but also an aching sense of social strain as well.

IN early 1812, writer and humorist James Kirke Paulding presented to the American public *The Diverting History of John Bull and*

Brother Jonathan. This boisterous satire depicted the troubled Atlantic world of the early nineteenth century by means of an elaborate allegory about life around a "great mill-pond." At one end of the pond lived the English representations, Old John Bull and his tenants, while at the other resided the French "Frogmoreans," who had recently deposed their landlord, "Lewis Baboon," and replaced him with the rambunctious "Beau Napperty." Between them stood young Brother Jonathan, the estranged son of John Bull and a prosperous farmer in his own right. The bulk of Paulding's tale followed the comic clashes between these clans on the great pond, complete with deflating caricatures of national ambitions and stupidities. [16]

Although certainly humorous, the story also betrayed an underlying tone of uneasiness. Its rendering of Brother Jonathan—the figure representing the United States—was far too barbed to be harmless. In Paulding's text, the young republic appeared wracked with divisions between Jonathan's various tenants, who were compared to a pack of "barking dogs." Among the most vocal were the "Southlanders," who "by reason of their having so many slaves, were great sticklers for universal freedom" and the "Yankey-landers," a shrewd group who monopolized "the fruits of the earth" and loved to "sing psalms through their noses." "Mrs. Jonathan," Paulding's symbol for the American government, appeared "whimsical, cross-grained, contradictory, and bedevilled" while she spoke with "the confusion of Babel." And Jonathan himself, it seemed, "loved profit rather better than honour." Although a young man of caution and good sense, "if anything could make him angry it was meddling with his pocket." [17]

Paulding's swipes at American society gave satirical form to the more serious and troubled meditations of many Americans of the early republic. Social divisions, money-grubbing values, and degeneracy of character were no laughing matters to many observers. The growth and mobility that accompanied liberalizing social change provoked deep dismay as well as exhilarating hope. The same ethos of the self-made man that raised expectations for material improvement also engendered fears of spiritual degeneracy and social brutality. So while certain literati might poke fun at America's post-1790 prosperity, more solemn citizens grew distressed by certain developing features on America's social landscape. [18]

A distrust of prosperity's moral effects comprised a constant lament in both public and private discourse of early-nineteenth-century America. The concept of "avarice" was used most often to convey a general apprehension of American descent into rampant materialism, and this social fear radiated in several directions. Winthrop Sargent, for instance, sadly wrote in the 1805 *Monthly Anthology and Boston Review* that many of his fellow citizens had become mere creatures of greed and materialism. "They have a national maxim which the infant is taught to lisp in its muse's arms; it is very long, and I do not recollect it; but I know it is equivalent to 'get money.'" Sargent sadly pictured the ascendancy of this "idol" over "science," "charity," and "the social principle." Jeffersonian and Methodist minister Conrad Speece put the matter in even more striking terms in an 1812 sermon to his congregation in Petersville, Virginia:

> We seem to have taken up the notion that all happiness was included in being rich; and the rage of accumulation has spread its baneful infection into almost every heart. To this cause must be imputed the discontent which is felt in moderate circumstances in life; the restless pursuit of the world, which leaves us little time as inclination for attending to the duties of religion.[19]

The social critique of avarice often pinpointed several targets. First of all, the scramble for wealth and status in a liberalizing society seemed to be raising a social ethic of dishonesty—or so it seemed to concerned viewers of economic speculation and business scams in the America of the early nineteenth century. Critics often described and condemned such activity as acts of unrestrained passion that approached mental derangement. Methodist minister James B. Finley recalled in his *Autobiography* memories of the newly settled areas of the West after the mid-1790s. He wrote, "A money mania seemed to have seized, like an epidemic, the entire people." Republican Governor Daniel Tompkins voiced a similar complaint to the New York legislature in 1812 about the dangerous growth of "bank mania." One of the baleful consequences of banks, Tompkins argued, was the way unscrupulous entrepreneurs often duped honest men. Having gained bank credit through the medium of a responsible endorser, "the fictitious capital thus acquired by a man, inspires confidence in all descriptions of dealers and mechanics, who consequently trust him." But when such a scalawag ran into trouble, continued the governor, his property was transferred to the endorser to secure the bank demand, while "more humble creditors, who have trusted the insolvent in consequence of imposing appearances, with which that very bank invested him, lose the utmost farthing of their dues." New Englander Jeremiah Mason extended the accusation of dishonesty even to wealthy merchant investors who lived only on the interest paid on their loans. "When the rich capitalist can by lending his stock obtain as much profit as he can by retaining it, and bestowing his industry upon it," wrote Mason to a correspondent in 1811, "he will lend the whole and become an idle drone living on the industry of others."[20]

Critics of avarice also anxiously pointed to the narrowing of life's possibilities in a society growing profit-mad. These commentators in the early republic frequently expressed misgivings over what social theorists would later call the "cash nexus." With individual ambition and pecuniary reward becoming the engine of social advancement in the young nation, money too frequently appeared as the standard by which all things were to be judged. For instance, complaints often surfaced in Jeffersonian circles that many citizens' political positions, and even their patriotism, emerged from selfish considerations of profit and social advancement. In May 1812 the *National Intelligencer* ran a front-page item that underlined the consequences of money-madness. The story related the career of a man who grew prosperous from farming, keeping a tavern, and distilling whiskey. But in accumulating a great estate he began to hoard his money, refuse credit to close friends, and even neglect the education and needs of his own family. With the consummation of a bad business deal, the tale of the miser came to a dramatic and moralistic close: "On receiving an account of this sale, he walked through his farm, went to his distillery, and gave various directions to his people. He then went to his wagon-house, and—hanged himself." Hezekiah Niles summed up many misgivings about America's emerging social relations in the summer of 1812:

> In private life the mere calculating spirit of trade, and sole attention to dollars and cents, sinks an individual to the level of a brute, and renders him the most miserable wretch in society. If we look around us we may discover many such. . . . Money is his god; and all the passions that prevail in hell are his ministers. The charities of his heart are concentrated on himself.[21]

Perhaps most frightening, the ascendancy of avarice on the American social scene seemed to threaten the vitality of republican virtue. In the eyes of uneasy critics, both deference to the public good and private regard for others' welfare were in danger of extinction. A newspaper contributor contended in the 1810 *Richmond Enquirer*, "An extended commerce . . . is incompatible with pure republicanism. Wealth is the sole end of commerce . . . and the natural effect of great wealth, unequally distributed, is the introduction of aristocratic manners and principles." Another anonymous correspondent took up this theme in the same paper, noting, "A preference of wealth to virtue, is an alarming symptom. . . . Honor, honesty, patriotism, virtue, yield without a struggle to the potent powers of avarice."

Condemnation of the greedy character of Americans frequently compared early-nineteenth-century avarice to the nobility of the Founding Fathers, each of whom stood "ready to sacrifice his personal
interest for the security of the rights of his country and of his posterity." The Jeffersonian *Philadelphia Aurora* expressed a common sentiment in an 1812 editorial discussion of profit-seeking in America's
emerging market society. It admitted that with practically everyone
"from the petty dealer in the market, to the great marketplace of
power, the conduct exhibited throughout every stage, appears to be
governed by the previous supposition, that there is no *honesty*, or
probity, no *private*, no *public virtue*."[22]

Yet the various sins of avarice—dishonesty, rampant materialism,
selfishness—perhaps shaped a painful awareness of moral ambiguity
more than anything else. Approbation or condemnation of social
conduct became increasingly difficult judgments to make in the society of the early republic. The desire for profit and prosperity seemed
to have hopelessly muddled social standards by combining industriousness with greed, virtue with riches. An anonymous article in
the 1810 *Kentucky Gazette* sensitively explored this growing moral
confusion in a liberalizing society. Americans, noted the author,
condemned aristocratic extravagance but admired commercial
wealth. In fact, there was little difference between the two.

> The man . . . who lives upon wealth acquired in dealing, lives upon the
> advantages which he has obtained from other individuals: for what are
> *profits*, what the *gains* of trade, what the income of *speculators* but *advan-
> tages* which cunning men derive in their dealings from men less cun-
> ning? . . . I allude to the gains which accrue from the *artifices* of shop-
> keeping, and of dealing, in general, the doctrine of which is not a
> reasonable advance on the article sold, as a compensation for trouble and
> labor, and risk; but which is, "as much as you can." . . .
>
> Thus are our understandings deceived by *modes;* and one man shall
> pick your pocket in one way, with applause and with impunity; whilst, if
> he were to do it in another way, he would be whipped, pilloried, or sent to
> the penitentiary.

The author could only conclude ruefully of his countrymen, "Wealth
lords it over the human mind. It seems to be the lever that moves
everything."[23]

Uneasiness over selfishness and materialism ultimately raised
alarm over social divisions opening among the American people in
the early nineteenth century. Social inequality and friction had existed
before 1790, of course, but republican deference and the community
model of traditional colonial society had worked to deflect and discourage resentment. But with the scramble for wealth becoming a

sanctioned social norm, and with competition raising the specter of chaos, many observers feared that emerging social factions would destroy the new republic. While public discourse did not exactly focus on social class by 1810, dismay over factions was acquiring social overtones. Uncomfortable memories of popular uprisings like Shays' Rebellion lingered, as did the scent of blood from the social upheaval of revolutionary France. Hamilton's financial programs and the Whiskey Rebellion brought home an acute awareness of economic manipulation by the elite and the violent possibilities of popular unrest. Such fears gave a dark cast to political and social divisions in the young republic.

By the late 1790s, in a highly charged atmosphere, polemicists were flinging about pejoratives like "monarchist" and "Jacobin" with abandon. Thomas Jefferson, writing to Edward Rutledge in 1797, observed sadly, "Men who have been intimate all their lives, cross the street to avoid meeting, and turn their heads another way, lest they should be obliged to touch their hats." A European traveler noted in 1799 that violent and hateful appellations had become the shocking stock-in-trade of American social and political intercourse. This bitterness, he continued, "infects the most respectable, as well as the meanest of men." Extreme socioeconomic and political divisions over the Embargo of 1808 further exacerbated these factional disputes. The New England Republican minister Solomon Aiken, for example, described his deeply rooted emnity toward the Federalists in 1811. It had become a sign of social turpitude, he wrote, "for us as it was for the Jews with the Heathen, to mingle with them; to give our Daughters to their Sons, or to receive their Daughters to our Sons."[24]

American factionalism—in both its social and political manifestations—found a witty critic in Washington Irving. He lampooned his countrymen's contentiousness in 1807 by pronouncing the republic a "logocracy, or government of words." In fact, he joked that argument was the only thing that held the nation together. Because of Americans' "gift of gab," Irving wrote,

> the country is entirely defended . . . by *force of tongues*. . . . Every offensive or defensive measure is enforced by *wordy battle,* and *paper war;* he who has the longest tongue, or readiest quill is sure to gain the victory—will carry horror, abuse, and ink-shed into the very trenches of the enemy, and without mercy or remorse, put men, women, and children, to the point of the—pen!

But a Jeffersonian writer in the 1811 *Philadelphia Aurora* warned more soberly that Americans should beware the tendency of particular groups to define an agenda of social well-being, organize around it, and "sacrifice the general interest to this particular interest." Such splintering, and selfishness, boded ill for a republican society.[25]

Frightened as they were of social faction and avarice, Americans perhaps feared most a deeper and less tangible consequence of ambition and materialism: a fundamental weakening of Americans' private character. Chasing after money and status, they feared, was producing a degenerating love of luxury and a flaccid fear of real work and sacrifice. For example, at a Baltimore Fourth of July oration in 1812, William Winder praised America's growing prosperity over the previous twenty years. But, he went on, "Dandled as we have been in the lap of prosperity, and enervated by an indulgence in the gratifications which rapidly increasing wealth and luxury afford, we had, I fear, begun to fall off from the spirit of our revolutionary fathers . . . [and] our jealous regard of national honor began to fade before the meretricious charms of inglorious ease and tranquility." Farther to the north a Boston essayist warned that growing familiarity with wealth had exposed Americans to "that enervating and debasing luxury, the object of which is sensual indulgence, its immediate effect, vice, and its ultimate issue, publick degradation and ruin."[26]

The dread of degenerating character in the early republic did not confine itself to the more rapidly commercializing areas in the middle states and the Northeast. Similar trepidation arose in the South, where the 1790s boom in commercial agriculture for foodstuffs had begun to transform into surging cotton cultivation by 1810. In the *Richmond Enquirer*, for instance, "The Old Bachelor" contributed some thirty articles in 1811–12 commenting on social manners and trends as well as public affairs. The thrust of his rambling discourses was that public morality was in decline. Surveying the prosperous farms and rapid immigration of settlers into the Old Southwest, he worried that "in our very prosperity is to be found the principle of our decay." America's post-1790s material growth, he admonished, had been "accompanied by a wealth, increasing so rapidly as to outstrip every other active principle that can influence the public mind." The destructive effects of such wealth burrowed into the very fiber of individual character, and the "Old Bachelor" anxiously queried, "How are we to stimulate men to exertion, on whom the love of ease and property has laid fast hold?" The *Enquirer* itself often extended this critique to the social character of the United States as a whole. America's foreign affairs difficulties during the embargo, an editorial maintained, stemmed from the fact that the weakness of her citizenry invited attack. Too many individuals had been "corrupted by the spirit of Avarice" and lapsed into lethargy and greediness.

Only time would tell, summed up the editors, if Americans could overcome money-grubbing and materialism and regenerate moral strength: "The People must minister to themselves."[27]

Even in the frontier areas of the West, consternation over the "weakness" of Americans had become acute by the first decade of the nineteenth century. A Kentucky citizen, for instance, writing under the pseudonym "Gregory Grindstone," contributed a series of essays to the *Kentucky Gazette* in 1812. The author lamented that "the rising generation" seemed to have become "too effeminate for republicans" and had fallen off from the virtuous and hardy race from which they sprang. Though but a recent arrival in the West, wrote Gregory, "Yet I can plainly perceive a decline of the republican spirit." In contrast to Revolutionary virtue, "the frippery of Europe and all her gewgaws are seen here." Americans appeared eager to "overleap their means," avoiding hard work but embracing idleness and calculation to demonstrate a high style of living. Congressman Richard M. Johnson of Kentucky aptly summed up Western fears of dissipating character in an 1810 speech. "I am desirous to see this nation grow. Nothing can stop its growth." Yet as Johnson described in an earthy and biting metaphor, the republic "has often reminded me of a swine confined in his pen—give it corn enough to eat and the animal will grow fat, although you kick it and cuff it for your amusement. . . . Let us recollect, that, like the animal, we may grow in fatness; but that fatness may soon be the spoil of others by slaughter."[28]

In a July 4, 1811, oration, Republican Jesse Bledsoe pulled together these scattered perceptions of social disarray in early-nineteenth-century America. In traditional fashion he began by lavishing praise on the social success of the American Revolution. "Upwards of thirty years have beheld the growth of our power and prosperity," he declared. Bledsoe halted, however, to warn of serpents that had appeared in the Eden of the early republic:

> Watch over these young vipers and strangle them in their birth. Faction which postpones our Country's good, to the love of power and self-aggrandizement . . . luxury, which bids us to give up our rights and ourselves, before we will forego present gratification; effeminacy, which shrinks from danger and death as the worst of evils; avarice, which places the supreme good in wealth; supineness, which blinds to danger, induces to false security, disarms us and invites the invader.

The path to social salvation, concluded the Kentuckian, lay in honoring Independence Day as "the sabbath of our political regeneration."[29]

As Bledsoe and many others indicated, the emerging ideal of a

liberal society of self-made men thus carried a twofold burden into
the first decade of the nineteenth century. Proponents of liberalizing
change—both enthusiastic publicists and practical-minded entrepreneurs—praised the felicities of individual enterprise and private ambition. And the young republic's post-1790 prosperity and
expansion seemed to fulfill these liberal expectations. Yet the very
process of affirmation barely concealed deep currents of doubt, fear,
and dissent. To many it seemed that avarice, faction, and weakness of
character threatened to corrode the dynamically growing republic
from within even as it reached the threshold of success. Thus, in
giving rise both to dreams and to disquietude, this liberal vision
created a social dynamic of intense and unstable stress among many
Republicans.

The immediacy of early-nineteenth-century social ferment is easily
lost, however, by recalling only the abstract discourse of speeches,
moral tracts, newspapers, and sermons. Its compelling importance
for individual lives can fade within the categories of generalization.
An attempt to recapture the social dilemmas facing Americans must
confront the experience of actual people to appreciate fully the emotional power of agitation for, and responses to, liberalizing change.
After all, the tension between hope and fear existed not only among
individuals but also *within* individuals. Philip Freneau, Henry Clay,
and Charles J. Ingersoll provide revealing vignettes of how thoughtful Jeffersonians responded to the social transformations of post-
Revolutionary America. They also help us understand how those
reactions became partially translated into war with Great Britain in
1812.

Philip Freneau: "Besotted by Prosperity, Corrupted by Avarice, Abject from Luxury"

In 1797 Philip Freneau founded and became editor of *The Time Piece*
in New York City, a newspaper devoted to contemporary belle-
lettres, social commentary, and politics. Freneau, a staunch devotee
of Jeffersonian principles since the early 1790s, penned for the paper
later that year a suggestive essay entitled "On Luxury and Commerce." "One might, perhaps not improperly, call this, *the trading
age*, to distinguish it from former ages; for certainly the spirit of
traffic never possessed all nations, at any period of time, more strongly than the present," he announced. Yet it was far from clear to
Freneau whether the benefits of this overgrown trade outweighed its
drawbacks. Several dangers for America seemed especially clear: "It
contributes extremely to the disproportion of fortunes; an inequality

which flints population; which prompts men to make improper uses of their riches, and consequently to abandon themselves to luxury." In 1815 Freneau was complaining still of an American society "where all the ideas of a people seem to be devoted to Commerce, Speculation, Bank Shares, & c." This rebuke of America's commercializing spirit—a critique that focused increasingly on the debilitations of avarice—came to play a strong part in Freneau's cries for war in 1812. Yet it sprang from deep roots in a controversial and varied career in the late eighteenth century.[30]

Philip Freneau had been born in 1752 into a prosperous merchant family—his father engaged in the wine trade—and he spent his early years on an estate in New Jersey. Schooled in New York City, he eventually attended The College of New Jersey (now Princeton), where he cultivated an interest in writing and poetry. Along with classmate Hugh Henry Brackenridge, Freneau co-authored in 1771 an epic poem, "The Rising Glory of America," that gained widespread notice as a vibrant expression of emerging cultural nationalism. After struggling with various trades and serving a stint in the Revolutionary navy, the young man finally turned to journalism as a vocational anchor in the 1780s. The 1790s, however, emerged as the most active, public, and controversial period of Freneau's life. As editor of the *Philadelphia National Gazette* from 1791 to 1793, this disciple of Thomas Jefferson and James Madison popularized Jeffersonian positions while castigating Federalists as monarchists, British minions, and manipulators of public money. It is little wonder that Freneau became a central figure in the political newspaper brawls of the era. In the latter part of the decade, this energetic journalist edited and wrote for several newspapers before withdrawing from public life in 1800. For the next two decades, poems and newspaper essays continued to issue sporadically from his New Jersey farm. He died in 1832.[31]

Freneau's reputation rests largely on twin achievements: his efforts as one of America's first serious poets, and his Jeffersonian political journalism. Yet his diverse career and wide-ranging essays, poems, satires, and polemics also nourished a sensitive social criticism. Freneau grew deeply apprehensive about the commercialization of American society after the Revolution, and a foreboding about avarice haunted his social and political meditations. As he admitted in 1809, commercial growth had benefited the young republic by enriching both farmers and merchants. Yet, "This love of lucre. . . . I fear it is dangerous to the happiness of the people—the desire of riches and to make a great show of it." This concern with the moral effects of economic growth and liberalizing change helped fuel not only his political activism in the 1790s, but also his vigorous endorsement of war in 1812. Freneau's criticism of commercializing trends first began to appear early in the 1780s.[32]

In 1782 Freneau contributed two revealing essays to the *Philadelphia Freeman's Journal*. Disturbed by the commercial cast of Philadelphia's social relations, the young journalist praised "The Advantages of Simple Living." He skeptically questioned an emerging social spirit of ambition where seemingly every parent pushed his child into "the learned professions," careers in "science," or business. Such activity not only removed men from productive labor in the earth, but created a situation where hordes of professional men clamored for advancement and "the ingenuity of the one ruined the other." With the typical agrarian bias of traditional republicanism, Freneau went on to defend the virtuous life of the yeoman farmer against the machinations of the shopkeeper and the merchant. The simple husbandman, he argued, worked hard and enjoyed the fruits of his labors by the winter hearth or the summer shade tree. In contrast, "the idle, scheming citizen" sat behind his counter "like a spider in the web, watching his commodities, and sedulously observing the steps of every passenger" because ensnaring customers was the basis of his existence.[33]

Several months later a much darker, even Gothic effort, entitled "A Midnight Soliloquy in the Market House of Philadelphia," appeared. Full of bizarre and grotesque images, Freneau's meditation suggested a deep, unconscious dread of a consolidating market society. The dominant images were of death and bestial behavior. The essay opened with Freneau sitting along in the abandoned marketplace observing, "Great residence of the dead, how empty are the shambles, to which in the tours of the day past flocked an innumerable host of flesheaters of all sizes, shapes, principles, and complexions!" Freneau continued the motif by describing the market as a "graveyard," a "receptacle of death," a "respository of ruin." His ostensible references were to the animals slain for their meat: "the tender lamb," "the suckling calf," "domestic poultry," "the poor mute fishes." But prompted by the approach of a drunk in the early morning hours, his elegiac theme transcended the brute world to include human beings. Freneau painted a gory picture of man as beast:

> It is a man, or the resemblance of one—he groans—he is sick—he reclines his head, as it were in anguish, upon one of the stalls—he vomits up a mass of mingled liquors and half digested viands—He is just returning from a midnight debauch—his senses are stupefied—his reason has forsaken him—he talks nonsense, and utters wild incoherent

sentences—Ah, like a swine wounded by a butcher's knife, down he falls into the midst of the loathsome fluids disgorged from his filthy stomach—he makes a feeble effort to rise, but finds it impossible—his face and nose are battered and bloody—and, trust me, a truer beast was never conveyed hither in a cart, nor cut into quarters, and impaled upon those iron hooks that were designed to support weight.

"The market house, like the grave," Freneau said, "is a place of perfect equality." These representations of the marketplace as an egalitarian but death-tinged chamber of "flesheaters" and "beasts" raised a submerged dimension of Freneau's suspicions about commercial relations. He suggested, perhaps in spite of himself, an image of a market society as a brutal arena for the killing of humanity.[34]

Freneau continued to develop this social critique in the 1780s, but often with a lighter touch. Writing under the pseudonym "Robert Slender" in 1788, for example, he composed the half-serious, half-facetious "Rules and Directions How to Avoid Creditors, Sheriffs, Constables." He posed as the treasurer of a club where no man could become a member unless he "laboured under actual persecution and harassment from his creditors and their emissaries, and had at least four writs of debt out against him at once." Disparaging the collection "schemes" of creditors—"Infernal harpies" and "our enemies" were favorite descriptions—Freneau went on to list rules for avoiding them by cunning and deceit. These included using alleyways for walking at all times, always sending your wife or child to answer the door, and maintaining a knowledge of your creditor's physical appearance to aid in quick flight.[35]

Two other 1788 essays elaborated Freneau's growing hostility to commercial values: "The Man in Business" and "The Man Out of Business." These sketches described contrasting character types. Freneau described the successful and prosperous commercial man as neat and smart of demeanor, reeking of confidence, and always walking fast, "not caring whose heels or toes he treads upon." If a stranger "answers to his ideas of man *in* business, he smiles upon you as a bone of his bone and flesh of his flesh; if not, he bids you an everlasting adieu, and walks off with as little ceremony as possible." The businessman, Freneau concluded, "is little better than a perambulating machine, till he comes to the scene of action, his counting house, or his law shop." In contrast, he rendered the down-and-out man in sympathetic prose. A "man out of business," wrote Freneau, often neglected his appearance and moved about aimlessly. His conversation "most commonly turns upon the scarcity of money or the peculiar and unparalleled poverty and rascality of the age." Yet the often pathetic posture of the unemployed man, Freneau observed, was animated by humanity and humility. He became acutely sensitive to the problems of his fellow man, and "his heart bleeds within him if he sees but a dog ill used." Commercial prosperity, the journalist thus decided, encouraged greed, insensitivity, and a callous disregard for other people. The fact that Freneau spent most of his life in debt undoubtedly added personal conviction to his critique.[36]

In the two decades after 1790, nothing happened to reduce Freneau's skepticism about the commercial expansion of American society. If anything, his social critique of avarice intensified and focused on two heinous groups: speculators and bankers. He poetically denigrated land speculators in "The Projectors," demanding "Base grasping souls, your pride repress; Beyond your wants, must you possess?" In 1792 Freneau facetiously offered a "Plan for a Nobility in the United States" to reward successful commercial charlatans. Hitting his stride as a satirist, he suggested with biting wit:

> The noble speculators of the lowest grade or rank, to be stiled "the order of the Leech." Their title to be "Their fulnesses." . . . The noble speculator of the next rank, to be stiled "The Order of modern Justice." The titles, "Their Rapacities." The arms, "A pair of scales." The motto, "Cheating no felony." The noble speculators of the next rank, to be stiled "The order of the virtuous League." Their title, "Their Huckster-ships." . . . The noble speculators of the next rank, to be stiled, "The order of Assumption," or if thought more suitable, "The Order of the Golden Fleece." The title, "Their Pirate-ships." . . . The motto, "the many made for the few."[37]

Bankers equally roused Freneau's ire. Their institutions, he frequently complained, not only legitimized greed but also worked to the advantage of those already prosperous. Writing in the 1802 *Philadelphia Aurora*, Freneau dismissed the public utility of banks. These institutions, he insisted, "benefit those who can command the funds, and rise upon their support." A few years later Freneau followed the familiar route of satire in announcing with mock horror an outbreak of "The Bank Distemper!!" Posing as "Dr. Sangrado," he analyzed the "mental malady" and "species of derangement" that afflicted those clamoring for the 1809 recharter of the Bank of the United States. He dismissed analysts who claimed that mass bankruptcies would follow the failure of recharter. "Some *few* have taken place," wrote Dr. Sangrado, "but in no greater ratio than what happens almost every year, and which is the inevitable result, of speculations, and extending business to an amount unwarranted by real capital, or property possessed equal to the debts." To the doctor, more dangerous was the "bank distemper," a type of mental sickness that grew from the germs of avarice and unbridled ambition. When the vulgar man rises, his head turns, Sangrado diagnosed, and instead of fearing a fall he "becomes anxious to go higher, until everything becomes so indistinct below to his mind's eye . . . that he has no correct ideas, his head [is] full of notions—a man in this condition is mad."[38]

Although inactive politically after 1800, Freneau continued to scribble sporadically for several newspapers. By late 1808, war with Great Britain had become a favorite theme. Writing several public letters to American congressmen, the old Jeffersonian pointed out the degradations suffered by American merchant ships at the hands of European aggressors. "History does not furnish an example where provocation so loudly called a nation to arms," he continued, "nor is there an instance on record, where a nation had equal ability to support the contest." Ironically, this bellicose stance violated many of Freneau's long-standing principles with regard to war. In his earlier career, influenced by currents of Enlightenment rationalism and republican ideology, he had regarded war as unnatural, archaic, and corrupting. As the ultimate in human irrationality, violent conflict offended Freneau's basic sense that man was naturally good and "a mild, a beneficent, and humane creature." More particularly, the urge to war had always seemed "rather artificial than natural, and introduced thro' the vice of government rather than instilled into the human constitution thro' the immediate design of the creator." For Freneau, that "vice" was especially monarchy. In numerous places throughout the 1780s and 1790s he had asserted that monarchy originated in murder, violence, and robbery and that royal governments thus encouraged war by their very nature. "Royal" pride and power, and "regal" desire for fame and immortality, produced in great measure the scourge of war. Republics should avoid it, he concluded.[39]

So what drove Freneau to abandon these precepts by 1812 and endorse, even demand, the young republic's war with the English? His rhetoric indicated that it was in part a simple matter of national pride, a pride that bristled at Great Britain's bullying treatment of American commerce in the Atlantic. But the real emotional edge to Freneau's anger came from his criticism of commercializing trends within post-Revolutionary *American* society itself. His social critique of avarice slowly shaped a vision of war as an exercise in purgation and regeneration for the United States. By 1812 Freneau entertained a vague belief that the sacrifices of war would abate the passion of Americans for material pursuit and revive devotion to virtue and the commonweal.

This personal commingling of concerns—over the American spirit of avarice and American difficulties in foreign affairs—became clear in 1809. Freneau, angry over the repeal of the embargo by Congress, saw the move as an admission of weakness prompted by commercial greed. He wrote contemptuously of "our *darling commerce,* for which the national character has been so *scandalously sacrificed.*" "The solemn truth, gentlemen," he told Congress, "is that the honor of the nation has been immolated on the altar of avarice." The failure of Congress to declare war, he sneered, made the republic appear "to drop the sword and take up the skirt—to muffle the derrière, against the future kicks of our adversaries."[40]

For Freneau, the dry rot of avarice had weakened the very foundation of American republican society. "Can it be at all wondered at, that Americans are despised all over Europe," the old Jeffersonian wrote, "that our people are no longer the brave men which they were wont to be—that the inordinate pursuit of commerce has rendered us effeminate and cowardly, and that if they attempt it, they will find no difficulty in conquering us, and reoccupying the land of their ancestors?" With the United States having "tamely borne so much, that every petty power in the world may think we shall submit to abuse with impunity," Americans had given themselves an uncomfortable choice. The nation could act as a brave man whose character "entitled him to honorable reconciliation and peace," or it could act as a coward who turns his back and "invites insults from cowards like himself." For Freneau, war offered the only honorable answer.[41]

Freneau began to envision such a war as a regenerating crusade for a people nearly sunk in selfish materialism. He praised the principle that "it is sweet and glorious to die for our country" and claimed it as "the height of virtue and the perfection of felicity." Entranced by this prospect of wartime patriotism, the Jeffersonian poet argued that citizens of the growing young republic needed to abandon greedy pursuits and join hands in a common effort. Freneau appealed to the example of the Revolutionary heroes and contended, "If we were unanimous at home, we should be able to command that justice, which has been denied to us, principally because our divisions have prevented the execution of measures either prohibitory or hostile." Asking Congress to "restore our character as a nation," he urged "a war which will unite the virtuous of every political denomination, whose onset will be vigorous, and whose conclusion will be glorious."[42]

A curious rhetorical habit revealed the social sources of Freneau's war fever in a different way. He half-consciously began to project his greatest fears about American avarice and rampant commercialism on to the British enemy, and also on to domestic opponents of the impending conflict. The English appeared in his writings as a decadent people sunk in "avarice and commercial gluttony." In August 1809, for example, Freneau wrote a long newspaper article castigating the British system of public finance. Their government, he argued, ran up huge national debts and then a corrupt alliance of "money lenders"—cabinet ministers, merchants, bankers—foisted on the public worthless national stock. In this way "are the people of England cheated out of their money" as lenders busy themselves "picking the pockets of the public." Against this commerce-mad brute, Freneau opposed an idealized version of the young republic. Eager to accept the distinction between an industrious America and a gluttonous, decadent Old World society, he wrote, "The great object of the American people has been and is to have an honest and free trade to all parts of the world; England, and England alone has been interested in interrupting it."[43]

Envisioned as creatures of pecuniary self-interest, Federalist opponents of the war also felt Freneau's lash. In a ferocious essay Freneau described them as "men who having long since sacrificed every noble and ingenuous feeling of the heart, at the accursed altars of avarice, and political bigotry, are now willing to sacrifice their country." Their "career of accumulation" had set them against the embargo, Freneau believed, and now with "their Baal" the "honor of the nation is an object of no consequence when put in competition." This material greed had become manifest in Federalist opposition to war, and the Jeffersonian stalwart warned that domestic divisions would bring only failure and disgrace. Freneau could only appeal to the Federalists to abandon profit and embrace war, "hoping that there was remaining virtue in that party sufficient to bring them back to unity with their countrymen, when danger from without made union more desirable."[44]

Thus by 1812 Freneau had completed his portrait of the war as a purifying, unifying movement against the agents of avarice both at home and abroad. "Cast off, therefore, all minor considerations, *ye who wish the public weal*," he proclaimed in behalf of the war. "Unite, like freemen, in the bands of affection and thus prove yourselves invincible." The ascendancy of public spirit over selfish materialism had become paramount, as Freneau indicated a few weeks after war was declared, and any attempts to "impede the measure, or divide the people, are treasonable." Freneau had best summed up his position a few years earlier in describing the United States as "besotted by prosperity, corrupted by avarice, abject from luxury." The war, he fervently hoped, would rouse citizens of the young republic from these social ills.[45]

Henry Clay: "The Tranquil, Putrescent Pool of Ignominious Peace"

In January 1812, Speaker of the House Henry Clay stepped down from his chair to address his colleagues, who had adjourned themselves into a committee of the whole. The young "War Hawk" leader spoke vigorously and eloquently—his fame as an orator had already begun to build—in behalf of increased support for the United States Navy so that it could better face British might at sea. He discussed particulars of this pending appropriation, but more striking was the premise of Clay's argument. The dynamic young Kentuckian sought to allay the fears of more timid congressmen by vividly picturing the American republic as a growing young giant.

Clay refused to be intimidated by the threatening maritime power of Great Britain. He insisted that America "only required resolution and a proper exertion of its immense resources to command respect, and to vindicate every essential right." To those who reminded the House that Congress had nearly plunged a weak republic into a disastrous war with France in 1798, he offered a rejoinder that resonated with confidence:

> But the state of things is totally altered. What was folly in 1798 may be wisdom now. At that time we had a revenue only of about six millions. Our revenue now, upon a supposition that commerce is restored, is about sixteen millions. The population of the country is greatly increased, nearly doubled, and the wealth of the nation is perhaps tripled. . . . Independent of the extension of our commerce, since the year 1798, we have had an addition of more than five hundred miles to our coast, from the bay of Perdido to the mouth of the Sabine.

Noting that the trade down the Mississippi was "a commerce that is destined to be the richest that was ever borne by a single stream," Clay concluded his assessment of American prospects with a flourish: "Diversified as are the interests of its various parts, how admirably do they blend together and harmonize!" he declared. "We have only to make a proper use of the bounties spread before us, to render us prosperous and powerful."[46]

As this speech indicated, Henry Clay unequivocally endorsed American economic and geographic growth in the decades after 1790. This exuberance over the expansive society of the young republic so dominated his sensibility that a strong countercurrent of fear—that a weak, vacillating American character had emerged in concert with commercialization—often remained submerged. And Clay's life matched his rhetoric. His early career seemed to epitomize the successful self-made man in a liberalizing society.

Born in 1777, Henry Clay grew up on the five-hundred-acre Virginia farm of his mother and stepfather. When his parents pulled up stakes and headed for the fertile, cheap farmland of Kentucky in 1791, young Henry was placed as a clerk in a Richmond mercantile house. Shortly thereafter he began reading law with the famous jurist George Wythe and served a legal apprenticeship in the office of the Virginia attorney general. A fledgling politician, Clay also spread his wings as an outspoken partisan of the Jeffersonian Republicans. Then in 1797 he abandoned his rising position among the Richmond gentry and crossed the mountains to Kentucky. Settling in Lexington, Clay became a member of the Kentucky bar in 1798 and quickly emerged as a political mover and shaker in the state. He actively opposed the Federalist Alien and Sedition Acts in the late 1790s, electioneered for Jefferson in 1800, and involved himself in a reform movement calling for the gradual abolition of slavery in Kentucky. In the early 1800s Clay became both an outstanding trial lawyer and a skillful negotiator of land litigations. Moreover, he solidified his position in Kentucky's growing commercial network. Serving as business agent for a wealthy Baltimore merchant, Clay also married the daughter of Colonel Thomas Hart, a local merchant, manufacturer, and land speculator. By 1805 his legal practice was focusing increasingly on the vexations of the Mississippi commerce to New Orleans—insurance, finance, marketing, shipbuilding—while his personal investments flowed into salt and iron works and the manufacturing of paper, hats, rope, and bagging.[47]

Clay's rapidly growing fortune reflected his success in the pioneer society of Kentucky. An 1805 tax list revealed his ownership of eight horses, six slaves, several lots in Lexington, and nearly thirteen thousand acres of land. An acquaintance from New Orleans wrote to Clay that same year, "On all hands it seems agreed by such of your countrymen as visit us that you are at the head of your profession, and are rapidly growing rich. Indeed some accounts assure us that you are acquiring money 'as fast as you can count it.' All that I infer from this is that you are doing extremely well."[48] As a shareholder and attorney for the Kentucky Insurance Company—and its affiliate, the Lexington Bank—Clay played a prominent role in defending these institutions against the attacks of Felix Grundy and other agrarian radicals. Deflecting criticism of the elitism and profit-mongering of banks, the Kentucky lawyer insisted on their utility as providers of the capital and credit necessary to economic development. As the candidate of businessmen, merchants, and planters in the Lexington area, Clay subsequently won a seat in the 1804 Kentucky State Assembly, and his political career skyrocketed. Chosen in 1806 to fill an uncompleted term in the U.S. Senate, he returned to become Speaker of the state assembly in 1807, completed another unfilled Senate term in 1810, and then was elected to the U.S. House of Representatives later that year. Arriving in Washington to take his seat in November 1811, the freshman congressman was chosen Speaker of the House by his colleagues at age thirty-three. Charming, magnetic, and spectacularly successful, the young Kentuckian caught the nation's eye— and would hold it for some forty years—as "Harry of the West."

Clay's personal success and buoyant faith in the prospects of a liberalizing society laid the foundation for his rhetoric of confidence. His speeches on the eve of war with Great Britain passionately appealed for Americans to realize the vitality of their prosperous republican society. Yet the inflammatory rhetoric could have misled the casual listener, because from beneath these paeans to American strength flickered flames of doubt about the character and moral fiber of the self-made American. While not strong enough to incinerate the larger structure of confidence in American society as a whole, these misgivings caused the Kentuckian considerable discomfort. Clay's own words revealed that by 1812 he had grown deeply afraid that commercial prosperity had inadvertently rendered Americans a dissipated, flabby, even contemptible, people. This fear of American weakness, often advanced in only indirect or half-conscious fashion, drove the Kentuckian to endorse war as an exercise in regeneration of character as much as a demonstration of national strength.

Clay clearly indicated this ironic juxtaposition of social strength and weakened character in the same naval armament speech of January 1812. He argued that Americans had grown wealthy since the Revolution but had lost their vigorous spirit in the process. It seemed that the lust for material goods had overcome even the desire for self-protection. This apparent degeneration of will caused Clay to observe, "The source of alarm is in ourselves." War might be legitimately feared, but it could not always be avoided, especially by a commercial society. "Sir, if you wish to avoid foreign collusions you had better abandon the ocean—surrender all your commerce; give up all your prosperity." The same concern had surfaced two years earlier when Clay served temporarily in the Senate. Remarking on the republic's ongoing foreign policy crisis, he expressed growing reservations about the effects of commercialization on American character. At one point he described "Dame Commerce" in terms of sensual temptation for the American citizen, noting, "She is a flirting, flippant, noisy jade, and if we are governed by her fantasies, we shall never put off the muslins of India and the cloths of Europe." At another point he condemned the effect of commerce on personal honesty, assailing the "fraud, perjury, cupidity, and corruption with which it is unhappily too often attended."[49]

In more passionate terms, by 1810, Clay revealed the true depth of his uneasiness over commerce and degeneracy. Arguing for a more vigorous policy against European aggression, he demanded, "Is there not danger that we shall become enervated by the spirit of avarice unfortunately so dominant?" He lashed out, "Are we to be governed by the low groveling parsimony of the counting room?" These signs of degradation brought Clay to the heart of his concerns. He feared that a weak, vacillating, profit-obsessed American character would render citizens of the republic contemptible not only to the world but to themselves as well. Calling up the image of the self-sacrificing and willful Founding Fathers, Clay saw a need for "a new race of heroes to supply their place, and to animate us to preserve unviolated what they achieved." By the eve of the war, Clay was determined that "we shall at least gain the approbation of our own hearts." If Americans failed to strengthen their character by defending their rights, "we forfeit the respect of the world, and what is infinitely worse, of ourselves."[50]

Clay's exhortations for regeneration of the American character eventually solidified in a program of political economy. In an 1810 address on domestic manufactures, the then-senator from Kentucky unveiled the prototype of his famous "American System." His remarks made clear the social fears that underlay it. In urging the advantages of manufacturing establishments and their encouragement through bounties and protective duties, Clay carefully distanced himself from the wretchedness and vice of English factories in Manchester and Birmingham. Instead, he cast his arguments in terms of self-sufficiency and social discipline for a society suffering from commercial dissipation. Certainly no one wished to displace agriculture, "that first and greatest source of our wealth and happiness," Clay stated. But a system of manufactures limited to domestic need would strengthen American character in several ways. "The invention and improvement of machinery," contended the young Kentuckian, would prompt "the employment of those persons, who, if we are engaged in the pursuits of agriculture alone, would be either unproductive or exposed to indolence and immorality." He also extolled the likely reduction of imports and "the gewgaws of Europe" and predicted a decline of the "Freaks" of commerce with their elevation of profits over national well-being. The growth of domestic manufactures—"not to the extent to which they are carried on in England, but to such extent as will redeem us entirely from all dependence on foreign countries"—would foster hard work and self-discipline for Americans. Clay thus offered his agenda as a reform to encourage "our own industry" whereby "the whole national family is furnished by itself with the clothing necessary for its own use."[51]

Near the end of his remarks, the Kentucky senator added another argument in favor of support for increased manufactures. An important consideration, he declared emphatically, was the capacity "to furnish ourselves with articles of the first necessity, in time of war." This observation transported Clay toward a more seductive solution for degenerating American character: violent confrontation with Great Britain. Impending war appealed partly to the aggressive, gambling instincts that had fueled the Kentuckian to the top of a liberalizing society. Clay himself admitted that he paid particular attention to "Dame Chance," "that fickle Goddess." As an acquaintance once noted, "When Mr. Clay was in doubt about what course to pursue, he acted on the principle of Hoyle, and took the trick." But war beckoned to Clay even more as a means for repairing the weakened will and moral fiber of the commercialized American. As an early biographer astutely observed of Clay and many of his compatriots, they stumbled toward the notion that only war "would arrest their degeneration into a mongrel race of stock-jobbers, despised by the world—and by themselves."[52]

Clay's prowar rhetoric suggestively utilized frequent and extended metaphors of "energy." Where the commercializing society of the early republic often fostered a vapid character concerned only with moneymaking and material comfort, thought the Kentuckian, war promised an elixir of invigorating action and reckless self-sacrifice. Clay noted in arguing for the raising of American troops in December 1811, "The American character has been much abused" and the confrontation with Great Britain would provide a test. The republic could act decisively and wage "a war of vigor, or a war of languor and imbecility." He clearly came down "in favor of the display of an energy correspondent to the feelings and spirit of the country." From 1810 to 1812 Clay doggedly demanded "an exertion of the national energies in every form, in prosecution of the war in which we are about to engage." He pictured the war variously as "the

combined energies of a free people . . . wreaking a noble and man-
ful vengeance upon a foreign foe," "a gallant effort, which called
forth the whole energies of the nation," and a crusade of "firmness
and vigor becoming freemen." The extent to which Clay saw the war
as an invigorating crusade appeared a few weeks after its declaration
in a private critique of his party's President to a friend. James
Madison, the Kentuckian asserted, was too benevolent to withstand
"the rough and rude blasts" of war. America's hope must rest on "the
vigor [of others] which he may bring into the administration."[53]

Clay's notion of war as vigor came as an antidote to America's
private and collective weakness. He queried rhetorically in late 1811,
"What are we to gain by war, has been emphatically asked. In reply,
he would ask, what are we not to lose by peace? Commerce, character,
a nation's best treasure, honor?" Several weeks later the issue of
private character again surfaced when the Kentuckian, addressing
injuries and abuses received by Americans, told his colleagues,
"What would disgrace an individual under certain circumstances
would disgrace a nation. And what would you think of one individual
who had thus conducted to another, and should then retreat?" By early
1812 Clay saw the crisis with Great Britain as testing the mettle of a
people on the edge of commercial debility. "It exists," he wrote of
this challenge, "and it is by open and manly war that we can get
through it . . . and if we are decided and firm, success is inevitable." The republic's greatest hope, he concluded, should be directed
to a marshaling of "that patriotism, to that spirit and display of those
qualifications, which are so honorable to the human character." Dismissing older Jeffersonian reliance on negotiation and peace, Clay
enthusiastically declared his hope "to see, ere long, the *new* United
States embracing not only the old thirteen states but the entire country
east of the Mississippi."[54]

Beyond the anticipation of energy and vigor, young Harry of the
West foresaw two particular agencies by which war would help
Americans overcome a commercialized weakness of character. The
first was the infusion of a martial ethos into a society addicted to peace
and profit. In January 1810 he explicitly rejected the pacifist thrust of
traditional Jeffersonian doctrine, asking in mocking fashion whether
"the art of war, the martial spirit, and martial exercises should be
prohibited—and that the great body of the people should be taught
that national happiness was to be found in perpetual peace alone? No,
sir." A month later Clay predicted that a happy effect of war would be
"the re-production and cherishing of a martial spirit among us." The
Kentuckian carefully noted, however, that only the self-discipline

and honor of a military ethos could be cherished. He made clear his opposition to a "diffusive military character" that might elevate "some ambitious chief" or "prostrate the liberties of the country."[55]

In addition to raising a rigorous military spirit, war promised to engender a spirit of self-sacrifice in the eyes of Henry Clay. Intense self-regard, especially concerning matters of profit, underlay the weakness of character produced by liberalizing social change. Hence the Kentuckian believed that the republic would benefit from a war rousing "the feelings of the whole American people." He predicted that Americans would gladly bear war taxes in the common interest. "When the most inestimable interests of the country are at stake, the nation would be unfaithful to itself if it withheld the requisite supplies," he wrote to a correspondent. Clay envisioned a crusade in the common interest and concluded, "Surely no man will hesitate to contribute his just *part* when *all* is at stake." Six months after the war declaration, Clay inspired his countrymen to sacrificial effort by declaring the imperative to join "together in one common struggle." "If we are united, we are too powerful for the mightiest nation in Europe, or all Europe combined," he concluded. "If we are separated and torn asunder . . . our country will not be worth preserving."[56]

Thus, while Henry Clay in the two-score months before June 1812 elaborately embroidered the political reasons for war with Great Britain—free trade, impressment, British encouragement of Indian agitation in the West—a deeper dynamic also drove the Kentuckian to embrace the conflict. As both exemplary product and vigorous defender of the entrepreneurial ideal emerging during the early republic, Clay felt compelled to prove that prosperity had not fattened and enfeebled the self-made American. At issue, perhaps, was the republic's survival with "this new and untried experiment to which the only free government upon earth is about to be subjected." Clay appeared brazenly confident that American firmness and fortitude would reappear to triumph in war. Yet in weaker moments he worried that commercial enervation might prevail. "It requires a great struggle for a nation, prone to peace as this is, to burst through its habits and encounter the difficulties of war," Clay spoke in early 1813. "Such a nation ought but seldom to go to war." But despite his occasional wavering confidence in American fortitude, Clay's resolve to strengthen American character by fire remained constant. "No man in the nation desires peace more than I," he insisted. "But I prefer the troubled ocean of war, demanded by the honor and independence of the country, with all its calamities, and desolations, to the tranquil, putrescent pool of ignominious peace."[57]

Charles J. Ingersoll: "Deep in the Slough of Faction"

The author of *Inchiquin, the Jesuit's Letters, During a Late Residence in
the United States of America* remained a mystery for several months in
early 1810. This clever, energetic defense of American society
against European detractors had garnered considerable attention
since its appearance as a forceful expression of confidence in the
young republic.[58] Published in New York City, *Inchiquin's Letters*
had spread quickly up and down the eastern seaboard and raised
comment from people as diverse as Timothy Dwight and James
Madison. Finally its anonymous author revealed himself to be
Charles Ingersoll, a twenty-eight-year-old Philadelphia lawyer. This
young writer, in fact, had begun to attract notice on other fronts as an
essayist, playwright, poet, orator, and politician. But it was as a social
observer that Ingersoll stood unsurpassed in the early-nineteenth-
century republic. His astute critique of the American social sensibility, his awareness of larger changes reshaping America since the
Revolution, and his determination to pursue a firm course against
Great Britain in 1812 disclosed much about the liberalizing society of
the early republic.

The son of a prominent Philadelphia attorney, Charles Ingersoll
had studied at Princeton in the late 1790s before himself entering the
legal profession. His heart, however, lay in belle-lettres, as he became a published playwright and poet in the early 1800s and, slightly
later in life, an amateur historian. Forced to support himself through
minor offices in the Pennsylvania state government, Ingersoll slowly
combined his talents to emerge as a social and political writer. In
1808 he presented a lengthy popular pamphlet on American foreign
policy. Then in 1810 *Inchiquin's Letters*, a vindication of the American national character and a prod to American self-respect, appeared.
With a growing reputation in Pennsylvania politics, Ingersoll won
election from a Philadelphia district to the U.S. House of Representatives in 1812 as a Republican. There he became an outspoken
advocate of war with Great Britain. His tenure in Congress initiated a
long career of public service—as a Jacksonian Democrat he would
later agitate both for American expansion and for gradual abolition of
slavery—that ended only with his death in 1862.[59]

In the early nineteenth century Ingersoll showed himself to be
acutely sensitive to currents of commercial growth and liberalizing
change remaking the young republic. He frequently commented on
"the prodigious and unexampled progress this country has made in
prosperity, population, and power since the adoption of the federal
constitution." The young writer noted that Americans' intrepid sense

of enterprise had flourished in the 1790s and propelled them to the first rank among commercial nations. Moreover, as he observed in 1812, after the imposition of European commercial restrictions Americans had retrenched and "advanced then, in three years, from a state of manufacturing helplessness to a very respectable manufacturing competency, together with an amazing excellence of internal improvements, both by water and land." In assessing America's destiny, Ingersoll seemed almost awe-struck by "an advancement in population and affluence, an improvement in the sciences and the arts, in agriculture and commerce, an exuberance of the products of the earth, and an accumulation of the profits of the sea, transcending all example, all calculation, all hope."[60]

The young Philadelphian acutely sensed in the early republic an atmosphere of burgeoning opportunity, a society on the move. Its citizens were paragons of industriousness, and the typical American appeared to be an independent and resourceful seeker of success. Ingersoll wrote of his countrymen in 1810:

> In the occupations of trade, agriculture, and the sea, persevering industry, almost without a risk of disappointment, leads to comfort and consequence. . . . Everyone is a man of business; everything in the progress of emulation and improvement. Universality of successful employment diffuses alacrity and happiness throughout the community. No taxes, no military, no ranks, removes every sensation of restraint. Each individual feels himself with the concentration of all this elasticity, rejoices in its growing greatness.[61]

This felicitous reading of American entrepreneurialism and social progress led Ingersoll to conclude that commercial spirit and political liberty were nearly identical. He wrote in 1808: "Ours is the first experiment ever made of leaving [commerce] to find its own vents and level, undisturbed by the projects of statesmen, or the monopolies of favorites." This American experiment had shown "that without liberty commerce cannot move with the enjoyment of its natural elasticity, or find its proper summit." Moreover, Ingersoll utilized this notion of the natural harmony of market pursuits to construct a blueprint for the ideal republic. The essence of America's social success was not a revolutionary equality of social condition, he argued, but equality of opportunity. A republican society should enact no leveling principle because "fortune will make her own selections, and laws cannot control them." Government should favor neither the rich nor the poor, Ingersoll stipulated, but should "maintain a perfect equality in all civil enjoyments and impositions." This classic expression of early-nineteenth-century liberalism, with its emphasis

on government protection only of fair opportunity, prompted Ingersoll to state what would become a compelling myth of the official
American creed for the next century. The American people, wrote
the Philadelphian, comprised but one class of society: "Luxury has
not yet corrupted the rich, nor is there any of that want, which
classifies the poor. There is populace. All are people."[62]

This liberal vision intoxicated Ingersoll and prompted optimistic
predictions. He foresaw, for example, a glorious American future of
geographic and commercial expansion. On July 4, 1812, the young
orator enticed a Philadelphia audience by describing a future republic
where Canada was annexed, settlements were extended to the Pacific
Ocean, river commerce flourished with steamboats, the Indians were
pacified by "paternal solicitude," and the eastern states were engaged
in massive and profitable free trade overseas. "When the day shall
arrive, and it cannot be very distant, when the ports of South America
and China shall be thrown open to American enterprise," he had
written in 1808, "the physical resource of this country will enable its
foreign trade, by means of the valuable new markets presenting
themselves, to exceed incalculably its present limits." The visionary
young writer added to this early rhetoric of manifest destiny a conviction that the republic was God's special nation. "It is here, and here
only," Ingersoll assured in 1812, "where the God of Nature seems to
have opened his bountiful hand without reserve." The fortunes of the
young republic, he continued somewhat later, had been enhanced "by
an especial Providence, to give irresistible splendor and attraction."[63]

Like many other early-nineteenth-century Jeffersonians, Ingersoll
sporadically grew troubled over the costs of the republic's material
prosperity. He feared that his countrymen's commercial spirit may
have shaped a taste for fraud and made them bearers of a "huckster's
heritage." Ultimately, however, Ingersoll quieted this dismay with
the reassurance that growth of commerce, trade, and manufactures
had actually magnified this American individual by increasing his
information and freedom, calling forth his entrepreneurial courage,
and broadening his horizons for learning. But if the Philadelphian
eventually downplayed the menace of greed and dissipation of character, another consequence of commercializing change continually
haunted him: the emergence of social and political faction in public
life. Observing the growing American fondness for all varieties of
religious, political, and professional associations, he described it as "a
passion more easily diverted than subdued." So for Ingersoll the
social critic, "the evils of faction and fanaticism" offered the greatest
danger to the liberalizing republic.[64]

Ingersoll feared particularly the possibilities for anarchy lurking in a factionalized popular politics. Writing to Rufus King in 1809, he wearily affirmed, "Nothing but perplexities abroad—nothing but democracy at home." For illustration he described to King a mob scene in Philadelphia where a dinner party of prominent citizens was confronted by a noisy crowd demanding the removal of a decorative "crown" adorning a window of the dwelling. When two shots were fired, Ingersoll reacted with fear and disgust, telling King, "I have no doubt if the Mayor of the City had been acquainted with the affair, he would have been the principal rioter." Yet even more disruptive than such agitated common citizens were Federalist machinations after Jefferson's election in 1800. After their removal from national power, Ingersoll sneered, they had become "a *fungus* of party opposition," "a malevolent and traitorous conspiracy to withhold and impede the national resources."[65]

Inchiquin's Letters, Ingersoll's lengthy social critique of the American republic, boiled up from this cauldron of concern over rising factionalism. The Philadelphia Republican made clear his motives for the book in two letters to James Madison in early 1811. A desire to elucidate and defend the American journey to affluence since 1790 provided one inducement. As he told Madison, his commentary appeared as a vindication of the republic's growth: "our prosperity, national character, resources, and virtue." But more important, Ingersoll clearly hoped to heal some of the lacerations of American factionalism by constructively assessing American society and downplaying issues of controversy. In this patriotic task, he wrote, "much minor matter was cast aside in the course of preparation for the press, in order that nothing might be published which would be objectionable or personal or political." Perceiving Americans' fears of weakness, this young Jeffersonian man of letters tried to bolster American confidence and put "this country in good humour with itself." *Inchiquin's Letters,* as its author could have realized only dimly at the time, also forged a connecting link between social criticism and the declaration of war less than two years later, a conflict for which Ingersoll became an outspoken and eloquent defender.[66]

Ingersoll opened *Inchiquin's Letters* with a series of fictitious letters from Europeans. While their remarks ostensibly expressed European prejudices about the young republican society, they actually served as vehicles for displaying and neutralizing the author's own concerns. A "Greek" correspondent made the central criticism of the early-nineteenth-century republic: "Instead of being managed by the people, [it] is too subservient to various contradictory interests." An imaginary Frenchman elaborated Ingersoll's concern. American society, he observed, was "composed of heterogeneous and militant materials" absorbed in economic pursuits and political disputes. This "assemblage of mixed tribes cannot speedily coalesce into a nation."[67]

Such anxiety over factionalism led Ingersoll—speaking through the priest Inchiquin—to devote much of the book to a promotion of American unity. Inchiquin analyzed at some length various divisions in American society between sections, labor systems, uses of capital, and cultural influences. Yet he tried to defuse the explosive potential of such fractures by explaining them as a natural stage in American social development. America's early settlers, explained Inchiquin, had "a fierce and enthusiastic devotion to certain principles, in religion and politics." Only partly diluted over the decades, these notions still "infused the fanatical morality, the factious republicanism, and the general enthusiasm, for which, I think, the Americans are remarkable." In other words, Americans had always been unshackled and enthusiastic freethinkers, and the republic's economic boom after 1790 only intensified this characteristic. As Inchiquin pointed out, "It is natural . . . that a commercial people should be enterprising and ingenious—that a republican people, whose press is free, and whose government is a government of laws and opinion, should be intelligent and licentious—that an adolescent and prosperous people should be aspiring, warlike, and vainglorious."[68]

Ingersoll believed that Americans could overcome factionalism in part by cultivating their common principles and habits: "a hearty hospitality, great achievement in the province of utility," a "general dissemination of common learning," and a "plentiful mediocrity." Ironically, however, his ultimate hope for American solidarity came from the very commercial prosperity that had helped to foment social divisions. In a judgment perhaps reflecting desire as much as conviction, Inchiquin contended that the republic's continued commercial growth likely would heal its own social wounds. He believed that Americans were destined to become "a great commercial people" due to a plethora of advantages: vast territory, rich soil, internal highways, the natural protection of oceans, growing population and prosperity, and native "industry, freedom, and affluence." Moreover, this commercial destiny had been brought into view by policies of free trade in the post-Revolutionary republic. With this spirit of commercial freedom, Inchiquin predicted, markets throughout the world "will be unlocked to the researches of christianity and civilization and under the auspices of universal peace, ten thousand times the traffic . . . will cover every sea, connecting and ameliorating all nations."[69]

Inchiquin also foresaw an eventual healing effect of free trade on the faction-ridden United States. The priest observed hopefully that in the American republic "the spirit of its freedom is impassioned, perhaps factious, but not furious or bloody." Moreover, he trusted that since the United States was "the natural offspring of commerce and liberty," both its republican sensibilities and its convergence of economic interests would keep it from splintering apart in the long run. Inchiquin harmonized these notes of commercial growth and republican institutions to trumpet a clarion call for American unity. The centerpiece of this "free, republican, commercial federation," he insisted, was "commercial liberty: not mere political liberty, but positive freedom; geographical absolution from all but the slightest restraints." In other words, social factions could unite in the greater cause of economic expansion.[70]

Near the end of *Inchiquin's Letters* the author touched on a threatening problem. Writing in a tense atmosphere caused by America's foreign relations with feuding European powers, he gingerly approached the topic of war. Inchiquin denounced war in general as flowing from scurrilous attempts at commercial monopoly, as an "infatuation which would establish national greatness on the perverted and tottering basis of navigation projects of exclusive aggrandizement." But Inchiquin also moved subtly to connect the prospect of war with his social critique of factionalism in the young republic. He noted of Americans:

> A long interval of profound tranquility, and multiplied commerce may have tarnished the fame, perhaps relaxed somewhat the tone of their people. But . . . the same spirit which was once displayed, is still ready to show itself when summoned into action. The same valour, good faith, clemency and patriotism still animate the bosoms of America, as the first bursts of their hostilities whenever it takes place, will convince their calumniators.

Inchiquin went a step farther to suggest that prosperity and the desire for social unity may be served by war. Reflecting that occasional wars may be necessary to assure long-term peace, he concluded, "A dominant republican empire, with military force enough to defend its rights . . . just and respectable abroad, free and just at home, forms the most glorious consummation of national prosperity." Thus he encouraged Americans "to cultivate so much of a warlike spirit as may not be incompatible with their republican institutions."[71]

Inchiquin's brief reflections on war and American society in 1810 portended Charles Ingersoll's justification of war with Great Britain. By the summer of 1812 the Philadelphia writer—by then a popular politician and orator—had become a vigorous proponent of hostilities. In 1808 he had written in favor of "a manly republican repulsion of our wrongs . . . to proclaim to the world our resolution and our ability." His rhetoric grew more intense thereafter. As a U.S. congressman he reiterated the political justifications for war: British impressment, the encouragement of Indian border attacks, and consistent violation of American free trade. But he moved significantly farther afield to describe the hostilities as "indispensable to the welfare, the character, the union, the existence of the nation." In 1813, after hostilities had begun, he privately asserted, "This holy war has advanced us a century per saltem in power and character."[72]

Confrontation with Great Britain became a holy war to Ingersoll, primarily because of one central feature. As a catalyst for American solidarity, it promised a solution to the vexing problem of social faction in the commercializing republic. Ingersoll's rhetoric at the time of the war declaration resonated with appeals for unity. Speaking before a mass meeting in Philadelphia on May 21, 1812, he characterized American resistance to British infractions: "All parties, all classes, were united, and the voice of the country descended by acclamation." He appealed to the Founding Fathers for inspiration, praising their "common sympathy and common enthusiasm" during the Revolution. The young orator pursued this theme even more tenaciously in remarks made a few weeks later. Speaking on July 4, he urged each listener to emulate the example of the Revolutionary generation and support the war "in purer singleness of heart—in a more devoted immolation of himself on that altar which is next in dignity to the altar of the Most High—I mean the shrine of patriotism." Writing to a friend from Washington, D.C., during the summer of 1812, he praised the sentiments of most Americans who were navigating around "the shoals of faction" and rallying around the national flagship. Ingersoll came to believe that without war "we might still have amused ourselves with furious factions and . . . unrelenting parties." This juxtaposition of war and social faction led him to speculate, "I have no doubt . . . that declaration [of war] will be recorded by the historian as the wisest and most fortunate act in the annals of America."[73]

This notion of the war as a unifying crusade prompted Ingersoll to envision it as an act of national regeneration. His flamboyant metaphors of social renewal pictured Americans throwing off domestic faction and commercial slumber to embrace the vigor and brotherhood of battle. As he explained in 1812, the war directed American contentiousness outward against a foreign foe, as citizens sprang from "the ease and enjoyments of profound relaxation, to grasp the rusted sword, and brighten it in the blood of their aggressors." Ingersoll excitedly portrayed a conflict from which Americans would emerge with "the vices of their prosperity chastened, . . . their character restored, their tranquility secured." Great Britain, Ingersoll hoped, would act on the United States as the wars of the French Revolution had acted on France, by prompting "the grandest and most stupendous effort of national regeneration ever exhibited in history, ancient or modern." The United States, he told an audience in 1812, comprised "a populous, powerful, and martial republic, whose citizens need nothing but to be resolved and justly confident in themselves." The war with Great Britain would not only affirm the young republic's political experiment, but also provide an object lesson to Europe "from the adolescent west, and under the auspices of republicanism and toleration, the world regenerate and live anew."[74]

   In October 1809 Charles Ingersoll had written in disgust to a friend that, while his fellow Americans were "deep in the slough of faction," he anticipated "a reformation at no very remote period." The opportunity for such reformation arrived in less than three years with the War of 1812. "After thirty years of fat, fastidious peace" Ingersoll rejoiced at this trial where "our institutions are to be put to their first great test." The war, he argued, would surely bond together a republic splintered by social faction. "It has snatched us from the trance of a tame listless peace. . . . It is substituting the strong bonds of national feeling and national glory for the degrading avarice which had become the national characteristic." A few days after war was declared, Ingersoll shared with a Philadelphia audience his vision of a republic reunited by war. Imagining the successful conclusion of the 1812 conflict, he looked ahead to the year 1850, where a factionalized society had achieved a transcendent unity. America at mid-century, he predicted, would integrate various interests and groups into a society where all would be "mainly alike, speaking one and the same language, alive to the same national sympathies . . . [and] in the daily interchange of thoughts and opinions." Still alive to hear the guns of the Fort Sumter in 1861, Ingersoll lived long enough to see this unifying vision ironically shattered by another war.[75]

War as Social Crusade: Civism and Renewal

Appeals for unity and self-sacrifice composed a constant refrain among Republican war advocates in the months surrounding the declaration of war. In late May 1812 a mass meeting in Baltimore of "democratic citizens" approved a series of resolutions castigating the British and demanding war. The group implored, "Let us act with

one heart, and with one hand; let us shew to an admiring world, that
however we may differ among ourselves about some of our internal
concerns, yet in the great cause of our country, the American people
are animated by one soul and one spirit." The *Western Intelligencer* of
Worthington, Ohio, confidently echoed, "Nothing united the public
mind so much as danger." Richard Rush, in a grand oration before
members of the Madison administration and both houses of Congress
on July 4, 1812, proclaimed, "May there be a willing, a joyful
immolation of all selfish passions on the altar of a common country."
Niles' Weekly Register approvingly described mounting war fever:
"From all quarters of the country—from the mountain tops of the
interior, we have a common expression of the public will." The
Richmond Enquirer urged Americans to embrace war with a spirit of
unanimity and "like wise men sacrifice minor objects to the great end
we have in view." The editors put the matter even more succinctly in
another editorial: "Forget self, and think of America."[76]

Such invocations may be dismissed in part as jingoistic rhetoric
common to any national crisis. Yet the singular social pressures in the
early American republic bestowed on such appeals a deeper urgency.
While a liberalizing society of self-made men had raised dreams of
ambition among early-nineteenth-century Americans, it also had created disquieting fears of greed and dissipation. As the cases of Freneau, Clay, and Ingersoll suggest, such tensions helped shape a complex social desire for war as a means of surmounting avarice,
weakened character, and social faction. The experiences of these men
reveal a pattern of compensation: war's appeal in 1812 involved twin
seductions of sacrifice to the common good and social regeneration.
As Michael Walzer observed, the often brutal race of life in a capitalist society engenders sporadic desires for "civism," or immersion
of self in a larger common purpose. Consequently, calls for widespread citizen involvement can appeal to a submerged yearning for
solidarity.[77] Thus war emerged partly as a social movement in early-
nineteenth-century America. In a liberalizing society riven with tension, war against Great Britain beckoned as a crusade for civism, and
hence renewal.

Notions of war as an adhesive for America's social factions featured prominently in the political discussions preceding the conflict.
Like Charles Ingersoll, many Jeffersonians hoped that the threat of
foreign power would weld together feuding combinations in the
liberalizing republic. "War . . . if called for must be gone into
with a vigor that will give the nation but one arm," editorialized the
National Intelligencer in May 1812, and success would depend on
"the undivided exertions of the whole nation against a common en-

emy." Governor William Plumer, addressing the New Hampshire legislature on the impending war less than a month later, put the matter even more forcefully. "Union is the vital strength of a nation, particularly so of a republic, whose authority rests on *public opinion*," he proclaimed. "Our union is our safety—*a house divided against itself cannot stand*."[78]

Polemicists and orators consistently envisioned war as an instrument for extinguishing party rancor. In December 1811 Governor Benjamin Smith urged the North Carolina legislature to endorse a national policy of armed resistance, declaring, "Let us strive . . . to discard all party bickerings, and promote a spirit of harmony and good will." Much farther to the north, Massachusetts Governor Elbridge Gerry made a similar appeal to citizens of his state in early 1812. Speaking in favor of war preparations, he argued that party spirit should vanish. Instead, liberty demanded that Americans "consecrate at her shrine a COALITION OF PARTIES." Prowar newspapers concurred, urging submersion of party bickering in the larger national war crusade. Republican organs like the *Kentucky Gazette* and *Niles' Weekly Register* admitted that "party contentions may be necessary to keep up the public stamina, and secure the government from corruption—but when the question shall be fairly put—for, or against our country—the honest man will not hesitate on his course."[79]

Advocates often depicted the War of 1812 as a gratifying and transcendent commitment for the liberal individual. In contrast to the mean pursuit of self-interest, war appeared to its supporters as an exercise in traditional republican virtue, or self-sacrifice to the public good. One newspaper, on the eve of hostilities, praised "a war, to which not one distillation from the subtle, anti-republican essences of ambition or aggrandizement has contributed." The *National Intelligencer*, in a series of editorials from May to July 1812, unfolded this notion of war as noble sacrifice. On May 5 it urged Congress to go beyond private interests and formulate a more aggressive policy in behalf of the *"general welfare."* The June 6 edition implored, "Let all transient or local feeling be merged in energetic measures against this common foe." The most unadulterated entreaty for self-sacrifice ran on July 4. "It is now no longer a hostile contest of counties and wards—of local claims and distinctions—of state rights—of honest differences of opinion—of who should or should not be the leaders of our high destiny," wrote the editors. "No, minor considerations must and shall be absorbed by the PUBLIC GOOD."[80]

While certain proponents beheld war in 1812 as a healer of social faction, others embraced it specifically as a means to overcome avarice. Whether prompted by guilt or disapproval, many enthusiasts came to see war as a regenerating alternative to pecuniary greed. A newspaper missive by "Americanus" defined war as an exercise in self-sacrifice and an antidote to luxury. "This kind of virtue stands opposed to *selfishness*—or to that principle by which a man is influenced to seek his individual welfare, without regard to the public good." Thus when war demanded closing "the avenues of luxury for a season," it was the citizen's duty to support it.[81]

Some Jeffersonians went even further to pose war as a noble contrast to an emerging cash matrix. Congressman Widgery of Maryland, for example, told his colleagues in early 1812 that even though war would be very expensive, "What is money? What is all our property, compared with our honor and our liberty? . . . [I] could not, however, believe that the free-born sons of America would lie down, under a calculating avarice." The *Richmond Enquirer* also endorsed war to counteract the pernicious influence of cash in a commercializing nation. "We speak, in the spirit of the Democracy of Virginia," the paper declared in January 1812, "when we assert that they are prepared to submit to the greatest sacrifices of *money*, rather than patiently submit to the wrongs of England." In a newspaper letter, Kentuckian Jonathan Roberts similarly testified: "In the contemplated state of war . . . some sacrifice of profit and convenience the nation must make, but they will be offered on the altar of public good and national independence. . . . The American people I feel confident are incapable of bartering virtue for gain."[82]

Many war supporters came to believe that violent conflict would help purge the republic of excessive pecuniary temptation. Several weeks after war was declared, Hezekiah Niles attacked bankers and wealthy merchants with Old Testament fervor. "One of the happiest effects of the war will be—the cleansing of the republic of such abominable rubbish," he avowed. "Heaven speed the day when the money changers shall be expelled from the political temple!" William Hendricks, speaking in Cincinnati at a July 4 Republican gathering, sadly pictured a young republic "engaged in accumulation of wealth," corpulent and in decline. But with war, he promised, again "the martial spirit of freemen is aroused to action" and "the falling greatness of our country is renovating." A letter from William O. Allen to Andrew Jackson in early 1810 indicated that such hopes were appearing privately as well as in public discourses. Describing his mustering out as part of the western militia, Allen first complained that military service would undermine his business affairs and exhaust his funds. Yet he quickly added, with great emotion, "If it should be asked, what is it that you would not do, for the benefit of your Country? I would unhesitatingly answer, *every thing,* that is within the *reach* of my *physical* or *mental* powers! No Sir! for so long as my nerves or mind would act, so long I *attempt* to search for the interests of this beloved Union!"[83]

The Rev. Joseph Richardson may have put the matter best in a sermon in early 1813. Speaking on war and the theme "The Christian Patriot Encouraged," he noted that America had been blessed with unprecedented prosperity since the Revolution. Yet he wondered, "Have we been governed by selfishness, by the cravings of avarice?"

> And may it not be a serious question whether our prosperity has not been too great to be continued, lest we should be led into such excesses as are inconsistent with the political health of the nation, and are dangerous to all the obligations of piety and virtue? We have reason to lament the propensity of our nature to degeneracy. . . . This is a favorable opportunity to commence a reformation that will be unspeakably happy to our friends and glorious to ourselves.

For Richardson as for many others, the civism and martial spirit endemic to war promised to dampen the pecuniary appetites of America's prosperous republicans.[84]

This impulse to curb avarice melded with a final dimension of the war as social crusade: a yearning to revitalize an American character weakened and bloated by commercial pursuits. Although usually less eloquently, many Jeffersonians agreed with Henry Clay that prosperity had sired private dissipation as its offspring in the early republic. This widespread apprehension of a softened moral fiber prompted repeated calls for willful regeneration through preparation for war. The *Richmond Enquirer* breathlessly concluded in April 1812, "The whole policy of America is now comprised in one word—Energy." In fact, "energy" emerged as a Jeffersonian code word for a rekindling of strength through war. Republicans contended that war would "demonstrate to an unbelieving world, that a free government is no less resistless in energy and power than it is free in principle." Congressman Robert Harper of New Hampshire agreed, warning his colleagues in January 1812, "The nation demands measures of spirit, of energy . . . it requires us to turn our energy against the enemy, not against ourselves." In the summer of 1810 the *Kentucky Gazette* reported a similar restless desire for revitalizing energy when it listed Republican toasts at a local Fourth of July banquet. According to the newspaper, enthusiastic Jeffersonians drank to the people's "unshrinking spirit," the "firmness" of the government, and the hope that "a NEW SPIRIT will animate the next Congress." For many of its backers, war became a test of American character, an opportunity for proving that Americans were not crippled by commercial enervation. A Jeffersonian newspaper put the issue starkly in April 1812: "The great question on which the United States have to decide, is, whether they will relinquish the ground which they now hold, or maintain it with the firmness and vigor becoming freemen."[85]

Thus war beckoned as the perfect vehicle for revitalizing America's weakened will. By 1810 growing numbers of Republicans were eager to plunge into conflict. They savored the prospect of Americans rousing from their commercial lethargy to face the bracing winds of war. Such desires for revitalization inspired portraits of war as intense, galvanizing activity, and images of renewal abounded in prowar discussion. Those of Hezekiah Niles were among the most colorful. Writing in April 1812, he compared war to the pruning knife of the husbandman that would cause the national character to "flourish with renewed vigor." A month later he offered a metaphor that was even more striking:

> The thunderstorm, black and tremendous, disturbs the calm serenity of the summer evening, and sometimes rives the mighty oak to tatters—it comes unwished for, excites general apprehension and frequently does partial damage—but it purges the atmosphere, gives a new tone, as it were, to listless nature, and promotes the common good. Thus it may be with war, horrid and dreadful as it is.[86]

So at least in part, many influential Americans urged the prosecution of war in 1812 to relieve the social tensions accruing to liberalizing change. War with Great Britain offered a means to objectify and overcome the specters of avarice, faction, and dissipation that were haunting commercial development. Yet it is important to note that this social impulse to war did not fundamentally challenge consolidating liberal capitalism in the young republic. Instead, by offering only temporary catharsis for dissent, war actually reinforced emerging liberal hegemony. It is striking that in endorsing the War of 1812 Americans often combined yearnings for self-sacrifice and regeneration with the enterprising, ambitious spirit of a liberalizing age. From this amalgam emerged war as a social crusade for ennobling unity *and* entrepreneurial striving, patriotism *and* profit.

This powerfully ambivalent affirmation of, and dissent from, commercial development sprang up everywhere in the emotional heat of prowar rhetoric. On the day war was declared, for example, a Republican congressman from New York articulated an interesting argument to support the war by buying Treasury notes. He made a patriotic appeal, but he also shrewdly observed that they "are better than cash itself." For the thrifty individual, "money, vested in a Treasury note, becomes immediately productive . . . [and] the industrious and prudent man may cause his capital to work and gain a little." The *National Intelligencer* similarly combined war, civism, and gain in calling for an enlarged army that would work as well as fight. By making roads and canals in addition to fighting and teaching an ethic of hard labor, a working army would create "a new era in the military character." The editorial pictured this soldier-as-liberal-man: "He will produce as much as he consumes. . . . Enured to regular habits of labor, his physical system will be nerved, he will, when necessary, be capable of making greater military efforts, and will be freed from the dangerous vices of indolence."[87]

Such Jeffersonian enticements combining ambition and profit with patriotism and sacrifice appeared everywhere in the republic. In June 1812 the *New Hampshire Patriot* launched a recruiting drive to gather the most promising and respectable young men. It advertised that "aside from the holy flame which fires the breast of every true American son, the offers held forth by the government in a pecuniary point of view are in a high degree advantageous; for there are but few kinds of business that will in five years put in a man's pocket 336 dollars, feed and clothe him, and leave him in possession of 160 acres of land worth at least 500 dollars." The *Richmond Enquirer* adopted an even broader social perspective by depicting war as a focusing of individual drives for success. Since the Revolution, argued the editors, industrious and enterprising Americans had achieved prosperity and independence. While intent on "the promotion of their own interest," they had overlooked the vitality and strength resulting from "an aggregation of individual resources. Now war has called forth these resources."[88]

So spoke many prosperous and ambitious Jeffersonian Republicans on the eve of war with Great Britain. Having cut themselves loose from familiar social moorings in an era of liberal transformation, they were drawn to war as vessels to a harbor in a storm. They hoped to demonstrate a capacity for civic unity and strength of character, while at the same time meeting imperatives of liberal ambition. By the summer of 1812 a social vision of war had fused instincts for success, civism, and regeneration. Spokesmen like Hezekiah Niles were proclaiming the new spirit that was invigorating the government and the people and rejoicing that "narrow local prejudices are sacrificed on the shrine of the republic, 'one and indivisible.' . . . We have everything to hope for, if united with energy." Polemicists such as the anonymous "Quintus" were urging their fellow citizens to avoid avarice and faction, endorse the war, and show the world that "we are not the degenerate people they would have us." Social critics like "The Old Bachelor" were declaring that war would bring forth "talents and virtue on their grandest scale" and provide a corrective to the commercial feebleness of "a long and prosperous peace." Through violent conflict "the very principle from which our vices spring, the love of distinction from some cause or other, might be wielded in such a manner as to make us all that the warmest patriot could wish."[89]

The social crusade for war in 1812 revived traditional veneration for virtue. It promised to strengthen weakened commercial character. It advanced nobler strivings in addition to those for profit and social betterment. But the venting of dissatisfaction, uncertainty, and strain over liberalizing change into the emotionally charged atmosphere of war had consequences that were even more far-reaching in the long run. It allowed early-nineteenth-century Americans to indulge both the entrepreneurial energy of ambition and the sacrifices of civism. Relegated to the war arena and ensconced in the armor of national survival, dissenting impulses were removed from day-to-day American social life. By relaxing the tension between dreams and disquietude for the self-made individual, purging him of guilt, and regenerating him, the War of 1812 comprised a long step toward assuring the hegemony of liberal society in America.

III

Religion and Repression:
War and Early Capitalist Culture

*American moralists do not pretend that one must sacrifice himself
for his fellows because it is a fine thing to do. But they boldly assert
that such sacrifice is as necessary for the man who makes it
as for the beneficiaries. . . . The doctrine of self-interest
properly understood does not inspire great sacrifices, but every day
it prompts some small ones; by itself it cannot make a man virtuous,
but its discipline shapes a lot of orderly, temperate, moderate,
careful, and self-controlled individuals.*

ALEXIS DE TOCQUEVILLE
Democracy in America

*The return of the repressed makes up the tabooed and subterranean
history of civilization. And the exploration of this history reveals
not only the secret of the individual but also that of civilization. . . .
Repression is an historical phenomenon. The effective subjugation of
the instincts to repressive controls is imposed not by nature but by man.*

HERBERT MARCUSE
Eros and Civilization

*Confidence is the indispensable basis of all sorts of business transactions.
Without it, commerce between man and man, as between country and
country,
would like a watch, run down and stop.*

HERMAN MELVILLE
The Confidence Man

In 1758 Benjamin Franklin published "The Way to Wealth" as an extended preface to his yearly almanac. This brief colloquial essay gathered many of Poor Richard's sayings, condensed and combined them, and offered Americans a prototype advice piece on secular success. This prophet of liberalizing change sketched out what would become the staples of the genre: "Industry, Frugality, and Prudence" for the striving individual. He urged the wise use of time, the avoidance of silly amusements, and diligence against the temptations of sloth. Franklin only once moved beyond advice to aspiring individuals to comment on the nature of relations between them. Yet when he did so he focused on monetary matters, intuitively grasping that such would be the stuff of much liberal social intercourse, and his tone took on a darker hue. He somberly warned against the danger of debt in a society of pecuniary ambition and cautioned of the likelihood of deceit and distrust. Debt, argued Franklin, gave to another "power over your liberty" and often reduced the debtor to excuse-making and lying. Avoid this obligation, he instructed, and "maintain your independency."[1]

For Franklin, homilies against debt sufficed for reassurance against the future. Yet this prescient commentary on relations in a commercializing society only began to appreciate the complex cultural problems that were to emerge with liberalizing change. On what basis, if any, could one approach and trust fellow strivers in the competitive race to success? How could a society of ambitious individuals and impersonal market modes hold together?

When the liberal society that Franklin envisioned actually began to coalesce in the decades after the Revolution, such problems grew increasingly painful. By the end of the eighteenth century, concern over social disarray and distrust of ambitious individualism had become a central topic of cultural discussion. John Adams' depiction of citizens in "masquerade," Hugh Henry Brackenridge's anger over the deceptions of "Teagomania," and John Taylor's emotional attacks on the "family of cunning" reflected fears of growing social and financial deceit. Similar sentiments mushroomed everywhere. The Rev. James B. Finley described the Western territories in the mid-1790s: "Immigration poured into Kentucky like a flood, and vast multitudes engaged in land speculation. Whole tracts of country were sold by these speculators with or without title, and thousands were stripped of their all." These land speculators, Finley recalled, "were looked upon generally as a class of villains." In the Northeast the young diplomat and essayist John Quincy Adams complained in 1795 to his diary, "Is it impossible to deal with a trading man without being deceived or imposed on?" On the literary scene, by the late 1790s, Charles Brockden Brown began tracing a shadowy social arena of calculating avarice, unscrupulous ambition, and deceptions in novels like *Arthur Mervyn*. Brown described the young rustic Arthur newly arrived in an urban marketplace: "He stept forth upon the stage, unfurnished by anticipation of experience, with the means of security against fraud . . . [or] the wiles of an accomplished and veteran deceiver." Farther to the south, *The Georgia and South Carolina Almanack for 1811* warned its readers against financial entanglements with ruthless lenders. "Keep a sharp look out, lest the credit price too much exceed the ready money price," it counseled. "Consider whether there be a moral certainty that you can meet your payments punctually without distressing yourself. . . . Multitudes are undone by taking, as well as giving too much credit." Nervous discussions of private character and public trust usually followed several themes.[2]

Anxious commentators frequently focused on the deliberate deceiver, or the "confidence man," as he would come to be known by the mid-nineteenth century. In a liberalizing society of expanding geographic and economic vistas, the "speculator" in lands, stock, and bank notes emerged as a villainous prototype. Solomon Aiken, speaking in 1811, excoriated those dishonest figures "who make it their business to buy and sell, and net gain, in the most useless manner to society." This activity, he complained, had "a tendency to break down all barriers to common honesty."[3]

The schemes of the con man, however, often went beyond the manipulation of novel financial instruments like credit, insurance, and public stock. They also involved outright scams by which the clever sharper would dupe the innocent, take the money, and run. For example, in a period of six months in 1811–12 the *National Intelligencer* ran two public warnings about such dishonest bubbles. In October 1811 the legitimate proprietors of a lottery office in Baltimore took newspaper space to notify readers that a fake lottery had been advertised under their auspices but without their knowledge or approval. Describing the charlatans who had set up a false office address from which to collect money, the outraged businessmen fumed that some people were so unscrupulous that "most gross libels seem to drop from them with as much freedom and assurance as if they had never cultivated the least acquaintance with the truth." In April of the next year, a certain James MacDonald ran a public letter entitled "Beware of Misrepresentations." He exposed as fraudulent a recent advertisement that claimed there was a revolutionary new process of making weather-resistant bricks. "Daniel French's machine for making bricks will be found on investigation to be merely an improved form of pressing clay into the form of a brick," MacDonald related. The author of this attempt to deceive the public, he indignantly concluded, had given birth to "a palpable falsehood" only further "detracting from his character."[4]

The conniving escapades of the con man, however, proved less frightening than a more widespread and corrosive process. The general shape of the American character itself seemed to be assuming a maleable, even amoral, cast under the pressures of liberal ambition. The con man, critics began to suggest, might be only an extreme type in a whole society of unscrupulous parvenues. As usual, Washington Irving sublimated fear into satire. In the 1807 essay "On Greatness," he mockingly pictured moral elasticity, not integrity, as the key to distinction and success in the young republic:

> To be concise, our great men are those who are most expert at crawling on all fours, and have the happiest facility in dragging and winding themselves along in the dirt like very reptiles. . . . It is not absolutely necessary to the formation of a great man that he should be either wise or valiant, upright or honorable. On the contrary, daily experience shows, that these qualities rather impede his preferment; inasmuch as they are prone to render him too inflexibly erect, and are directly at variance with that willowy *suppleness*, which enables a man to wind and twist through all the nooks and turns, and dark winding passages that lead to greatness.[5]

Others went even further to warn that this "supple" American character seemed to be in danger of disintegrating altogether in the scramble for success. Moralists like Caleb Bingham discerned a tendency among his fellow citizens to pursue "knowledge of the world" with its assertive and flexible qualities. But this worldly knowledge, he asserted in the 1810 *American Preceptor*, too often comprised "little arts of simulation and dissimulation," "follies and vices," and "immoral and indecent behavior." Bingham warned: "A most fatal mistake is made by parents of all classes in the present age. Many of them seem to think vice and irregularity the marks of sense and spirit, in a boy; and that innocence, modesty, submission to superiors, application to study, and to everything laudable, are the signs of stupidity." An attenuation of moral fiber promised other consequences. If prosperity came easily, according to commentators like Congressman Peter Porter of New York, self-indulgence and luxury would sully individuals who were able to appreciate only material gain. Western farmers provided a case in point, as

Porter postulated in 1810. Their land was so fertile and resources were so plentiful that minimal labor brought comfortable circumstances. "They are therefore, naturally led to spend the other part of their time in idleness and dissipation." On the other hand, if failure attended the striving individual, results could be even more devastating for a weak, materialistic character. As an almanac pointed out in 1810, unexpected problems could derail the calculating success-seeker. If unprepared for privation, their "pleasing dream is dissolved, and they awake out of it in consternation."[6]

Ultimately the notion of "moral free-agency" defined both the thrust and the difficulty in this maelstrom of culture and character in early-nineteenth-century America. In an atmosphere conducive to ambition and pursuit of the main chance, the individual was taking shape as the conceptual building-block of society. Older notions of an organic social order and traditional republican commitments to the commonweal were disappearing as restraints on individual action. The solitary citizen, many Americans became convinced, thus had to take responsibility for his own actions and destiny. For example, Parson Mason L. Weems contended in his 1810 pamphlet *God's Revenge Against Gambling* that virtue or vice could only be voluntary. "To act voluntarily man must be free; acting freely he may offend; that is, he may prefer darkness to light, and vice to virtue." Charles Brockden Brown confirmed moral free-agency but characteristically gave it a darker reading in his 1799 novel *Ormond*. At one point Ormond explained his beliefs and discussed the duties incumbent on individual conduct, arguing that duty consisted only of self-interest. "A man may reasonably hope to accomplish his own end, when he proposes nothing but his own good," contended Ormond. "Any other point is inaccessible." In 1802 the Rev. Alexander McCleod, a Reformed Presbyterian, confirmed man as "a moral agent" and "a free agent." The individual, he insisted, had a God-given right "to dispose of himself, and be his own master in all respects, except in violating the will of Heaven."[7]

The moral free-agent's unprecedented powers of decision—over vocation, salvation, political loyalty, material attainment—brought new burdens of responsibility. The problem was how to manage these responsibilities, and anxious discussions permeated American culture in the early republic. At the private level, the free individual faced the task of how to shape a stable and resilient character. Such a character was necessary for sustaining dependable work habits in a vocation, maintaining a steady course toward success, withstanding the blows of fortune and competition, and thus controlling effectively the direction of one's own destiny. At a larger social level, the mass of free individuals also confronted the difficulty of how to restrain the excesses of ambition. The bridling of un-scrupulous greed and passionate self-interest increasingly appeared essential to avoiding viciousness, fraud, and even anarchy in a liber-alizing society.

As these private and public tensions began to converge in early national America, they gradually activated a campaign for indi-vidual self-control, a cultural crusade that was popularized by Jeffersonian spokesmen. The "character ethic," which later became a cultural dogma in the Victorian decades after 1830, emerged as the most basic goal of this movement. In the two-score years after the Constitution, Republican cultural commentators especially began to publicize self-control as a virtue involving *both* command of person-al destiny and repression of libidinous instincts. David Riesman suggested an interpretive context here with his description of the "inner-directed" character types that slowly emerged throughout the early modern West in response to a society "characterized by in-creased personal mobility, by a rapid accumulation of capi-tal, . . . and by an almost constant expansion." With the splinter-ing of traditional restraints and growing social demands for initia-tive and choice-making, Riesman has contended, the individual had to develop an internal "gyroscope" that made him "capable of main-taining a delicate balance between the demands upon him of his goal in life and the buffetings of his external environment." By the early nineteenth century, Jeffersonian moralists and success writers were constructing this gyroscope in terms of a character ethic of self-control. In this important period of American cultural formation, they began promoting it as an indispensable aid to both personal success and social harmony.[8]

Most moral tracts began by urging the individual to engage in a steady process of self-inspection. George Bruder, for example, au-thor of the 1810 *Closet Companion; or, An Help to Serious Persons, in Self-Examination*, instructed citizens of the early republic to subject themselves to constant, intense self-scrutiny. He presented a litany of questions for the individual that blended traditional matters of salvation and religious standing with newer social concerns about passion and fraud:

> Do I avoid all intemperance? Do I resist passionate tempers? Do I labour to promote the welfare of men's souls? . . . Do I earnestly strive to preserve my own, and my neighbor's chastity, in heart, speech, and behavior; avoiding all incentives to lust. . . . Do I use the lawful means of moderately procuring and furthering the wealth and outward estate of myself, and others? . . . Am I strictly and conscientiously honest in

all my dealings, not over-reaching or defrauding any persons, in any degree?[9]

Moral writers usually supplemented such strictures by persuading individuals to self-consciously cultivate qualities of inner strength and integrity. Richard Johnson's *Blossoms of Morality Intended for the Amusement and Instruction of Young Ladies and Gentlemen* (1810), for example, explicitly adopted a horticultural metaphor. Comparing human life to a garden, the tract urged readers to encourage the "culture of the rose," Johnson's symbol for morality. "The rose reaches its highest perfection in the garden of Industry," continued the text, "where the soil is neither too luxuriant, nor too much impoverished. Temperance fans it with the gentle breezes, and Health and Contentment sport around it." Johnson insisted that the mind was the seat of happiness or misery and that the individual had the power to determine which would predominate. The individual should strive for self-control by attempting to "maintain a uniform conduct, through all the varying stations of life—to content ourselves with what comes within our reach, without pining after what we cannot obtain, or envying others what they possess—to maintain a clear unsullied conscience."[10]

Many moralists explicitly posed the self-controlled character as an antidote to wild ambition and greed. Caleb Bingham, writing in the 1810 *American Preceptor*, typically advised that wealth and social standing "can never produce happiness, unless the mind, on which all depends, be taught to enjoy them properly. Fortune, without this, will but lead . . . to more abandoned sallies of extravagance." He urged Americans to pursue an "even course of right conduct." Enos Hitchcock's allegory *The Farmer's Friend; or, the History of Mr. Charles Worthy* (1793) addressed the same idea more pointedly. After outlining the excellence of hard work and frugality for triggering a rise to success, Hitchcock added a stern warning that character formation mattered far more than any gain in status or material comfort. Riches and social advancement may command external respect, he wrote, but "he who possesses real worth may always expect the inward homage of the heart." Only with this self-respect could "true dignity of character be found."[11]

For popularizers of the character ethic, however, the "passions" of the unfettered individual comprised a large stumbling block. These dangerous emotions took a number of forms. *The Youth's Guide to Wisdom, Containing a Choice Selection of Maxims and Morals for the Rising Generation* (1812) bluntly defined one of them: "Nothing is so inconsistent with self-possession as anger. It overpowers reason, confounds our ideas, distorts the appearance, and blackens the colour of every object." Sensual gratification too came under attack. The passions of "gluttony, drunkenness, and debauchery," wrote one secular moralist, undermined spiritual life while weakening physical health as well. He concluded, "The sensual indulgences in general, when they are inordinate and excessive, debase, corrupt and brutalize. Their delights are transient, their pains severe and of long duration."[12]

Ultimately, however, proponents of the character ethic were forced to walk a thin line. The passions could not be muffled altogether because the struggle for success required a certain crude energy and lust for competition. Yet neither could such impulses be allowed to get out of hand, lest the engine of success overheat and explode. Thus shapers of the self-controlled character tried both to prompt and to harness instinctual power. As one moralist described, his text strove to "correct the passions" while also invigorating the "mental faculties" of Americans. Andrew Law's *Thoughts and Instinctive Impulses* (1810) lucidly discussed this integration of instinct and character. He began with the assumption of moral free-agency, arguing that "freedom of will" was the essence of humanity "without which we should be mere machines, incapable of all virtue." Law went on to note, however, that many writers overlooked the role played by emotions and impulses in human action. He urged the realization that "all our instinctive impulses are given by our creator for our benefit and happiness, and that education in conformity with them would render us more perfect." Law concluded that the individual should attempt to control rather than obliterate the passions, to "cultivate all his instinctive impulses and restrain all their excesses, till he becomes worthy of so amiable a being."[13]

Writers of didactic moral tracts unanimously agreed that youth comprised the best time for internalizing the ethic of self-control. *Moral and Prudential Maxims and Sayings* (1810), for example, instructed that good and bad habits were framed in childhood: "Virtuous youth gradually brings forward accomplished and flourishing manhood." Another tract typically placed the responsibility for teaching self-restraint on the parents of young Americans. For children to embark on a steady path of self-control, "the infant minds must be carefully watched, and the unruly passions made to give way to the reason and authority of the parent." But Caleb Bingham's "Address to Students" at the end of the *American Preceptor* charged youth as well with the task of developing self-control: "You are placed here for two purposes; the improvement of the understanding, and the formation of virtuous principles for the guidance of your moral conduct. . . . It is your burden to unite these estimable objects."[14]

John Foster's *Essays in a Series of Letters to a Friend* (1807) provided perhaps the most comprehensive expression of the character ethic in the early republic. Foster, a contemporary English Baptist preacher and essayist whose tracts were widely dispersed in nineteenth-century America, skillfully synthesized various elements of didactic advice and made a powerful case for shaping personal self-control. Noting the importance of "habitual self-observation," he urged readers to explore "what our character was, and what it was likely to become." In the letters entitled "On Decision of Character," Foster carefully instructed his audience in the particulars of fashioning control over the self.[15]

He envisioned first that the human mind was "a half-fluid substance, in which angles, or circles, or any other figures, may be cut, but which recovers, while you are looking, its former state, and closes them up." Yet Foster believed that for everyone this substance took some kind of definite shape in early life. If "a man have some leading and decided propensity, . . . it will be surprising to see how many more things he will find, and how many more events will happen, that any one could have imagined, of a nature to reinforce it." Foster thus surmised that it was critical for the individual to gather moral influences and form "an internal authority." This would provide guidance when one left behind early moral teachers to enter the world.[16]

Yet an internalized authority could not result from intellect alone, Foster maintained, since "passions easily beguile this majestic reason into neglect, or bribe it into acquiescence, or repress it into silence." Rather, the most effective tactic was to make "a decision of character" that focused the will, harnessed instinctual energy, and activated reason to control the self. Foster decreed it imperative that the vital individual's "passions are not wasted," but rather guided so as to "augment the force of action." The essay conveniently provided a formula for shaping self-control: a lucid analysis both of one's goals and of the barriers to success, followed by cultivation of "a conclusive manner of reasoning," disciplining of the imagination, putting oneself in situations where firm decision is required, and restraining the licentious pursuit of self-interest. Foster's decisive character embodied a "vigorous health" for "great exertion and endurance" and maintained "complete confidence in his own judgment." He sought a variety of experiences and cultivated a "systematic energy" where "the passions are exactly commensurate with the intellectual part."

Finally, the self-controlled character endeavored to present "a mildness of manner" and "tenderness" to the world, since it made a man more efficacious in worldly affairs. The man of internal strength did not require bombast. [17]

For John Foster, the contrasting fates of the strong and weak characters in a dangerously competitive society illustrated the need for self-control. On the one hand, the man of indecisive character depended on the whim of others and failed to gain self-possession. "He belongs to whatever can seize him," wrote the minister. "An infirm character practically confesses itself made for subjection, and passes like a slave, from owner to owner." With the recognition of a firm, decisive spirit, however, "it is curious to see how a space clears around a man, and leaves him room and freedom." Others quickly sense such an individual's inner strength and grasp that "he wills with extraordinary force." This character of self-control, Foster believed, promised respect and success:

> Such a man will not re-examine his conclusion with endless repetition, and he will not be delayed long by consulting other persons, after he has ceased to consult himself. He cannot bear to sit still among unexecuted decisions and unattempted projects. We wait to hear of his achievements and are confident we shall not wait long. [18]

The crusade for the character ethic, however, was not simply a secular movement in American culture. It also received indirect support from another quarter in the decades of the early republic. It was no accident that the Second Great Awakening began to gather force around the turn of the century with its evangelical emphasis on moral free-agency, the individual's decision for salvation, and personal regeneration. As Donald G. Mathews described, the Awakening in its social aspects was "an organizing process that helped to give meaning and direction to people suffering in various degrees from the social strains of a nation on the move into political, economic, and geographical areas." Indeed, many religious writers began to mirror their secular counterparts in exhorting the values of the character ethic. William Burkitt's *The Poor Man's Help and the Young Man's Guide*, a tract whose first edition appeared in 1811, urged godliness in every aspect of life, temperance in all things, and an ethic of industriousness. John Foster was a Baptist minister, and the fourth number of his *Essays in a Series of Letters*, called "On Evangelical Religion," sang the praises of "the Christian character." Even the *National Intelligencer*, normally a dedicated secular publication, suggested the intersection of evangelical and secular didacticism in the social ethic of self-control. On July 1811 appeared a brief poem entitled "To Religion" that began "Welcome, Evangelical stranger, Welcome to my lone retreat; In thy presence lurks no danger, In thy smiles dwell no deceit."[19]

By the first decades of the nineteenth century, the burgeoning crusade for self-control had begun to effect a significant *embourgeoisement* of American cultural standards. Jeffersonian moralists and ministers were welding traditional Protestant and republican values— godly industriousness, virtue, individual independence—to a secularized character ethic molded by a rapidly liberalizing society. Hard work and material comfort, Christian morality and steady habits, willful energy and sensual restraint—all began to congeal into a creed of bourgeois virtues that became the cultural foundation for middle-class America in the nineteenth century. Everywhere by the early 1800s appeared agendas for temperance and control directed at scrambling seekers of success in the young republic, especially the young and pliable ones.

Paeans to bourgeois stability and prosperity arose in didactic tracts like *The Youth's Guide to Wisdom* (1812). There attributes of virtue, honest, industry, diligent use of time, and control of the passions received hearty endorsement. Other moral guides praised to young readers the learning of any trade or business for "procuring their future livelihood." It also inculcated an ethos of honesty in this worldly catechism: "Truth shall regulate my words, and equity my actions. If I am engaged in a profession, I will do the duties of it; if in mercantile, I will take no advantage of the ignorant, nor debase my character, nor would my conscience for the sake of gain." Other pamphlets, like *The Reward of Avarice* (1810), contrasted the virtues of steady work and slow gain with a dangerous get-rich-quick mentality. It contained the sad story of the curiously named "Whang the Miller," who abandoned the steady income of his mill to dig for gold. Failing to find any, he succeeded only in undermining and collapsing the mill that provided his only means of support. Early nineteenth-century almanacs throughout the young nation also helped disseminate bourgeois values. A Virginia number urged readers to pursue "steady hours" and "well paid industry," while a Kentucky counterpart featured "Poor Robert the Scribe" lecturing on punctuality and the avoidance of alcohol. *The New England Almanack for 1813* pronounced: "A strict regularity in business is necessary to warrant success—and industry and integrity, will almost insure prosperity."[20]

As part of the consolidating bourgeois creed, the notion of "benevolence"—the voluntary performance of good works by individuals or by special organizations of individuals—began to achieve new prominence. In a society where deference to the common good was declining before the attractions of success, many began to seek a corrective to the potentially brutal side-effects of competition. The benevolent principle became such, as Caleb Bingham's *American Preceptor* suggested. The security and happiness of society flowed from the "benevolent affections" of its individual members, Bingham informed his readers. He praised the principle of "universal benevolence" and urged the responsible citizen to "prove his sincerity by doing good, and removing evils of every kind." Offering a beatific summary to his restless compatriots, Bingham wrote: "Benevolence, from its nature, composes the mind, warms the heart, enlivens the whole frame, and brightens every feature of the countenance. . . . We are bound to it by duty; we are invited to it by interest."[21]

Lyman Beecher's 1812 sermon "A Reformation of Morals Practicable and Indispensable" captured, in all its complexity, the *embourgeoisement* of American culture in the era of the early republic. Beecher, a Connecticut Congregational minister, had emerged from Yale College in the late 1790s determined to invigorate traditional Calvinist doctrine with the dynamism of the revival. By the 1820s he was to become a popular preacher, author of tracts against dueling and drinking, and an outspoken proponent of voluntary societies. Three of his children—Catherine, Harriet, and Henry Ward— would become pillars of American Victorian culture by mid-century. But in 1812 Lyman Beecher only was beginning to trumpet a message of energetic evangelical morality and bourgeois respectability.[22]

In "A Reformation of Morals" Beecher proclaimed a crisis of American values in terms that reflected problems of liberalizing social change. On the one hand, he beheld the forces of darkness: values of "avarice and cupidity," drunkards with dissipated "morals" and weakened "productive labor," Sabbath-breakers, and "another class of men . . . too exclusively occupied with schemes of personal enterprise. . . . If *their* fields bring forth abundantly, if *their* profession be lucrative, if *they* can buy and sell and net gain, it is enough. . . . The stream of business hurries them on, without the leisure of a moment, or an anxious thought concerning the general welfare." On the other hand, he beheld the as yet unmarshaled forces of light: "integrity," "industry, and temperance, and righteousness." But Beecher saw a strong basis for hope in two developments. Pointing to the growing strength of the evangelical movement, he praised the "revival of religion," "effusion of the Holy

Spirit," and "missionary spirit" spreading throughout the republic as with its reforming influence. He believed that "the nation is beginning to learn righteousness" with these early-century stirrings of the Second Great Awakening.[23]

The other encouraging tendency for Beecher was the emergence of "local voluntary associations of the wise and the good." Noting that "men freed from restraint will be wicked, and will not be peaceable," the New Englander praised these moral associations that used sermons, public reports, and conversation to diffuse moral instruction. According to Beecher, "they constitute a sort of disciplined moral militia, prepared to act upon every emergency." By the early nineteenth century this "moral militia" of associated individuals had begun to march all over the nation—in missionary societies, lyceums, temperance groups, Sunday School unions—carrying a message of moralism, steady industry, and self-restraint to foot-loose Americans on the make.[24]

An equally clear and comprehensive statement of emerging bourgeois standards came from the pen of Tench Coxe. In 1810 the Philadelphia merchant, political economist, and Jeffersonian essayist contributed to the prestigious *New Edinburgh Encyclopedia* a section called simply "America," in which he attempted to present European readers with a trenchant analysis of the character and values of the young North American republic. Coxe turned first to the mutually supporting influence of Protestantism and republicanism. Praising Americans' commitment to freedom of religion, he noted the popularity of the Episcopal, Calvinist, and Methodist denominations. Coxe also described the powerful attachment of Americans to "republican principles" as an opposition to "the power of a few" in behalf of "the rights of the whole of the members of the community." For Coxe, both Protestantism and republicanism were species of "reformation," the one opposed to arbitrary ecclesiastical power, and the other to tyrannical political power.[25]

The Philadelphian then launched a probing exploration of the American character. He described an ambitious people who by industry, economy, and skill had conquered an unproductive wilderness and risen to great prosperity. "Every male youth is taught some occupation, trade, calling, or profession," Coxe wrote admiringly, "for it is held that independence is highly favourable, if not absolutely necessary, to virtue." Echoing popularizers of the character ethic, he maintained that Americans had derived their institutions and principles "from their own will, mind, and power." Coxe extolled the independent spirit of self-made Americans with their confidence in "their own good sense, the knowledge of their own situation, and the lessons of their own experience." And as he carefully added, the "crafty devices, and wild ambition" of men on the make were being tamed by the widespread "scholastic and religious instruction of the rising generation."[26]

Coxe concluded with an insightful reading of the composite features of the American people after twenty years of nationhood. Surveying the rise and integration of several trends in American values, he perceived "a perfect civil uniformity." This vibrant synthesis of ambition, self-control, and justice, Coxe argued, was expressed in *"The piety of our politics—the true religion of our civil institutions."* Operating under the natural favor of Divine Providence, Americans had found in their cultural values and political standards "a glorious substitution for an established church." Thus Tench Coxe in 1810 articulated a consolidating bourgeois creed for a liberalizing society. He had grasped, however roughly, the cultural convergence of evangelical Protestantism, success rhetoric, a character ethic of self-control and temperance, and civil institutions that strove to maintain individual rights and opportunity. And indulging a growing habit for Americans, he wrapped this cultural ideology in the mantle of special approval from God.[27]

Men like Tench Coxe, Lyman Beecher, Caleb Bingham, and John Foster were present at the creation—either in body or spirit—of the official cultural standard that came to dominate the entrepreneurial America of the nineteenth century. By establishing the terms and popular boundaries of cultural discourse, these and other moralists and ministers inspired the shaping of self-control and the *embourgeoisement* of values during the decades of the early republic. Yet this process followed no tidy and efficient formula. It emerged from the private struggles of individuals trying to cope with the effects of the liberalizing change that they encountered and often encouraged. The experiences of three men—Spencer Houghton Cone, Benjamin Rush, and Mason Locke Weems—illustrate particular ways by which Jeffersonians synthesized religion, repression, and ambition and moved to the fore in molding the criteria of early capitalist culture. Their lives demonstrate the difficulties and struggles endemic to emerging liberal individualism in this era: the determination of vocation and destiny, the evolving demands of self-restraint, the integration of profit and moralism. They suggest as well how the cultural shift toward self-control eventually became entangled with the Republican war crusade in 1812 and issues of discipline, character, the passions, and the "moral militia."

*Spencer Houghton Cone: "I Will Be a Living Worker in the World—
I Will Play No More"*

Spencer Houghton Cone began his life as a Baptist minister in 1814
under remarkable circumstances. He had abandoned a promising
career as an actor amid an avalanche of guilt and self-doubt and, even
more recently, had aborted a stint in journalism after being fenced in
by creditors. His life in disarray, Cone had undergone a religious
conversion and felt a call to the ministry. Now having repaired to
Washington, D.C., to accept a minor clerkship in the Treasury
Department, the young lay minister was invited to speak at a small
church in the Navy Yard.

To his surprise he arrived to find an immense crowd gathered to
see the novelty of a former actor preaching. Cone later recalled, "I
reached the pulpit steps with difficulty. This was the greatest trial I
ever had as a preacher, in view of an audience." But while singing the
opening hymn "the worth of souls was presented to my mind with
irresistible force; I never once thought of the want of words to tell the
story of the Cross . . . and spoke for an hour with fervor and
rapidity. Wonderfully did the Lord help me that day." The congregation's enthusiastic reception cemented Cone's ministerial ambitions, and he rose rapidly to become a leader of his denomination over
the next four decades. He became chaplain for Congress in 1815, was
pastor at two large Baptist churches in New York City from 1823 to
his death in 1855, served as president of the Baptist General Convention from 1832 to 1841, and played leading roles in the American
and Foreign Bible Society and the American Bible Union.[28]

Cone's life before 1814, however, remains perhaps the most fascinating part of his career. In many ways his early years recapitulated
larger social and cultural trends in the young republic. His journey to
the ministry confronted many obstacles to success, followed several
tortuous vocational twists, and ultimately involved a profound personal crisis. Moreover, Cone's embrace of the Baptist ministry was
deeply enmeshed in his emotional endorsement of war with Great
Britain in 1812. He had been born in 1785 in Princeton, New
Jersey, to parents of stern Calvinist background. His boyhood was
shaped by a love of learning and family pressures for religious conversion, while adolescence saw a mentally unstable father become
violently deranged. When the older man finally required incarcera-
tion in 1799, young Spencer dropped out of Princeton College after
two years. Forced to abandon his beloved study of poetry, Latin, and
mathematics, the promising young student found himself the sole

provider for his mother and five younger siblings. He was fourteen years old.[29]

Like many other fledgling self-made men, although in far more dramatic and painful fashion, young Cone appeared on the social stage stripped of support and utterly dependent on his own resources. Just as typically, he came face-to-face with two pressing problems: finding a suitable vocation and escaping the snare of debt and pecuniary pressure. Cone did not lack industrious instincts. By all accounts he manfully shouldered his responsibilities and went to work, first as a Latin instructor at Princeton Academy, then as a schoolmaster at Burlington, and finally as an assistant principal at an academy in Philadelphia. Finding that schoolteaching barely allowed him to meet family expenses, and growing restless intellectually, Cone decided to study law at night. He entered the office of a Philadelphia lawyer as a clerk and student and often read legal tracts until the early morning hours after completing his teaching duties. Following several months of intense labor, the young man's health began to wane, while his meager salary "barely kept us alive." "Though I lived at that period with the strictest economy," he recalled later, "I found we were sinking daily more and more into debt—but I still persisted in keeping my family together." Consequently, in 1805 Cone made a curious but decisive vocational decision. He became an actor.[30]

At his first public speech at Princeton College, the school's president had told him approvingly, "Young man, your voice will be your fortune." Apparently this rich, mellifluous speaking voice prompted Cone's friends to urge him to take up a stage career. He grudgingly acquiesced, secured a role, and made his first appearance in July 1805 in *The Tragedy of Mahomet*. Cone's success was nearly instantaneous, and he became a regular in the company of the "old Chestnut Street Theatre" in Philadelphia. He rapidly developed as a performer and adopted a florid, romantic style characterized by "grace and majesty," grandiloquent use of pantomime, and quick changes of emotion from pathos to fiery anger. Cone became so popular that his poor Calvinist mother became the unwitting hostess for a salon of admirers and artists in her home. His salary increased substantially, and in the five years after 1805 he made frequent appearances in Philadelphia, Baltimore, and Alexandria, Virginia.[31]

In many ways acting met several of Cone's deepest needs. Monetary necessity was one obvious motivation. Cone recalled in 1810, "It was the only way by which I had a hope of extricating myself from my pecuniary embarrassments," and his salary provided support for a hard-pressed family. The stage also offered a forum for Cone's obvious talents and assets: elocution, energy, vivacious personality, love of literature and poetry. Yet equally significant, acting gave the young man an escape from the massive burden of hard work and responsibility that had nearly crushed him from 1799 to 1805. He revealed this in an emotional letter dated September 5, 1810:

> The cup of life to me has been a cup of bitterness. I came into the active world at fourteen years of age, overburdened with duties and difficulties. I beheld my mother, and my little sisters left completely destitute— without the means of procuring a comfortable subsistence—without a friend or a father to support and protect them. . . . It would only give a useless pang to your sympathizing heart, to tell you how I struggled, and what I suffered, during those delightful years when nature wears no mask. Those years of happy youth, that by most are merrily spent in study or amusement, to me brought nothing in their train but vexation and disappointment.

Thus the stage gave Cone both a fresh chance at success and a much-needed outlet for intense personal frustration.[32]

Yet the actor's mantle weighed increasingly heavily on Cone's shoulders. The tension between attraction and guilt proved excruciatingly painful, and in 1810, at the zenith of his success and popularity, the young thespian decided to quit the stage. Several factors forced this action. Cone's Calvinist background had never blended easily with the sensuality and frivolity of the theater. Moreover, he came to see acting as intellectually demeaning, something that "destroys all reflection which alone can improve and enlighten the human mind." But in an intriguing way Cone also betrayed growing uneasiness with the deceptions of the stage player. In language akin to the emerging critique of the "con man," he ruminated that the actor's adoption of fictitious characters somehow muffled, masked, or perverted genuine personal character. "If, by the exercise, merely, of the power of simulating the passions of courage, love, virtue, and whatever . . . I have obtained such power over the affections of any portion of my fellow man," he wondered, "how much nobler and more worthy of an American it would be to live the reality of heroic virtues—to act [out] instead of mimicking the deeds of greatness." As he burst out with considerable agitation and apprehension to a friend in 1810, "You know me as I really am. . . . Filial duty and brotherly love have formed my rules of action. I have too often swerved from their principles, but I trust they have for the most part directed my course through life." Cone the actor had entered a crisis of confidence.[33]

Beginning sometime in 1810, the weakened rafters of Cone's emotional structure began to cave in. Vocation, his old dilemma, was the first to go. Determined to leave the theater, Cone struggled to

find an outlet for his obvious talents. Like many young men in a
liberalizing society, he had internalized the rhetoric of self-made
success. Writing in 1810 of the search for "happiness," he contended:

> As free agents we have an undoubted right to make use of whatever means
> are honorable to attain, if possible, this desirable object. Reason and
> judgement were given us in vain, if we are not to be allowed the privilege
> of exercising them; and even our hearts are of no value if they can be
> disposed of as the whim or caprice of another may direct.

But he could find no suitable calling, first attempting and then abandoning attempts to start a circulating library in Baltimore and a
young man's academy in Philadelphia. Unable to secure funding for
either project he lashed out bitterly at monied men, "whose under-
standings could scarce aspire to the composition of a cabbage-net, and
whose hearts are as impervious to human feelings as their heads to a
Greek epigram," who would not believe "that an actor might be an
honest, intelligent being; and not of necessity, either an idiot or a
vagabond!"[34]

Romantic involvement at this time also threw Cone into a state of
emotional agitation. During 1810 he met Sally Morrell at the theater
and fell in love. As the daughter of a rich Philadelphia merchant and
a society girl of the city's upper crust, the young lady stepped down
socially in becoming attached to an actor who was dashing but had no
real position. Her family strongly resisted the match for some three
years. This trauma of upward mobility only exacerbated Cone's
struggles with vocation as he searched more frantically than ever for a
career that would support a family. It also drove him toward an
embrace of a bourgeois ethic of middling prosperity as he fled both
the poverty of his own past and the arrogant wealth of his fiancée's
family. He wrote to Sally:

> I shall yet, I hope, be possessed of a peaceful home to shelter her in—neat
> if not splendid—where, though we may be deserted by the votaries of
> fashion, we shall still enjoy the bliss which flows from perfect esteem and
> sympathy of soul. . . . A bliss, in my opinion, far preferable to the
> midnight revels, or the boisterous merriment of those whose lucky stars,
> and not their merits, have raised them to the gilded couch of affluence
> and luxury. Happiness does not depend on riches.[35]

Vocation and romance combined to awaken in Cone an anxious
yearning for self-control around 1810. Confronted with a treacherous social maze, the young man began to turn inward in hopes of
finding direction for and control of his life. In a letter written in

October 1810 Cone replied to a friendly inquiry about his condition: "You ascribe to me a greater depression of spirits than is really true. I am indeed rather more thoughtful than formerly, and care for the future frequently induces serious reflection." Cone went on, however, by trying to reassure his correspondent—and probably himself— that success would come only from within. In a sentence replete with the injunctions of self-control, he bravely maintained, "By reflecting upon our moral duties, the troubles incident to humanity, the native energies of the mind, and the great reward that perseverance never fails to receive, we acquire a confidence in ourselves, which, joined to a consciousness of habitual rectitude, can alone enable us not only to meet undismayed, but at last triumphantly to surmount the direst distresses."[36]

Cone's struggle with himself began to surface in the guise of a profound religious crisis. Sometime in late 1810 he had a remarkable dream that remained imprinted on his mind even thirty-five years later. In an 1844 sermon, the by-then distinguished Baptist leader told his congregation of how God "was pleased to visit me in a dream" one night in 1810 where he was falling, terrified, down a well shaft backward. While looking upward he saw a man standing at the top. "I recollect his countenance as distinctly as though I had seen it but yesterday," remembered Cone, and the stranger offered to help him climb out of this deep hole. Cone refused and "resolved to save myself," when unaccountably "the well immeasurably widened, like the mouth of hell, and was lost in a bottomless pit." With the flames leaping about him and his strength drained, Cone looked "up to the good Being at the top of the well; he stood there still, regarding me with the tenderest compassion; in unspeakable anguish I cried, 'Save me! save me!' and in a moment I was at the top of a well—I was safe!" This vision marked a psychological turning point in Cone's life. "I have never regarded dreams as worth remembering," he stated, "and yet this dream told me the story of my life in such vivid colors, that I could not drive it from my mind. I was oppressed—terrified—at the prospect of Hell, and began to pray and read the Bible diligently."[37]

This awakening of religious fervor began to fuse with Cone's quest for command over his own destiny. In an 1810 letter he divulged this process in urging a course of study and self-improvement to a friend. Bringing God to support of the character ethic, Cone argued that intelligence and industry should be utilized to cultivate "an improved taste and cultivated understanding. . . . How can we better thank the Author of our existence, than by improving the noble faculties He has bestowed upon us?" In other letters Cone lamented the attractions of "fashionable folly and vice" and proclaimed a duty to "prevail on ourselves to cultivate wisdom and virtue, to ensure us content and peace." Some two years later still seeking salvation, Cone clearly had melded religious yearnings with denial of sensuality and become primed for a "decision of character." He confessed to a friend in 1812:

> We try the world—we tread all the giddy mazes of pleasure—we taste of every sweet that promises enjoyment; till at length the overburdened appetite sickens with satiety, and the fascinating allurements that once captivated our senses, charm us no more! . . . We have kept company, and fiddled, and danced and sung, till we can do so no longer; and then, making virtue of necessity, we religiously determine to become good, and serve our Creator. But, will he receive us, then? . . . The present moment is ours—the next is the womb of futurity, and we may never live to realize it.[38]

By the summer of 1812 young Spencer Cone arrived at the threshold of resolution to his personal predicament. His restless energy, his yearning for suitable vocation, and his struggle for self-control found an explosive release in the emotional catalyst of war with Great Britain. In the spring of that year, Cone began to exhibit a heightened interest in public affairs and the growing foreign crisis with England. He joined a Baltimore artillery regiment and took up the study of military science and discipline. "We talk of nothing but the 'mailed Mars, up to the ears in blood.' We hear nothing but the martial drum, the shrill fife, and the warrior . . . with enthusiastic zeal, buckles on the armor of resistance with all a freeman's wonted alacrity! Success to our cause!" he wrote to a friend. The generally agitated state of his emotions fed this new-found war fervor. He confided his belief that "the expediency, propriety, and absolute necessity" of war with Great Britain reflected "the best passions and affections of my soul." Cone concluded the letter with an emotional flourish: "Farewell, and oh remember!—it is sweet to die for our country."[39]

The young soldier spent much of 1812–13 drilling with his artillery company. This martial displacement and focus of frustrated energy supplemented another critical change in Cone's life. Sometime in the spring of 1812 he became treasurer and bookkeeper at a local newspaper, the *Baltimore American*. This position fulfilled two immediate needs. It gave Cone a respectable profession with which to support a wife, and it provided a gratifying regimen of self-discipline. He related after several weeks of employment, "I rise regularly at five in the morning, from necessity, and not from choice, you'll say. No matter—I do it—and wend my way to the office, and post my books." The young scrivener became so infatuated with journalism that he joined with his brother-in-law, John Nowell, and purchased the *Baltimore Whig* in 1813. During this time Cone admitted that "politics and war completely engrossed my mind." Writing vigorous editorials against "the Hartford Conventionists and Federal anti-war party," the fledgling Jeffersonian editor noted, "We sustained the Madison Administration with all our powers."[40]

As 1814 approached, Cone's war fervor and continuing religious quest intensified and became almost inseparable. In the *Baltimore Whig* he agitated editorially for an invasion of Canada, an expedition of which he hoped to be a part. And in the spring of 1813 he began anew to seek salvation. The religious crisis appearing in 1810 had ebbed and flowed over several years before finally washing over Cone's psychic defenses. Once more taking up the Bible, he read and meditated inconclusively for several months, a period that also saw his marriage and brief active stint with his Baltimore regiment. Finally, in November 1813 Cone's religious anxiety came to a head. In that month he went to a book auction, casually picked up a volume that happened to be the *Works of John Newton,* a Protestant minister studied by Cone at Princeton. "In an instant my whole life passed in review before me," he described, and thus began a conversion ordeal lasting some two months. Haunted by his earlier "dream of the well," hearing a voice saying, "This is your last warning," unable to conduct work, Cone suffered intense private anguish. In February 1814, after spending a prayerful, tearful night alone in the garret of his house, he finally experienced a vision of godly beneficence. "I felt as if plunged into a bath of blood divine—I was cleansed from head to foot . . . [and] from that hour to the present, a doubt of my calling and election of God has never crossed my mind." In a few days he was baptized in the Patapsco River—a hole was cut through the foot-thick ice—and he joined the First Baptist Church of Baltimore.[41]

Within a few months Cone ventured onto the battlefield with renewed personal spirit. When the British invaded the Chesapeake in August 1814, his regiment fought with the American army at Bladensburg. The disorganized force of the Americans was crushed, and Cone fled with them to Washington, D.C., where he had a harrowing escape from capture. Returning to Baltimore, he was appointed captain of a rifle company in September. He then served at Fort McHenry during the unsuccessful British bombardment and fought in several skirmishes around the city.[42]

Cone's support of the war had always contained a religious dimension. In July 1812 he had exhorted, "Let us confide in the God of battles, who will ultimately crown the cause of virtue with success."

But by 1814 the military crusade of the young republic began to seem but a larger reflection of his personal spiritual crusade. Shortly before his conversion experience, while in the throes of religious uncertainty, Cone had explained his war fervor as something in which "I must embark my life and honor, which constitute my all." But by 1814 his "all" embraced personal salvation as well as war, and Cone took the field as a Christian Soldier. The months after conversion saw a fascinating mingling of religious and martial metaphors in Cone's discourse. The young man who proclaimed the sweetness of noble death in wartime now rapturously described his baptism as "a glow of warmth and animation . . . while buried beneath the wave." The excited admirer of a "mailed Mars, up to the ears in blood" now proclaimed the joy of being "plunged into a bath of the blood divine" and thanked God for "the lamb that was slain" and his "blood-bought, free reward." The blessed soldier in the field now urged his unconverted wife "to enlist under the banner of the great Captain of our Salvation." For Cone, war and religious conversion converged as a consuming ritual of individual purgation and rebirth.[43]

The religious enthusiasm of the young Baptist became so great that by war's end he complained, "My soul pants to become engaged in the work of the ministry." As the final act in his drama of success, however, Cone had to extricate himself from a web of debt before settling into his true calling. The *Baltimore Whig* had been unable to collect money owed to it because of wartime exigencies, and in turn it fell victim to its creditors. Cone and his wife were forced to give up their house and possessions at auction. Finally, amid these "pecuniary embarrassments" and "entanglements of business," the debt was largely liquidated and settlement was reached. The former editor procured a minor position in the Treasury Department, began lay preaching, and finally moved toward the dramatic religious episode in the Navy Yard.[44]

Ultimately Spencer Cone's early life was a miniature portrait of the larger cultural panorama of the early American republic. His struggles to find a suitable career, his difficulties with credit and debt, his hunger for self-control, and his contention with religious conversion as a moral free-agent typified—if perhaps more dramatically than most—the travails of emerging liberal man in the early nineteenth century. Typical too were the ways in which his individual experience with American cultural realignment fed the Jeffersonian instinct for war in 1812. Cone perhaps best summed up his situation, and that of many others, in an 1810 comment. About to abandon the insincerities of the stage in a search for vocation, salvation, and self-control, the anxious young man vowed, "I will be a living worker in the world—I will play no more."[45]

Benjamin Rush: "I Consider It as Possible to Convert Men into Republican Machines"

Benjamin Rush passionately condemned war throughout most of his life. In the 1790s he had published *A Plan of a Peace-Office for the United States*. This humanitarian essay proposed the establishment of a Department of Peace in the new national government and the appointment of a Secretary of that department who was "a genuine republican and a sincere Christian." This Department of Peace, argued the eminent Philadelphia physician, should strive to establish "free schools" that teach moral principles as well as academic subjects. Moreover, it should furnish every family in the United States with a Bible. As for the already-existing War Department,

> In the lobby of this office let there be painted representations of all the common military instruments of death, also human skulls, broken bones, unburied and putrefying dead bodies, hospitals, crowded with sick and wounded soldiers, villages on fire, mothers in besieged towns eating the flesh of their children, ships sinking in the ocean, rivers dyed with blood, and extensive plains without a tree or fence, or any other subject, but the ruins of deserted farm houses.

Yet in the summer of 1812 Rush endorsed war with Great Britain and bitterly attacked its opponents. "Alas! what dead weights are banks, whiskey distilleries, and the funding system in the opposite scale to that which contains the patriotism, the justice, and the honor of our country!" he complained to John Adams. "We are indeed a be-banked, a bewhiskied, and a bedollared nation." The reasons for Rush's turnaround were both complicated and revealing. As with many other Republicans, war, although abhorrent in the abstract, in 1812 culminated a long personal campaign in behalf of self-control. This central compulsion in Rush's life took root in the years after the American Revolution.[46]

Rush had been born in 1745 near Philadelphia, took a degree from Princeton in 1760, and returned to his native city to study medicine for several years. From 1766 to 1769 the young medical student completed his education at the University of Edinburgh and then trained at London's St. Thomas Hospital. After his return to the colonies, Rush pursued an amazingly varied career over the next four decades. He became America's leading physician, was the author of several medical texts, and taught hundreds of students chemistry, theory, and medicine at the University of Pennsylvania. He won the title "Father of American Psychiatry" for his work with the insane at the Pennsylvania Hospital and for his influential text *Medical Inquiries and Observations upon the Diseases of the Mind* (1812). Rush also took an active role in politics as a member of the Continental Congress, a signer of the Declaration of Independence, and a leader of the 1787 fight in Pennsylvania to ratify the new Constitution. Finally, as one of the busiest social reformers of his age, he wrote and organized in behalf of Bible societies, prison reform, a public school system, antislavery, control of smallpox and yellow fever, and temperance. Benjamin Rush epitomized the intellectual energy and breadth of the American Enlightenment.[47]

The political and social thought of this American *philosophe*, like that of most contemporaries, had taken shape in the mold of the American Revolution. Although first politicized by the controversy over the Stamp Act, Rush's introduction to republican theory actually came in Scotland. There he "heard the authority of Kings called in question" and became convinced that "no form of government can be rational but that which is derived from the suffrages of the people." As an agitator for independence, the young doctor urged Thomas Paine to write a revolutionary pamphlet and then read and criticized portions of Paine's *Common Sense* as they were composed. In the two decades after independence, Rush's republicanism became more solid and refined. He came to believe that a government where sovereignty resided in the people rested on a tripod of support. "Virtue"—the sacrifice of private interest to public good—formed the first leg. Rush's notion of virtue tended toward the extreme, as he noted in 1787: "Every man is public property. His time and talents—his youth—his manhood—his old age—nay more, his life, his all, belong to his country."[48]

Evangelical Christianity comprised the second supporting leg of Rush's ideal republic. As a boy he had attended Rev. Samuel Finley's boarding school and then fell heavily under the influence of Princeton's president, the Rev. Samuel Davies, both of whom were leading preachers of the First Great Awakening. He also heard the revival preaching of the Rev. George Whitefield. Having visited Whitefield while in London studying medicine, Rush recalled in his *Autobiography*, "He and Mr. Wesley [John Wesley] constituted the two largest and brightest orbs that appeared in the hemisphere of the Church in the 18th century. Probably they were exceeded only by the apostles in zeal and usefulness." By 1786 Rush would contend in his famous essay *Thoughts Upon the Mode of Education Proper in a Re-*

public that the "foundation for a useful education in a republic is to be laid in religion. . . . A Christian cannot fail of being a republican." Although flirting with "Universalism" in later years, Rush's evangelical fervor remained high throughout his life. In August 1800 he still enthused to Thomas Jefferson, "It is only necessary for republicanism to ally itself to the Christian religion to overturn all the corrupted political and religious institutions in the world."[49]

The final leg of Rush's republican tripod consisted of a sturdy work ethic. He straightforwardly declared in his 1786 essay *Enquiry into the Influence of Physical Causes upon the Moral Faculty*, "Idleness is the parent of every vice. . . . Labor of all kinds, favors and facilitates the practice of virtue." Industrious values, he insisted, must be learned when one is young, because the "effects of steady labor in early life, in creating virtuous habits, is . . . remarkable." Rush personalized both the social felicities and the private satisfactions of hard work in his 1801 *Account of the Life and Character of Christopher Ludwick*. The life of this successful Philadelphia citizen, Rush assured his readers, showed both the happy influence of religion on moral conduct and the necessity of "habits of industry and economy upon success in all enterprises." Rush hoped that his story would "inspire hope and exertion in young men of humble employment, and scanty capital, to aspire to wealth and happiness."[50]

The Philadelphia physician summed up much of his early thinking about republicanism in 1786. Writing on the ideal education for the young republican citizen, he urged the teaching of industry, virtue, piety, and restraint:

> He must be taught to amass wealth, but it must be only to increase his power of contributing to the wants and demands of the state. He must be indulged occasionally in amusements, but he must be taught that study and business should be his principle pursuits in life. Above all he must love life and endeavor to acquire as many of its conveniences as possible by industry and economy, but he must be taught that this life "is not his own" when the safety of his country requires it.

If such values were internalized, Rush believed, citizens would create a republic of unsurpassed "energy" and "strength."[51]

By the later 1780s Rush's bright republican idealism began to fade. The agitations of that decade—Shays' Rebellion, widespread lawsuits, constant commercial bickering between the states—provoked fears of long-lasting social chaos. He wrote to David Ramsay in 1788 that Americans had been seduced by vice and warned of "their degenerating into savages or devouring each other like beasts of prey." Rush described the problem in medical terms in his 1789 text *Medical Inquiries and Observations:* "The excesses of the passion for liberty" raised during the Revolution, he argued, "constituted a form of insanity, which I shall take the liberty of distinguishing by the name of *anarchia.*"[52]

In the 1790s the progress of American commercialization only aggravated Rush's concerns. For example, his *Commonplace Book* for 1792 overflowed with complaints that growing speculation and frenetic commercial exchanges were exacerbating "anarchic" tendencies. He lamented those "immense debts" so "disgraceful to moral character," "the spirit of speculation" which led to "numerous failures," and the "great distress" of unlucky investors who "weep in the streets." The Hamiltonian funding system—a plan to stabilize national credit by recognizing Revolutionary certificates at face value, whether they were held by the original holders or by wealthy speculators—epitomized this disgraceful trend for Rush. By "robbing" the original holder of his property and giving it to men "who had neither earned nor deserved it," this plan succeeded only in "drawing the capital of the country into speculation." Rush's disgust with these commercializing trends grew so profound that he made the following notation without comment in his 1799 journal: "Burke's character of a merchant: Gold is his God, the exchange is his church, his counting house is his altar, an invoice his Bible, and his only trust is in his banker."[53]

Rush's own conduct fed his consternation over liberalizing change. The young doctor's personal ambition had involved him in several undignified imbroglios in the 1780s and 1790s. As "Surgeon-General of the Middle Department" during the Revolution, he was forced to resign after being involved in a plot to replace George Washington. Rush's aggressive advocacy of a novel theory of disease—he believed that all ailments originated in excessive agitation of the blood vessels and could be treated by "bleeding"—triggered nasty clashes with other doctors. It also brought a painful, years-long lawsuit for libel against journalist William Cobbet. This English immigrant had taken some well-aimed shots at Rush's medical pretensions in the 1790s. He sarcastically praised Rush's bleeding treatment as "one of the great discoveries . . . which have contributed to the depopulation of the earth." He referred to the physician as a "poisonous trans-Atlantic quack" and termed him "the remorseless Bleeder." He approved Rush's reputation as the "Samson of Medicine," arguing that the "Rushites" indeed "have slain more Americans with it, than ever Samson slew of the Philistines." But Cobbet also hit uncomfortably close to home in assessing Rush's ambition. "Rush had constantly endeavoured to place himself at the head of something or other," wrote the Englishman: "He had ever been upon the search for some discovery, some captivating novelty, to which he might prefix his name, and thus reach, at a single leap, the goal at which men seldom arrive but by slow, cautious and painful approaches." The outraged Rush finally won the libel suit in 1799 and an award of five thousand dollars.[54]

Lapses in personal conduct proved even more disconcerting to Rush than the travails of professional ambition. For all his complaining, Rush himself became involved in land speculation. Beginning in the mid-1780s he bought up numerous tracts of land, most of them in counties in central Pennsylvania, and employed several land agents to buy and sell them according to exigencies of the market. In 1795, for example, his holdings totaled more than forty-one thousand acres in six counties. Rush also had an acute awareness of how personal passion threatened to overwhelm the restraints of virtue. His sexual appetite as a young man left a lasting impression, and he confessed to an affair with a married woman as well as other vague indulgences. Rush noted in his autobiography, "The early part of my life was spent in dissipation, folly, and in the practice of some of the vices to which young men are prone. The weight of that folly and those vices have been felt in my mind ever since."[55]

By the last decade of the eighteenth century, perhaps from personal introspection as well as from social observation, Americans appeared to Rush as a people running wild. The scramble for individual success and a dangerous disregard for authority in the young nation profoundly challenged his ideal of the virtuous republic. Hence, the Philadelphia *philosophe* slowly mounted an unrelenting, multifront campaign urging the individual to restrain the impulses of gratification. As the 1790s unfolded, self-control steadily subsumed religion, virtue, and industriousness to become Rush's republican icon. It linked his endeavors in psychology, social reform, and politics as Rush struggled to shape the requisite republican citizen. The nature of his response to unsettling social change—a crusade for mental and physical self-regulation—moved the doctor onto new cultural ground. Rush became a leading apostle preaching the character ethic of self-control.

In 1798 the physician analyzed the crucial cultural problem for overly ambitious Americans. In the essay *Thoughts upon the Amusements and Punishments, Which are Proper for Schools*, Rush perceptively described the erosion of external authority over the individual in the early modern West. In the medieval past, he observed, transgressions had brought "civil, ecclesiastical, military, and domestic punishments . . . of a cruel nature," but with "the progress of rea-

son and Christianity, punishments of all kinds became less severe."
With this shift away from being "governed by force," the burden of
regulation fell increasingly on the individual himself. Recalling his
own childhood training in his *Autobiography*, Rush stressed the importance of "shame" for internalizing moral values and Christian
principles. And of his regimen of "constant labor and self-denial" in
learning medicine, Rush admitted, "I owe much to it. It produced in
me habits of industry and business which have never left me."[56]

In raising his own children, Rush refined techniques for teaching
self-control. After the age of three or four, his children suffered no
corporal punishment but rather "SOLITUDE as a means of reformation." Once having confined his son John to a room for two days,
Rush argued that the effects "will never wear away, nor do I think it
will ever require to be repeated." He concluded that a youthful
transgressor's "thought should recoil wholly upon himself" and other
disciplines were but "light punishments compared with letting a
man's conscience loose upon him in solitude." Rush's interest gravitated toward the cultivation of the "moral faculty," that "power in the
human mind of distinguishing and choosing good and evil." As Rush
wrote in a 1786 essay, *An Enquiry into the Influence of Physical Causes
upon the Moral Faculty*, "I believe in the freedom of moral agency in
man because I conceive it to be essential to his nature as a responsible
being." But the key to molding restrained individuals, he suggested,
lay in "proper modes and places of education."[57]

Thus, for Rush, internalized moral restraints became central to a
stable, prosperous republican society. Quoting Rousseau that "a well
regulated moral instinct is the surest guide to happiness," Rush prepared a variety of techniques for instilling self-control outside the
family. He argued for the importance of a "virtuous education" for
the young, where the schoolmaster would exhibit "a prudent deport-
ment," "command his passions and temper at all times," and utilize
shame and guilt in teaching moral principles to his young charges.
Rush extended the same principles to the treatment of criminals. He
contended that the goal should be "reformation," not punishment per
se, and that that object could best be met in a "penitentiary system."
These institutions, Rush contended, should inculcate restraint among
inmates by both teaching "the principles and obligations of religion"
and by utilizing "bodily pain, labour, watchfulness, solitude, and silence."[58]

The good doctor, however, did not stop there. Not content with
setting a new moral agenda for institutions like schools and prisons,
he extended his crusade for self-control into the physical body itself.
As he wrote exultantly in 1786, cultivation of the moral faculty now

had become the business of "the natural philosopher" and "the physician," not just parents, teachers, and ministers. For Rush, "a physical regimen should as necessarily accompany a moral precept, as directions with respect to air, exercise, and diet generally accompany prescriptions for the consumption and the gout." This linking of bodily function and moral instruction reached its conclusion in his famous book of 1812, *Medical Inquiries and Observations upon the Diseases of the Mind.* The culmination of some twenty-five years work with the insane at the Pennsylvania Hospital, this ground-breaking work argued that diseases of the mind and "derangement of the moral faculty" were closely related to physical malfunctions. Most mental illness, Rush believed, would be improved by manipulation of certain environmental stimuli: diet, exercise, warm baths, active labor, and of course bleeding to relieve the agitated "blood vessels of the brain."[59]

Rush's concern for physical self-control and a healthy moral faculty led him in *Diseases of the Mind* to focus on the dangers of human sexual desires. He believed that if this natural appetite designed for propagating the species were allowed to become excessive, it would bring "disease both of the body and the mind." The danger of excess usually appeared in either an "undue or a promiscuous intercourse with the female sex, or in onanism" (the eighteenth-century term for masturbation). In both cases the consequences were appalling: "seminal weakness, impotence, dysury, tabes dorsalis, pulmonary consumption, dyspepsia, dimness of sight, vertigo, epilepsy, hypochondriasis, loss of memory, manalgia, fatuity, and death." Rush also connected such sexual derangements to other physical indulgences like excessive eating, intemperate drinking, and idleness. The only solution, Rush insisted, was a regimen of disciplined self-control. He recommended matrimony, or at least the "company of chaste and modest women," a diet of "vegetables and other simple foods," temperance, "constant employment in bodily labour or exercise," and the always dependable "cold bath." As a last resort, Rush proposed "avoiding all dalliance with the female sex," assuring readers, "I have heard of a clergyman, who overcame this appetite by never looking directly into the face of a woman."[60]

Dr. Rush's unique "tranquilizer" device became the ultimate symbol of his obsession with controlling the physical passions. For deranged patients at the Pennsylvania Hospital who were physically agitated, he designed a restraining chair with a head block, straps for the arms and legs, and a cut-out seat for relief of bodily functions. This tranquilizing chair made unnecessary the application of direct "human force," Rush noted, while reducing the patient's "force of pulse" and "muscular action." It also enabled the physician to bleed and apply cold-water treatments with greater proficiency. Such concerns with repression of bodily gratifications seems to have become ever more important to Rush. Conscious of "the few sands that remain in my glass," he informed Thomas Jefferson only a few weeks before his death that his next book would carry the title "Hygiene, or Rules for the Preservation of the Health Accommodated to the Climate, Diet, Manners, and Habits of the People of the United States."[61]

Rush ultimately gathered his scientific sermons on the moral faculty and self-control and began to preach a sweeping bourgeois gospel by the early nineteenth century. In 1799 he told scientific audiences, "The *will* should never be idle in those persons, who wish to possess great vigour and activity of mind." In 1803 the doctor instructed his son James, "Labour is the lot and destiny of man, and . . . must be submitted to by all young men who are not born to inherit large estates." In 1798 he argued that frivolous activities for schoolchildren were wasteful. "The Methodists have wisely banished every species of play from their college," he said approvingly. In 1811 he published a stinging attack on alcoholic consumption entitled *An Inquiry into the Effects of Ardent Spirits upon the Human Body and Mind.* Rush equated intemperance with the destruction of morals, self-control, work habits, and property. Moreover, he related "the case of a notorious drunkard, having been sadly destroyed in consequence of the vapour discharged from his stomach by belching, accidently taking fire by coming in contact with the flame of a candle."[62]

Rush accompanied these bourgeois nostrums with explicit attacks on the sensuality and laziness of certain social groups. He complained that aristocratic "courts create servility, insincerity, idleness, vice of every kind, particularly seduction." And his *Autobiography*, written in the years after 1800, linked the French ("the highest degree of civilization") with the North American Indian ("the savage life") in their contempt for labor and commerce, their preference for revealing attire and makeup, and their lack of restraint in sexual matters. Rush leveled most of his criticism, however, at the poor. In efforts like *An Address to Ministers of the Gospel* (1798) he denounced the attraction of the lower class to alcohol and taverns, fairs and horseracing, gaming and fighting, and weekend frolicking resulting in the wastefulness of "St. Monday." Moreover, the doctor asked rhetorically, "How many young men and women have carried through life the sorrowful marks in their consciences or characters, or their being initiated into the mysteries of vice, by unprincipled servants of both sexes!" In a 1787 *Plan for Free Schools,* Rush worried about the "children of poor people." Their ignorance and vices were bad enough in themselves, he wrote anxiously, but it became even worse when "they associate with and contaminate the children of higher ranks of society." For teaching moral restraint to children of the poorer sort, Rush found inspiration in the child labor practices in growing British industrial cities. "The wealth of those manufacturing towns in England, which employ the children of poor people, is a proof of what might be expected from connecting amusement, and labour together in our schools." For control of their parents, the Philadelphia sage suggested "the house of God," which "winds up the machine of both soul and body, better than anything else, and thereby invigorates it for the labours and duties of the ensuing week."[63]

These acute social and cultural vexations in many ways primed Benjamin Rush for war in 1812. In part he remained skeptical, describing warfare as "nothing but duelling upon a national scale." Rush also recognized that war might encourage the social values that he despised. Surveying "the evils of war" in his *Commonplace Book,* he noted that "1, it begets debt. 2, idleness. 3, drunkenness. 4, extravagance in dress. 5, dissipation. 6, quarreling, duelling, heavy taxes." But Rush's anxiety over social anarchy, and his determination to nourish self-control among ambitious Americans, gradually overwhelmed his hesitancy about war. It began to seem a useful therapeutic tool to the physician distressed over the social ills and diseased characters of Americans.[64]

By the summer of 1812, Benjamin Rush had grown despondent over the "selfishness" of Americans and their "canine appetite for wealth." Complaining to John Adams that money hunger had "reduced regular industry and virtuous economy to the rank of sniveling virtues," he recommended placing an ad in leading European newspapers: "For Sale, to the highest bidder, the United States of America." Even more, Rush was convinced that commercial values had undermined the self-control and sanity of many of his countrymen. "In the United States, madness has increased since the year 1790," he wrote in the 1812 *Diseases of the Mind.* "This must be ascribed chiefly to an increase in the number and magnitude of the objects of ambition and avarice, and to the greater joy or distress, which is produced by gratification or disappointments in the pursuit of them."[65]

This army of social and psychological anxieties led Rush to embrace war in 1812 as a chastening, disciplining ritual for a people careening toward the abyss of unrestrained "madness." The old Jeffersonian began to see war, like religion or education, as a means for cementing self-control within ambitious Americans of the early nineteenth century. The rationale Rush mustered was superficial, of course. Wars, he admitted, were sometimes unavoidable and probably inevitable, and "to expect perpetual peace therefore among beings constituted as we are is as absurd as to expect to discover perpetual motion." But he made a more revealing statement to John Adams a few weeks after the declaration of war. "It is too high an honor to call us a nation of shopkeepers. It would be more proper to call us a nation of peddlers," he wrote. "A city in flames kindled by the hand of war is not so melancholy a sight as a whole nation absorbed in the love of money." Rush expanded this explanation in a later letter to Jefferson picturing the war as a corrective to pecuniary greed. "A nation debased by the love of money and exhibiting all the vices and crimes usually connected with that passion, is a spectacle far more awful, distressing, and offensive" than any battlefield carnage. "War has its evils, so has a long peace," he concluded.[66]

Rush gave several hints in 1812 of the extent to which he saw war as a means of fostering self-control among citizens of the young republic. A military crusade, he believed, would comprise an acceptable, socially useful means of channeling off the libidinous urges of Americans. "One of the most necessary ingredients in the apparatus of war is still wanting in our country," he wrote in July 1812. "I mean *war passions*. . . . Without an *inflamation in our passions*, nothing effective can be done in the mighty contest before us." Rush propounded this theme more carefully in *Diseases of the Mind*, recommending the embrace of an active military spirit that would "predominate over the sexual appetite." "The love of military glory, so common among the American Indians," Rush pointed out, "by combining with the hardships of a savage life, contributes very much to weaken their venal desires." For those opponents of the war unwilling or unable to triumph over sensuality in this fashion, Rush had another alternative. "Alas! the *madness* of party spirit! Where—where is my tranquilizer?"[67]

Years earlier, in the 1780s, the idealistic young doctor had excitedly described the young republic as being in a plastic state where "the benefactor of mankind may realize all his schemes for promoting human happiness." Thirty years later such enthusiasm had waned somewhat. Americans' instinct for gain and gratification had proved to be an unexpectedly formidable opponent, and Rush brooded over "derangements in the will" that led his fellow citizens to "lying," "drinking," and pursuit of "their animal existences." At times he even despaired of the past and his attempts to teach the necessities of self-control. He asked Jefferson in 1813, "From the present complexion of affairs in our country, are you not disposed at times to repent of your solicitudes and labors and sacrifices during our Revolutionary struggles for liberty and independence?" But in the end Rush remained devoted to the central task he had set for himself. "I consider it as possible to convert men into republican machines," he had written confidently in the 1786 *Thoughts upon Education Proper to a Republic.* "This must be done if we expect them to perform their parts properly in the great machine of the government of state." Near the end of his life—he died in 1813—Rush's only regret was that he might have adopted certain tactics earlier to shape these self-controlled, morally self-propelled "republican machines." "Were we to live our lives over again, and engage in the same benevolent enterprise," the Philadelphian mused to John Adams in 1811, "our means should not be reasoning but bleeding, purging, low diet, and the tranquilizer chair." In 1812 Rush added war to his list of remedies.[68]

Mason Locke Weems: "Sacrificing Their Gold to Gamblers, Their Health to Harlots, and Their Glory to Grog"

Mason Locke Weems appears to us as a cultural hobo from early-nineteenth-century America—a traveling man, benevolent and smiling, yet slightly grimy and scheming and loaded down with a knapsack of contradictory impulses. As the didactic "Parson Weems," he wrote the immensely popular and priggish *Life of Washington,* a book full of saccharine platitudes to do good. But as the hard-nosed, traveling book salesman he greedily demanded that his publisher clear out the old editions of *Washington* and distribute the new. "You have a great deal of money lying in the bones of old George if you will exert yourself to extract it," he wrote irreverently, "and perhaps some good fluent Hawker wd. aid as much." As the pious moralist, Weems could ask his reading audience, "What motives under heaven can restrain men from vices and crimes, and urge them on, full stretch, after individual and national happiness, like those of religion?" But the good parson would horrify the Rev. William Mead by selling both religious tracts and Thomas Paine's blasphemous *Age of Reason* at the same public meeting. When confronted, Weems simply held up both books and replied audaciously, "Behold the antidote. The bane and the antidote are both for you."[69]

Historians have found it difficult to understand this multifaceted and elusive figure. One study labeled Weems "an amiable charlatan" and "one of the first great national boosters." Another emphasized his role as a pioneer in the nineteenth-century literature of both "child nurture" and the mythology of the American "Union." Marcus

Cunliffe, probably the most penetrating modern student of Weems, has described him as a likeable "confidence man" and a trailblazer for American cultural nationalism, humanitarian reform, popular literature, and marketing techniques.[70] While each of these sketches catches a color of the chameleon-like Parson, the essential man remains obscure. However, he assumes a more clear and coherent shape by the reflected light of liberalizing change in the decades of the early republic. In his most inclusive role, Weems served as a captain in the swelling moral militia of bourgeois culture in early-nineteenth-century America. Through his strenuous efforts to reconcile profit and philanthropy, money and moralism, he became the greatest popular theorist of the character ethic of self-control before the Civil War. And these cultural endeavors led him to fervent support for the War of 1812. To understand this fascinating and frustrating man fully, one must go beyond the worshipful chronicler of "Washington and the cherry-tree" and explore his moral struggle with historical change.

Mason Weems was born a Marylander in 1759, the youngest of nineteen children. Information on his early life is sketchy, but we do know that he had some schooling as a child and spent considerable time on the trading vessels of two older brothers. Weems seems to have been in the British Isles between 1777 and 1779 studying medicine, probably in London or Edinburgh. He did not serve in the American Revolution, but reappeared in England from 1779 to 1784, preparing for the ministry. After ordination in the Episcopal Church, Weems served as rector at two Maryland churches until 1793. He then took the first steps toward a new career as a promoter and seller of books, contracting as an agent for publisher Mathew Carey of Philadelphia. Marrying in 1795, he settled in Dumfries, Virginia, a small tobacco port in Prince William County. As a salesman on commission, Weems traveled in Maryland, Pennsylvania, and Virginia and eventually north into New York and New Jersey and south deep into the Carolinas and Georgia. He spent much of his mature life on the road. Weems gradually began to write popular books on his own, the first being the famous *Life of Washington*, initially published in 1800 before going through countless reprintings in the nineteenth century. Over the next two decades he churned out other mass-market biographies of Francis Marion, Benjamin Franklin, and William Penn. Weems also composed numerous moral pamphlets denouncing gambling, drinking, dueling, and bachelorhood. He died in the 1820s, destined to be one of the most widely read authors in antebellum America.[71]

Two concerns in Weems' early adulthood emerged to set the course for his later career. The first was religion. Although trained as an Episcopal priest, by the late 1780s he had become attracted to evangelical Protestantism. Superiors complained that Weems "introduced ye Methodists' Hymns & Tunes in ye Public Service," while fellow priests raised their eyebrows over his "method of working up the passions that pays no respect either to reason or decency." Then in the 1790s Weems turned to bookselling, a move that caused him to reject doctrinal rigidity in favor of a vague, uplifting message of love and benevolence. Preaching and selling books simultaneously, the Parson reportedly thought "love the sum and essence of Christianity," and it was noted that "his doctrines are said to have approached universal salvation." For Weems, this combination of amiable theology and business was a happy one. "I hope that, at my preaching appointments, of which I have made a fine chain for next week, I shall get pretty nearly clear of my cargo," he told a correspondent in 1803. One observer put it less kindly, "After a congregation have heard a sermon for nothing, they will seldom be so hard-hearted as not to pay for a book."[72]

This commingling of religion and sales eventually led Weems a step further. By the late 1790s he had initiated a campaign to make the gaining of profit morally acceptable, even virtuous. Befitting his sensibility, the parson turned first to practical benevolence. In concocting various schemes to sell books—and the parson was nothing if not ingenious—he fell into the habit of promoting humanitarian projects with profitable by-products. He petitioned the Virginia State Legislature, for example, to establish "charity schools" by way of a lottery with "the prizes payable in books." "To all good Christians the education of the poor and fatherless is a *primary wish*," he said, informing his publisher of his plan, before adding, "I have no doubt but I shall be enabled to sell you $16,000 worth of books more briefly than you apprehend." Weems urged the establishment of "circulating libraries" for similar reasons of public uplift and private gain.[73]

When discussing money, Weems adopted the language of the moral imperative. He explained in 1802:

> Next to health of body and virtuous mind, wealth is one of the first of this world's goods. . . . By wealth, a good man takes up the orphan in his arms, wipes away his tears, feeds and clothes his little trembling body, and by pious instruction leads him safe to his God. Hence, among all sensible people, who have had any true *self* love or *social*, gold has ever shone with the most inviting lustre, and every exertion, that conscience could approve, has been made to obtain it.

Even religion itself became a moral and material commodity to
Weems. As the traveling Parson Weems explained to Carey in July
1812: "I have just come to the fullest conviction that if I were clear of
all other Books under Heaven and gave my whole undivided attention to the Bible I shou'd in 5 years make a fortune for us both."
Weems' original idea for the Washington biography arose from this
convergence of benevolence and profit. Writing of his plans for the
manuscript in 1800, he revealed both his moral intent—"to show
that his unparalleled rise and elevation were owing to his Great
Virtues"—and his material hopes—that "we may sell it with great
rapidity." Weems perhaps best summarized his creed of philanthropy and profit in December 1811. Goading Carey to establish a
chain of bookstores in the eastern states, he exclaimed, "O what
might not be the results in Good to the Country, & in Gold and Glory
to Ourselves."[74]

Weems' personal resolution of money and morality emerged publicly in a message of success. His Washington biography, in fact,
resembled nothing so much as a success manual for young Americans. The Revolutionary hero emerged from its pages preeminently a
self-made man. Washington, the rather imaginative author insisted
from the outset, was not "born with a silver spoon in his mouth."
Realizing that he had "no chance of ever rising in the world but by his
own merit," he embraced "Industry . . . the queen mother of all our
virtues and of all our blessings." Washington's ethos of hard work,
Weems maintained, was responsible for his success: "And what is it
that raises a young man from poverty to wealth, from obscurity to
never-dying fame? What, but *industry*." Hard work and achievement
determined the real worth and merit of individuals, and Weems
lashed out at social groups who rejected his doctrine. Young gentlemen "in powder and ruffles" who believed work to be fit only for
the "poor and slaves" were burdens on society and easy prey for
creditors. The lazy poor roused Weems' contempt equally. "For
whence do all our miseries proceed, but from lack of industry? In a
land like this, which heaven has blessed above all lands . . . why is
any man hungry or thirsty, or naked, or in prison?" lectured the
parson. "Why but for his own unpardonable sloth?"[75]

Going beyond the simple message of hard work, Weems established two additional moral canons for citizens of the early republic.
He went to great lengths to explicate Washington's supposed aph-
orism "There exists in the economy of nature, an inseparable connexion between duty and advantage." Weems illustrated this notion by
describing George's tender care of his ailing half-brother Lawrence.
"Well, what was the consequence? Why, when Lawrence came to

die, he left almost the whole of his large estate to George, which served as another noble step to his future greatness." In addition to such assurances that virtue would bring material success, Weems also warned that virtuous hard work was necessary to survival in a commercializing society. He praised the man of "honest industry" as one who could meet "his creditor with a smiling countenance, and with the welcome music of gold and silver in his hand; who exerts an honest industry for wealth, that he may become a watercourse in a thirsty land." In a moral tract some twenty years later, Weems glorified the successful self-made man in a liberal society. "His riches were not of the hereditary and effeminating sort; they were the brave and healthy offspring of his own virtues," he wrote. "The credit which his HONESTY commanded, was doubled by his INDUSTRY, and trebled by his providence."[76]

Like many others, however, Weems found that the gospel of self-made success inspired some unruly converts. He grew concerned that ambitious individuals in the new republic, in grasping their own destiny, were abandoning all restraint in the scramble for advancement. Hence, by 1800 Weems was punctuating his writing with warnings about the dangers of uncontrolled self-gratification. He expressed great fear—both in his biographies and in his didactic pamphlets, which began to appear in the early nineteenth century—over the consequences of indulging libidinous cravings. For example, Weems perceived social chaos lurking in the sexual impulses as he inveighed against adultery and excessively long bachelorhood. He anticipated danger in the aggression and anger of the unrestrained liberal individual and wrote nervous tracts like *God's Revenge Against Murder*. The American appetite for alcohol also threatened to destroy Weems' idealistic social vision. Drunkenness, he wrote in 1812, "beyond doubt, is the Apollyon or the Grand Destroyer of the Land, in all its dearest interests, its *population*, its *genius*, its *health*, its *wealth*, its *morals*, and whatever, in conjunction with a free government, would exalt our country to the first rank among nations."[77]

Weems' growing dread of unregulated desires found a special target in gambling. This vice particularly frightened the Parson because the typical gambler both indulged his greedy passions and preyed on his fellow man. Horrified by these charlatans who would "swallow your substance, and chuckle over his accursed gains," Weems described them as "burnt with strong liquors and still fiercer passions: with fever-heated brains, exhausted purses and black despair" and ready to "rush into fierce disputes and brawls." But perhaps more important than their bestial behavior, gamblers directly challenged the self-made ideal. Weems readily admitted that self-interest formed the mainspring for the actions of many individuals in the young republic. But the problem lay in the gambler's desire for wealth without the moral discipline of hard work. "Human wisdom is best marked . . . by a steady pursuit of its *true interest*, and on principles that can reasonably insure it," Weems contended. While a cobbler, for instance, followed a steady course to success, the gambler "has no reasonable security at all, but still trembles . . . [that] he may die a beggar at last." The gambler, the parson concluded, would do anything to get your money: "If fair play will not do, you must cheat; if cheating will not do you must lie."[78]

Yet near the end of *God's Revenge Against Gambling*, Weems slipped in his criticism of the scheming gamester. Speaking of the gambler, he attempted to contrast him with a more praiseworthy figure. "I can tell him of honourable merchants, who thirty years past opened shop with hardly more than peddler's packs, and now drink as good wine as the great"—and here Weems stumbled—"and parry, with a shrug only, the loss of 50,000 dollars, on a cotton speculation." The failure to see the obvious—that the cotton speculator himself has engaged in a form of gambling—revealed the moral blind spot in Weems' critique. This limitation was even more apparent in his own career. The parson would seemingly try anything to make a dollar on his books, and apparently he suffered few twinges of conscience. Preaching and humanitarian boondoggles, as we have seen, always presented lucrative possibilities. And for all his condemnation of gambling, Weems was not above working the crowds at horse races. He wrote to Carey in December 1809, "I mean, as I always told you, to take a room on the public street, and sell away for Life during the very great Concourse of Men & Horses in February." Perhaps his most tasteless scheme surfaced in 1801, shortly after Weems preached a funeral sermon for a deceased young woman. Praise for his effort set the wheels in motion, and the parson immediately envisioned going to press with *The Lovely Wife, an Oration Pronounc'd over the Honor'd Dust of a Sleeping Angel*. The coins already jingling in his pocket, Weems dashed off a breathless letter to Carey imploring, "If you cou'd get me a *superlatively lovely female likeness* . . . touch'd off in his best style by Tanner [a New York engraver] you'd greatly oblige."[79]

In fact, Weems' private circumstances displayed many of the gambler's characteristics that publicly he found so abhorrent. He constantly fell into debt. He gave "too liberal credit to purchasers of Mr. Carey's books" and fell in arrears some nine hundred dollars; he "deposited with Mr. Mullen some books, these were all seiz'd for house rent"; he suffered under "the multitude and Rapacity of my

Wife's Relatives"—such were the constant laments in his correspondence. Carey wrote to Weems in 1801 of an even greater financial difficulty: "It will be necessary if you visit us this fall, to be on your guard against an arrest, which, I have strong reason to suspect, is designed for you." In rare moments of introspection, the parson also revealed a gambler's grandiose ambition. "I have never made much—owing to want of knowledge of Men & business. I am getting knowledge and therefore money," he told Carey in 1807. "I am sure—very sure—*morally* and *positively* sure that I have it in my power . . . to make you the most Thriving Book-Seller in America." Even more suggestively, the Virginian once described himself as having the flexible character of the con man. He wrote in 1810 of vast opportunities for

> a man of Intelligence, activity and popular manners: One who can dash around with his books to the Courts; preach with the Preachers, reason with the Lawyers & Doctors, and render himself dear to the Leading Characters of Society, themselves purchasing his books and recommending them to all their Friends and Neighbors.

Sometimes Weems went further. The title page of *The Life of Washington* described him as "The Rector of Mount Vernon Parish." Weems never held the post, because such a parish never existed.[80]

Weems ultimately responded to the social sins of liberalizing Americans, including himself, by mounting the cultural pulpit as a minister of self-control. An awareness of unrestrained ambition, never-sated passions, and greedy deceit led the parson to inject his basic message of hard-working success with forceful appeals for Americans to censure their own conduct. *The Life of Washington*, for example, attributed the general's remarkable success not just to industrious habits but equally to his iron self-control. At the beginning of the volume, Weems explained that Washington's love of virtue "enabled him first to triumph over *himself*, then over the British." He constantly contrasted the Founding Father with scoundrels "who have *no command over their passion*" and praised his "True Heroic Valour which combats malignant passions—conquers unreasonable self." As an instructive example of Washington's self-command, the reader saw the general rejecting the temptation to overthrow the civilian government and assume personal control at the end of the Revolution, "scorning to abuse his power to the degradation of his country."[81]

From Weems' fertile imagination Washington sprang forth as a full-blown purveyor of the character ethic. "Early aware of the importance of character, to those who wished to be useful," the young hero assumed responsibility for himself. Washington's decision of character gave "such uncommon strength to his constitution, such vigour to his mind, such a spirit for adventure, that he was ready for any glorious enterprise, no matter how difficult or dangerous." According to the parson, the general's commitment to industriousness and self-control directed his treatment of poor neighbors. "Character was the *main chance*. Mount Vernon had no charms for lazy, drunken, worthless beggars. Such knew very well that they must make their application elsewhere." As Weems summed up near the end of this didactic biography, Washington's mother "threw over him her own magic mantle of *Character*. And it was this that immortalized Washington."[82]

Weems' stress on the character ethic underlay a larger campaign for bourgeois values in *The Life of Washington*. The author pictured young George successfully overcoming a selfish spirit while learning love of truth and piety. He lauded the general's "*benevolence* which he so carefully cultivated through life." A perfectly rationalized man strode out from Weems' pages. Washington, eager to make every moment productive, "divided his time into four grand departments, *sleep*, *devotion*, *recreation*, and *business*," the parson wrote admiringly. "On the hours of business, whether in his own or in his country's service, he would allow nothing to infringe."[83]

This bourgeois ethos received continuous refinement and reinforcement in Mason Weems' later writings. *The Life of Benjamin Franklin* (1815), for instance, acclaimed its subject's hard work, thrift, sobriety, and success. It directly addressed "young men! young men! you with segars in your mouth, and faces flushed with libations of whiskey" and urged them to press on for "*Virtue* and *Knowledge* and *Wealth*" by studying Franklin's example. Many youth never learn self-control, warned the parson, instead succumbing to the lure of "*immediate gain*." What was "honey in the mouth," however, quickly turned to "gall in the bowels." The theme of postponement of instinctual gratification flavored other pamphlets like *God's Revenge Against Adultery* (1820), in which Weems castigated those who "riot and revel in the [pig] sties of brutal pleasure." The parson instructed parents to take a special responsibility in preparing respectable young men for society. "Pleasures your son *must* have: God intended, God *created* for them: he will never be easy *without* them," wrote Weems in the 1807 *God's Revenge Against Murder*. Thus parents had two choices: they could abandon their child to the "infamy and ruin of *drinking, raking, gambling,* and swindling," or they could mold "an early relish for the refined and elegant pleasures of KNOWLEDGE and VIRTUE."[84]

Several pamphlets urging moral reform in the early decades of the nineteenth century also carried forward Weems' crusade for self-control. In *The Drunkard's Looking Glass* (1812), the parson advocated temperance as a remedy for the varied licentiousness—violence, abuse of family, loss of money—of the inebriated man. A decanter filled with whiskey and set near a group of men, he suggested, was "a moral thermometer." *God's Revenge Against Duelling* (1820) demanded self-restraint among hotheaded individuals who "murdered" in the name of "honor, courage, magnanimity." In an intriguingly titled effort, *Hymen's Recruiting Sergeant* (1805), Weems agitated in behalf of early marriage as an aid in gaining command over the sexual passions. A final section of the parson's temperance tract, however, best expresses his sense of moral reform: "Thus idleness leads to gambling, gambling to losses, losses to sorrow, and sorrow to drunkenness and ruin. In this way thousands of young men of the first families and fortunes are annually brought to an early dunghill, a whipping-post, or gallows."[85]

Thus Weems arrived at the summer of 1812 flushed from the heat of strenuous moral campaigning. Swept away by his success in making profit-seeking virtuous and in shaping a self-controlled character among ambitious compatriots, the parson had begun to behold America as God's Republic. Weems drew upon the "city on a hill" tradition of colonial Puritanism and the idealism of Revolutionary republicanism and combined them with his enthusiastic bourgeois moralism. What emerged was an ecstatic, panoramic mural of a republic of hard-working, wealth-seeking, but morally restrained citizens enjoying the special sanction of God. He reported:

> While others have been over-run with devouring armies, and doomed to see their houses in flames, and the garments of their children rolled in blood, *we*, like favoured Israel, have been sitting under our vine and fig-tree, none daring to make us afraid; *we* have been advancing in riches and strength, with a rapidity unequalled in the history of man; we have been progressing in arts, manufactures, and commerce to an extent and success that has astonished the most enlightened Europeans.

These American Israelites, he reflected, comprised the "*last best* trial of a free and equal government . . . who have received this *Covenant of Mercy*, signed by the finger of heaven . . . whom God has thus raised up as an ensign of hope to the nations, that here the oppressed of other lands might find a place of rest."[86]

By and large, Weems' vision of the Godly Republic did not translate easily into the language of political ideology. Although fancying himself a Jeffersonian, he ventured into the political arena only twice in his political career, and each effort demonstrated his inclination to neutralize controversy under the weight of moral didacticism. The 1802 *True Patriot; or, An Oration on the Beauties and Beatitudes of a Republic* urged Americans to quiet political discord and recognize the "excellencies" of a republic. With a spirit of unity, Weems assured, Americans could "derive that plenitude of good things which heaven intended for them." From 1799 to 1809 there appeared ten editions of *The Philanthropist; or, Political Peace-Maker Between All Honest Men of Both Parties.* Here Weems denounced excessive party spirit and acclaimed "mutual dependence," "social affection," and "harmonious co-exertion." This volume, as the parson informed a correspondent, was "my political Placebo, my . . . political Anodyne," designed to "soothe and comfort the nerves of all honest Republicans."[87]

But Weems subscribed more explicitly to a kind of cultural politics, and these led him to advocate war in 1812 as an exercise to strengthen self-control in God's Republic. He had laid the foundation for such support in his earlier writing. *Hymen's Recruiting Sergeant,* for instance, proclaimed poetically on its second page, "Marry and raise up soldiers might and main; Then laugh you may at England, France and Spain." *The Philanthropist* had noted that internal discord would tempt the European powers into attacking American commerce and inciting rebellion among slaves and Indians. Weems, in the 1810 *Life of General Francis Marion,* contrasted the sacrifice and discipline of patriotism with the avarice of those who hid their money from the Revolutionary cause.[88]

Once again, however, *The Life of Washington* proved the most prescient guide for Weems' understanding of affairs in 1812. There war appeared as an acceptable "passion" because of its influence on Washington's moral stature: "Joined to a very manly appearance, and a great dignity of character, [it] could scarcely fail to attract on him the attention of the public." The general, Weems observed, "behaved with the firmness of a soldier and the resignation of a christian," and he pictured Washington in wartime as the supreme example of those who "have cheerfully sacrificed their own wealth to defeat the common enemy." In the 1809 edition of the biography, Weems took another step in preparing for war by defending Jefferson's embargo. The embargo was, he argued, a necessary demonstration of self-denial, and its opponents were "inexpressibly absurd . . . to put the loss of trade, for a year or two, in competition with the peace and happiness, the independence and sovereignty, of our country."[89]

Weems stamped his final approval on the war effort in September

1812, observing to Carey that it had "acted on our Patriotism, like the water & Bellows application to a coal-fire, have given it a prodigious heat." But more important, the war reflected the parson's post-Revolutionary struggles to reconcile profit and virtue. On the one hand, as he complained at one point, "the War & rumour of war have produced the effect I fear'd. No money, no selling." But on the other hand, Weems saw the war as a stand of godly, self-controlled Americans against the forces of licentiousness. In a letter of 1814 to President Madison, he described the British as violent barbarians, as the "modern Goths, our Enemy." An earlier communication to the President made even clearer Weems' perception of the British as part of the forces of "passion" to be resisted. Sending Madison a copy of his recently published *God's Revenge Against Gambling*, Weems wrote, "Tho' I cannot fight the British into their better senses I am at least endeavoring to do something with those Deluded ones of our own People, the Gamblers." Some years later, the parson reiterated this notion of a war for self-control as he recalled Andrew Jackson's heroic troops facing at New Orleans an unrestrained British army of "blustering courage," "flush and stout as beef and porter could make them" and "in full march for Booty and Beauty."[90] As Parson Weems had taught since the 1790s, the moral free-agent's greatest enemy lay within himself. The individual must gain command over his passions to be successful morally and materially. Or, as *The Life of Washington* had urgently prescribed, ambitious Americans must achieve self-control to avoid "sacrificing their gold to gamblers, their health to harlots, and their glory to grog." In his writing endeavors, Weems had tried to abate sensual gratification—and turn a profit as well—through moral instruction. Now war against the British, he hoped in 1812, would fortify both the character ethic and the redoubts of God's Republic. At the war's happy conclusion in 1815, Weems reaffirmed this cultural compound of money, morality, and civil religion. Writing to Carey, he acknowledged that thanks were due to "God, the Conservator of the Republic." But, he added impatiently, "Measures for our own emolument after the nip tides of War must be adopted." Then, in a typical burst of commingled piety and profit, the parson eagerly offered, "I am willing to assist you in your Bibles and Washington."[91]

War as Cultural Crusade: Self-Control and Civil Religion

As an example of the ornate public oratory of early-nineteenth-century America, Ephraim P. Ewing's *Oration* seemingly offered little beyond the cadence of ringing, hollow platitudes. Yet this 1810

speech by the Transylvania University student to his fellows animated its pomposities with a vibrant cultural message. Printed in
Lexington's *Kentucky Gazette*, the young Jeffersonian's speech displayed the expansive success ideology of a rapidly liberalizing society.
But more important, it forcefully expressed the concomitant character ethic of self-control formulated by theorists like Benjamin
Rush, popularized by moralists like Parson Weems, and lived by
men like Spencer Cone. Most intriguing, the oration clearly revealed
the way many Republicans translated the cultural drive for self-
control into the language of war in 1812.

Ewing emotionally described the sense of opportunity, at once
exhilarating and frightening, that faced the aspiring young man in
the 1810 republic. Society, he suggested, was "an alluring but
treacherous world," but he quickly assured his audience that the
voyage to success lay open to any individual of "assiduous industry."
Elevated birth was not necessary, Ewing explained, because in America often "the most brilliant talents sprang from the humblest cot-
tage." In the buoyant spirit of the self-made man, the young speaker
insisted, "Merit will meet its reward from a just and generous people." Yet Ewing paused to warn of the carnal, luxurious dangers
threatening any sojourner to success. Certain activities that promised
to satiate the senses would in the end dissipate the individual: "Dice,
billiards, cards, and many other games. . . . Theatrical exhibi-
tions. . . . Frolics, revels, and gallantry." The only correct course,
the young orator insisted, lay in "retirement" and "solitude" and
"conversing with our own hearts and with good authors."

The youthful student eventually pushed his point to its final conclusion. The decision of character, he argued, was not just a private
necessity but a public responsibility because an older Revolutionary
leadership was fading away. It now was the responsibility of the
young "to forsake the low gratifications of sensual enjoyments, and
learn wisdom that we may be prepared for this momentous task."
Facing the looming possibility of foreign war, Ewing neatly connected it to the character ethic. The republic, he concluded, now
appealed to her sons "to forsake the debilitating pursuits of dissipation and idle sports, and to invigorate their minds with knowledge
and their limbs with activity and strength . . . to prop up her tottering frame."[92]

Ephraim Ewing's appeal, like that of numerous others, helped set
the cultural stage for war in 1812. Jeffersonians who urged self-
control on individuals in a liberalizing society slowly and often half-
consciously became receptive to the notion that war could be an
adjunct in their cultural crusade. Some came to see military conflict as

an acceptable, socially useful outlet for libidinous drives. Others perceived the rigorous demands of wartime as a builder of character, as a mold in which to cast values of restraint. Overall, bourgeois moralists and their momentous message helped formulate the war as a dramatic clash of God's Republic and her "moral militia" with the dark forces of licentious passion.

By the summer of 1812, discipline and self-restraint had become watchwords of Republican prowar rhetoric. Military service appeared as precisely the sort of activity by which restless, ambitious Americans could learn discipline and self-command. The newspaper writer "Anti-Royalist," for instance, in January 1812 penned in the *National Intelligencer* an essay arguing that military life and "the manual exercise" would straighten out wayward young men. Drawing upon scenes of his own youthful army training, he recalled, "The most awkward boys became straight and graceful; puny ones were soon restored to health; strength and vigor attended upon all; the most untractable boys became obedient, and boys, who before ill comprehended the obligations of juvenile life, became strenuous asserters of and practical observers of every honourable institute of society." William Henry Harrison echoed these sentiments. He urged the rising generation to enter military service, absorb its discipline, and internalize its "minute observances, which collectively form a beautiful and connected system."[93]

In addition to generating this sobering jolt of military discipline, the war crisis promised to mold an American character of energetic strength, sensual restraint, and focused will. The Rev. Philip Mathews, for example, posed the war as a moral struggle between controlled self-made men and the forces of licentiousness. "Depravity sickens at the sight of virtue and purity," he announced, "and the restless malignity of its nature makes it pant to demolish what it is conscious it does not possess, and cannot hope to rival." Conrad Speece, in a fast-day sermon in Petersville, Virginia, in August 1812, refined this notion of war for moral character. Liberties in a republic depended on private morality, he insisted. "In vain does the licentious man, who daily spreads moral corruption around him, boast the venerable title of patriot."[94]

Jeffersonian hopes for wartime shaping of personal resiliency often led to an anticipation of its effect on collective moral fiber. Many citizens backing the war saw it as an energizing, strengthening influence for a national character gaining notoriety for weak indecision and gratification of avarice. One anonymous writer noted worriedly in the 1810 *Richmond Enquirer*, "Our character is sunk in the eyes of Europe—many exertions are necessary to restore it to its elevation." War with Great Britain, he speculated, "is calculated to call forth the resources and energy of the nation." Congressman William Lowndes of South Carolina agreed, arguing "Important will be the effect of manly resistance on the character of the country." Complaining about those Americans who only "compute the money-value of rights," Lowndes pictured the coming war as a contest between moral fortitude and the passions. The object of war "is the preservation of that character without which neutrality would be a burden," he affirmed on the floor of the House. As one newspaper contributor summed up, Americans' "supineness of charac- ter . . . will not be extirpated until suitable excitement is applied to causes of resentment . . . the attainment of that object alone would almost justify a war."[95]

Some Republicans hoped that war, like a reservoir, would catch, control, and make socially useful the surging streams of passion running strong among ambitious individuals in America. The *Boston Patriot*, a prowar newspaper, put the matter sharply in calling for war in June 1812. Americans, it noted, were "bold, restless, and independent, and to be gratified with activity and exertion of some kind or other." With such enthusiasm so prominent, "a government which rightly understands their character will give them something to do." Thus armed conflict would indirectly aid the crusade for bourgeois restraint and focusing of the will.[96]

This notion of a war for character and self-control became es- pecially evident in Jeffersonian depictions of the foreign enemy. In the eyes of many war advocates, the British symbolized all the dark passions that Americans were struggling against in the quest for self- regulation. If such perceptions often involved the projections of fantasy rather than fact, they nevertheless appeared quite real to their holders. Older ideological fears in the Puritan and republican tradi- tions formed some of the foundation for this moral critique. Like Presbyterian minister Samuel Knox of Baltimore, Americans were fond of contrasting, in time-worn fashion, the peace and prosperity of America with Old World nations that drenched their lands in "human gore" and dealt in "injuries, violence, and bloodshed."[97]

Yet the cultural crusade for character also raised more recent and more particular targets for American moralists. Castigations of Great Britain often employed the image of the con man. President Madison, in an 1811 letter to Joel Barlow, complained of Great Britain's "crafty contrivance, and insatiable cupidity" and con- trasted it with the "open, manly, and upright dealing" of the United States. Two 1812 editorials in the *Richmond Enquirer* grew quite overheated in denouncing British trade policies as "so abominable a fraud upon a whole nation" and then asked, "Shall we be cheated as well as insulted out of our rights?" The editors bitterly concluded, "So little regard is paid to morality in their commercial dealings, that their trade resolves itself into a system of fraud, forgery, and perjury."[98]

This thrashing of the British con man often accompanied attacks on England's affectation of religious morality. Joseph Richardson, in *The Christian Patriot Encouraged*, scoffed at Great Britain's "high boasted pretensions to religion" in light of her government's practice of injustice, oppression, and cruelty. The Rev. John Stevens similarly dismissed those who upheld Great Britain's piety as a barrier to the atheism of the French Republic. "From such a bulwark, may the Lord in his mercy save us and our posterity," he proclaimed. "I do believe in my heart, that there is not a more corrupt and wicked government on earth than the British. . . . They have, in my opinion, caused more wars, bloodshed, misery, and desolation in the earth than any other."[99]

The British, however, ultimately represented enemies that were even more threatening to many nervous Republicans. They came to embody those animalistic passions that required chaining in the name of self-control. The often outlandish American rhetoric on this point suggested the magnitude of emotional agitation involved in the struggle for repression. The British Army offered a favorite target for commentators like Samuel Knox, who described it as a "mercenary band of despots" committed to no other principles but organized murder and looting. The English aristocracy provided another foul symbol. Philip Mathews, in denouncing the profligacy and immorality of the British nobility, worked himself into a paroxysm of rhetorical rage when he beheld the royal family. They comprised, he fumed, "a deep and loathsome sink of moral putrescency, through all of its ramifications: from the stupid, moping drivelling idiot on the throne, down to the scullion in the kitchen, it is one unvaried, disgusting, distorted picture of bloated depravity."[100]

Some Americans, such as Charles Ingersoll, focused on the British alliance with Indian raiders on the western frontier to raise images of violence, carnage, and lust. In a very long letter to his constituents defending the war, which was widely reprinted in eastern Republican newspapers, the congressman drew upon his stockpile of adjectives in condemning British libidinous outrages: "The massacre of captives and the poisoning of wounded," "foul and hellish slaughter," "refinements of barbarity which no savage ever exceeded," "rapine, rapes, and indiscriminate outrages," "their game of ruin, spoil, and havoc." Even Hezekiah Niles, a man who seldom ventured from issues of political economy or foreign policy in his commentary, adopted the rhetoric of self-control in upholding the war. Writing in *Niles' Weekly Register* several weeks after the declaration of war, he described British commercial goods as "the flesh-pots of Egypt" and condemned the earlier American attraction to them as "momentary and individual gratification." Martial conflict was forcing Americans away from this "sensual gratification," Niles wrote approvingly:

> Our people have been drunk with foreign trade—it is true they were exhilarated by it, and felt strength from it—but the issue is, that the public mind is debased, and too ready to submit to any indignity or insult to obtain a little more of same intoxicating material. . . . Every time that the many, many thousand spindles, now in motion [in new American manufactories] go round, this harkening for the flesh-pots is diminished, for it increases the treasure at home and keeps the heart from wandering.[101]

This Republican reading of the 1812 conflict as moral struggle received a significant twist from John Stevens. Proclaiming *The Duty of Union in Just War,* and obviously confident about his own talents, he announced he would "judge of God's mind and will, from a view of his moral character." "I think it is a clear case, that God approves of the war in which we are now engaged for the defense of our just rights," Stevens declared confidently after assuring himself of the Deity's moral uprightness. Although a bit more brazen in tone than most such comments, Stevens' conviction reflected a widespread belief among Jeffersonians that the struggle with Great Britain enjoyed divine sanction. Their cultural campaign for morality, character, and sensual restraint—when combined with older Puritan and republican beliefs in the sacred destiny of the American "errand into the wilderness"—gave a strong boost to what one scholar has called the "civil religion" of the United States. In 1812 war summoned the republic's Christian Soldiers.[102]

Samuel Knox, a Presbyterian minister and principal of Baltimore College, put the matter bluntly in August 1812. Speaking on the day appointed by President Madison for national humiliation and prayer, he proclaimed, "Our national cause is a religious cause." In a July 4 discourse, Reformed Dutch minister Peter Van Pelt drew a more elaborate picture of divine participation in a titanic moral clash. The British were a force of darkness, he argued, combining royalty, corruption, and a sordid history of bloodshed. With the forces of light in 1812, Van Pelt contended, stood a virtuous citizenry as "a monument of American wisdom, union, and virtue." Rapturously describing the divine destiny of the young American Israel, he proclaimed, "An all-wise God in His providence, has established in this western world, that just and equal form of government which from henceforth is the model of all nations." Other Republican ministers and moralists embroidered this motif of God's active intervention in a just war. Urging Americans to found their patriotism in love of God, one assured, "I have confidence that no weapon formed against us will be permitted to prosper." The conflict raised "the sword of the Lord and Gideon" in "a just and righteous war; a war which God approves."[103]

But while some Jeffersonians found inspiration for war in an already-existing American Israel, others were attracted to it as a formative, chastening, revitalizing experience for the republic's religious character. Employing God in the service of bourgeois moralism, they recounted the sins of a people turning against him: pride, profanity, intemperance, lying, gaming and vain amusements, Sabbath-breaking, lewdness, and avarice. A Virginia Republican, for instance, in August 1812 contended that war was a punishment for sins that had tainted the moral character of America. He spoke at length on three of the most grievous: a lack of religious fervor, the growing use of liquor, and "the thirst for wealth." Prowar minister Solomon Aiken soberly explained the impending conflict in similar terms:

> It is for our iniquities and the abuse of divine favors. God hath given us the greatest liberty, civil and religious, of any Nation on earth. But what astonishing returns of ingratitude have we made. We have abused our liberties to great licentiousness, like Jeshurun of old, we have waxen fat, and kicked; we have rebelled against our God.

For these religious warriors, war offered a way for the republic to *renew* its divine covenant, and public discourse resounded with appeals for Americans to humble themselves before God, to gain victory. The Rev. Conrad Speece implored of his congregation in preparing them for a war, "Let us then repair to his throne of grace, to confess before him, with humble and contrite hearts, our own sins, and the sins of our country."[104]

This overlapping of evangelical and martial impulses helped forge a direct link between personal salvation and national victory in 1812. God's dominion over nations was similar to his power over individual sinners, wrote one minister in urging forward patriotic American Christians. "In our national as well as our individual capacity, we must be forgiven or we must suffer." The preface of an 1810 republication of an older work, *The Christian Solder*, stated simply that because the life of a Christian is "a life of warfare," Heaven would be "inherited by the *violent*. Our life is military, Christ is our Captain, the gospel is the banner, the graces are our spiritual artillery." In a note preceding this long treatment of "holy violence," the American editor expressed his hope that "it may be the happy means of converting some from the miserable ways of sin and death, to the paths of righteousness and everlasting life."[105]

Many evangelical circuit riders observed that war fever in 1812 seemed to be appropriating religious enthusiasm. Peter Cartwright recalled decreasing membership in the western Methodist Church as many members "volunteered and helped to achieve another glorious victory over the legions of England, and her savage allied thousands." The Rev. Jacob Young described Methodist Bishop Francis Asbury meeting American volunteers near Chillicothe, Ohio. After a stirring sermon in support of the administration and the war, Asbury tearfully blessed the assembled troops and their commander and "stood there till he shook hands with every soldier in the company." Rev. James B. Finley reported in 1812 that the war spirit also swept away most of his congregation: "Many that once walked with us to the house of God and took delight in the services of religion, now marched off in rank and file to become disciplined in the arts of war." Like Spencer Cone, large numbers of Americans seemed to be venting private religious yearnings into the emotion-charged atmosphere of war.[106]

Perhaps the ultimate amalgamation of American civil religion and war in 1812 occurred through the agency of the Founding Fathers. Still awe-struck by the legacy of the Revolution, early-nineteenth-century Americans looked back on it as an achievement directed by the Deity in alliance with a group of republican demigods. According to figures like Peter Van Pelt, the Founding Fathers had gained divine interposition in their struggle for independence because of their "trust in God" and "public virtue." This Dutch Reformed minister and New York Republican urged Americans to remember that they "are descendents of fathers who resolved to live free or perish, who stuck to the resolve, until they conquered the legions of arbitrary power, and drove them from our shores." Such sentiments were not restricted to the clergy, as Congressman John Clopton of Virginia indicated. In a circular to his constituents, he urged them to realize that the same God that had ordained victory in the Revolution stood behind them now. Clopton concluded pointedly, "I trust that the spirit which animated the heroes of the revolution, will not be less ardent and vivid in the bosoms of their sons."[107]

The various cultural elements of the 1812 crusade against Great Britain—discipline and self-control, bourgeois morality and the character ethic, evangelical and civil religion—carried different weights of motivation according to individual sensibility. But figures like Joshua Lacy Wilson demonstrated how such strands could intertwine to provide a compelling moral rationale for war. Speaking to the Cincinnati Light Companies in May 1812, this Presbyterian minister and Jeffersonian enthusiast argued that the Bible pictured war as inevitable. He quoted from the Bible (Ecclesiastes 3:1–8): "To everything there is a season, and a time for every purpose under heaven; a time to kill and a time to heal; . . . a time of war, and a time of peace." If anything, the American government had erred in exercising too much patience with those who violated her rights. Such temperate discourse fell quickly to the wayside, however, as Wilson launched a scathing moral assault on Great Britain. The English, he pronounced, manifested "all the infernal principles of devils incarnate" in their violent attacks on American commerce and their stirring up of the Indian "heathen." The domestic dissenter against the war, he continued, was little better than an animal "brute" for abandoning the duties of citizenship in the face of such evil: "He is not fit to live, he is not fit to die. Let him rank with the terrapin and snail." Wilson called down heaven's curse on moral slackers who refused to fight because of "the love of ease, the tenderness of connexions, or the fears of his enemies."[108]

Wilson then climaxed his speech by picturing war with Great Britain as a challenge for Americans seeking moral regeneration. He juxtaposed the idleness and ease of "lazy men" with the toughening "fatigues and dangers of the field." The militia—the supposed "boast of the American nation"—symbolized for Wilson the weak character and will among his fellow citizens that needed to be strengthened:

> Officers we have who know their duty, but such licentiousness and indolence of the soldiery they will not submit to command. It is truly painful to attend our musters. What do we see and hear? While men are in the ranks unarmed, some with sticks and some with their hands in their pockets, we hear some gabbing, and some grunting, and some yawning; we see some sitting, and some lolling, and some standing more like oxen than like men. And is this the bulwark of our nation?

The war, Wilson hoped, would instill a corrective discipline. His address culminated with a call to "a more important warfare—a warfare against sin." "The subjugation of lust and passion is of vast moment," Wilson told his audience, and the army did not have to be "a school of vice." To the contrary, it could be an academy instilling moral vigor. The minister reminded in closing, "Abraham and

David . . . and Washington, were all military men, and all men of eminent Piety and virtue."[109]

In such ways war in 1812 comprised an emotional, compelling episode in the process by which American moral free-agents erected a bourgeois culture of self-control in the early republic. For its Jeffersonian supporters the discipline of war promised to inculcate the energy, focused will, and self-restraint of the character ethic. And yet the vision of conflict with Great Britain allowed legitimate expression of libidinous passions otherwise thwarted. Thus the war mustered the swelling ranks of the young nation's "moral militia" and sent them against the minions of licentious depravity. By offering a dramatic opportunity for proving the moral preeminence of God's Republic, it engaged the electric impulses of American civil religion. The War of 1812, through this powerful combining of religion and repression, magnetically attracted the Republican majority in the early nineteenth century as a compelling, legitimizing expression of America's early capitalist culture.

IV

Founding Fathers and Wandering Sons: War and the Masks of the Personae

*Madame Merle: There's no such thing as an isolated man or woman;
we're each of us made up of some cluster of appurtenances. What
shall we call our "self"? Where does it begin? Where does it end?
It overflows into everything that belongs to us—and then it flows
back again.*

*Isabel Archer: I don't agree with you. I think just the opposite. I don't
know whether I succeed in expressing myself, but I know that
nothing else expresses me. Nothing that belongs to me is any measure
of me; everything's on the contrary a limit, a barrier, and a
perfectly arbitrary one.*

HENRY JAMES
Portrait of a Lady

*All visible objects, man, are but as pasteboard masks. But in
each event—in the living, the undoubted deed—there, some unknown
but still reasoning thing puts forth the mouldings of its form
behind the unreasoning mask. If man will strike, strike through the mask!*

HERMAN MELVILLE
Moby Dick

*All the other stuff, the love, the democracy, the floundering into lust,
is a sort of by-play. The essential American soul is hard, isolate,
stoic, and a killer. It has never yet melted.*

D. H. LAWRENCE
Studies in Classic American Literature

On the afternoon of July 4, 1812, Richard Rush, the second son of Benjamin Rush, strode to the podium in the hall of the House of Representatives. A zealous and eloquent Jeffersonian, the young comptroller of the treasury had been chosen by President James Madison to defend officially the two-week-old declaration of war against Great Britain. Looking out at this grave celebration of American independence, the orator's eyes met those of the President, his cabinet, numerous congressmen, and assorted public officials and dignitaries. Carrying a heavy rhetorical burden, the young Philadelphian opened by castigating the British for their violations of American neutral rights and their instigation of Indian unrest on the frontier. Turning homeward, he also admonished his countrymen that decades of peace since the Revolution had created in America "an inordinate love of money, the rage of party spirit, and a willingness to endure even slavery itself rather than bear pecuniary deprivations or brave manly hazards." Thus Rush presented war not only as a defense of American rights but also as a regenerating cure for commercial dissipation. Nations and striving individuals were alike, he insisted, in that their well-being came only through "severe probations . . . by a willingness to encounter danger and by actually and frequently braving it."[1]

Yet as it unfolded, Richard Rush's address put forward two other striking images that raised a submerged layer of meaning in his calls for war. First, he described the American republic as a young man struggling to find vigor, direction, and moral purpose. He contended that in the aftermath of revolution a young nation still in "the feebleness of youth" had been forced to submit to European economic regulation and foreign affairs structures. But now with war, Rush hoped, the growing republic "shall stand upon a pedestal whose base is fixed among ourselves." Military action proclaimed that "in the hope and purity of youth, we are not debased by the passions of old age." In the ringing words of the orator, war would make "ourselves more independent—privately and politically."[2]

This imagery of youthful independence and destiny foreshadowed a second motif in Rush's symbolism. He queried rhetorically and emotionally that if Americans did not go to war in 1812, "where would be the spirit, where the courage of their slain fathers? Snatched and gone from ignoble sons?" Weaving a psychological fabric that contrasted the "noble" Founders with "the base conduct of those sons for whom they so gallantly fell," Rush vowed passionately to uphold the inheritance of the older generation: "We will wipe away all past stains; we will maintain our rights by the sword, or, like you, we will die! Then shall we render our ashes worthy to mingle with yours!"[3]

Rush's emotional contrast of heroic Founding Fathers and searching, dissipated, death-seeking sons might seem histrionic and peculiar. Yet for such an important occasion—and for such an imposing and discriminating audience—Rush must have sifted his metaphors carefully for those most likely to find an emotional affinity. That he chose wisely was reflected in the fact that on the eve of war with Great Britain this refrain of Fathers and Sons sounded over and over again in Republican discourse. Moralists like Mason Weems, for instance, utilized a cult of the Founding Fathers to aid in establishing a character ethic of industriousness and self-restraint among young Americans. The Fathers' Revolutionary exploits also proved invaluable to early-nineteenth-century shapers of the republic's "civil religion." The example of the Founding Fathers provided as well an ideal for social critics like Philip Freneau, Henry Clay, and Charles Ingersoll, who wished to stem the tide of social selfishness and degenerate character in the commercializing republic. Such instances, however, comprised but the tip of a rhetorical and psychological iceberg.[4]

Early-nineteenth-century Independence Day celebrations habitually admonished, "Sons, remember the glory of your fathers." Reverent words for the Founders, however, did not occur only on July 4, and they did not just reflect the gloss of patriotic generalities. In newspapers, letters, and sermons, citizens often went to great lengths to contrast the selflessness and virtue of the Fathers with the degeneracy of their sons into ambition and avarice. Thomas Rodney complained in 1808, "Is the Patriotism of 1776 no more? Is it all converted into Fish, Wheat, Flour, Rice or Cotton, or into the love of profit and gold? The nation is surely paralyzed by these sordid motives, or they would speak a language that would operate like thunder and Lightning over the Land and the Sea." Virginia Congressman John Roane expressed similar sentiments in the 1810 *Richmond Enquirer*. "What did our fathers do, at the Revolution?" he asked of his constituents. "Were privileges calculated down by dollars and cents, or a barter proposed, to exchange liberty of conscience . . . for delusive prospects of great wealth, with its concomitants, splendid equipages, fine buildings, and sumptuous repasts?" Baltimore minister and educator Samuel Knox concurred on August 20, 1812, the day appointed by President Madison for national humiliation and prayer. "He, who can trace among us, no marks of degeneracy from the first principles of the Fathers of this

nation . . . who formed and established it, under the special bless-
ing of Divine Providence," he argued, "must be blind indeed." As
other Republicans added, the spirit of 1776 had all but vanished in
cold calculations of profit and loss as ambition had "degenerated the
sons of patriot fathers, into abject followers of fortune, and made
them ashamed of the virtues, as well as the religion of their ancestors."[5]

These widely expressed perceptions of the Son's degeneracy often
accompanied broad references to the "youth" of the republic. Like
Richard Rush, Jeffersonians constantly compared their polity to a
young man entering the world in search of personal distinction and
destiny. Congressman Peter Porter, for example, spoke to his colleagues in December 1811:

> Our situation was not unlike that of a young man just entering into life,
> and who, if he tamely submitted to one cool, deliberate, intentional
> indignity, might safely calculate to be kicked and cuffed for the whole
> of the remainder of his life; or, if he should afterwards undertake to
> retrieve his character, must do it at ten times the expense which it would
> have cost him at first to support it.

James K. Paulding provided a whimsical literary version of the
same motif in 1812 as he characterized the republic as young
"Brother Jonathan." The son of old "John Bull," Jonathan "became
a tall, stout, double-jointed, broad-footed cub of a fellow" with "the
promise of great strength when he should get his full growth."
Paulding pictured the young man as falling out with his father,
entering the world on his own, and becoming prosperous and successful. Although Jonathan's coat and pants always looked too short
because of rapid growth, the author assured readers that "he had not
come to half his strength as yet, and that when his sinews were a
little more strengthened, and his joints stronger knit, woe be to the
blockhead that should wantonly provoke him to raise his fist." As
Philip Freneau summed up this metaphorical tendency in 1808,
while the Revolution had witnessed Americans "in our infancy,"
now "we are in a state of manhood, or we shall never be so."[6]

What should be made of this recurrent symbolism in Republican
prowar discussions of America as an aspiring youth, of this consistent depiction of Founding Fathers and degenerate Sons? First, it
suggests an anxious awareness among American citizens of living in
what R. R. Palmer has called "the age of democratic revolution."
Veneration for the Founding Fathers—and anxiety over the ability
to match their exploits—reflected in part Americans' consciousness
of the path-breaking, unproven "republican experiment" in which

they were engaged. In addition, these images also seem to reflect an awareness, however inchoate, of historical change in the early years of nationhood. Both the Sons' self-castigation for falling prey to profit and private gratification, and the association of the republic's success with that of the youthful self-made man, embodied the social and cultural tensions accruing to commercialization and the growth of a liberal society.

The power of these rhetorical fictions, however, also flowed from a deeper psychological source. Philip Rieff has suggested, "As cultures change, so do the modal types of personality that are their bearers." But historically these changes have been neither quick nor smooth, he continues, because people's "comprehensive interior understanding was cognate with historical institutions, binding even the ignorants of a culture to a great chain of meaning."[7] The consolidation of liberal capitalism in the early nineteenth century, by generating significant shifts in the most basic "historical institutions," thus set off loud repercussions in the recesses of private experience. The family, for instance, the entity most responsible for socialization as "the mediating agent between psychic and social structures," began changing fundamentally in the era of early American nationhood. According to many family historians, the organization of traditional family paternalism shifted noticeably toward the modern, privatized, conjugal household in the decades after the American Revolution.[8] Work, as numerous labor historians have recently added, also began to transform dramatically by the late eighteenth century. It increasingly moved out of the isolated matrix of the household economy and into the competitive market whirl of a rapidly commercializing economy. The impact of such developments on personality structure was profound.[9]

On the one hand, the decline of paternalism in work and family liberated individuals and encouraged autonomy. As many scholars detected, this departure from traditional structures created a "modern personality" of great ego strength and attuned not to fatalism but to choice, opportunity, new ideas, and participation. But on the other hand, the liberation of the individual created tremendous new psychic pressures. Choosing and shaping one's own destiny in a fluid society could be a lonely and frightening task, as David Riesman has observed:

> Under the new conditions the individual must decide what to do—and therefore what to do with himself. The feeling of personal responsibility, this feeling that he matters as an individual, apart from his family or clan, makes him sensitive to the signals emanating from his internalized ideal. . . . What must he do to fulfill the injunction? And how

does he know that he has fulfilled these different self-demands? . . .
Little rest is available to those who ask themselves such questions.

In other words, the liberal individual's vaunted ego strength often
comprised but a shell, behind which lay a dark domain of lonely
insecurity and harsh, unsatisfiable self-demands.[10]

Evidence from the early republic suggests that from such social
and private transformation emerged three psychological difficulties.
First, demands for the repression of instinctual gratification in the
name of social harmony and individual success greatly heightened
private anxiety. The mandates for self-control issued by moralists
like Benjamin Rush, John Foster, and Parson Weems required
severe personal repressions. The psychological cost could be heavy,
as many social theorists have observed. Max Weber concluded
darkly of this rationalizing impulse that its "most urgent task [was]
the destruction of spontaneous, impulsive enjoyment." Sigmund
Freud, of course, in *Civilization and Its Discontents* maintained that
the ever-tightening instinctual strictures on man in modern, liberalizing society made it "hard for him to be happy in that civilization." In a passage from *The Economic and Philosophic Manuscripts of
1844*, Karl Marx waxed eloquent on the alienating thrust of repression in early market man. He wrote of liberal values:

> Self-denial, the denial of life and of all human needs, is its cardinal
> doctrine. The less you eat, drink, and read books; the less you go to the
> theatre, the dance hall, and public house; the less you think, love,
> theorize, paint, fence, etc., the more you *save*, the *greater* becomes your
> treasure. . . . The less you *are*, the more you *have*.[11]

Fragments of evidence from Jeffersonian commentators in the early
nineteenth century disclose this picture of an American psyche
straining under the pressures of repression. Praise for the Fathers'
sacrifices and condemnation of the Sons' sins—selfish ambition,
"dollars and cents patriotism," sensual indulgence—revealed guilt
over the inability to control the self. Yet swelling praise for the
Fathers' blood sacrifice during the Revolution—and equally persistent appeals for the Sons to match it—suggested the ambiguous
appeal of violence over that very process of self-denial. Henry Clay,
for example, consistently contrasted the vigor and strength of the
Revolutionary warriors with their Sons' anemic materialism. Other
Republican spokesmen offered similar paeans to "deceased fathers"
who gave their children "freedom with the loss of their blood." An
1810 editorial in the *Richmond Enquirer* posed a simple but haunting question: "Our sires . . . they gave their blood for independence. . . . Are their sons unworthy of their sires?" Such widely

expressed wishes to escape rationalizing strictures and engage in the spilling and shedding of blood indicated a deep, regressive yearning to satisfy instinctual cravings.[12]

Benjamin Rush, the American pioneer of self-control, provided one glimpse of the costs and contradictions of repression in a consolidating liberal culture. He recorded in his *Commonplace Book* a singular and curious dream that occurred probably in 1811. Triggered by a sermon on the necessity of "acquiring habits of virtue, and the danger of contracting habits of vice," the dream impressed on Rush a powerful series of images that he transcribed without comment or analysis. The fantasy unfolded around a "resurrection" motif, where the dead arose and exhibited the moral qualities with which they had been entombed. Rush imagined himself walking around Philadelphia on the day of this Second Coming and stumbling into the city graveyard. There he mingled with the risen and encountered several bizarre scenes. First, in the doctor's dream the rejuvenated corpses addressed him as "Tom." This different name—perhaps an identification with Tom Paine, his notoriously unrestrained old colleague—possibly reflected Benjamin Rush's unconscious desire to escape the rigidity of his own identity and doctrines. Second, the resurrected figures hungrily expressed their libidinous cravings. They told the doctor of their desires for various things: a tavern, sexual fulfillment, bank stock, gambling wheels, political rallies, stage performances, and titillating novels. Others engaged in hateful feuds, spitefully denigrated the character of others, or engaged in conjugal violence, like the man who was kicking his wife and dragging her by the hair of her head along the ground, and then leaving her, saying, "There, take that, you bitch." It is significant that Rush in his dream did not condemn, or recognize any special punishment for, these sensual and violent creatures. "Contrary to my expectations," he admitted near the beginning of his dream narrative, "I saw neither confusion nor distress among them."

Rush's dream ended when he encountered "a plain-looking little man" and accompanied him to the Pennsylvania Hospital. Upon entering the door, patients surrounded the small gentleman, called him "father," and lavished praise on him for saving their lives. Rush had in real life been directing the mental ward at the Pennsylvania Hospital for some two decades. Moreover, another private and more painful fact of the doctor's life undoubtedly sprang forth here. His eldest son, John, had served as an early subject for Benjamin's theories of repression before coming to an unhappy end. Arguing that "*solitude* is the most effective punishment that can be derived for them [children]" to learn self-control and industry, the elder Rush had employed it rigorously. He once confined John to his room for two entire days, and reported with some pride, "My eldest son . . . has more than once begged me to flog him in preference to confining him." John, after years of vocational indecision, drifted into the U.S. Navy, killed a fellow officer, and went completely mad in 1804. His father committed him to his ward for the mentally diseased, where he remained for twenty-seven years until his death. Thus Rush's fantasy encounter at the hospital conjured up a final, complex image of paternalistic, altruistic "Fathers" and dependent, constrained, even mentally deluded "Sons."[13]

If struggles with repression bedeviled Jeffersonians in the early republic, a concern with reconstructing authority defined a second major psychological issue. The steady crumbling of traditional paternalism in family, social, and political structures evident by the late eighteenth century raised painful dilemmas of sovereignty and loyalty for nascent liberal individuals. Did the determination of obedience emanate solely from within? If not, where did authority lie? If so, on what basis could the sovereign individual legitimate authority and protect himself from the assaults of other self-driven men? As Fred Weinstein and Gerald M. Platt pointed out, the breakdown of external structures of authority in the modern West involved the loss of a traditional "reciprocal understanding of obligations and rewards, wherein personal orientations were consistent with the organization of power." While one consequence might be greater ego strength, less felicitous results also appeared. "This need to make choices on the basis of personal morality, the pressures deriving from the desire to accept or reject different levels of autonomous activity, and the struggle for inclusion [in society]," Weinstein and Platt argue, have prompted "persistent feelings of discontent." Elizabeth Fox-Genovese added that the demise of "embedded paternalism, whether social, governmental, or religious, engendered regressive longings for paternal or organic authority." Liberalizing society, in other words, might demand individual dominion, but it could not totally eradicate longings for external, socially rooted authority. Individuals thus endured severe inner trials in the process of legitimizing self-sovereignty and in determining questions of relationship and obedience to one's fellow man.[14]

Shreds of evidence suggest that anxiety over the establishment of legitimate authority indeed preyed on the psyche of many Republicans by the early 1800s. The rhetoric of the Founding Fathers and degenerate Sons, for instance, usually pictured the offspring as struggling mightily to match the moral authority of their progenitors. Like Richard Rush, they confronted the Fathers and wondered how they might replicate their "noble achievements." Spencer Cone, his father made penniless and mad by Revolutionary service, presented another kind of search for authority in his years-long struggle with and final submission to godly direction in his life. The yearning for legitimate authority found a separate voice in "Quintus," an anonymous writer of a long essay in the summer of 1812 in the *Philadelphia Aurora*. Describing America in the decades since the Revolution, he constructed a family allegory of "a band of thirteen brothers." Having associated together in common defense, "each brother went his way" after independence and "success attended all their undertakings, and prosperity crowned their industry." Yet Quintus concluded this sketch of "family" diffusion by picturing a disintegration of authority as well. In contrast to the Revolutionary era, the brothers were in later years attacked by Indians, insulted and degraded by the British, and able to muster only a weak and vacillating response. Their dominion had vanished.[15]

Mason Weem's *Life of Washington* gave cleaner form to the psychological crisis of authority in the early republic. Washington emerged from these pages as the supreme "Father of his Country," and Weems self-consciously strove to present the General-President-Father figure of unquestioned authority as "a pure Republican" of exemplary virtue. But in depicting the authoritative Washington as a model of self-control and eminence, Weems brought into the open his anxiety over sensual, materialistic, and quarrelsome Sons. The first President, lectured the parson, had always sought union and order in the affairs of his country and hence "ever yielded a prompt obedience to her delegated will." Yet by the 1790s America's selfish Sons seemingly rejected all authority, reveled in serious political disputes, and raised "the awful idea of DISUNION." Each "needlessly irritates his brother" while engaging in "a discourse worse than devilish." The point of Weems' oedipal drama of emulation and succession struck home. Washington, without children of his own, had become Father of his entire people, and his wayward Sons must strive manfully to imitate his virtues and hence internalize his authority. As the parson summed up near the end of the biography, "Young Reader! go thy way, think of Washington, and HOPE. . . . Like him, honour thy God, and delight in glorious toil; then like him, 'thou shalt stand before kings.'"[16]

Problems of repression and authority ultimately fed perhaps the most overriding psychological issue of the early republic: a tendency toward the diffusion of personality and identity. The development of modern values of the market, the privatized family, achieved status,

and political participation may have fostered ego strength and individual autonomy in the early republic. But again, disintegrating
tendencies swirled beneath the psychological surface. As Erik Erikson demonstrated, identity "connotes both a persistent sameness within oneself . . . and a persistent sharing of some kind of essential
character with others." Therefore, he continues, there is a definite
link between "ego qualities, social institutions, and historical eras."
When a society in flux after the Revolution created new uncertainties—antithetical pressures of home and work, success and morality,
ambition and repression—true autonomy and firm identity in fact
became extremely problematical. Instead, as some observers have
suggested, liberal individuals scrambled to adopt a series of self-
manipulative masks allowing for self-survival. Social theorist Max
Horkheimer has contended that the emergence of modern capitalism
was linked with

> the development of a kind of pluralistic personality structure,
> or . . . "personae." . . . Education, whether in the family, the school,
> or the outside world, seems to provide the individual with a set of masks
> rather than a coherent, integrated personality. He is one person in the
> barber shop, another in the interview situation; a tender husband and
> father at home and a hard boiled, hard-driving businessman from nine to
> five.[17]

This figure of the "personae"—consciously struggling for self-
control, unconsciously tormented by an incoherent identity, consequently agitated and tending toward destructive release—consistently appeared in the discourse of early-nineteenth-century Jeffersonians. The career and writings of Hugh Henry Brackenridge, as
we have seen, offered superb expression of the anxiety, anger, and
self-defamation of the fractured self. Another example is Parson
Weems, who on the first page of his *Life of Washington* admitted, "A
public character is often an artificial one. . . . It is not then in the
glare of public, but in the shade of *private life*, that we are to look for
the man. Private life is always *real* life." The "personae" of the good
parson, of course, publicly condemned gambling while privately
working the crowds at horse races, and decried money-mongering
while pursuing every financial scam he could concoct. Such psychological confusion over virtue and the profit motive led some to harsh
expressions of self-loathing. An 1810 newspaper article, for instance,
praised the Fathers who "gave their treasure" in the Revolution and
derided their Sons who could calculate patriotism only in "shillings
and pence." Yet only a few sentences later the authors turned and
asked of the Sons, "Are they so blind to Interest, as to see their rights

invaded, their trade cut up and the future means of acquisition destroyed by British avarice. . . . What sort of economist is he, who would save a dollar today, to lose twenty tomorrow?" The logical and emotional tension in this essay ultimately prompted an image of self-destruction: "This is a bastard spirit of parsimony, that destroys its own view—it is an economy that devours itself." Other anxious undercurrents of self-hate pulled at the edges of early-nineteenth-century Republican consciousness. An anonymous 1810 essay by "Vindex" quivered with psychological tension. Noting that self-respect was the basis of public esteem, the author praised the Founding Fathers, who had risked everything to achieve liberty and then "dropped successively into the grave" in the postwar decades. Now the avarice and cold calculation "has degenerated the sons of patriot fathers," he bemoaned, and "the survivors are to be pitied!" Richard Rush expressed a death wish more directly in exclaiming to the Fathers, "We will wipe away all past stains . . . or, like you, we will die!"[18]

These prominent psychological issues in the early republic—identity, repression, and authority—occasionally converged and intertwined. William Selden's July 4, 1811, oration in Richmond, Virginia, clothed such an example of complex inner turmoil in the language of the Fathers and Sons. The Republican speaker began with an accustomed appeal to the example of the Revolutionary generation, worrying, "We shall never attain their dignified endurance of sufferings; shall never reach their elevated grandeur of character." But Selden also approved Americans' liberation from authority, declaring that the individual citizen was "no longer threatened with the trammels of inglorious thralldom, [and] may give free action to every one of his faculties." He halted, however, and anxiously admonished American free-agents to heed the maxims of self-control and chart the course of their destiny by "striving to *improve* what they [the Founders] successfully labored to *obtain*," by prosecuting "the grand work of moral, political, and intellectual improvement." Selden finally admitted, however, that the Sons probably could not match the virtues of their predecessors, but only "permanently evince our gratitude for their noble exertions in the cause of freedom." Observing that the American Revolution had provided heroes whose achievements were awe-inspiring, the Virginian payed homage to the overwhelming presence of the Founding Fathers. Acknowledging the psychological burden they represented for their Sons, Selden instructed, "Appreciate their labors; imitate their celestial virtues; and cultivate the glorious heritage which they have left you."[19]

The vicissitudes of inner life in an era of profound historial change are most firmly grasped, however, through probing scrutiny of individuals and their private trials. Though evidence is fragmentary and interpretation is somewhat speculative, as both must be in this type of inquiry, the lives and words of Charles Brockden Brown, Alfred Brunson, and John Quincy Adams reveal some of the private traumas of early liberal individualism in America. In the experiences, reflections, confessions, and actions of these Jeffersonian sympathizers[20] can be seen the psychological dramas involving Fathers and Sons, authority and repression, and identity and coherence. Furthermore, these figures reveal how the quiet desperation of the liberal self, as an underground spring feeds a great river, flowed into the war movement in 1812. Like Richard Rush in his grand speech of the first war summer, they divulge the secret that countless wandering sons embraced the war crusade for reasons they understood only vaguely, or perhaps not at all.

Charles Brockden Brown: "I Am Conscious
of a Double Mental Existence"

John Bernard, the British actor and comedian, was surprised when he met Charles Brockden Brown in Philadelphia in the early 1800s. Familiar with Brown's passionate, bizarre, and violent novels, the Englishman had expected to encounter a wild-looking aesthete. But "Brown gave very little idea of an imaginative writer in his appearance," Bernard recounted with some disappointment. "He was short and dumpy, with light eyes, and hair inclining to be sandy, while the expression of his countenance told rather of ill-health than of intellect." More provocative, however, were Brown's comments on the striking contrast between his sensual, agitated fiction and his pleasing, ordinary social presence. Bernard transcribed verbatim the novelist's musings:

> I am conscious of a double mental existence. When I am sufficiently excited to write, all my ideas flow naturally and irresistibly through the medium of sympathies which steep them in shade. . . . This I term, therefore, my imaginative being. My social one has more of light than darkness upon it, because, unless I could carry into society the excitement which makes me write, I could not fall into its feelings. Perhaps . . . the difference of the two may be thus summed up: in my literary moods I am aiming at making the world something better than I find it; in my social ones I am content to take it as it is.[21]

Hints of Brown's contradictory "double mental existence" did not go unnoticed by others. A contemporary, Paul Allen, read Brown's private journals after his death and concluded, "To all appearances, two persons are present." William Dunlap, a close friend and later biographer, elaborated. He reported that Brown, as a young law student, had entered opinions in the journals that were a model of dry prose and judicial argument. Yet hard on the heels of such essays would appear "a poetical effusion, as much distinguished by its wild and eccentric brilliance, as the other question was for its plain sobriety and gravity of style." "They are perfect opposites," Dunlap marveled, "and any one who perused them, would with difficulty be persuaded that so much eccentricity, and so much regularity, were the productions of one man; much less would he believe them to have proceeded from the same source with the interval of a few moments only."[22] Literary historians have attributed Brown's fluctuating sensibility to personal idiosyncrasy, or the overheating influence of the German "Sturm und Drang" early romantics, or the torment of writing fiction for a provincial and unsupportive American culture.[23] It seems more likely, however, that his divergent impulses were rooted far more deeply in the massive social and cultural dislocations of the early republic. An extremely sensitive, imaginative, and passionate individual, Brown partially buckled under the tremendous personal pressures of vocation, expression, and self-control engendered by liberalizing change. He emerged as an intensified example of the "personae" in early-nineteenth-century America, a fragmented self who sought cohesion and solace in the "enchantment" of writing, as he would call it. He would discover that another source of psychic consolation in the early 1800s lay in a vision of aggressive national expansion and war.

Charles Brockden Brown, usually considered the "Father of the American novel," was born in 1771 and grew up in a Philadelphia Quaker family. Drawn to books as a child, he developed wide intellectual interests even in grammar school: epic poetry, essays of all kinds, French, geography, fiction. As a teenager, he entered the legal profession and took a position reading law in the office of a Philadelphia attorney, all the while indulging his literary fancy in the local "Belle-Lettres Club." Then in 1792 the young man abruptly abandoned the law and drifted to New York City, determined to earn a living by writing. After publishing several essays and abandoning several fragmentary book manuscripts, Brown exploded in a burst of creativity from 1797 to 1800 and published four major novels. Unable to make an adequate living, however, the young novelist gradually turned to editorships and his brothers' mercantile importing company for sustenance. Although two minor novels appeared in 1801, as well as several essays and pamphlets somewhat later, Brown

gradually abandoned writing altogether. He died in 1810 of tuber-
culosis, at the age of thirty-nine, after being reduced to supporting
his family by running a small retail business alone.[24]

Brown's brief life pivoted on two episodes: the anguished decision
to leave the law for literature in the early 1790s, and his more gradual
but equally traumatic departure from fiction-writing to business and
editorships around the turn of the century. Each incident hinged on
key issues created by a consolidating liberal society—profit and success, morality and deception, repression and yearnings for escape.
Each brought serious bouts with depression and morbid, even at
times suicidal, self-deprecation. And each proved critical for shaping
the troubled "personae" evident in this figure of "perfect opposites."

Brown's initial crisis of vocation apparently emerged from two
sources. By 1789 the eighteen-year-old had grown despondent over
his legal studies, despising what he termed the law's "endless taut-
ologies, its impertinent circuities, its lying assertions and hateful
artifices." This concern with duplicity and deception became a preoccupation in his writing. In addition, a vague resentment of the profit
motive helped drive Brown from the law into writing. He bitterly
complained that for a lawyer, "intellectual ore is of no value but as it
is capable of being turned into gold, and learning and eloquence are
desirable only as the means of more expeditiously filling our coffers."
Nor did such values accrue only to attorneys, as Brown also admitted
"the despicable idea I have always entertained of the character of a
'Retailer.'" These two issues of social deception and profit-mongering reflected the commercializing trends of post-Revolutionary
America, and Brown found himself in a state of troubled alienation.[25]

In the autumn of that same year, Brown published a series of four
essays that provided an arresting contrast, even a challenge, to his
ostensible vocation of the law. Composed in evening spare time and
appearing in Philadelphia's *Universal Asylum and Columbia Magazine*, "The Rhapsodist" made integrity, imagination, and individual
judgment their main themes. "Truth is with me the test of every
man's character," he wrote. "Wherever I perceive the least inclination to deceive, I suspect a growing depravity of soul that will one day
be productive of the most dangerous consequences." Brown added,
"I am also careful to regulate my own conduct by the immutable
standard." The author's persona of the rhapsodist also described
himself as a figure of spontaneous and genuine expression. He spoke
in "artless and unpremeditated language," "pours forth the effusions
of a sprightly fancy," and "in his fondness for solitude . . . the
singularity of his character principally consists." However, the role
of the rhapsodist appealed most to Brown for its intensely dreamlike

sensibility. This figure "loves to converse with beings of his own creation" because to his "strong and vivid fancy there is scarcely a piece of mere unanimated matter existing in the universe." The author concluded, "The life of the rhapsodist is literally a dream." This fascination with half-conscious states, this implicit rejection of the rationalized self, would also become a key ingredient in his fiction.[26]

By the early 1790s the lawyer and rhapsodist within Brockden Brown had become irreconcilable. Unable to assimilate the narrow logic and profit-seeking of the attorney, the young man was infected with a prolonged crisis of vocation that festered for several years. Finally abandoning his law office in 1792, he sporadically taught grammar school while resisting offers to join the mercantile enterprises of his brothers. Brown gradually uprooted himself and began making extended visits to New York City to mingle with literary acquaintances like William Dunlap and Dr. Elihu Smith. He began to devote most of his time to writing fiction.[27]

This period of Brown's life proved equally notable for a prolonged crisis of passion. The struggling author went through several love affairs that concluded unsuccessfully. He became enamored of two young women in succession, but each relationship disintegrated under pressure from his Quaker parents—each girl was a non-Quaker—and from his inability to support a wife by writing. Moreover, Brown apparently developed a highly charged relationship with a male roommate, William Wood Wilkins. Although there is no direct evidence of physical liaisons, there does exist a series of emotional letters between them with definite homoerotic overtones. (Their suggestiveness would so disturb Brown's wife that she excised them from Dunlap's biography in the early 1810s.) Brown would not marry until 1804, when he wed Elizabeth Linn, the daughter of a Presbyterian minister, after a four-year courtship. For finally bucking the opposition of his family he was read out of the Philadelphia Society of Friends the following year.[28]

The burden of frustrated vocation and passion took its toll. From 1790 to 1795 Brown appeared as a young man suffering extreme stress, emotionally desperate, and possessed of a near-hysterical personality. He descended into a state of agonized self-absorption. He admitted to a friend, "I have not been deficient in the pursuits of that necessary branch of knowledge, the study of myself." That proved to be a dramatic understatement, as the aspiring writer engaged in theatrical outbursts of self-condemnation. "I utterly despise myself," he announced in January 1793. "I am the object of my most unbounded pity, the slave of a gloomy and distressful musing." At other times his moody self-analysis swung unpredictably from arrogance to self-loathing, as in a letter that said, "I am seldom inclined to question my own superiority, but . . . the phantom of superiority quickly vanishes and leaves me to regret my measureless distance from absolute excellence." Brown liberally sprinkled his correspondence with references to "the profound abyss of ignominy and debasement into which I am sunk by my own reflections," or to confessions that "the prospect of my mind, is the prospect of a desert. A scene of horror and insanity, growing hourly more desolate and gloomy." As he wrote to William Dunlap with much distress, "I am sometimes apt to think that few human beings have drunk so deeply of the cup of self-abhorrence as I have. There is no misery equal to that which flows from this source. I have been for some years in the full fruition of it. Whether it will end but with life I know not."[29]

Brown's internal struggles reinforced a tendency that had first surfaced in "The Rhapsodist" essays: an escape into a dream world of his own making. An early 1790s letter to Wilkins, for instance, offered an ecstatic free-association of unconsciousness, release from self-control, and androgynous sexuality. Describing himself as "The Sleeper," Brown described a fantasy where "I lost dominion of myself. First some spirit whispers in my ear the name of Wilkins," after which "the image is excluded only to admit the luminous idea of a gracious beauty" of "Henrietta G.," one of Brown's elusive love objects. In another letter the tormented young writer sought another kind of unconscious release. "Even my ambition is extinguished," he told a correspondent, "and all my views and wishes terminate in darkness and death." Brown frequently referred to his diary as "The Journal of a Visionary," and his absorption in private, dark fantasies eventually raised anxious reproaches from his friends. Dr. Elihu Smith in 1796 accused him of falling too much under the influence of "the example of J. J. Rousseau" and wandering "in a world of your own creation."[30]

These yearnings for escape into an unconscious state issued not only from dilemmas of vocation and passion, but also in reaction to the self-applied pressures of liberal individualism. A contemporary who read Brown's early diary noted frequent and strict injunctions to hard work. "He frequently congratulates himself on the resolution with which he encounters, and overcomes what he is pleased to denominate his *native indolence*," reported this observer. Young Brown also consistently, if not always successfully, strove to repress his vigorous sensuality. "I have been the child of passion and inconsistency, the slave of desires that cannot be honorably gratified, the slave of hopes no less criminal than fantastic," he guiltily burst out to a friend. But the process of restraining such desires was not a happy one, as Brown suggested in another letter to Wilkins in early 1793. "The passions are not *subdued* in manhood and old age; they are *extinguished*," he wrote. "But what is a being without passion?" Ratcheting tighter such demands for self-control, Brown slowly forced his personality structure into a schizoid shape. A contemporary commented after studying Brown's personal writings in the 1810s:

> His private journal offered a striking contrast to his familiar letters. By the former we discover his heart to be oppressed with gloom and dejection; while if we cast our eyes on a letter of the same date, we shall find him entering into all the gay and cheerful feelings of his friends, abandoning the contemplation of his own sorrows for a moment.[31]

Thus the trained lawyer and the instinctive rhapsodist, the guilty servant of passion and the remiss master of restraint, the private Brown and the public Brown, embarked on a literary career in the mid-1790s as a profoundly divided and troubled young man. Grimly determined to attempt a living by means of his pen, he began to pour out fictional prose. Some dealt with social issues, like *Alcuin* (1797), a long fictional dialogue on the rights of women, and *The Man at Home* essays, a desultory attack on the injustices of imprisonment for debt. A fragmentary and unpublished first novel, *Skywalk*, apparently swerved closer to Brown's own psychological turmoil. It took place in a wild frontier setting, and the plot revolved around sleepwalking and Indian atrocities. It also displayed the suggestive subtitle "The Man Unknown to Himself—An American Tale."[32]

Beginning in 1798, Brown published over the next two years the four novels on which his literary reputation rests. *Wieland; or, The Transformation* told the shocking story of a growing religious obsession that drove a young man to madness and the murder of his family. *Ormond; or, The Secret Witness* followed a youthful heroine's attempts to overcome her family's destitution from a commercial swindle and her struggles against a willful and rapacious "superman." *Arthur Mervyn; or, Memoirs of the Year 1793* detailed a boyish rustic's removal to the city and his hazardous adventures with the yellow fever, a sinister "con man," and a bizarre maelstrom of murder and money. *Edgar Huntly; or, Memoirs of a Sleep-Walker* explored a tangled maze of unconscious states, mistaken identities, and violent confrontations on the edge of civilization. Writing at an astonishing clip, Brown frantically spun into these narratives threads of personal anguish and inchoate criticism of emergent liberal values. The fictional fabric that resulted startled the senses with its brilliant and emotional intensity and otherworldly texture. The young Philadelphian seems to have half-consciously created these novels as a therapeutic release, as an exorcism of the private demons of frustrated vocation, repressed passion, and thwarted truth-telling that had tormented him since late adolescence.[33]

Brown's novels suffer in common from certain defects: rambling narratives, unconvincing climaxes, abrupt endings, superficially developed characters. Yet several thematic and emotional motifs give a raw power and compelling unity to these works. First, the fervent young novelist used shadowy depictions of America's growing market society as fictional settings. He often unfolded his tales against commercial backdrops darkened by financial intrigue, avarice, indebtedness, and embezzlement. In both *Arthur Mervyn* and *Ormond*, for example, much of the narrative action revolves around the business manipulations of unscrupulous self-made men. *Edgar Huntly*, after learning of an acquaintance who had lost a significant amount of money through an unfortunate loan, echoed Brown's misgivings about the growing obsession of Americans with going "in search of fortune":

> Our countrymen are prone to enterprise, and are scattered over every sea and every land in pursuit of that wealth which will not screen them from disease and infirmity, which is missed much oftener than found, and which, when gained, by no means compensates them for the hardships and vicissitudes endured in the pursuit.

Brown affirmed this consolidating business culture a couple of years later in an editorial preface to *The American Review and Literary Journal for the Year 1801*. The people of the United States, he wrote, were "more distinguished than those of Europe as a people of business, and by an universal attention to the active and lucrative pursuits of life."[34]

Additional probing of the moral problems of work and profit added depth to Brown's portrait of America's commercializing society. Characters like Theodore Wieland, Stephen Dudley, and Arthur Mervyn, for example, rejected "employment of which the only purpose was gain." Brown's condemnation of a narrow bourgeois calculus of material and social gain found life in his character of Balfour, a petty merchant and suitor of protagonist Constantia Dudley in *Ormond*. This figure concerned himself only with those qualities in a spouse that "lay upon the surface"—"her admirable economy of time and money and labor, the simplicity of her dress, her evenness of temper"—while remaining ignorant of "her intellectual character, of the loftiness of her morality." As a self-made man, Balfour could appreciate little beyond "the efficacy of industry and temperance to confer and maintain wealth" and only desired a wife "that would aid him in preserving rather than enlarging his property."[35]

Armed with this half-formed critique of market values and relations, Brown set out to explore in his fiction the rocky terrain of individual choice in an expanding liberal society. All four novels of the 1790s were preoccupied with the motives, nature, and consequences of actions taken by tormented individuals. *Ormond*, for example, featured both the hard-working Constantia Dudley, determined to support her family, and the nefarious Ormond, concerned only with self-gratification. Arthur Mervyn, however, stood as Brown's fullest representative of the liberal individual in the early republic. Young Arthur was a rural adolescent who abandoned the countryside to seek fame and fortune in the city. Pausing to meditate on his subsequent isolation from family and community, he admitted, "I was now alone in the world, so far as the total want of kindred creates solitude. . . . I was destitute of all those benefits which flow from kindred in relation to protection, advice, or property." Upon entering the city, thieves quickly pilfered Arthur's money and possessions. But he remained confident of his internal resources and eventual success, arguing that life can be appreciated "only by those who have tried all scenes; who have mixed with all classes and ranks; who have partaken of all conditions; who have visited different hemispheres and climates and nations."[36]

The young man's self-confidence began to wane when he became the employee and protégé of a seemingly wealthy merchant named Welbeck. This gentleman turned out to be the propagator of a massive financial scheme involving stolen money, misrepresentation, and murder. As Mervyn began to untie this knot of fraud, in the process discovering his own unintended part in the scheme, he pondered the problematic nature of individual agency. Good intentions without knowledge might "produce more injury than benefit," he concluded, but "we must not be inactive because we are ignorant." As an older friend noted shrewdly of Mervyn, "He stept forth upon the stage, unfurnished, by anticipation or experience, with the means of security against fraud."[37]

Brown's murky portraits of individual free-agency grew positively frightening as he ventured deeper into the liberal individual's soul. The alarming character of the lying sharper, the dangerous deceiver, the "con man," became a hallmark of his fictional tales. The young novelist's long-standing concern with "truth" became manifest in a rogues' gallery of characters that revealed the dark underside of the self-made man. Carwin, the mysterious ventrilo-

quist in *Wieland,* was portrayed as "the double-tongued deceiver."
Arthur Mervyn's Welbeck appeared as another such sinister figure.
Although admittedly averse to "the labour of my hands, to perform
any toilsome or prescribed task," Welbeck burned with ambition. To
fuel his way upward he embezzled money, entered into a huge mercantile scam, and eventually murdered. All the while he chuckled
over "the facility with which mankind are misled in their estimates of
character." Thomas Craig—the defrauder of the Dudley family in
Ormond—exhibited similar instincts. As the business partner of Stephen Dudley, he embezzled Dudley's stock, used the company's
credit to procure payments to himself, and then ran off as a wealthy
man. Brown described his character: "Craig was one of the most
plausible of men. . . . There were few men who could refuse their
confidence to his open and ingenuous aspect. . . . Deception was so
easy a task, that the difficulty lay, not in infusing false opinions
respecting him, but in preventing them from being spontaneously
imbibed."[38]

This fictional deployment of grasping con men raised to the surface several of Brown's underlying social concerns. First the author
consistently used the con man to portray commercial activity in the
early republic as a rather nasty affair. He pictured Welbeck, for
instance, with his "aversion to labor" as advancing a commercial
scheme where "the profits would be double to original expense." In
Arthur Mervyn, a description of another merchant/con man appeared. "[He] was one of those who employed money, not as the
medium of traffic, but as in itself a commodity," wrote the novelist of
this stock manipulator. "In short, this man's coffers were supplied by
the despair of honest men and the stratagems of rogues."[39]

Brown generalized from such perceptions that artifice and elusion
had permeated the very structure of social relations in the early
republic. Thus the con man merely embodied a larger troubling
necessity: discerning the truth of *anyone's* character or actions in a
society of liberal individuals. "Masks" and "deceptions" stood out as
an overriding social motif in Brown's novels. "What are the bounds
of fraud?" wondered one character in *Arthur Mervyn.* "A smooth
exterior, a show of virtue, and a specious tale, are a thousand times
exhibited in human intercourse by craft and subtlety." Even individuals like the philosophical Ormond—who claimed "that in which
he chiefly placed his boast was his sincerity"—wore duplicitous
masks. Having developed a talent for imitating the voice and gestures of another, Ormond often "assumed a borrowed character and
guise, and performed his part with so much skill as fully to accomplish his design." In Brown's words, Ormond was a man of "as-

sumed characters" in whom "appearances were merely calculated to mislead and not to enlighten." Amid this tangle of hidden motive and deceptive appearance, moral judgments of right and wrong became exceedingly difficult. Brown, describing himself as a "moral painter," attempted to explore these "latent springs and occasional perversions of the human mind." He found no easy answers. One of his characters observed, "Wickedness may sometimes be ambiguous, its mask may puzzle the observer; our judgement may be made to falter and fluctuate."[40]

This complex reading of emerging market society, private ambition and perception, and the specter of the con man finally led Brown into the most secluded recesses of liberal individualism. His major novels, as numerous readers have seen, frequently entered the realm of abnormal psychology. The Philadelphian himself once explained: "The chief point is not the virtue of a character. The prime regard is to be paid to the genius and force of mind that is displayed. Great energy employed in the promotion of vicious purposes constitutes a very useful spectacle. Give me a tale of lofty crime rather than of honest folly."[41] Indeed, his narratives overflowed with misled or demented characters committing murder, rape, theft, and all manner of outrage. Yet two related impulses have been overlooked. First, Brown's psychological themes flowed directly from the private anguishes of consolidating capitalist culture, and second, they clearly reflected a shaping of the personae's "double mental existence."

A recurring motif in Brown's psychological musings pictured the individual suffering in a pressure-cooker of isolation. Each of his four major narratives, for instance, had its young protagonist facing the destruction of his or her family. Clara and Theodore Wieland were orphaned after their father slowly went mad and died, and their mother wasted away from grief. Constantia Dudley, in *Ormond*, watched as her defrauded father grew blind and then was murdered, while her mother died of shame over their poverty-stricken condition. Arthur Mervyn departed for the city following his mother's death, while his father expired as an alcoholic a short time later. Edgar Huntly's parents were killed when he was a young boy. Thus, each of Brown's major characters stood dramatically alone in society, somewhat dazed from the trauma of destroyed family ties.[42]

Brown often magnified the distressed and solitary state of his characters by involving them in unresolved oedipal disputes. Theodore Wieland was obsessed with his father. His sister explained: "His father's death was always regarded by him as flowing from a direct and supernatural decree. It visited his meditations oftener than it did mine. The traces which it left were gloomy and permanent."

The sinister Carwin, from the same novel, resentfully described his father's attempts to thwart his intellectual proclivity. Carwin recalled that he "would make the most diligent search after my books, and destroy them without mercy, when they were found; but he could not outroot my darling propensity. I exerted all my powers to elude his watchfulness." Brown, however, reserved for Arthur Mervyn the most striking oedipal conflict. After the death of his much-beloved mother, Arthur grew disgusted with "that feebleness of mind which degraded my father, in whatever scene he should be placed, to be the tool of others." Having embarked for the opportunity of the city, young Mervyn eventually fell in love with and married an older woman, Ascha Fielding, admitting, "Was she not the substitute for my lost momma?"[43]

If act 1 of Brown's psychological dramas involved scenes of lonely, resentful, struggling individuals, act 2 presented scenes of their personalities coming apart altogether. This young novelist, the man of "perfect opposites," seasoned his narratives with symbols of deep internal division. Much of _Arthur Mervyn_'s tangled action, for example, revolved around Arthur's uncanny resemblance to Lodi, a rich young man who had died before Arthur entered the city. In _Wieland_, Carwin spoke mysteriously of his own ventriloquist powers as if they comprised a separate, inner, hostile entity: "He is my internal foe; the baffler of my best concerted schemes."[44]

Brown deepened such schizoid images by constantly delving into the explosive, hidden dimensions of his characters' personalities. Ormond presented at first appearance a calm, benevolent, and supremely rational sensibility. But as the novelist revealed more and more of this antagonist, he emerged from behind this facade as a man of fiery and uncontrolled passions who engaged in murder and then attempted to rape Constantia Dudley. Theodore Wieland, of course, summoned dormant savagery to kill his wife and children. Confronting his sister Clara, and about to stab her, he came face-to-face with his own murderous delusion. Theodore objectified his agitated libido into the figure of Carwin and cried out, "I was indeed deceived. The form thou hast seen was the incarnation of a demon."[45]

In addition to creating creatures of bursting passion, Brown also consistently employed "closet" images to suggest dark, hidden attributes. Upon arriving in the city, Arthur Mervyn spent the night in a closet as a result of a prank, but while he was there the young innocent was astounded to overhear the details of a financial fraud. At another point in the novel, Arthur began to uncover the unsavory truth about his patron Welbeck while in the cellar of the house they shared. In _Ormond_, Constantia was resting in a closet hideaway when her sinister suitor rode up to her house determined to satisfy his lust. Perhaps most memorable, *Wieland* contained an incredibly suspenseful scene where Carwin hid in the closet of Clara Wieland's bedroom, threw his voice into the night-darkened room, and scared her terribly. Opening the closet door, Clara discovered that "whoever was within, was shrouded in darkness." When Carwin emerged with only vague explanations, the young woman became convinced of his violent potential.[46]

Edgar Huntly, however, served as Brown's most expansive and outlandish vehicle for exploring the diffusion of personality. The young novelist packed the story with images of the divided personae. In its opening scenes, Clithero, a mysterious immigrant and murder suspect, appeared in a rural community and intrigued Edgar as a shadowy reflection of his own personality. In narrating the story of his own life, Clithero told the story of Mrs. Lorimer, his patroness, and her twin brother Arthur Wiatte. "The resemblance between them was exact to a degree almost incredible," Brown related, but while the lady was the picture of virtue, her brother "exceeded in depravity all that has been imputed to the arch-foe of mankind." Waldergrave, the murder victim of the suspect Clithero, prompted more images of intertwined personalities. Edgar confessed, "Connected with the image of my dead friend was that of his sister," while yet another acquaintance declared, "With his life, my own existence and property were, I have reason to think, inseparably united."[47]

A fascination with the violent underside of personality also appeared prominently in Brown's *Edgar Huntly*. Again, Brown frequently used the familiar image of the closet-like enclosure. When Clithero disappeared into the wilderness, Edgar determined to help him but could find only a locked "trunk" as a source of possible information. "A thousand conceivable motives might induce him to prevent or conceal the truth. If he were thoroughly known, his character might assume a new appearance," Edgar reflected. "It was possible that his box contained the means of this knowledge. . . . I determined to examine, and, if possible to open it." Having decided to pursue Clithero and prove his innocence, Edgar then found himself newly awakened on the floor of a dark "cave," bruised and bloody and not knowing how he got there. Emerging from this "abhorred darkness in the heart of the earth," the young protagonist began to uncover a side of himself that he knew not before.[48]

The cave sequence brought into focus another aspect of Brown's psychological portraiture. *Edgar Huntly*, as one critic has quipped, was "not so much written as dreamed." Both Clithero and Huntly were sleepwalkers, and as manifestations of Brown's long-standing

interest in unconscious states, these figures suffered suggestive tribulations in the novel. Clithero was aware of his affliction and worried
that "my steps wandered forth unknowingly and without the guidance of my will." But Edgar himself became Brown's most striking
representation of the liberal individual's divided consciousness.
Emerging from the cave where he mysteriously awakened, young
Huntly began what can only be described as a nightmarish journey
into the unconscious. Finding himself nearly naked and ravenously
hungry, he became beast-like. "My heart over flowed with cruelty,
and I pondered on the delight I should experience in rending some
living animal to pieces, and drinking its blood and grinding its
quivering fibres between my teeth," he declared desperately. After
killing and eating a panther, Edgar emerged from the cave into the
midst of an Indian raiding party. Calling up unknown strength, he
killed several of the savages and escaped. He then attempted to work
his way home, but was himself mistaken for an Indian and hunted by
white settlers. Amid these travails, he slowly grew proud of his new-
found wiles: "I disdained to be outdone in perspicacity by the lynx, in
his sure-footed instinct by the roe, or in patience under hardship, and
contention with fatigue, by the Mohawk." Shortly before his return
to white civilization, Huntly indulged a final outburst of libidinous
energy. Having killed an Indian, he made a half-crazed gesture of
carnal triumph. "I left the savage where he lay, but made prize of his
tomahawk," Huntly announced defiantly. "Prompted by some freak
of fancy, I stuck his musket in the ground, and left it standing
upright in the middle of the road." But upon arriving at his home,
the young man discovered with amazement not only that Clithero was
a homicidal maniac but also that he himself was a sleepwalker and the
perpetrator of several mysterious actions. Completely baffled by his
own deeds, Edgar proclaimed at the novel's end, "How little cog-
nizance have men over the action and motives of each other! How
total is our blindness with regard to our own performances." If
Brown's other novels featured the deception of virtuous characters by
con men, in *Edgar Huntly* the protagonist so utterly deceived himself
that the hard core of self threatened to disintegrate entirely.[49]

Thus Charles Brockden Brown's novels echoed with the crashes of
shattering identity, and the novelist's array of tormented, fragmented
characters often turned to violence for cathartic relief. Some directed
it inward, and the list of characters either contemplating or per-
forming acts of suicide was lengthy: Arthur's father and Welbeck in
Arthur Mervyn, Ormond's lover Helena Cleves and Constantia in
Ormond, Clithero in *Edgar Huntly*. *Wieland*, however, exhibited the
most spectacular cases of self-destruction. The elder Wieland, unable

to reconcile his quest for religious purity with the contaminations of the everyday world, literally exploded and burned, in Brown's phrase, from "spontaneous combustion." His son Theodore, with a psyche rubbed raw from a similar tension, erupted in a homicidal fit and then slit his throat in front of his sister. Yet just as frequently Brown's characters directed their aggression outward. Ormond and Constantia were but two of many examples. The former, having killed and prepared to commit rape, assaulted the latter while she, in a near-hysterical convulsion, stabbed him to death. Edgar Huntly, after an orgy of killing man and beast alike, perhaps best explained Brown's suggestion of violence as regeneration. "Never was any delight worthy of comparisons with the raptures which I then experienced," the young man disclosed. "Life, that was rapidly ebbing, appeared to return upon men with redoubled violence. My languors, my excruciating heat, vanished in a moment, and I felt prepared to undergo the labours of Hercules."[50]

After this frenzied burst of fictional writing, Brown paused wearily around 1800. The four novels, although brilliantly illuminating the public and private pathology of consolidating capitalist culture, nevertheless failed to provide an adequate living for their creator. So Brown entered the second major crisis of his life as the exigencies of market society once more forced the lawyer-rhapsodist personae to choose. A private letter indicated an ebbing of creative vitality. Upon his return to Philadelphia, Brown told a correspondent, "All the inanimate objects in this city are uniform, monotonous, and dull. I have been surprised at the little power they have over my imagination, at the sameness that everywhere reigns." He slowly began to drift from the calling of novelist to that of editor, with the object of financial security looming large. He told friends that editing a Philadelphia magazine would bring "clear profit to me," but the transition was expensive in terms of Brown's personal unity and self-regard. He bitterly affirmed in an 1801 poem, "Fame! I abjure thee, hate thee; thou has nought Worthy calling into life. . . . Come, blest Obscurity!" This self-loathing emerged even more strongly two years later. He wrote in an editorial preface to the *Literary Magazine*, "I should enjoy a larger share of my own respect, at the present moment, if nothing had ever flowed from my pen, the production of which could be traced to me."[51]

Brown entered the last decade of his life in retreat from creative writing and divided within himself as well. On the one hand, he moved uneasily into a business milieu that he had previously despised. He became not only an editor but also a partner in his family's mercantile firm. In the 1805 essay *On Classical Education*,

Brown conceded with a bitter twist of irony that "if a boy be intended for trade or business, a classical education will be injurious to him . . . [and] inimical to the mechanical processes of trade and to the activity and bustle of a man of business. . . . The dull uniformity and confinement of a shop or accounting room are irksome to men of genius and studious minds." Yet Brown also married, settled into the comfort of domestic routine, and became an advocate of bourgeois respectability. As he promised in the *Literary Magazine*, he strove to be the "ardent friend and the willing champion of the Christian religion," the proscriber of "everything that savors of indelicacy or licentiousness," and the foe of "intemperance of party," "personal altercation and abuse," dueling, gambling, and undue sensuality in women's clothing. Brown flatly assured William Dunlap of his happiness in 1805. "There is nothing to disturb my felicity but the sense of the uncertainty and instability that sticks to everything human," he wrote. "I cannot be happier than I am."[52]

After 1800 Brown did find one new outlet for his confined, restless emotional energy. He sporadically entered the realm of public affairs as an essayist. From 1803 to 1809 Brown wrote three pamphlets on the cession of Louisiana, American navigational rights on the Mississippi, and Jefferson's embargo. In these writings, especially the first two, the Philadelphian urged a vigorous policy of expansion, trade, and if need be, war. But most compelling was the way the vision of a prosperous, cohesive, martial republic became a unifying attraction to the personae of the frustrated novelist.

Surveying the United States since the Revolution, Brown was awestruck by the young republic's tremendous growth. "During this period, the American nation has increased in numbers and opulence, in a degree far beyond any known example," he exclaimed, "[and] it is not easy to set the due limits on it. We can discover no material obstacle to the continued extension of our settlements to the Pacific Ocean, nor can the increase be less than double in every twenty years." Moreover, Brown saw clearly the expansion of America's market networks. He declared flatly, "Trade is the principal employment of the American people," and praised its "wonderful power of annihilating, in its usual and natural effects, even space itself." But Brown retained much of his old distrust of commercial, liberal values. Writing in the guise of a French counselor to Napoleon, he offered these scathing remarks in the 1803 *Address on the Cession of Louisiana:*

> This is a nation of peddlers and shopkeepers. Money engrosses all their passions and pursuits. . . . Their ruling passion being money, no sense

of personal or national dignity must stand in the way of gratification. They are an easy sacrifice to the lust of gain.[53]

For Charles Brockden Brown, war became in the early 1800s both a social and a personal corrective to such tawdry impulses. While demonstrating convincingly America's commercial destiny, it offered also an opportunity for shaping virtuous values. He recognized, of course, the evils of war: "the neglect of agriculture, the ruin of sobriety, the pollution of morals, the waste of human life." But as a commercial nation, Brown argued, America was "liable to those disputes which flow from clashing interests and irritated passions, both on land and water." The Mississippi commerce and unrestricted foreign trade were vital to the growing republic's future, so Brown believed that such issues should be forced. "With what front can men talk of expense on occasions like these? Is money, levied on the people, and employed in the prosecution of a just war, thrown away?" he demanded. "Compare the expenses of the most formidable expedition with the losses accruing from the cessation of commerce." In addition, war would bring "advantages, not to be bought by mere money, in the salutary fear and respect which our conduct will impress upon foreign nations." The "motley character" and "forward passions" would be chastened. War would mold character, Brown argued, because "the odium of indolence and cowardice . . . will be washing away."[54]

Brown ultimately utilized a governing metaphor of "unity" in contending for war. His argument took shape in ostensibly social terms, but the former novelist's long-standing involvement with the fragmentation of personality added another resonance to the language. Brown wrote of his fellow Americans: "The utmost force of all the wisdom they possess, is exerted in keeping the hostile parts together. These parts are unlike each other, and each one has the individualizing prejudices of a separate state." The American Revolution served for the Philadelphian as an admirable example of cohesion. "It was then evident," he stated, "that the ploughman and the mechanic at either end of the continent, could recognize a common interest with each other; could sacrifice their ease, their fortunes, their lives, to secure a remote and general benefit." Now, Brown believed, expansion and war could reestablish that bond. "By unity of manners, laws, and government is concord preserved, and this unity will be maintained . . . by the gradual extension of our settlements." Brown stridently insisted as early as 1803 that Congress prepare to fight a crusade for solidarity: "*The iron is now hot;* command us to rise as one man, and strike!"[55]

We will never know if Brown would have supported so ardently the War of 1812. By 1809 his bellicose rhetoric had softened. Brown opposed the embargo as a crippling blow to American commercial vitality and generally held that the United States should stall for time—and hence greater strength—in her foreign affairs difficulties. His last words on the subject, however, maintained, "If foreign war must come, those who labored most to avert it, ought, by inculcating submission, and promoting unanimity, to save us from its worst evils." Then in 1810 Brown died suddenly. So if one can only speculate that he would have endorsed the 1812 conflict, one must recognize the novelist's definite attraction to violence that flowed largely from a fragmented, agitated personality.[56]

The personae of Charles Brockden Brown always had created intense personal pressure and always had sought a healing remedy for its torment. Fiction had provided one means of escape and fusion for Brown's tortured self. He perceived writing as a passion of intellectual energy that would "enchain the attention and ravish the souls of those who study and reflect." This creative muse, the Philadelphian described at another point, was "the enchanter" that always promised to seduce him "to a greater distance from the tract of common sense than I am at present desirous of being." A vision of violence and war—as it wound its way through Brown's fiction and burst forth in his militant rhetoric of the early 1800s—proved equally alluring as a ritual for psychic regeneration and unity. But Brown once had reflected earlier, "All my views and wishes terminate in darkness and death." Thus in 1810 the anguished, divided rhapsodist found a final wholeness far greater than anything tendered by either writing or war.[57]

Alfred Brunson: "Either Rise to Distinction or Fall in the Attempt"

In many ways Alfred Brunson was a rather ordinary citizen of the early republic. A native New Englander, he decided as a young man in the early nineteenth century to pull up stakes and head west. Like many others, he became attracted both to Jeffersonian politics and Methodism. Converting and then preaching in the Mississippi Valley, he felt compelled to leave a memoir of his religious work in the West. Thus in 1872 appeared *A Western Pioneer; or, Incidents of the Life and Times of Alfred Brunson . . . Written by Himself,* a long account of the trials and tribulations of this Methodist man of God. But through its rich psychological texture this volume made the ordinary life extraordinary. Brunson provided there an unusually detailed description of his agitated experience as an adolescent in the early 1800s when he struggled mightily with vocation, salvation, and self-control in a milieu of expanding opportunity. Even more uncommon, he made a long transcription of a dream during the height of this crisis that vividly portrayed the prominent psychological issues facing the fledgling liberal individual. Finally, Brunson's account of the War of 1812 revealed both intentionally and unintentionally the knot of private, emotional motivations that tied together his enthusiastic participation in that conflict.[58]

Brunson was born in Connecticut in 1793 as the eldest of seven children. The account of his early years disclosed a youth dominated by the imposing presence of his father. Apparently the elder Brunson had been fond of "good living and the higher class of society" and had squandered away his modest inheritance as a young man. After marriage, he followed several paths in trying to make a living for his family. He opened an inn, then a brickyard, picked up occasional money as a wrestler—he was a man of extraordinarily large and robust physical stature—and finally opened a ferry service on the Hudson River at Sing Sing, New York. Young Alfred helped in these various enterprises and became especially adept at handling the ferryboats.[59]

Then in March 1806 tragedy struck. Alfred's father, already afflicted by the early onset of rheumatism, fell overboard from the ferry in late winter while wearing heavy woolen clothing. Alfred rushed from the bank with a friend and attempted to rescue him from a rowboat. While the companion maneuvered the craft close to the struggling man, Alfred—not a good swimmer himself and afraid of being pulled under—attempted to grab his father by the hair and hold him afloat until more help could arrive. Unfortunately the small boat, while bobbing in the choppy water, collided with the elder Brunson and the son lost his precarious hold. With Alfred frantic but helpless, his father sank out of sight. By the time more boats arrived, it was too late. The corpse floated to the bank a bit farther downstream the next day, the body hardened in a crawling position as if the victim had hit bottom and attempted to creep to the surface. This episode left the entire Brunson family in a state of shock, but young Alfred especially so. Overcome with grief at his loss, and burdened with the heavy load of guilt over his own failure at rescue, the thirteen-year-old was traumatized. Moreover, at the funeral his mother and certain of her relatives—all of Calvinist background—induced further anxiety by lamenting that his father was a "worldly man" and unlikely to find salvation. Thus Alfred recalled, in language painfully reflective of his guilt over failure to "save" his father, "At this event I felt the first sense of my own sinfulness, and the need of a Savior, and resolved, with my mother to seek him." This religious yearning subsided momentarily, but it would later arise again with even greater intensity.[60]

The Brunsons moved to Danbury, Connecticut, later in 1806 to enjoy the support of family, and the mother with her seven children were baptized into the Congregational Church. Alfred consented gladly because of lingering nervousness over the state of his soul. The young man's life in New England, however, quickly became a travail of religious and vocational struggle. He became an apprentice shoemaker in the shop of his uncle and grandfather and, in his own later words, was lured into "the snares of vice." Both relatives were avowed skeptics and deists, influenced by Tom Paine's *Age of Reason*. In this atmosphere Alfred eased into "dancing and other amusements" with his fellow shoemakers. Yet his mother's religious admonitions prompted recurring nightmares that he "should wake up in hell before morning." He was "deeply impressed with the necessity of religion," if only intermittently.[61]

Alfred's nervousness over salvation combined with another subject of private uncertainty—what to do for a living. As a boy, young Brunson had entertained military dreams, and his father had decided to prepare him for "West Point Military School" by sending him to a local academy. The elder Brunson's death destroyed such plans, however, and Alfred began a five-year apprenticeship in shoemaking with his mother's brother, Ezra Starr Crozier. Although mechanically talented, the adolescent's gaze went beyond the craftsman's bench. Taken with the Jeffersonian idealism of his late father, his uncle, and his grandfather, young Brunson grew ambitious. Spurred on by the examples of Roger Sherman and Benjamin Franklin—both of whom had risen from humble mechanic to statesman—he decided "to study law, and, as soon as possible, enter upon its practice." When his uncle refused to release Alfred from his apprenticeship, they had an altercation and the young man impulsively left Danbury in 1808. He recalled, "My design was to go to Ohio, study law, and rise, if possible, with the young state to whatever distinction merit might entitle me to." Weaned from the succor of family and community, the fifteen-year-old Alfred entered the society of the early republic as a mobile, aspiring, but intensely anxious self-made man.[62]

Surreptitiously leaving his kin and career behind, Brunson set out for the West. He stopped in Carlisle, Pennsylvania, on the way to Ohio, intending to work there for a while and replenish both his funds and his energy. But once more he entered into private turmoil. Alfred began to hear a godly voice whispering that since he had left his old companions, and had no new ones to hinder him, it was his "last call" to be saved. Becoming quite unsettled, he sought God anew and engaged in intense self-examination and prayer. He began to attend the local Methodist church. His life became an emotional pendulum. Brunson found work in a shoemaking shop, but he swung erratically between sensual attractions and the ever-tightening demands of his religious calling. He remembered of his struggle for self-control,

> I was naturally of a lively and jocose turn, and, in the shop, I would indulge in light conversation, crack jokes, tell yarns, debate questions, and endeavor to play my part in the good humour of the company; but this I found to be injurious to devotional feelings; for, after such indulgence, or retiring for prayer, I found great deadness of feeling. . . . I resolved to break off from it, but, before I was aware of it, I would catch the spirit of the company I might be in and launch out in this playful pastime. . . . To remedy this I would sit down, or kneel, and meditate on my sins and sinfulness, and repent.

Brunson's vivid description of inner tension mirrored the heightened repression and rationalization that characterized early capitalist culture. These demands that melded work, religion, and character formation drove the youthful New Englander into personal crisis. He partially resolved it on February 3, 1809, in a dramatic conversion experience at a Methodist prayer meeting. Alfred, while earnestly singing a hymn, suddenly felt a great burden of sin falling away, heard a voice whispering "You are converted," and was washed over by a wave of peace and love.[63]

Brunson bounded home feeling ecstatic and light-headed, but it soon became evident that conversion met only some of his psychological needs. This reborn Christian still faced the problem of vocation. Moreover, he had the continuing task of inculcating self-control, once the flush of salvation had faded, into the permanent structure of his character. While sorting out his life in this agitated and anticipatory state, Brunson wrote later, "I had a singular dream, warning me of approaching danger." This he interpreted as an "extraordinary call" from God both cautioning of religious trials and testing his mettle for the ministry. But more intriguing, this remarkable dream gathered from Brunson's unconscious a cluster of images that lucidly conveyed the psychological pressures enveloping the liberal individual in early-nineteenth-century America. It was to be a turning point in his life.[64]

The dream, occurring about a month after conversion in March 1809, presented a setting that strongly suggested Brunson's inner confusion and sense of disorientation: "In my dream I was traveling over ground, the like of which I never saw. . . . At length I came to the foot of a high and steep hill, up which my path led. At this moment the scene was changed from warm weather and bare ground to Winter, with snow about two feet deep. . . . The hill became so steep as to hang over me." If this hostile geographical scene seemed clearly to depict the imposing barriers facing Brunson in his journey to success, equally revealing were two other images. The first concerned "family," while the second was that of an elusive "path." The only other people in the dream were a "Brother" of the church and "my eldest sister." Both family figures proved to be messengers of adversity. Near the end of the dream Brunson's sister would assist at his own burial, while nearer the beginning his church brother "made a path in the snow in which I was to follow him . . . [but he] was going out of my sight, leaving his trail in the snow plainly to be seen; but it seemed to be impossible for me to follow him." The metaphor of the path continued as Brunson then discerned "a road that went round the hill, and ascended by an easier grade." The dreamer, however, found himself unable to follow this trail either. Thus the general dynamic of this fantasy disclosed Brunson's anxiety over frustrated success, waning self-confidence, and isolation from family.

As Brunson's travail with finding and following the path further unfolded in the dream, other compelling images surfaced. The young shoemaker related an episode of striking phallic significance. "In crossing a plain, or meadow, I saw numerous mats of grass; under which rattle-snakes were coiled in great numbers, and I had to use great caution to avoid being bitten by them as they thrust their heads out at me." This scene seems a clear reflection of Brunson's fear of, and ongoing attempts to repress, his own sensuality. Then, he continued, in struggling to follow the path in the snow, "I fell on the ice and frozen ground with such violence as to kill me." This act of self-destruction prefaced a clear expression of divided personality. Brunson reported, "I seemed to stand by and look upon my dead body for a while." Then appeared a final jolting vision. Brunson helped his sister pick up his own corpse and laid it in a wagon, when the body transfigured and "it seemed to be my father." This concluding picture not only conveyed the young man's disturbing impulses toward suicide and personality diffusion, but also connected them with oedipal memories of patricide. Brunson awoke in a cold sweat. Emotionally unhinged, he entered upon several weeks of anguished introspection and religious devotion. He prayed to God for death rather than to fall from grace. The dream proved to be a catalyst, however, as Brunson quickly heard a voice instructing, "Stay here, and preach the Gospel!" Having confronted his inner demons in this "most singular dream," the young New Englander moved closer to psychological peace by flying to the vocational haven of the ministry.[65]

This harrowing resolution of vocational crisis led Brunson to several concrete decisions. "Feeling now that I was called to preach," explained the young convert, "I gave up all my projects for the law, and military glory, and devoted my studies to a preparation for the work before me. I bought a Pocket Bible, and commenced reading it by course." Brunson also completed a move away from his family's Calvinist heritage. He joined the Methodist Episcopal Church in April 1809 and began reading Methodist "Doctrinal Tracts." Brunson defined this shift in terms of expansive spiritual energy. He recounted, "I desired to *live* while I did live, and to have religion enough to make and keep me happy. The idea of having just religion enough to make one miserable . . . enough to be a servant, but *not enough to be a son* [italics added]—did not suit my views of propriety or safety, nor the nature of my regeneration."[66]

With renewed vigor, Brunson confidently reentered the battle for self-control. He admitted that his besetting sin was a passionate "impetuosity of character, which often led me into hasty acts or words, for which I was afterwards sorry." But this time young Brunson was victorious after "a severe contest which lasted three weeks." He proudly observed of this hard-won triumph of character, "My nature was not changed, as to its impetuosity, but that being in subjection to the grace of God, it was under control from angry passions." The young man was at last able to implant an internal moral gyroscope in place. He noted of himself, "When anything presented itself to be done, or if solicited or tempted to do anything, I first look inwardly and to God, to see whether my conscience approved or disapproved."[67]

Brunson made manifest this self-control by returning to Connecticut to make amends and reorder his affairs. He first reconciled himself with his mother and then took work as a shoemaker to pay off the apprenticeship debt to his uncle. At age sixteen Alfred became his own man. Within a few months he married Eunice Burr, a distant cousin of Aaron Burr, and became a petty entrepreneur making shoe "stockwork" for the New York City market. But Brunson did not abandon his ministerial aspirations. In 1810 he was "licensed to exhort" by the local Methodist conference and thereafter, in addition to holding prayer meetings, he constantly badgered his superiors to become an itinerant preacher. Much to his frustration, they just as consistently refused because of his youth. In addition, the embargo and nonimportation measure of this period slowly destroyed his shoemaking enterprise. So the old pressures of vocation surfaced once more. Brunson first contemplated entering the navy, but then took advantage of an opportunity to buy a tract of land in Fowler, Ohio. He and his wife moved there in the summer of 1812.[68]

The young religious enthusiast went west with bright hopes. The goal of being an itinerant preacher remained foremost in his mind, but the economic prospects for shoemaking and even farming also seemed promising. When Brunson was refused ministerial status once more, however, he became dejected and conceded, "My religious ardor was so dampened that my enjoyment was greatly lessened." Then in the fall of 1812 war came to the Old Northwest as the U.S. Army surrendered at Detroit without a shot and the British threatened to invade southward. Impulsively, Brunson enlisted in the army for a year. His ostensible reason was national pride—"my patriotic blood was up to fighting heat" at the thought of British invasion—but his own narrative revealed a deeper complex of emotions.[69]

First, it was clear that the war and military service served as an object for Brunson's vocational frustrations. His "dampened" preaching ambitions found another outlet in hopes for military advancement. As he declared in 1814, he expected that "merit would be rewarded in the army." But as well as ventilating repressed anger, military service promised to soothe the young man's battered psyche in another way. Brunson quickly came to see the war as a test—even an opportunity—for the further molding of his Christian character of self-control. As he quickly discovered at the "recruiting rendezvous," his fellow soldiers were definitely an unvirtuous lot. "The first time I . . . saw what kind of company I was to be associated with, conviction, like a clap of thunder, struck my mind that this is not the company Providence designed for you. . . . I saw that I had erred in entering the army instead of preaching," he remarked remorsefully. But Brunson quickly turned this moral challenge to his psychological advantage:

> I resolved that at the end of my term of service, if spared, I would return to duty and preach the Gospel of Christ. I had no fears of death in the army, either by the sword, a bullet, or by disease; for the conviction was strongly fixed in my mind that I had to preach, and that God would preserve me to do the work.[70]

The young convert thus transformed the war into a personal crusade. Brunson hoped to temper under fire his moral character and thereby both prepare and justify himself for another attempt at entering the ministry. He began his duties enthusiastically. As an "Orderly Sergeant" in an infantry company, he campaigned throughout the Old Northwest under William Henry Harrison. He saw action at Lake Huron, Sandusky Bay, and Fort Stevenson, observed Captain Oliver Perry's naval victory on Lake Erie, and was present at Harrison's great victory over Tecumseh at the Battle of the Thames. But the bulk of Brunson's efforts in the army focused on a personal moral imperative. While in camp he engaged in lonely sessions of "secret prayer" and "formal secret devotions" in the evenings behind the breastworks. He read portions of the Bible every day. The regiment's "Quartermaster Sergeant" stopped Brunson one day and guessed the Ohioan must be a Methodist because "you mind your own business, perform your duty punctually, but never join in the amusements of the men, nor use any of their bad language." When the quartermaster expressed friendly skepticism that such conduct could continue, Brunson only grew more inspired. The older man later admitted that the "religious integrity" of his Methodist friend had proved worthy of honor and respect.[71]

Apparently Brunson's campaign experience, obvious intelligence, and moral steadfastness also raised him in the eyes of both peers and superiors. Having grown quite popular and respected among the troops, he was promised a field promotion to an officership. For reasons that are not clear, it never came, so when his term of service expired, the resentful Brunson quit the army. He turned a deaf ear to the appeals of regiment officers, but his genuine attraction to an army career surfaced in his bitter reply. "My merit had been acknowledged and promotion promised," he recorded, "but it had not come, and I should trust to uncertainties no longer." Although vocationally frustrated once more, Brunson found ready solace this time in a larger perception of the war as a moral challenge. "I had promised God, if he would spare me to the end of my term, I would return home and give myself to the work to which he had called me," the young man reminded himself. "I took my discharge and went home."[72]

Alfred Brunson left the war believing that it had prepared him for the ministry. He saw the hand of God at work. "I thought, probably, He had controlled, and prevented my promotion," said the pious young man, "lest if it had occurred, the inducement to remain in the service might be too strong for resistance." Brunson may have been right. Returning to Fowler and again applying to become an itinerant preacher, he first encountered neighbors who accused him of wartime sins common to the soldier. But after a few months he reported triumphantly, "It had to be admitted that I had sustained my Christian character unsullied, and came home unscathed by the corruptions of the camp." In 1815 Brunson finally was authorized as a traveling minister by the Methodist Western Reserve Conference. He began traveling circuits in Ohio, and before his long career was over he had preached throughout much of the Mississippi Valley, evangelized among Indians, founded dozens of "missions along the middle border," and served as a chaplain in the Union armies during the Civil War. He died in Wisconsin, his home of many years, in 1882.[73]

Brunson's encounter with the War of 1812 thus served as a pivotal affair in his private life. Tormented by the psychological pressures of success-seeking, repressed sensuality, loss of social and family roots, and frustrated ambition—all captured in his "singular dream"—this adolescent had suffered first an anguished crisis of salvation. When conversion only partly settled Brunson's convulsed psyche, war offered another means of relief. By supporting and participating in this violent conflict, Brunson was able to release pent-up frustrations over vocation, identity, religion, and self-control. Amid these private struggles in the months before the war, the young man had vowed rather desperately at one point "not to do anything that I would not be willing to die in the act." He successfully tested this commitment to virtue or death in the army and experienced war as a kind of catharsis. As he had claimed earlier, if war came with England he would "enter the army, and either rise to distinction or fall in the attempt." By coming through the conflict to a pastorate, and in the process only stumbling rather than falling, the troubled psyche of Alfred Brunson found 1815 to be a year of personal as well as national peace.[74]

John Quincy Adams: "Two Objects the Nearest to My Heart, My Country and My Father"

John Quincy Adams was always difficult to like, often easy to admire, and sometimes impossible to understand. But seldom was he to be pitied, as he was in May 1829. Brilliant, relentlessly industrious, and unbending in his integrity, the New Englander had shaped a monumental record of public service to the American republic on the way to the presidency. In the process his fiercely independent character and clenched-jaw morality had often left a wake of exasperation and acrimony among his colleagues. Yet even his bitterest enemies must have felt compassion when, in the flowering of spring as he prepared to leave the White House for Boston, the stern old statesman received horrifying news. His oldest son, George Washington Adams, had committed suicide.[75]

While presenting a stoic mask of mourning to the public, the

President poured out bitter anguish and guilt in his diary over the next several weeks. High hopes for his talented, sensitive son had begun to fade long before 1829 because of the steady progress of mental instability in young George. But the suicide dashed those hopes with crushing finality. Moreover, it tragically highlighted two emotional compulsions in John Quincy's own life: a deeply felt obligation to the legacy of the Founding Fathers, and an equally profound commitment to the necessity of self-control. His son, named in memory of the "Father of his Country," had been the subject of constant paternal exhortations to self-discipline, study, temperance, and hard work. George's self-destruction thus brought together, in a wave of emotional introspection, these two private issues for the President as they had not been for some two decades.[76]

As a young man, John Quincy Adams had shouldered the same twin burdens as his ill-fated son. He proved to be made of sterner stuff. Growing up in the shadow of John Adams, Thomas Jefferson, George Washington, and other Revolutionary luminaries, he had embarked on a determined quest to fulfill their hopes and match their achievements. Urged to the task of self-control by demanding parents, he had engaged in a protracted, dramatic, eventually successful struggle to master an impulsive nature. But John Quincy discovered, as his own son never did, an outlet for venting the pressures resulting from such personal struggles. Like many contemporaries in the early republic who endured both the imposing legacy of the Founding Fathers and the private costs of self-control in a liberalizing society, he read these psychological issues into a highly charged agenda of public affairs. Also in typical fashion, he ultimately attempted to absolve them in an emotional crusade against Great Britain in 1812.[77]

Born in 1767, John Quincy Adams had grown up in the turmoil of Boston during the Revolution. Educated at his mother's side, he constantly heard tales of John Adams' glorious accomplishments at the Continental Congress. Then in 1778 the eleven-year-old boy joined his father on a diplomatic mission to France. He would stay on foreign soil for some six years, almost half of those as John Adams' private secretary.[78]

While in Europe the adolescent Adams became acutely sensitive to the commanding presence of the Founding Fathers. He spent considerable time in the Paris households of Benjamin Franklin and Thomas Jefferson, so much so that his father would later write to Jefferson, "Our John . . . appeared to me almost as much your boy as mine." Yet John Adams' achievements loomed largest in his son's mind. John Quincy's admiration grew so great that he adopted his father's mannerisms, causing bemused relatives to quote Joseph Addison's words, "Curse on the stripling, how he apes his Sire." Equally important, however, the years in Europe prompted the first skirmishes in young Adams' long campaign for self-control. On the one side beckoned the theater, the opera, and the sophisticated women of cosmopolitan Paris. On the other appeared stern admonitions from both parents to "curb that impetuosity for which I have frequently chided you" and to cultivate "the character of the Hero & the Statesman." Apparently steering a troubled course between temptation and restraint, an anxious young man decided to come home in 1785. He felt compelled to escape financial dependence on his parents. But having decided to enter Harvard and then pursue a legal career, he evinced rather mixed feelings about his future prospects and the likely demands of rigid self-discipline. Although "dry and tedious study" were less than attractive, John Quincy confided to his diary that he could never support himself "if I loiter away my precious time in Europe." The only consolation was that with hard work and common sense "I can live *independent* and *free,* and rather than live otherwise, I would wish to die."[79]

Upon returning to America as almost a foreigner in his own country, the young man's anxieties did not subside but instead intensified. The next seven or eight years proved to be the stormiest period of John Quincy Adams' personal life. On the surface things went smoothly. Once in Massachusetts, young Adams decided to press for admission to an advanced class at Harvard because of his extensive European education. He spent several months of hard study with his aunt's family at Haverhill and after examination was admitted to Harvard's junior class in March 1786. Over the next two years he appeared as a diligent, stand-offish, and brilliant student. After graduation he studied law with his usual intensity in the office of Theophilus Parsons in Newburyport.[80]

Beneath the superficial calm young Adams' passage from adolescence to manhood was beset by gnawing frustrations over vocation and character. While expressing a wish to settle into a comfortable and productive life, at the same time his surging ambition undercut the prospects for tranquillity. Standing in the long shadow of his father, John Quincy wrote anxiously, "I often wish I had just ambition enough to serve as a Stimulus to my Emulation, and just Vanity enough to be gratified with small Distinction. But I cannot help despising a fellow of such a character. I esteem a Man who will grasp at all, even if he cannot keep his hold." Added problems came from a growing aversion to the law and an attraction to literary pursuits that would survive as an unrequited passion throughout his life. Struggling with his own career, he lashed out at the manipulative social-climbers "who have no characters at all." Scribbling angrily in his diary, he denounced those who "secure the favour of their superiors by an hypocritical kind of modesty," or the man whose "genius is imitation, and his skill is cunning." By 1788 young Adams had grown frequently despondent—"my prospects appear darker to me every day"—and indulged in gloomy meditations on "Nothing" as the meaning of life.[81]

This anxiety over his future barely concealed another seething controversy in the private life of John Quincy Adams. The few years after 1785 witnessed an explosion of what he would term his "passions." To the surprise and discomfort of the Adams scion and his family, if not to modern students of the typical "identity crisis" of late adolescence, the young man became extremely argumentative, fell in and out of love with great rapidity, and took to drinking and rakish behavior. Like a rudderless ship, he drifted from emotional self-indulgence at one extreme to fits of harsh self-reproach at the other. Adams soberly reported in a 1786 address to the Harvard "A.B. Club" that natural man's progress in society required the curbing of instinct. As a creature that is passionate by nature, he argued, the individual in society must fall "under restraints, and in proportion as he advances in that he learns the Duties which he owes to those that surround him." But as he confessed with more anguish in his diary, "How despotically they [the passions] rule! how they bend, and master, the greatest and the wisest geniuses! 'Tis a pity! 'tis a pity!"[82]

John Quincy's difficulties with passion burst to the surface especially in affairs of the heart. While in Haverhill studying for Harvard, he was smitten by several young women. With uncertain career prospects looming and parental warnings ringing in his ears, the young man wrestled with his libidinous drives and impetuous nature. "I have still more reason, than I ever had, to repress my feelings," he confided in his diary. In Newburyport, young Mr. Adams' amorous tendencies came to full flower as he moved into a social whirl of parties, dancing, drinking, and numerous flirtations. His diary from this period abounds with commentary on the town's young women. Then in late 1790 John Quincy fell passionately in love with Mary Frazier, a move denounced by his parents as imprudent. It nearly broke his heart, but the young man broke off the relationship and retired to Boston to practice law. The struggle with "passion" persisted, however, as the fledgling lawyer revealed in a privately kept poem of 1792. "Imperious Beauty's over varying forms, / By turns assume their empire o'er the heart. / Each new attraction my fond bosom warms, / Now Nature's bloom, and now

the grace of Art," he wrote. The verses went on to detail his indiscriminate fondness for girls of fifteen, widows, the "fair Coquette,"
the learned maid, and the "gentle nymph" and magnanimously concluded of women, "All colours please me, black or brown or
white."[83]

Young Adams' difficulties with females and libido prompted a
litany of self-reproaches by the late 1780s. He drove himself relentlessly. "I cannot, must not be negligent," he wrote in his diary.
"All my hopes of going through the world in any other, than the most
contemptible manner, depend upon my own exertions, and if I continue thus trifling away my time, I shall become an object of charity
or at least of pity." An address before his Harvard debating society
upheld the proposition that "nothing is so difficult, but it may be
overcome by Industry." Constantly calculating the moral consequences of his behavior—"Can I boldly say to myself, that my
improvements have been in proportion to the moments that have
flown?"—he consistently fell short of his own harsh standards. The
morbidly introspective, guilt-ridden youth often lamented, "Every
day to him is lost which does not render him more capable of fulfill-
ing the duties for which he was created. Such however have been
many, many of my days."[84]

The young man's painful problems with career and self-control
were further exacerbated by a persistent psychological specter hang-
ing over his head: the exacting image of the Founding Fathers, and
his own father in particular. Having returned to Massachusetts to
pursue his future, John Quincy wrote rather pathetically to his absent
father in tones mixing admiration and self-doubt.

> Should you return home next spring and be yourself at leisure to instruct
> me [in law], I should prefer that to studying anywhere else. But if you
> are still detained in Europe, I should wish to live in some place where
> there might be society sufficient for relaxation at times, but not enough to
> encourage dissipation.

That John Quincy labored in his father's footsteps was indicated in
newspaper accounts of his Harvard graduation speech, which characterized the 1780s as a "critical period." The *Massachusetts Centinel*
noted the high "public expectation from this gentleman, being the
son of an Ambassador" and reported, "He is warmly attached to the
republican system of his father." As the young New Englander indicated on his twenty-first birthday, both resentment and reverence
colored his own mental portrait of his prestigious sire. "This
day . . . emancipates me from the yoke of paternal authority which
I never felt, and places me upon my own feet, which have not

strength enough to support me. I continue therefore still in a state of dependence." The burden of his paternal legacy grew so heavy that in December 1787 he wondered despondently whether "the blind, unreasonable affection which Nature has given to parents for their children" was not simply a "humiliating" instinct of "brute creation." The young diarist carefully added, however, that love was "rational" "which a child owes to his parent . . . from gratitude for obligations received."[85]

John Quincy's emotionally unsettled state reached a climax in an intensely self-conscious, anxiety-ridden speech to the Harvard Phi Beta Kappa society in the fall of 1788. With his parents in attendance among other Boston dignitaries, the youthful orator analyzed the situation of a typical "youth about to enter upon the scenes of an active Life, a view of the prospect before him, and of the Fortunes which expectation leads him to imagine." He opened this transparently autobiographical meditation by acknowledging a young man's tendency to envision his future "through the deceptive medium of fancy, or the passions." Soaring upward in fantastic dreams or plummeting into undue gloom, the young striver suffered the pain of mental agitation. Arguing to himself as much as to his audience, John Quincy proposed an agenda for overcoming such difficulties. First, the neophyte citizen should demonstrate "indefatigable industry," "rigid economy," and "great exertions" in his pursuit of success. Second, he should seek to achieve self-control in two senses of that term: both to "circumscribe our desires with rational bounds," and to make oneself "independent of external circumstances." Finally, a young man should commit himself to a "well-filled station" of vocation, or to a private calling wherein ambition and virtue would combine to further "the improvement of mankind." The necessity of all these measures, young Adams insisted, came not only from private yearnings for advancement. It also came from the heritage of "the late revolution" which had created heroes whose exploits were known to the "boundaries of the civilized world." Thus it was "incumbent upon the rising generation to maintain in all its lustre the splendid reputation which our country has acquired." The young speaker emotionally appealed to other Sons in the audience, "Suffer me to express my ardent desire, that you may cherish the generous flame."[86]

By the mid-1790s John Quincy Adams had dampened many of the sparks of personal friction from his late adolescence. Following a brief stint as a practicing lawyer in Boston, his European experience led to an appointment in 1794 as Minister to the Netherlands at The Hague. Over the next several years he subsequently performed diplomatic services for the American republic in England, Portugal, and Prussia. Thus settling career difficulties, the young diplomat also gained greater sway over his passionate impulses. In a typical entry in his 1796 diary, he wrote that idleness and flirtation had begun to give way before a disciplined regimen of reading and moral instruction: "I have not yet become perfectly studious and busy according to my wishes, but I am gradually verging towards it . . . since I adopted this species of self admonition."[87] So the New Englander became a public man as he largely resolved his "identity crisis" of early manhood. Yet the weighty legacy of the Founding Fathers and the onerous burden of self-control did not vanish. Instead, they cut a new channel in influencing the direction of his life.

Some two years after the termination of the Mary Frazier romance, John Quincy had written resentfully to his mother that the decision, although a wise one, had shaped in him "the dullness of blunted sensations rather exempt from pain than conscious of pleasure." Thus partly conscious of the psychic distress issuing from self-denial, he redirected repressed emotion into the arena of public affairs in the 1790s. Politics became a way to honor the ideal of self-control, but also a way to sublimate inarticulated yearnings for release from its dominion. On a number of fronts, the younger Adams demanded the exercise of restraint in political life. He argued in 1793:

> In a state of civil and political liberty, parties are to the public body, what the passions are to the individual. . . . Like the passions, too, it [the spirit of party] is a prolific source of misery as well as of enjoyment: Like them it requires a severe and continual exertion of restraint and regulation, to prevent its breaking out into excesses destructive to the Constitution.

This politics of repression obligated him to condemn the "licentiousness" of the French Revolution and the "malignant passions" of party politics in his own country. As he suggested in a private letter, political popularity is akin to the seductions of a beautiful woman, because "she cannot grant it without exciting all the evil energies of those whose ardor aims at much more familiar caresses." But young Adams also leaped into political frays with a rage that strained the cords of genteel restraint. He angrily defended the theater against Boston provincials and he bitterly denounced advocates of French-style radicalism. He savagely characterized opponents: "No half-fledged spurless chickling on a dunghill, could strut and crow, and flap his wings, with more insulting exultation."[88]

As John Quincy Adams practiced this ambivalent politics of self-control in the 1790s, he also emerged as a defender of the pristine tradition of the Founding Fathers. His earliest political forays were dedicated to upholding John Adams' career. The young man's famous "critical period" speech of 1787 was read as a defense of his father's "republican system," his original opposition to the Constitution folded before his father's advocacy of that document, and his widely reprinted "Publicola" letters of 1791 were issued to defend his father from pro–French Revolution critics. Moreover, as John Quincy ruefully admitted in 1796, his father was "far more solicitous for the extension of my fame, than I have ever been." In domestic affairs, he followed John Adams' principles of republican "balance" and personal rectitude in the face of "private malice and public faction." In foreign affairs, he held strictly to George Washington's—the father of his country—policy of neutrality. Not only was the policy a wise one for the survival of the infant republic, young Adams believed, but the general's character made it nearly impossible to oppose him. Washington was "one of the greatest names that ever appeared upon earth for the pride and consolation of the human race," he informed a correspondent. "I feel it is an inestimable happiness to have been the contemporary of that man."[89]

John Quincy Adams came home in 1801. With the election of a new administration in 1800, President John Adams ordered his son back to America. After returning, the young diplomat practiced law in Boston for a couple of years before being elected to the U.S. Senate in 1803 by the Massachusetts legislature. He appeared first as a maverick Federalist in the national councils in the nation's capital, pursuing a typical Adams path of lonely self-reliance. The New Englander, for instance, was the only man from his section in either house of Congress to uphold the acquisition of Louisiana. He also supported Jefferson's embargo, and by 1808 he had grown so sympathetic to Jeffersonian politics that he attended the Jeffersonian's Congressional caucus. His Federalist support at home crumbled.[90]

John Quincy's role of stubborn independence in the Senate materialized in part from his hard-won self-control. His personal reflections from the period contained strict injunctions against indulgence of the emotions. "My self-examination this night gave rise to many mortifying reflections," he wrote typically in 1803. "Pride and self-conceit and presumption lie so deep in my natural character, that, when their deformity betrays them, they run through all the changes of Proteus, to disguise themselves to my own heart." Often this cultural compulsion spilled over into personal disdain for colleagues, as when Adams described Congressman Claiborne of Virginia as "a man of ruined fortune and habitual intoxication." Most of all, however, self-control translated into political independence for Senator

Adams because of party passion. He became convinced that rational, moral judgments of merit had retreated before the "furies of faction" as both Federalists and Jeffersonians gave free rein to "impetuous violence" and "political phrenzy." Although admitting a "strong temptation . . . to plunge into political controversy," he resisted and strove to "set aside all party spirit." For Adams, political self-reliance, even at the sacrifice of popularity, became a matter of personal character. As he wrote in his diary shortly after entering the Senate in 1803, with the republic "so totally given up to the spirit of party," he stood ready to give up advancement and reputation, while remaining "determined to have the approbation of my own reflections."[91]

This lonely role, however, also found inspiration from Adams' reverence for the Founding Fathers. In 1807 a poem entitled "A Winter's Day" set down a brief but suggestive description of his Senate labors: "There with the fathers of the land, / I mix in sage deliberation, / And lend my feeble voice and hand / With equal laws to bless a nation." Yet again, this desire to tread in the footsteps of the Fathers followed most faithfully the trail of old John Adams. As John Quincy made clear on numerous occasions, his lonely avoidance of party affiliation was partly an attempt to emulate the admirable course of his father. He wrote to the elder Adams in 1805, "I have never in my gloomiest moments considered my situation as of so trying or severe a nature as was yours during the whole period of our revolutionary controversy." This paternal identification also appeared in letters to friends, many of which stoically noted the unrelenting persecution coming from "personal enemies of my father and myself." Unpopularity that resulted from "passions, and prejudices, and personal enmities" became a badge of honor for continued loyalty to the virtuous politics of the Founders. John Quincy assured William Eustus in 1809, "I have no fear that either my father or myself will leave to after ages a name, at which my children will ever have occasion to blush."[92]

Abandoned by the Federalists, half-heartedly seduced by the Jeffersonians, John Quincy Adams stood alone in his own mind as a heroic practitioner of the politics of virtue. He often wrote to his father for psychological support. Noting his frequent selection by the Republican majority to play crucial committee roles in the Senate, he described himself with bitter irony as "a leader without followers." "I am compelled, therefore, to lean upon my own judgement more than it will always bear," John Quincy told his paternal confidant. "My only consolation is in the consciousness of good intentions and unwearied attention to my duty." He proudly defied the "accumulated personal malignity borne me, both on my father's and my own account." Writing to William Branch Giles in 1808, he proudly explained his political "martyrdom"; "I consider every calumny cast upon me, as the tribute of profligate passions to honest principle." His Senate career thus became a private proving ground for commitments to self-control and the legacy of the Founding Fathers. His Senate resignation in 1808 confirmed this loyalty. He rejected Republican political overtures in Massachusetts and determinedly warned himself, "In the dreams of others' fancies, may the reality of my own situation be present to myself, and teach me the steady possession of myself."[93]

By 1808 another highly charged issue gradually began to engage the private politics of John Quincy Adams. Unresolved tensions with England and France—especially the former—made armed conflict an increasing possibility for the young republic. Adams had supported the Republican embargo—this move had finalized his ostracism by New England Federalists—as a measure that would preserve American neutrality, give the republic time to gather strength, and allow for a negotiated settlement of commercial disputes. But the Massachusetts statesman became steadily preoccupied with the question of war. He typically moved with great caution and rationality. War, Adams observed, unfortunately seemed to be the spirit "of the age upon which we have fallen. This spirit of ambition, of glory and of conquest burns in Europe with an intenseness beyond all former example." In the manner of his father, he acidly noted that war remained "far from being extinguished by the flood of philosophy which poured upon that self-conceited dupe, the eighteenth century." Nevertheless, the younger Adams cautioned his countrymen against hasty involvement in martial adventure. The immature American republic, he believed, would likely suffer intense internal divisions and total destruction of her commerce in a conflict. An 1808 public letter to Harrison Gray Otis outlined his position. He condemned English impressment and commercial depredations, chastised the Federalists for subverting a unified American response, and upheld the American right to resist English "pillage." Yet he rejected extreme alternatives of "voluntary servitude" or dangerous war. The embargo, he continued to believe, offered a reasonable course of resistance. As late as January 1812 Adams warned against "a war in which we could gain nothing and could not fail to lose something of what is worth more than all other possessions to nations, our independence."[94]

Between 1808 and 1812, however, Adams moved by fits and starts toward endorsement of armed conflict with England. He characteristically rejected a rationale of anger, arguing that war should not be undertaken "presumptuously, nor impelled by passion, nor without a precise and definite object for which to contend." The issue of impressment came to meet that criteria. In 1811 the New Englander asserted that while he still believed it "better to wait the effect of our increasing strength and our adversary's more mature decay," if necessary "I would advise my country to declare war explicitly and distinctly upon that single point [of impressment]." This was the perfect war issue for the stern advocate of morality and self-control, an issue that offered a rationale both private and national. "If ever there was a *just* cause for war in the sight of Almighty God, this cause is on our side just," he wrote to Thomas Boylston Adams in 1813. "The essence of this cause is on the British side *oppression*, on our side *personal liberty*."[95]

Beneath this veneer of statecraft and rationalization, however, gathered a compulsion to war that was intensely private, emotional, and moving. Long-standing personal predicaments crept into John Quincy Adams' advocacy of armed conflict. The severely repressed man spoke first. "The time is apparently coming when the temper and character of the American people will be tried by a test to which, since the war of our revolution, they have been strangers," he reflected in 1811. "The school of affliction is, however, as necessary to form the moral character of nations as of individuals. I hope that ours will be purified by it." But while this rational, self-controlled voice depicted a contest for the strengthening of "moral character," the passionate man beneath also sensed in war an opportunity for emotional release. He wrote in March 1812, "It is quite time for us to show, what for my part I never doubted, that there is among us a latent energy capable of being roused into action . . . [of which] a large portion of our own people have [not] any suspicion." Adams' prowar discourse resonated with calls for regenerated "martial ardor" and a legitimate venting of American wrath. He explained to his mother:

> There are great and glorious qualities in the human character which as they can unfold themselves only in time of difficulty and danger seem to make war from time to time a necessary evil among men. . . . God grant that in suffering the unavoidable calamities we may recover in all their vigor the energies of war!

The fact that Great Britain had come to symbolize a licentious, "infamous compound of robbery, perjury, and fraud"—ruled by "the maniac" George III—further justified Adams' righteous crusade of the passions. "The only temper that honors a nation is that which rises in proportion to the pressure upon it," he wrote, "and I trust our enemies will find our country in the day of trial true to herself."[96]

The anxious heir of the Revolutionary legacy joined the man of emancipated passion in 1812. While the obedient offspring of the Founders counseled neutrality and a measured building of strength to preserve the republic he inherited, the self-deprecating, insecure, and vaguely resentful Son discerned an occasion for equalizing, and possibly even surpassing, the achievements of the Fathers. Writing to his brother in the summer of 1812, John Quincy Adams hoped that "the spirit which conducted us through that [war] of our revolution may again lead us in triumph through all its evils." The intensity of this oedipal complex revealed itself more clearly yet in a letter written after hostilities had commenced. Corresponding with William Harris Crawford, Adams wrote emotionally, "If our countrymen are not all bastards, if there is a drop of the blood flowing in their veins that carried their fathers through the Revolutionary War, the prolongation of hostilities will only be to secure ultimately to us a more glorious triumph." In a rare lapse into sentimental confession—here to his brother Thomas Boylston Adams—John Quincy disclosed at some length the highly personal and familial dynamic that helped drive him to support the 1812 conflict. He recalled scenes of Revolutionary Boston and prayed that a new conflict would not expose his children "to such perils as those which surrounded your childhood and mine." But his final prayer was that a righteous war, to his own progeny "as to me," would heighten their patriotism and "mingle the remembrances of evil overcome and of deliverance from distress with all the first traces of conscious existence and of opening intellect."[97]

If Adams understood the 1812 war to be a vindicating demonstration of Revolutionary virtue, he hoped that it would ultimately give the Sons a secure identity of their own as heroes of the republic. In 1811 Adams had paid tribute to his father for his long struggle to have "*balance* established as the great and fundamental principle of the American Constitution." He explained to old John a few months later his own quest:"*Union* is to me what the *balance* is to you, and . . . without this there can be . . . no good government among the people of North America in the state in which God has pleased to place them." "I look to the *Union* of our country as to the sheet anchor of our hopes," he had informed a friend years earlier. His 1808 *Letters to Harrison Gray Otis* had been intended "to promote Union at home, and urge to vigor against foreign hostile powers." The second war with Great Britain, he made clear to William Plumer in 1813, was a crusade for union. "If in such a war we have not been able to unite," he declared, "it is evident that nothing can unite us for the purpose of war." But perhaps most important, he went on, a war for union would establish the Sons' authority in the eyes of *their* offspring, since "the question is not how many of our children we shall sacrifice without resistance to the Minotaur of the ocean, but whether our children shall have any security to protect them from being devoured by them."[98]

In 1793 a younger John Quincy Adams had revealed the complex psychological dynamic that would drive him over the next two decades, and perhaps over his entire life. Presenting a July 4 oration to the citizens of Boston, he observed that much of the audience at the time of the Revolution had like himself been too young "to partake of the divine enthusiasm which inspired the American bosom." They felt only slightly "the passion for the public [that] had absorbed all the rest." But the youthful orator implored older paternal patriots to reject the notion that America's sons "have degenerated from the virtues of their fathers."

> Let it rather be a subject of pleasing reflection to you that the generous and disinterested energies, which you were summoned to display, are permitted to remain latent in the bosoms of your children. . . . Should the voice of our country's calamity ever call us to her relief, we swear by the precious memory of the sages who toiled, and of the heroes who bled in her defence, that we will prove ourselves not unworthy of the prize, which they so dearly purchased.

By 1812 America's voice indeed began to call, and the son of John Adams rushed to her martial standard. The prospect of war offered a series of private remedies: legitimate expression for tightly bound passions, a scaffolding for erecting a younger generation's authority, and an arena for rivaling the exploits of the Founders. After all, John Quincy Adams had confessed several years earlier that "a profound anxiety" persistently tormented him. He confided to his diary, "The situation of two objects the nearest to my heart, my father and my country, press continually my reflections." The War of 1812 would go far toward relieving that pressure.[99]

War as Personal Quest: The Inner Healing of the Liberal Individual

In the summer of 1812, Asa Aikens addressed the Republican citizens of the small town of Windsor, Vermont. Endorsing war against Great Britain, he quickly established a generational tone for his argument. "Fathers and Fellow Citizens," he began. Gazing at the young faces in the audience, he described "American sons, who retain the first love of their fathers," and exhorted them to "unite in the celebration [of independence] as our fathers united in the achievement." The Vermont orator then raised his speech to its climax by depicting the 1812 conflict with England as a generational provingground. "We are now commencing another war, in vindication of those sovereign rights which our fathers bled to acquire," he declared. He emotionally pressed on the Sons their obligation to fight for the republic.[100]

At nearly the same time in the middle states, Hezekiah Niles wrote a passionate editorial in *Niles' Weekly Register* entitled "War with England." The ruling metaphor of the piece was also familial, but slightly altered. Niles depicted the American republic as a maturing youth, and the war as a test of its manhood. During the Revolution, this war advocate argued, "we were as children, devoid of arms and munitions of war, destitute of everything but patience and courage." The next thirty years, however, had witnessed tremendous development in the United States. "In 1812," Niles pointed out, "we have a stable and solid government . . . [and] are abundantly supplied with weapons of defence." The Jeffersonian journalist aggressively concluded, "We are in a state of comparative manhood, and will meet the enemy with confidence over whom we triumphed in infancy."[101]

Even farther south in Virginia, the citizens of Fauquier and Prince William counties met in a raucous July 4, 1812, celebration of war with the English. The *National Intelligencer* reported that the crowd "drank with repeated plaudits" the first two toasts of the evening. The tributes that attracted such boisterous enthusiasm mixed images of America-as-growing-youth, intimidating Revolutionary Fathers, and insecure Sons eager to justify themselves and straining toward violence. The Virginians raised their glasses to

> 1st. The Congress of '76—The patriotism which dared to proclaim the independence of America, while in her infancy, weak, defenceless, & invaded by a powerful foe, we will not disgrace, in the second generation, by shrinking from a contest, now, when we are in the strength of manhood, and our resources are an hundred fold increased.
> 2d. The Memory of the Heroes, whose blood stained the fields of the Revolution—Their spirits shall fire the bosoms, and nerve the arms of their sons in the day of battle with their ancient army.[102]

By the spring of 1812 similar appeals echoed throughout the length and breadth of the United States. Jeffersonian discourse resounded with metaphors of Founding Fathers and wandering Sons, in a generational drama that promised a denouement in war against an external, "ancient" enemy. The taut rhetoric of Fathers and Sons channeled several emotional currents into the war movement. Chaf-

ing under the restraints of self-control, anxious over the establishment of personal authority in a fluid liberal society, and struggling
for identity beneath the masks of the personae, troubled liberal individuals succumbed to the varied seductions of armed conflict. Psychologically, Republican Sons had several things to prove in 1812,
both to themselves and to others.

In a compelling sense the offspring of the Founders felt a strong
need to demonstrate their resilient virtue. Lured by the material
attractions of liberalizing change in post-Revolutionary America,
they could show through war that they had not become unworthy
creatures of ambition and avarice. As a Congressional committee
declared after William Henry Harrison engaged the Indians in early
1812, the Battle of the Wabash offered proof that the Revolutionary
spirit "has not been diminished by more than thirty years of almost
uninterrupted peace, but that it has been handed down unimpaired
to . . . posterity." As many newspapers constantly assured, "the independence established by the valor of our fathers will not be tamely
yielded by their sons." The *Kentucky Argus* echoed this message in
December 1811. The republic should be inspired to wartime effort
by an illustrious example from the past, wrote the editors: "The
departed spirits of the heroes of the revolution, will not discourage
exertions and courage in so noble a cause."[103]

Yet if American Sons seemed eager to prove what they were not,
they also were driven in 1812 to establish what they were. In many
ways, war with Great Britain took shape as an oedipal struggle. Both
respectful and resentful of their "heroic" Revolutionary forebears—
and themselves set loose as individuals in the highly pressurized
atmosphere of a competitive society—many early-nineteenth-century
Americans were desperate to secure personal authority. Like John
Quincy Adams, they sought to escape the paternal domination of the
past and ascend to prominence in their own right. War promised a
heroic means to do so. Hezekiah Niles, for example, acknowledged
in 1811 that America's youth should try to emulate their fathers, but
he added pointedly, "Most of the actors in the great scenes of those
times have departed; a new generation supplies their place." An
anonymous essayist in the summer 1812 *National Intelligencer* further
illuminated this instinct for replacing the Fathers. The national crisis
demanded that all Americans rally to the war effort, he wrote. Yet the
author insisted that older patriots should now step aside for the
"young, active, and enterprising." The Fathers had "done enough
hitherto in preserving our liberties and nurturing us to manhood; let
their sons now resume their stations, and ease them of their toils."[104]

Underlying resentment of the legacy of the Founding Fathers

could not be directly expressed, of course, so early-nineteenth-century Sons often sublimated it into the war effort in complex ways. James Kirke Paulding, for instance, in a popular 1812 satire depicted war as a generational clash. "Brother Jonathan"—his symbol for the young republic—appeared as the "son" in the narrative. The threatening father-figure, however, was not American but old "John Bull," or Great Britain. Jonathan felt a deep affection for his father and would have responded to paternal kindness, Paulding suggested in a suggestive oedipal metaphor. "Still, when the father . . . makes use of his superior power to depress rather than exalt his offspring, it is not to be wondered at if the ties of relationship are broken forever." Jeffersonian commentators also made different connections or displacements regarding war and paternal resentment. Newspaper editorials, for example, lavishly praised the Revolutionary heroes for presenting their heirs with a free republican government. But nervously surveying a scene of overburdened and agitated Sons, they warned that brotherly friction might destroy that heritage. Rather than quarreling among themselves for dominance, urged one editorial, blades of anger "should be pointed against the enemies of our country." Whatever the path of sublimation, a war to establish new generational authority emerged as the common denominator. As John Giles urged young listeners in a prowar address of August 1812, they had to prove themselves worthy of the Founders: "Prove, that you not only inherit their names, but likewise their courage; that you will not detract from their glory, but maintain with your blood, undiminished, the fair inheritance which they have bequeathed you."[105]

This oedipal dynamic shaded a less obvious but equally important psychological urge to war. Driven to ever-greater efforts of repression by bourgeois strictures of self-control, liberal individuals also yearned for occasional release of libidinous energy. Like Charles Brockden Brown, Alfred Brunson, and John Quincy Adams, many citizens of the early republic found the struggle for self-dominion and instinctual restraint to be only intermittently, or superficially, successful. Thus war emerged in part as a violent "return of the repressed." As the *Western Intelligencer* suggested in January 1812, war promised far greater exhilaration than the "lucrative business" of everyday market pursuits. "Let there ever be an opportunity for activity and exertion, and men of more character will rally round the standard."[106]

This return of the repressed often appeared in primitive bursts of blood-lust. Like Charles Brockden Brown in his dark fiction, Americans becoming accustomed to marketplace rationalization often yearned for the gratifying expression of sensuality and violence. Charles Ingersoll, for example, relished the picture of citizens "springing from the ease and enjoyments of profound relaxation, to grasp the rusted sword, and brighten it in the blood of their aggressors." Some men, like Spencer Cone, grew obsessed by 1812 with war images of "a mailed Mars, up to the ears in blood." Or, like Henry Clay and Philip Freneau, others railed against the cringing softness created by American prosperity and envisioned the violent strength of angry American republicans in wartime. Even Parson Weems, that paragon of innocuous self-restraint, momentarily dropped his morals to expose a hidden core of violent fantasy. Writing breathlessly to President Madison, he urged him to turn American rage against the British by constructing primitive land mines. "Tar'd, Canvas hose, or tubes (one inch diameter) . . . filled with gunpowder and laid in deep furrows . . . w'd in a moment annihilate their Troops and their Hopes," he wrote with bright-eyed anticipation. Another minister concluded on July 4, 1812, that the Sons needed to follow in "the bloody tracks of . . . the heroes that fought and bled for the freedom of the states."[107]

Republican advocates also frequently utilized "fire" as an image for the release of instinctual energy in wartime. Sigmund Freud once pointed out that "tongues of flame as they shot upward" have traditionally been associated in Western culture with natural power and phallic assertion. Usually perceived as a force to be extinguished or controlled, fire when unrestrained represents the unharnessing of primal urges. A Pennsylvania Republican thus rejoiced in 1812, "The manly propensities of the American people are not longer confined, like hidden fires, to consume their own entrails, but kindled and directed against foreign aggression." "May the fire of our Fathers be transmitted to their Sons," declared a group of New York militiamen. Congressman Robert Wright of Maryland concurred in December 1811, proclaiming to his colleagues that if British outrages did not rouse the anger of American citizens, "I fear the sacred fire that inspired your fathers in the Revolution is nearly extinguished." The *National Aegis* graphically summarized of this straining toward release on the eve of war, "We believe . . . the revolutionary spark is not extinguished, the flame if once kindled again will blaze out; and we believe too, if it does it will blaze with consuming fury."[108]

A recurring refrain in these bloodstained and fire-singed calls to war stressed that conflict offered *legitimate* expression for libidinous instincts otherwise banned. Here the British emerged as psychological straw men, particularly regarding their alliance with the Indian.

Jeffersonian newspapers habitually presented the atrocities of English-style war as justifications for American violence. They blasted British pretensions to religious morality by sarcastically noting "the practical correspondence between the *bible societies* and the *tomahawk*—between *vital religion* and the *scalping knife*." Parson Weems, urging adoption of his "land mine" scheme, suggested that British barbarity richly deserved such a murderous tactic. "The Modern Goths, our Enemy, think it no harm to employ rockets, bombs, and red hot shot," he wrote warmly. "Why not follow their example?" William Hull, a frontier general and Republican partisan, gave a cold and quietly furious rationale for this legitimation of American libido in war:

> If the barbarous and savage policy of Great Britain be pursued, and the savages are set loose to murder our citizens and butcher our women and children, this war will be a war of extermination. The first stroke of the tomahawk—the first attempt with the scalping knife will be the signal of one indiscriminate scene of desolation. No white man found fighting by the side of an Indian will be taken prisoner; instant destruction will be his lot.[109]

This cathartic "war of extermination" ultimately promised to correct perhaps the largest psychological difficulty of emerging liberal individualism. The violence of war—sometimes in actuality, more often in fantasy—offered a means to the achievement of cohesive identity for the diffuse personality structure of the "personae." For ambitious Jeffersonian individuals anxiously struggling with the manipulative masks of success, war tendered the possibility of personal unity in several ways. First, historical analysts of emotion and personality believe that an "unintegrated personality," like that of the "personae" exudes a regressive kind of "rage" as a consequence of inner tension and unresolved anxiety.[110] Bloody visions of martial violence in 1812, like the gory fantasies of Brockden Brown's novels, indeed suggested a playing out of such unconscious fury. Apocalyptic visions of "extermination," "desolation," "consuming fury," "up to the ears in blood," and "annihilation" emerged as cathartic, outward explosions of primitive rage by emancipated but deeply divided individuals.

Yet according to the language of war in 1812, the schizoid structure of the liberal "personae" also turned primitive rage inward. Tormented by a fragmented personality, isolated individuals saw in self-destruction a means of personal peace and formulated a death wish as a halcyon resolution of inner incoherence. Thus many Jeffersonian appeals in 1812 promoted war as a legitimate, sanctioned

ritual of death and presented seductive expressions of self-annihila-
tion. Both Philip Freneau and Spencer Cone rejoiced that "it is sweet
to die for one's country," and Freneau judged such a demise to be the
"height of virtue and the perfection of felicity." Alfred Brunson
vowed "not to do anything that I would not be willing to die in the
act" and subsequently entered the army to "either rise to distinction or
fall in the attempt." Republican newspapers, such as the *National
Intelligencer*, added simply a recommendation "to live free, or die."
It is little wonder that Richard Rush, in rallying war support from his
fellow citizens in 1812, pledged to his forefathers "to wipe away all
past stains or . . . we will die. Then shall we render our ashes worthy
to mingle with yours."[111]

However much war may have vented the primitive rage of the
liberal "personae" in 1812, drawing anger inward as well as throwing it outward, war also proved attractive as an identity catalyst in a
more positive sense. Rather than merely projecting or internalizing
the frustrations of unintegrated personality, the martial crusade
against Great Britain ultimately promised to weld together the fragments of the "personae" through a sort of primal, genuine experience
that would overwhelm the materialistic, duplicitous masks of social
intercourse in a liberal society. Nearly all appeals to war in the
months before the summer of 1812 paid homage to the straightfor-
ward energy and vitality of the battlefield. Usually this was contrasted with the serpentine, dissembling, calculating quality of
American commercial life. Republican critics warned that greed had
carried America to commercial degradation and loss of honor, and
that money-obsessed citizens needed to be "retrieved from the im-
putation of apathy." With war, they proclaimed, "the martial spirit
of freemen is aroused to action." Prowar newspapers commonly
spoke of war as comprising "the regenerated spirit of freedom." It is
significant that Republican rhetoric also consistently displaced on the
British enemy the imagery of deceit. The English appeared as representatives of "fraud, forgery, and perjury," while analyses of British
aggression carried titles like "The Mask Thrown Off." Domestic
war opponents earned the epitaph of "counterfeits" from war advocates who contended that "as soon as their [bank] drafts are dishon-
oured, their masks fall." One newspaper enthused that an 1811
Congressional call to war deserved applause as an invitation to genuine, forthright, spontaneous experience: "This manly appeal to the
People will go at once to their heart. It breathes the American
spirit."[112]

The fluid and perturbed "personae" found another congealing
element that tendered immediate cohesion in 1812. As Erik Erikson

has argued, stages of the human life cycle involve working through a series of endemic personal and environmental difficulties toward a full sense of identity or "wholeness." Wholeness, defined as the ability of a strong ego to accommodate and integrate disparate experiences, marks the securely maturing personality. This personal process is reinforced throughout life by social institutions like the church, the family, the community, and the work group. But in periods when social structures become unstable or diffuse, Erikson continues, the achievement of wholeness becomes unusually problematic and an alternative strategy for psychic survival beckons: the gaining of a pseudo-wholeness through "total" solution. Isolated, anxious, and distrustful, the individual constructs identity not through integration but by paranoid definition. Instead of cohesively binding together life experiences, the ego defines itself by separating the world into good and bad, friend and enemy, objects of hatred and identification, "me" and "not-me." In 1812 their discourse suggests that the troubled "personae" of many early-nineteenth-century Jeffersonians embraced war as being a "total" means to identity.[113]

The tenor of discussion and the use of certain images among war enthusiasts offered fleeting glimpses of this delusory process of inner definition. For example, an anonymous newspaper contributor styling himself "An Enemy to Submission" argued that the issue of war raised questions for the individual American as "an independent man": whether he could protect and support his family, whether he could pursue the career of his choice, whether he "may be justly charged with submission." Commentators also frequently utilized a metaphor of emerging manhood—the classic age of identity crisis—to sanction war with Great Britain. According to one, "In our infancy we humbled their pride. . . . If we achieved such exploits in our infant state, what shall we not, through providence, be able to do now, in our manhood." Even James Madison pursued this theme. "If our first struggle [the Revolution] was a war of our infancy," he wrote, "this last was that of our youth."[114]

Emotional expressions of paranoid definition further seasoned Republican war appeals. Outlandish, overheated messages portrayed Great Britain as the embodiment of all evil in the world. Anxious and insecure critics pictured England as a "disgusting, distorted picture of bloated depravity" and proclaimed her an ally of "the flesh pots of Egypt." Agitated speakers flailed its government as "founded and cemented in blood, and its tottering state, still upheld by blood." Congressmen declaimed against Great Britain's "diabolical brutalities on our seaboard—their rapine, rapes, and indiscriminate outrages—their game of ruin, spoil, and havoc" and "refinements of

barbarity which no savage ever exceeded." With such a psychological
view of their enemies, Americans adopted a looking-glass image of
themselves as robust defenders of humanity, morality, and civilized
values. Citizens of the republic collectively comprised a growing
young "hercules," assured one Republican newspaper, and "let the
serpents of despotism attack us, and our strength will be manifest."
Henry Clay elaborated the dynamic of identity, telling his fellow
Kentuckians that 1812 provided an opportunity to show they were not
"savages." They could establish themselves in war, he contended,
"by shewing their calumniator that they were not only brave, but
humane and merciful when circumstances permitted." Hezekiah
Niles perhaps best reflected the search of the liberal "personae" for
"total," oversimplified identity in war. The conflict, he proclaimed
to Americans, would benefit them by "giving us a NATIONAL CHAR-
ACTER, and separating us from the strumpet governments of Europe."[115]

The cathexis of armed violence in 1812 thus summoned several
haunting apparitions from the psyche of early-nineteenth-century
liberal men: the desperate need to establish generational authority, the
yearning for a "return of the repressed," the straining toward integration of fragmented personality. By these psychological currents
they could not fully see, many Jeffersonian Republicans were carried
toward war. They knew only that they stood in the shadow of the
Founding Fathers and felt compelled, in the words of one war advocate, to become "a band of American brothers" to defend their inheritance by force. About such Americans of the early 1800s D. H.
Lawrence once made a shrewd observation:

> Always the same. The deliberate consciousness of Americans so fair and
> smooth-spoken, and the under-consciousness so devilish. Destroy! de-
> stroy! destroy! hums the under-consciousness. Love and produce! love
> and produce! cackles the upper consciousness. And the world hears only
> the Love-and-produce cackle. Refuses to hear the hum of destruction
> underneath. Until such time as it will *have* to hear.

The world might have begun to hear in 1812 as the "hum of destruction" built to a roar, but Lawrence was only half-right regarding
Americans of that era. Sensitive ears also would have detected a
lower-pitched, more pathetic groan issuing from the under-con-
sciousness of Jeffersonian Americans. While war exploded with the
exhilarated shouts of physical destruction, a quieter and more desperate voice sought also in it psychic peace and inner coherence. In this
latter, deeper sense war promised to heal the troubled spirit of the
early liberal "personae."[116]

V

Politics and Productivity:
War and the Emergence of Liberalism

A new political science is needed
for a world itself
quite new.

ALEXIS DE TOCQUEVILLE
Democracy in America

Political economy, this science of wealth is therefore
simultaneously the science of renunciation, of saving. . . .
The science of marvelous industry is simultaneously
the science of asceticism,
and its true ideal is an ascetic.

KARL MARX
Economic and Philosophic Manuscripts of 1844

The White Whale swam before him as the monomaniac incarnation
of all those malicious agencies which some men feel eating in them,
till they are left living on with half a heart and half a lung. . . .
all evil, to crazy Ahab, were visibly personified,
and made practically assailable in Moby-Dick.
He piled upon the whale's white hump the sum of all
the general rage
and hate felt by his whole race from Adam down;
and then, as if his chest had been a mortar,
he burst his hot heart's shell upon it.

HERMAN MELVILLE
Moby Dick

In many ways Joel Barlow had pivoted as an intellectual weather-vane in the post-Revolutionary American republic. In early man-hood a "Connecticut Wit" of Calvinist and Federalist leanings, this man of letters evolved in later life to become an ardent friend of both the French Revolution and Jeffersonian principles. Now in 1809, as he presented a Fourth of July oration to the "Democratic Citizens" of Washington, D.C., this unofficial adviser to Presidents Jefferson and Madison conveyed a curiously mixed message. He mixed bombast about the republic's potential with jeremiad-like brooding over her future and transmitted overall an unsettling sense of crisis.[1]

Events since the Revolution, Barlow contended, had "only prepared this gigantic infant of a nation to begin its own development." With the inevitable demise of the Revolutionary founders, weighty responsibilities had descended on a new generation in a new century. "Yes my friends, we are now the nation," claimed the New England Republican. "As such . . . instead of looking back with wonder upon our infancy, we may look forward with solicitude to a state of adolescence, with confidence to a state of manhood." Barlow's assessment of the problems facing the republic in 1809, however, was sobering, even frightening. He noted the hostility of European powers "whose political maxims are widely different from ours" and surveyed the "vast extent" of wild territory to be encompassed within the United States. He viewed with alarm internal political divisions, the experimental nature of the republic's attempt at "representative democracy on a large scale," and her harried "commercial relations" on the high seas. With such pressing difficulties on all sides, the orator admitted his "anxiety" about a secure American future: "The difficulty of attaining it and the danger of losing it, are sufficient to cloud the prospect in the eyes of many respectable citizens and force them to despair."[2]

This volatile situation, Barlow insisted, required "new theories," "new and bold . . . experiments," and "deep reflection." Personally the New Englander believed that implementation of *"public improvements"* and *"public instruction"* would best guarantee the republic's survival. The former—and here he meant the building of roads, canals, and bridges—promised both to connect a far-flung citizenry and to boost "the value of property and the wealth of individuals." The latter project of education also would bind "members of the great community" while providing the citizen with "instruction necessary to enable him to discriminate between the characters of men." These undertakings were doubly important, Barlow concluded, because of the likelihood of war and the probable need "for money to repel foreign aggression."[3]

Joel Barlow's 1809 remarks typified the sense of urgency that dominated American political life by 1812. His perception of crisis, his emphasis on the construction of fresh ideological approaches, and his sensitivity to the role of war in this situation reflected widely held concerns. Various anxieties festering in the American body politic since the 1790s had grown acute in the early nineteenth century, especially among younger figures in the post-1800 Jeffersonian coalition. From the Embargo of 1807–8, through the nonintercourse acts that followed, to the bitter debates culminating in war in June 1812, there occurred in Jeffersonian discourse a profound questioning of the key ideals of traditional American republicanism: civic virtue, an organic notion of society blending popular sovereignty and deference, and a political economy committed to commercial agriculture, the export of surplus produce, and international free trade. Confidence in these tenets had been eroding subtly for some twenty-odd years from pressures of economic development and liberalizing change, but the gathering war crisis tightly focused a number of concerns that were previously inchoate. This disquietude over republicanism sprang particularly from three broad areas of ideological ferment.

The first area was a growing concern over republican political values that was rooted in the social and cultural changes issuing from the consolidation of liberal capitalism. The emerging creed of the self-made man, with its emphasis on ambitious individualism, had raised serious problems for American republicans. As we have seen, fears of avarice and ambition, "confidence men," and faction had grown pronounced by the early nineteenth century.[4] It is significant that such misgivings often were translated under pressure into political language. Republicans like Philip Freneau, Benjamin Rush, Henry Clay, Spencer H. Cone, and Charles J. Ingersoll frequently raised their voices in the context of Congressional discussions or in the forum of partisan newspaper debates. Social and cultural quandaries became politicized in several ways.

For many, what seemed to be a wholesale abandonment of republican civic virtue comprised the heart of the problem. While the fact of self-interest reluctantly had been granted by the Founding Fathers in their construction of the Constitution, they had hoped to negate its influence by balancing and checking selfishness in the internal structure of the American government.[5] But since 1790 the swelling spirit of individual gain seemed increasingly about to overwhelm republicanism itself. American politics threatened to degenerate into the negotiations of the countinghouse. The nation had fallen into disgrace, mourned one newspaper: "The love of money has prostrated our public measures—the spirit of commercial avarice has shed its malignant, stupifying venom upon our councils— A gold calf has stood up among us, and we have bowed down before the idol. We must arouse from our prostration." Congressman Peter Porter of New York added his own reservations in 1810. Granting the quantum leap in American "external commerce" over the previous twenty years, he worried, "Our citizens have not only grown rich, but they have gone almost mad in pursuit of this commerce."[6]

Anxiety over the political import of commercial values led some Jeffersonians to question whether Americans could be roused to any civic commitment above pecuniary gain. Concern for the good of the republic seemed to be vanishing as "our jealous regard of national honor began to fade before the meretricious charms of inglorious ease and tranquility." As a writer in the *Philadelphia Aurora* typically complained in 1811, many citizens seemed eager to "form an interest separate from and adverse to the general interest, and to sacrifice the general interest to this partial interest. This operation has already been felt with great severity." Critics like Washington Irving worried more that Americans had failed to integrate commercial prosperity into their republican ideology, but instead slipped into a petty political mode of parsimony and money-grubbing. His imaginary Turkish visitor "Mustapha" explained this political pollution in 1807. "ECONOMY" was "the watchword of this nation," he wrote, but it seemed to constitute "a kind of national starvation, and experiment how many comforts and necessaries the body politic can be deprived of before it perishes."[7]

If concern over the political impact of commercialized values provided one source of republican disquietude by 1810, uncertainty over the direction of American economic development comprised the second. The emergence of a commercialized economy and corresponding market structures had posed increasingly difficult problems for late-eighteenth-century American republicans. At one end of the spectrum, some had embraced commerce as a liberating instrument by which to pry loose the choking grip of a "feudal" past.[8] At the opposite end, others could not reconcile the private pursuit of profit with civic virtue and voiced fears that economic growth would lead the republic to "luxury" and "decline."[9] The great mass of American Jeffersonians, however, struggled to accommodate commerce to republicanism by endorsing—with varying degrees of enthusiasm—an expansive program of geographic expansion, limited commercial agriculture, household manufactures, and international free trade for the export of surplus commodities. This moderate "commercial republicanism," it was hoped, would allow the American polity to remain at a "middle stage" of economic development somewhere between barbarism and an overrefined, manufacturing society like that of Great Britain.[10] By the end of the first decade of the nineteenth century, however, the rapid evolution of America's commercial structure was straining the republican framework on which it was built. Among the Jeffersonian Republican majority, political economy became a subject for troubled ideological questioning in the years before 1812.

Few Americans sought to return to a precommercial past. Congressman Samuel L. Mitchill of New York admitted in 1811, "Our people . . . are bred to commerce; they are devoted to navigation; barter and sale are their delight; the spirit of business animates them. . . . It is not the question of whether our constituents shall be a commercial people or not. That die has long been cast. We are so." But anxiety over the consequences for the American body politic increasingly surfaced. Some worried about the survival of the small, independent, landowning farmer—the backbone of the virtuous republic. A Fourth of July toast in 1810 upheld "The Independent Yeomanry of the United States" and warned that "a bold peasantry, their country's pride, If once destroyed, can never be supplied." The *Richmond Enquirer* suggested in 1811 that the "marine mania" of foreign commerce was creating more problems than benefits—external clashes over navigation rights, internal discord over economic interests, the likelihood of war. Daniel Waldo Lincoln, in an 1810 speech in Boston, accurately portrayed slowly-growing suspicions of commerce, especially the overseas variety. "As a profitable servant of the common weal, let commerce be fostered and protected," argued this Republican, "but let not the independence of America be sacrificed in mercantile speculation."[11]

Some Jeffersonian Republicans began to question the civic commitment—at times even the loyalty—of American merchants involved in the Atlantic trade. Editors of the *New Hampshire Patriot* bitterly noted in 1811 that Republican administrations since 1800 had patronized overseas trade by enacting "discriminating Duties." "What use have the eastern nabobs, grown rich, immensely rich, under the protection of the government, made of their wealth acquired?" the paper demanded. "Has it not been employed as an engine to batter down the very fabric on which their whole prosperity has rested?" By 1810, Westerners like Richard M. Johnson

of Kentucky started to criticize the efficacy of Republican support
for free trade. Skeptical about whether "the merchants should be
permitted to go where and how they please without restraint," he
expressed misgivings about their "sordid and selfish views." Johnson declared emphatically, "The plain English to this objection
amounts to this, let the merchants dictate and govern the people of
the United States, and they will be satisfied, or sell the independence of this nation for gold." Such discontent with the minions of
overseas commerce prompted numerous Americans to consider new
avenues of economic endeavor. By 1810 many commentators were
urging "a judicious attention to the improvement of manufactures,
and the advancement of internal commerce." It was argued that
"domestic manufactures promote the real independence of our country . . . by establishing internal commerce and increasing their
[the states'] mutual reliance." European trade restrictions and violations only increased this sense that the republic's dependence on
commerce had come to a crucial juncture. In 1811 the *National
Intelligencer*, referring to the post-Revolutionary political economy,
stated, "A crisis must ensue. All temporizing must cease. Commerce must be abandoned or fought for."[12]

Yet for some early-nineteenth-century Jeffersonians, not commerce but republicanism itself gradually became the question at
issue. A vague but nagging sense of waning vitality in republican
ideology comprised a third great source of political uneasiness on the
eve of 1812. As an April 1812 editorial in the *National Intelligencer*
stated flatly, "That an important crisis has arrived in the U. States is
seen by everyone." European attacks on American neutral commerce, the failure of the embargo, and the reluctance of mercantile
groups to support a policy of resistance combined to undermine
American assumptions of republican vigor. A rhetoric of republican
emergency became endemic by 1810. Newspapers like the *Richmond Enquirer* dramatically proclaimed "the crisis that awaits us."
"The crisis will try the strength of our republican system," it stated
in May 1812. "Since the days of the Revolution, we have not
witnessed a crisis more important than the present." A few weeks
later the paper added: "The Embargo is repealed! every American
cheek is flushed with shame, our constitution is ridiculed for its
weakness." The editors of the *Philadelphia Aurora* consistently
chimed in on this chorus. "We consider the country this moment in
a situation which bears a strong analogy to the crisis of the revolution of 1776," they opined in 1812. "A state of things such as the
present, is not propitious to *republican government*." "Americanus,"
writing in the *National Intelligencer*, accurately expressed a wide-

spread perception of American republicanism at a crossroads. "The present crisis involves consequences to this nation of incalculable moment," he concluded in May 1812. "We are either to continue the happy possessors of liberty with its train of peculiar blessings; or we are to become enslaved and miserable."[13]

Domestic divisions combined with foreign affairs to challenge the resiliency of American republicanism from another direction. The political battles of 1800–1810—over the Louisiana Purchase, the embargo, commercial protection, and alliances with France or England—had cemented the trends of the 1790s and established the Federalists and Jeffersonian Republicans as organized, oppositional coalitions, if not quite parties. Yet ideological confusion increasingly muddied perceptions of the role of factions in a republican system. George Fowler's 1810 *Wandering Philanthropist*, for instance, in traditional fashion excoriated the antirepublican spirit of faction for distorting issues, inflaming public opinion, dividing the citizenry, and providing a vehicle for the power-hungry. Yet the author then pivoted to argue that perhaps party spirit "was destined to supply the place of pure disinterested benevolence, and so far as it answers this purpose it is valuable and salutary." Fowler conjectured that Americans "are so much governed by self-interest, so much engrossed in private concerns that a portion of party spirit is necessary to rouse the publick mind, to draw it from private concerns and give it a due attention to publick objects." Citizens like Washington Irving despaired more deeply about American republicanism and the problem of organized faction. His Turkish visitor "Mustapha" appeared in the 1807 *Salmagundi* sarcastically offering a unique plan of defense for the republic. The swelling legions of political writers, or "slang-whangers," should be marshaled and "exhorted to fire away without pity or remorse, in sheets, half-sheets, columns, hand-bills, or squibs—great canon, little canon, pica, german-text, stereotype—and to run through their enemies with sharp, pointed italics." The *Richmond Enquirer* summed up this sense of republican disintegration in February 1811. An editorial entitled "The Crisis" argued that because of American conduct "the tyrants of the old world ridicule the imbecility of republics. Our government is despised for its want of energy, and our people are held up to scorn for their unmanly sacrifice of rights at the shrine of money." With a glance toward the immediate future, the editors concluded that the vacillations of the republic "have left a stain upon our character, which some great and decisive effort is necessary to expunge."[14]

As historian Roger Brown noticed two decades ago, political

discourse in the years preceding the War of 1812 was saturated with
fears of "the republic in peril." The war, he argued, thus took shape
as a desperate defense of republicanism, an exercise that would
prove the efficacy of republican government and restore its luster as
a beacon to the world.[15] This argument, however, tells but half the
story. A sense of ideological crisis pervaded political discussions by
1810, but those seeking solutions did not just look backward and
seek a restoration of the virtuous republic. Social, cultural, and
economic change had made that impossible. Many concerned Jeffersonians peered uneasily into the future and asked hard questions
about the American republican tradition: Was the republic viable in
its present form? Did it deserve to continue? Did republican ideology need *somehow* to be altered or invigorated? So while the crisis
with Great Britain brought these issues to a head and while war
materialized in part as a test for the survival of the republic, it
comprised even more an emotional, fusing catalyst for latent impulses and tendencies of an emerging liberal ideology. The war
crisis served as an ideological bridge over which many Jeffersonians
walked—with varying degrees of sure-footedness—from the republican past into the liberal future. As a closer look at debates over
political economy and the republic's "strength" reveals, their political understanding had begun to shift critically but almost imperceptibly in the early years of the nineteenth century.

Tensions in Political Economy: Producers and the Home Market

The early-nineteenth-century crisis of republicanism raised new and
critical issues in American thinking about political economy. The
rapid development of overseas commerce in the 1790s first had
raised anxious questions about "speculation," "luxury," and "degeneracy" in American life. Then intensified European attacks on
American foreign commerce after 1803—initiated by the British
blockade of France and Napoleon's retaliatory Berlin and Milan
decrees—brought more immediate and pressing difficulties: declining prosperity, public outrage, ineffectual resistance by the American government. But most important in the long run, this dampen-
ing of the post-1793 trade boom prompted an uncertain, frustrated,
yet fundamental rethinking of Jeffersonian assumptions about the
direction of economic development.[16]

First there began to emerge a "producer" critique of commerce
that allied agriculture and manufactures while questioning both the
morality and utility of foreign trade. Second, an ideological coalition

gradually took shape favoring an integrated "home market." These two trends marked a significant departure from traditional Jeffersonian thinking about political economy. By altering the decades-old endeavor to keep the United States at a "middle stage" of development through geographically expansive agriculture and overseas commerce, this producer ethic and home-market sentiment helped shift developing American capitalism from an accumulative to an entrepreneurial stage. The dynamics of this shift also helped create a turbulent ideological atmosphere by 1812.

Producer concern over commercial speculation had arisen in Republican circles as early as the late 1790s. This skepticism grew to an angry censure of commercial groups by 1810 and echoed throughout much of the republic. For many citizens, mercantile interests came to represent the darker impulses of liberalizing change and economic development: avarice, selfishness, loss of virtuous character. James Madison, writing an anonymous newspaper piece on the "Embargo" in 1808, excoriated its merchant opponents as greedy men "who to personal dishonesty adds a total destitution of patriotism." Virginia governor John Tyler, in an 1810 message to the state legislature, also decried a "too great love of money, the prevailing passion of the times which would sacrifice the very independence of the country for a *Price*—for a mean and degraded commerce." In 1812 Asa Aiken of Vermont granted that "a neutral commerce was an honorable road to wealth and affluence" but questioned its role as a conductor for "foreign influence and foreign vices." Aiken concluded disapprovingly that because of its promise of wealth "the spirit of commerce keeps the passions of men in a state of perpetual effervescence."[17]

This fear of degraded commercial values prefaced a more serious analytical issue. Throughout the first decade of the nineteenth century, accusations steadily mounted that commercial endeavor was "unproductive" and hence of diminished value in American political economy. As early as 1794, Republican critics like John Taylor had described merchants as a "class unproductive," as "brokers, honourable and useful, whilst adhering to a steady line of commerce . . . but pernicious and dangerous, whilst speculating indiscriminately." Such sentiments had become rampant fifteen years later in many areas of the republic. Republican newspapers frequently observed by 1810 that "commerce is certainly beneficial to society in a secondary degree, but never should it have the ascendency over agriculture and manufacturing interests. These are our primary objects." The anonymous newspaper writer "Solon" concluded bluntly in 1811, "The merchant and the sailor constitute an *unproductive* class; and . . . they are only so far beneficial as they advance the interests of those classes that are productive."[18]

Thomas Cooper, an influential immigrant Jeffersonian, exemplified this Republican trend toward a producer critique of commerce around the dawn of the nineteenth century. Born in England and immigrating to the United States in the 1790s, he emerged as a leading Republican political economist and became a confidant and adviser to Presidents Jefferson and Madison. Cooper's background was both interesting and varied. It included an education at Oxford and broad training in scientific inquiry, especially chemistry and medicine. Moreover, in the early 1790s the young Englishman—he had been born in 1759—invested and lost much of his considerable family inheritance in a Manchester textile firm of "calico-printers." A growing interest in politics proved equally trying. Since his student days Cooper had been attracted to religious free-thinking and utilitarian political theory, and he emerged as a fast friend of the French Revolution. The author of several popular tracts favoring universal manhood suffrage, the right of revolution, and parliamentary reform, he was prosecuted for sedition in the 1790s and acquitted. Nevertheless, like other English radicals, such as Joseph Priestly, he succumbed to political pressure and removed to the United States. There Cooper gravitated toward the "Jefferson Circle" and immersed himself in Republican politics, science, and natural history. Working as a newspaper editor, he authored an important campaign pamphlet for Jefferson's 1800 election, and over the next few years he received a chair of chemistry at Carlisle College, was elected to the American Philosophical Society, and became a Pennsylvania state judge.[19]

It was as editor of *The Emporium of Arts and Sciences*, a position he assumed in 1813, that Cooper achieved his greatest influence. Although the journal pursued a wide variety of topics in history, science, and literature, its editor often focused on presenting his views, theretofore expressed in private correspondence and sporadic public essays, on what had become his primary intellectual interest: political economy. His theorizing typified the ferment occurring in Republican circles about issues of economic development and productivity in the early-nineteenth-century republic.

Cooper based his analysis in part on the doctrines of François Quesney, a French physiocrat and critic of mercantilism who had insisted that agriculture was "the sole productive labour, and the only source of revenue" for a nation. Adam Smith, however, provided an even greater influence. Said Cooper of *The Wealth of Na-*

tions, "It has been, and will in the future . . . continue to be *the book* on the subject of political economy." From such mentors this English émigré imbibed several principles that became the touchstones for his own musings on political economy. First, he insisted that self-interest—"the calculating foresight of individuals," he described it—must be acknowledged as the motivating factor in economic life. Cooper also stood convinced that the public good existed not in opposition to private gain, as traditional republicanism would have it, but rather as its culmination. "I am persuaded that the aggregate of individual [wealth], constitutes national wealth," he declared simply. Finally, this Republican theorist became firmly opposed to government guidance or regulation of economic endeavor. Government interference was misplaced "when it attempts to direct the capitalist what he shall do with his money," Cooper maintained. "Let the merchant, the manufacturer, the farmer, each carry his goods to market at his own risk." He emphatically stated in the 1813 *Emporium,* "Every treatise on political economy ought to have its first page occupied with . . . LET US ALONE."[20]

These tenets led Cooper by the late 1790s to several firm positions regarding American economic development. He viewed with considerable skepticism the post-1793 boom in the republic's foreign commerce that resulted from war between France and England. Denouncing an excessive reliance on foreign trade in 1799, he contrasted the merchant who "often gets rich by accident, by imprudent and unfair venturing, by sudden exertions" with those whose "gains can be made but slowly, gradually, and by the regular exertions of habitual, wholesome industry." While "a farmer, a mechanic, an engineer" worked to "increase the mass of consumable products," merchants were simply "unproductive persons." He wrote scathingly to Jefferson in 1806: "I know of no body of men, so ready to postpone the interests of their Country to their own Interests, as Merchants. They are truly a swinish multitude: touch but the bristle of one of them and the whole herd cry out murder."[21]

Though Cooper reviled overseas merchants as unproductive "swine," their ultimate danger lay in the short-lived, fragile prosperity they brought to the young republic. He argued in the *Emporium,* "It is a great misfortune when the existence of a people depends upon the sale of articles, which their customers can dispense with whenever they please and without inconvenience." Not only could foreign commerce be ended at any time by an external power, Cooper pointed out, but such endeavor—if relied on by the United States—would inevitably require government sustenance. Merchants continually clamored for "prohibitions and bounties," Cooper observed, while their speculations seemed always to involve "protection by engaging in wars on account of it, or manning navies for its defence." True to his laissez-faire principles, the political economist did not advocate banning or neglecting the foreign trade. He only wished that "it ought like every other losing scheme to be left to its own fate, without taxing the rest of the community and their posterity for its support."[22]

Another transplanted and prestigious Jeffersonian, Albert Gallatin, echoed the producer critique of commerce. Yet he did not content himself with mere intellectual influence. Gallatin actually grasped the reins of political power to implement, as well as shape, a fresh Republican political economy based largely on productivity. Coming to Pennsylvania from Switzerland in 1780, this Republican convert had risen through the ranks to become perhaps the party's leading spokesman on economic affairs by the late 1790s. Gallatin had been an entrepreneur in early manhood, and then had carved out a political reputation first in the Pennsylvania Assembly, then later on the Ways and Means Committee in the U.S. House of Representatives. Appointed secretary of the treasury in 1800—he would hold the post until 1813—he became, along with Presidents Jefferson and Madison, one of the powerful "triumvirate" who shaped national policy for the growing Republican consensus after the turn of the century.[23]

Before coming to this position of power, Gallatin had in 1796 given an important preview of his mature theory of political economy. Wearing the mantle of the opposition expert on public finance, the Pennsylvanian had published a comprehensive challenge to the fiscal programs of Alexander Hamilton and his Federalist successors in the Treasury Department. His *Sketch of the Finances of the United States*, a two-hundred-page critique of Federalist financial policy, became a manifesto for Republican congressmen. And its central motif—the encouragement of American "productivity"—revealed the fundamental assumptions and concerns that would preoccupy Gallatin over the next fifteen years.[24]

In attacking Hamilton's notorious policies for assuming, funding, and manipulating the national debt, *Sketch of the Finances* focused on the lack of "productive" incentive in the program. Gallatin argued that in seeking to bind wealthy investors to support of the new national government, Hamilton had in fact attracted mostly "speculators" and foreign capital. While there had been "some dazzling temporary effect" on America's economy, the primary result had been "an acquisition of wealth to speculators in stock alone, and not to the nation." Far better, argued the Pennsylvania congressman, for the labor and capital of American citizens to be placed in "the pursuits of private industry" where they would "increase the cultivation and improvement of lands, the erection of manufactures, [and] the annual income of the nation." Thus elimination of the national debt, which made "not the smallest addition either to the wealth or to the annual labor of a nation," became one of Gallatin's quests in political economy. As his *Sketch of the Finances* also announced, a reduction of the foreign trade and a boosting of domestic manufactures comprised another goal. The bulk of importations consisted of "luxuries," Gallatin pointed out, yet even with the infant state of America's manufactures "a great proportion of the most essentially necessary articles are made at home." Such productive endeavor seemed an attractive alternative to, in his words, "that most common evil in America, 'overtrading.'"[25]

Gallatin's criticisms of commerce became even more pronounced in a speech delivered before Congress two years later. Speaking against a measure to expand the American navy, Gallatin denied its necessity for "protection to our floating property on the sea," contending that foreign commerce was "a mere matter of calculation . . . a question of profit and loss" for its agents. Furthermore, it could not be understood correctly without dividing it into its productive and nonproductive elements. Useful overseas trade consisted of "that part of our commerce which consists of the exportation of our own produce," a trade where "the profits are divided between the merchant and the farmer" and which was "directly and immediately beneficial to the whole nation." On the other hand, Gallatin condemned the carrying and reexport trades as "not useful or productive," but only trafficking in "a sort of extraneous staple." Providing "no direct service to the farming interest, or to the nation at large," it served only the purpose of "increasing the wealth of these merchants." Unfortunately, however, the carrying trade comprised more than half the republic's commerce, and Gallatin could not see fit to grant it military protection. Not only would war be more likely, but the "enormous expence" of a large navy forced the question "to whom . . . that expence would prove most beneficial, and by whom it must finally be borne." It appeared clear to this Republican political economist that "unproductive" merchants would gain most, while "productive" farmers would pay most.[26]

Gallatin's critique of foreign trade led him to an additional assertion. He became convinced that "extensive commerce" did not promote national prosperity, contrary to the arguments of the proponents of extensive foreign trade. The "wealth of a nation," he insisted, depended on "internal industry" and those laws that encouraged it by protecting private property. Great Britain's navy and foreign trade had not produced her wealth but rather "the internal industry, and the protection afforded to manufactures and commerce, in that country." This fact led the Jeffersonian leader to conclude that an extensive navy would not contribute to "the encouragement of agriculture, manufactures, or anything really useful to society." This juxtaposition in 1799 of unproductive commerce with productive agriculture and manufactures, in the context of a vital domestic trade, emerged as the foundation of Gallatin's political economy and proposals over the next decade.[27]

Appointed secretary of the treasury in 1801 by the newly elected President Jefferson, Gallatin moved to put his notion of political economy into practice. Writing to Jefferson shortly after taking office, he noted their common struggle in behalf of "securing our republican institutions and of giving a proper direction to the operations of our government." He vowed to attempt in his position "the permanent establishment of those republican principles of limitation of power and public economy, for which we have successfully contended." Gallatin's primary goal was reduction of the public debt, "the principal object in bringing me into office." This reduction, he believed, would nail down the coffin of Hamiltonian finance. As late as 1809, with the ghost of Hamilton hovering in the background, Gallatin still heatedly denounced any secretary who could

> act the part of a mere financier, to become a contriver of taxes, a dealer of loans, a seeker of resources for the purpose of supporting useless baubles, of increasing the number of idle and dissipated members of the community, of fattening contractors, pursers, and agents, and of introducing in all its ramifications that system of patronage, corruption, and rottenness.[28]

Yet once in office, Gallatin demonstrated his intent to go beyond the merely negative goals of reducing the debt and destroying Federalist neomercantilist programs. He strove to harness what he perceived to be a certain crude vitality in the economic spirit of early-nineteenth-century Americans. He had described his fellow citizens in 1799 as ambitious, industrious individuals transcending the usual confines of the trades and professions to produce, buy, and sell among themselves. "Go into the interior of the country, and you will scarcely find a farmer who is not, in some degree, a trader," he had informed his colleagues in the House. "In a grazing part of the country, you will find them buying and selling cattle; in other parts you will find them distillers, tanners, or brick-makers." Several years later, Secretary Gallatin disclosed to Congress the happy effects of this liberated economic character among Americans. "No law exists here, directly or indirectly, confining man to a particular occupation or place," he exulted. "Industry is, in every effect, perfectly free and unfettered; every species of trade, commerce, art, profession, and manufacture, being equally opened to all. . . . Hence the progress of America has not been confined to her agriculture." This society of zealous self-made men—with their enthusiasm for domestic production and exchange—would become the bulwark of Jeffersonian political economy in the early nineteenth century.[29]

Such concern with productivity led growing numbers of Republican commentators to formulate a far-reaching new distinction in American political economy. Many began to contrast *both* agricultural and manufacturing interests—or productive elements in the republic—with a greedy and impotent commerce. As Congressman William Bibb of Georgia told his colleagues in 1812, agriculture and commerce were like sisters with sharply different personalities. "Agriculture, the elder sister, is contented, frank, and unsuspicious—always making sacrifices, never receiving any in return. Commerce, the younger sister, is cunning, avaricious, and rapacious—never satisfied unless her gains are commensurate with her desires." Republican organs like the *National Intelligencer* made similar arguments, although attacking commerce from the vantage point of manufactures. Praising in 1812 a new cotton mill in Rhode Island, the paper distinguished its owner as a man "who employs his riches in benefitting his country—in contributing to its real independence— . . . [not in] a cringing, servile foreign commerce which is draining the country of money."[30]

Thus many Republican critics of political economy began to propose an ideological coalition of productive farmers and manufacturers by 1810. As the *Philadelphia Aurora* noted angrily in 1812, since the Revolution merchants in the Northeast "have been enriched by exporting the *produce* of the middle and southern states, while they have had no *produce* of their own to export." Such resentment led to calls for alliance among those who "by the annual production of their labor at the plough, the loom, or the oar, constitutes an undeniable claim to all privileges and rights." A series of Fourth of July toasts in 1811 reported in the *Western Intelligencer* put the matter more forcefully. Commerce received grudging praise as "a valuable appendage to an independent state," but it also drew the warning that "it is the greatest civil curse that can happen to any nation" if occurring "according to the British model." Another toast paid simple tribute to "agriculture and domestic manufactures," "the two grand pillars of American independence."[31]

A growing Republican campaign for manufactures in the early 1800s stressed their productive function in contrast to the unproductive nature of foreign commerce and the carrying trade. It pictured both "household" and "extensive" manufactures as the natural offspring of hard-working, striving, liberal individuals. In 1812, *Niles' Weekly Register* proudly ran a letter from "a gentleman concerned in a woolen manufactory" in Middletown, Connecticut. "The woolen manufactories are indeed making great progress in the northern section of the union," the writer noted proudly, "and you may be assured that Europe will find the Yankees the most powerful rival in all her valuable manufactures." An 1810 letter in the *Kentucky Gazette* from "One of the People" argued that in the making of rope "one Kentucky boat may be loaded with three times the value of the manufactured article, than it could be with raw hemp. How absurd then to export the raw material." In an 1811 article entitled "Manufactures," the *Richmond Enquirer* detailed with pleasure the progress of cloth manufactories, paper and gunpowder mills, and glass and nail works in the state of Maryland. "We in Virginia are behind our sister states of the north in this patriotic career," the paper admonished its readers. "But the good work has commenced."[32]

This praise of manufacturing productivity often assumed a cast of nationalism. An 1810 public letter from "Dorothy Distaff" noted of household manufactures, "A hundred thousand spinning wheels put in motion by female hands will do as much toward . . . establishing our independence as a hundred thousand of the best militiamen in America." A newspaper observed with equal excitement in 1810 the plans for a large "manufacturing establishment" for cloth production. "Its capital is subscribed by 8 gentlemen—to the amount, if necessary, of $40,000," the report noted. "The Spinning machine is at work—and may be enlarged, if need be, to as many as 500 spindles." By such establishments, according to the editors, "instead of seeing our Cotton shipped to England, as it now is . . . we may see our own Yarn becoming an article of direct exportation to the markets of the continent."[33]

Lemuel Sawyer admirably synthesized the Republican case for manufactures. Presenting a July 4, 1810, oration in Lexington, Kentucky, he noted that the main objection to manufactures came from "the supposed superior productiveness of agriculture, that being assumed as the most beneficial and lucrative object of industry." Sawyer emphatically denied this point. "No one can be a greater friend to agriculture than myself," he declared, but to support exclusively American farming would be a mistake. Sawyer argued that the central question was "whether the surplus after defraying expences of a given capital employed in the purchase and improvement of a piece of land, is greater or less than that of a like capital employed in a manufactory." He found the answer to be obvious: "The inference must be drawn in favor of manufactures, of which there are scarcely any in the whole catalogue that do not furnish on the average, a profit of from 10 to 15 percent, whereas few lands will afford a common interest." Moreover, if "workshops would be distributed throughout the United States, a rivalry would ensue among them "that would stimulate production and keep prices low. The Kentuckian anticipated an American future "in which a manufacturing spirit should prevail and diffuse its wholesome vigor throughout."[34]

But equally important for Sawyer, manufactures also appeared as logical extensions of the republican spirit. Oppressive traditions, he argued, too long had supported "odious maxims of government" and crushed "efforts of reformation" in religion, science, and politics in the West, and this traditionalism "has been idly raised against the progress of manufactures." Thus associating manufactures with republican liberation as well as profit, Sawyer concluded that on domestic manufactures "rests the ultimate independence and prosperity of the country." More than any army, he contended, they comprised "the more effectual system of national defence."[35]

Arguments like that of Lemuel Sawyer helped set the stage for another new position in Republican political economy. Sentiment in favor of an integrated "home market" grew prominent in Jeffersonian circles by 1810. Like the cultural compulsion to individual self-control in this era, public attention focused on the felicities of internal, domestic economic development. The *Richmond Enquirer* ventured in September 1811, "The foreign commerce of the United States must undergo a great and perhaps permanent reduction." Because of risks in the foreign trade from rapacious European powers, "everything . . . impressively points to the policy of establishing within ourselves a market for our own productions."[36]

This market "within ourselves" proved increasingly attractive to Republican political economists for several reasons. First, a home market seemed to provide a secure basis for national economic independence. An editorial in the *Kentucky Gazette* put this matter forcefully in 1810: "The plain question . . . is this. *Shall we mutually combine to promote the interest of one another—or still make our industry subservient to the interests of foreign nations?* No American can have any hesitation upon the subject." In a poem of 1810, Philip Freneau appealed, "Americans! why half neglect / The culture of your soil? / From distant traffic why expect / The harvest of your toil? / At home a surer harvest springs / From mutual interchange of things." A newspaper editorial concluded in February 1810, so long as Americans "look up to the nations of Europe, for some of the necessaries, and many of the comforts of life, they cannot boast of that true independence. . . . Let us be Americans, not only in name, but in reality."[37]

This desire for the home market's "true" economic independence led many Republicans again to the topic of manufactures. It seemed obvious that production of finished goods would not only promote virtuous productivity, but also make possible an integrated domestic commerce. The *National Intelligencer*, for instance, after 1810 conducted a sustained campaign in behalf of domestic manufactures that utilized home-market sentiment. Economic self-reliance was within easy grasp of the American republic, its editors insisted: "We have only to turn our attention to the manufacture of the raw materials which we grow in abundance." The editors put the question of finished goods more frankly several months later, maintaining that Americans could either "get them from the British, or . . . *we may manufacture them for ourselves.*" Newspapers like the *Kentucky Gazette* also consistently praised "the progressive improvement of domestic manufactures" for "establishing internal commerce" among the states and thereby solidifying their "true independence." This paper announced to its readers in 1810, "Never until the U. States become a manufacturing, as well as a commercial and agricultural nation, can they be really independent."[38]

The promise of handsome profits and widespread prosperity made other converts to the gospel of the home market. Declaring that there was "abundant scope for enterprise at home," one public letter on internal transportation improvements contended that "public funds cannot be better employed than in bringing a market for every man's produce, as it were, to his own door." Newspapers like Cincinnati's *Western Spy* frequently praised the potential profit of the home market. The front page of the February 1, 1812, edition, for example, carried an excited advertisement for "Articles of Subscription" for two steamboats to travel "between Pittsburgh and the falls of the Ohio." Another article followed praising "commencement of a woolen manufactory" at Eleutherian Mills. Growth of the "highly interesting art of manufactures," the editors maintained, would allow Americans to rely on themselves for prosperity. An 1810 public address on internal improvements suggested the wider import of a profitable home market. "Some great system of internal navigation . . . is not only an object of the first consequence to the future prosperity of this country, considered as a measure of political economy," wrote its author, "but as a measure of state policy, it is indispensable to the preservation of the integrity of this government."[39]

A desire to connect the far-flung regions of the republic led many Republicans to a final justification of the home market. By 1810, appeals for promotion of domestic commerce were increasingly stressing the strengthening of American "union." Philip Freneau, for instance, writing as "Atticus" in the 1808 *Philadelphia Aurora,* urged his countrymen to "render ourselves completely independent of foreign nations, of external commerce" through development of internal economic networks. Both "individual and general prosperity" would ensue, but the greatest boon, he concluded, would result from "connecting the extremes of the continent together, and strengthening the bright chain of our confederation." Congressman Peter Porter of New York agreed in 1810. European attacks on America's foreign commerce, he wrote, ironically had proved useful by turning the attention of "the people of this country to their own internal resources." If this trend were encouraged, according to Porter, it would prove "much more profitable and advantageous than the most favored external commerce which we could enjoy." Moreover, he concluded emphatically, the home market would "be the means of producing a closer and more intimate union of the states."[40]

Once again, both Thomas Cooper and Albert Gallatin appeared as prominent architects of this new Republican edifice of political economy. Their blueprints appeared remarkably similar in integrating domestic manufactures with agriculture to promote internal exchange as the basis of a productive economy. Cooper's stinging attacks on foreign commerce, for example, cleared the way for his construction of an American "home market." As early as 1800, he began singing the praises of domestic commercial interchange. "Improve your roads, clear your rivers, cut your canals, erect your bridges, facilitate intercourses," he urged his new countrymen in his 1800 *Political Essays.* "No fear but if you will raise [both] produce and people they will find their market. It will soon be discovered what articles are wanted, what are the most profitable, and such will be supplied." Moreover, the home market required no expensive defense and encouraged national unity. Cooper pointed out, "The home trade . . . induces no national risk, produces none but home feelings, home interests, home predilections. These characters do not belong to the foreign trade."[41]

In addition to making America prosperous and less vulnerable to foreign exigencies, the home market for Cooper promised to unite "productive" elements in the American economy. Agriculture, of course, always had drawn praise from this admirer of Quesney. "If any profession is to be fostered," he wrote typically in 1800, "let it be the Tiller of the Earth, the fountain head of all wealth, and all power, and all prosperity." By the early years of the nineteenth century, however, Cooper had become a vigorous advocate of another productive activity: "home manufactures." Writing to Jefferson in 1808, he went so far as to amend his Smithian free-market principles. He suggested a protective tariff to encourage American manufactures, admitting that "there may be cases where necessity calls for this. . . . Our markets ought to be more at home; more under our command." A few years later Cooper painted a more explicit picture of a home market uniting productive agriculture and manufactures. "Employ yourself and your capital at home," he implored American entrepreneurs. "There are manufactures to establish without number; a population to be supplied incessantly calling for your articles; lands to cultivate without limits; employment for money and for people, that centuries will not satisfy."[42]

In his 1813 "Prospectus" for the *Emporium of Arts and Sciences*, Cooper summarized many of his conclusions on political economy arrived at over the previous decade and a half. A home market, he argued, would stop the flow of enervating luxury items—"velvets," "silks," "laces"—coming into the republic and remove the danger from "the prevailing madness of commercial wars." But even more important, domestic commerce would unite the "agricultural capitalist" with the "energetic, frugal, calculating and foreseeing character" of "a manufacturing people" and bind Americans "by all the ties of habit and of interest, to their own country." It would foster, in the confident phrases of the "Prospectus," a "general spirit of energy and exertion" and provide a system "the most *productive*, because . . . the capital is permanently invested and employed at home; because it contributes directly, immediately, and wholly to the internal wealth and resources of the nation." As Cooper predicted, flushed with enthusiasm for the benefits of liberal capitalism, this system encouraging "the exchange of agricultural surplus for articles of manufacture produced in our own country, will for a long time to come furnish the safest, . . . the most productive and the most patriotic employment of surplus capital."[43]

In like fashion, Albert Gallatin moved to implement a Republican economic agenda of domestic production and exchange. This course of action became most apparent in a series of economic reports submitted to Congress in the early nineteenth century. In April 1808 Gallatin sent to Congress a "Report on Roads and Canals." "The general utility of artificial roads and canals is at this time so universally admitted, as hardly to require any additional proofs," he began. They were "an object of primary importance" because they encouraged domestic commerce and thereby brought "a clear addition to the national wealth." After some two hundred pages spent surveying existing transportation routes, the secretary contended that the development of more roads and canals was critical to the young republic for two reasons. First, by building connections throughout America's "vast extent of territory," "good roads and canals will shorten distances, facilitate commercial and personal intercourse, and unite, by a still more intimate community of interests, the remote quarters of the United States." Second, a network of roads and canals "embracing the whole Union" would rouse "dormant capital" and "render the whole productive and eminently beneficial."[44]

Gallatin appended to his report a supporting letter from Robert Fulton. This testament supplemented in clear and forceful language the treasury secretary's rationale for an expanded system of transportation and a developed home market. Every republican citizen seeking his "true interest on subjects of political economy," Fulton wrote, must contrast those "non-productive citizens whose labor is not only lost, but who must be supported out of the produce of the industrious inhabitants" with "pursuits which multiply the productions of useful labor, and create abundance." The great advantage of "a general system of cheap conveyance" would be its support for productive citizens. Extensive roads and canals, wrote Fulton, would "enable every man to sell the produce of his own labor at the best market, and purchase at the cheapest." Moreover, such facilities would raise the value of surrounding land, including public lands. But most important, they would assist greatly in "cementing the Union, and extending the principles of confederated republican Government." Fulton concluded, "The United States shall be bound together by cheap and easy access to market in all directions, by a sense of mutual interests arising from a mutual intercourse and mingled commerce." For such reasons, Secretary Gallatin recommended the "early and efficient aid of the Federal Government" to supply "the capital wanted" for expanded road and canal construction.[45]

Another report helped to round out Gallatin's developing blueprint of political economy. In 1809 he suggested to Congress the recharter of the Bank of the United States. The treasury secretary believed that its affairs, for the most part, had been "wisely and skillfully managed" and that the institution itself performed several vital functions: safekeeping and transmission of public money, collection of revenue, making of safe loans. Moreover, Gallatin continued, the bank could meet those requirements better than various

state banks because of its superior capital and greater facility nation-
wide. Yet the greatest reason for recharter, he observed, was the
bank's role in binding the nation together economically. He concluded, "The bank itself would form an additional bond of common
interest and union, amongst the several states."[46]

Then in 1810 Gallatin presented to Congress a "Report on Manufactures," which sketched his mature vision of an American economy based on production and the home market. Calculating the scope
of infant American manufactures—both of the "household" type and
on an "extensive" scale—the treasury secretary calculated that "their
annual product exceeds one hundred and twenty millions of dollars."
Some of this growth he attributed to enterprising entrepreneurs, but
Gallatin also happily recognized that English and French attacks on
American commerce "by forcing industry and capital into other
channels, have broken inveterate habits, and given a general impulse,
to which must be ascribed the great increase of manufactures during
the two last years." This declining dependence on foreign commerce
was a trend to be encouraged, Gallatin believed, so he sought "the
plan best calculated to protect and promote American manufactures,"
especially "those manufactured for home consumption." Since want
of capital comprised the biggest barrier to developing manufactures,
Gallatin proposed that the federal government "create a circulating
stock, bearing a low rate of interest, and lend it at par to manufactures." This loan might go as high as twenty million dollars a year,
but as Gallatin stressed, this government provision of capital would
bear a rich return in the future by uniting productive sectors of the
economy in domestic interchange. "It is not improbable," he predicted, "that the raw materials used, and the provisions and other
articles consumed by the manufacturers, create a home market for
agricultural products not very inferior to that which arises from a
home demand."[47]

The emergence of a producer critique of commerce and support
for a home market reshaped Republican thinking about political
economy in the early 1800s. As the developing attitudes of men like
Thomas Cooper and Albert Gallatin reveal, long-standing commitments to a republican society based on expansive, commercial agriculture and foreign commerce had begun to shift subtly toward a
productive, entrepreneurial, domestic market mode by 1810. Such
tendencies in economic thinking did not occur in isolation, however,
but corresponded to another important trend in early-nineteenth-
century Republican ideology. By 1810 fear had begun to mount over
the vitality and durability of American republicanism itself, a con-

cern rooted in the tensions of the young nation's tense foreign affairs. In tandem with shifting assumptions about political economy, an anxious questioning of what Montesquieu had called the "spirit" of republicanism helped create an atmosphere of political crisis by the summer of 1812.

Strategies for Survival: From Enlightened to Energized Republicanism

Americans' confidence in the viability of their republican form of government began to erode in the early nineteenth century under the pressure of foreign affairs. Great Britain and France, bled white from the butchery of the Napoleonic Wars and each desperate for advantage, had turned to assault the neutral merchant vessels of the United States. The English first began to impress sailors from American ships in 1803. Then in a series of Orders in Council over the next few years they blockaded the European continent, denied to American merchants the wartime carrying trade, and began to seize American ships and their commercial loads. Napoleon responded with the Berlin and Milan decrees, edicts that blockaded the British Isles and prohibited all neutral trade with them. The French by 1806 also began to confiscate trade vessels of the United States. From 1803 to 1807 the Republican administration of Thomas Jefferson protested and negotiated in an attempt to moderate the maritime policies of the European belligerents. This strategy failed.

In December 1807 the Republicans took a new tack. Determined to find an effective American policy somewhere between war and submission, Jefferson and his followers in Congress enacted the famous embargo. This measure prohibited American ships from traveling to foreign ports, and foreign ships from gathering any cargo in the United States. Designed to bring Great Britain and France to reason by economic pressure, the measure instead prompted domestic economic hardship, political discontent among mercantile interests, and a widespread smuggling trade within the United States. The embargo's unpopularity and ineffectiveness brought its repeal in fourteen months and the subsequent enactment of weaker forms of commercial restrictions.[48] Such Republican policies, while influencing the European powers little, did succeed in creating a profound crisis of confidence at home over the vigor of American republican government. This foreign affairs conundrum not only helped raise tensions in American political economy and turn it inward toward production and the home market, but also raised larger and even more unsettling questions. Could the United States defend itself and

survive? And if it could not, did its republican structure deserve to
continue in its present form and based on its long-standing assumptions?

In this agitated state of uncertainty over the vitality and future of
republicanism, many Americans confronted the traditional republican strategy for international survival. A policy of neutrality and
peace, and the avoidance of war at almost any cost, always had been
central to the republican experiment. According to precepts rooted in
the republicanism of English "Country" ideology, war was a primary
instrument for aristocratic "Court" forces in their attempts to consoli-
date power. By raising taxes, running up the national debt, and
enlarging the standing army in wartime, the central government
would increase its powers of patronage, impoverish the citizenry, and
engage in liberticide.[49] Such republican fears of war joined broader
currents of thought emanating from the Enlightenment. According
to eighteenth-century *philosophes* like Montesquieu, "the spirit of
monarchy is war and enlargement of dominion; peace and moderation
are the spirit of a republic." Rather than engaging in war—that
"blind passion of princes"—enlightened republicans would better
serve their polity by pursuing two objectives. First, they should seek
to remove foreign affairs from the center of national political life by
stressing domestic tranquillity and the peaceful production of goods.
Second, good republicans should move to establish international free
trade, using commercial interchange to create a community of economic interests among nations. These general convictions led most
Americans to the position that war would undermine the structure
and corrupt the spirit of their republican government. Consequently,
first George Washington, and then his successors John Adams and
Thomas Jefferson, pursued peaceful neutrality as the foreign policy
necessary to both the survival and the virtue of the infant republic.[50]

By 1810, however, this traditional republican strategy had fallen
under a shadow. The failure of the embargo's "peaceful coercion"
and the continued violations of American commerce raised wor-
risome questions about neutrality and the ideological avoidance of
war. Many members of the Jeffersonian majority began to evince
extreme ambivalence over the "pacific genius" of republicanism. "If
this doctrine be true, that a Republican Government cannot stand the
shock of war, in vindication of its inalienable and moral rights, it is
bad, indeed worse than bad—not worth contending for—a Government not able to defend itself against all aggressions ought to be
changed," declared Congressman John Rhea of Tennessee. But as he
attempted to reassure, "the Government of the United States is not a
Government of this description. . . . This nation is as strong, if not

stronger, than any Government in the world." "A Republican," writing in the *Richmond Enquirer*, betrayed similar uncertainty. If it was true that "our republican institutions" were inappropriate to war, he speculated, "republics would be the most disgraceful of all forms of government, for they would be the most feeble." "But it is not the truth," he countered. "War has its evils. And we know it. But we ought neither to paint those evils greater than they are; nor to underrate our own means for carrying it on."[51]

This suspension between suspicions of republican weakness and confidence in republican strength, between the fear of war and the disgrace of an unjust peace, was nowhere more evident than in the troubled reflections of Thomas Jefferson and James Madison. As leaders of the Republican "revolution of 1800," a crusade that they perceived as a restoration of republican government after an "aristocratic" Federalist interregnum, they sought to establish policies that would realize their vision of the virtuous republic. On the domestic front they moved to reduce the national debt, weaken the standing military establishment, and secure western territories for an expansive commercial agriculture. In foreign affairs, they attempted to maintain American neutrality and free trade for the purpose of exporting the republic's agricultural surpluses. But of necessity, as European attacks on American neutral commerce accelerated after 1803, Jefferson and Madison were drawn into a vortex of strategic and ideological difficulty. They found themselves obliged to shape a strategy that would steer the young republic—with its virtuous character intact—through the gauntlet of foreign depredations.[52]

As intellectual heirs of eighteenth-century traditions, the two Virginians originally hoped to construct a foreign policy based on commercial leverage and avoidance of war. Drawing on republican fears and Enlightenment hopes, Jefferson consistently denounced the "armed despots of Europe" for using " 'the dog of war' for binding in chains their fellow man.' " As late as 1811, he contrasted the pacific spirit of republics with the rapacious violence of monarchy: "Peace has been our principle, peace is our interest, and peace has saved to the world this only plant of free and rational government now existing in it." James Madison concurred. In *The Federalist* of 1787–88 he had upheld the republic's militia as a "substitute for those military establishments which have subverted the liberties of the old world." As a congressman in the 1790s, he insisted that questions of war and peace must be left to the legislature, not the executive, because "of all the enemies to public liberty, war is, perhaps, the most to be dreaded." "War is the parent of armies," Madison explained. "From these proceed debts and taxes; and armies . . . [which] are the known

instruments for bringing the many under the dominance of the few."
Moreover, both men agreed that war's "field of lawless violence" was
simply a "resort from reason to force" that contradicted all "advances
in science and civilization" and undermined the "empire of morality." This convergence of republican and Enlightenment principles
led Jefferson and Madison to a general policy of neutrality, negotiation, and commercial pressure that culminated in the Embargo of
1807–8. Attempting a bold version of "peaceful coercion," these
Republicans sought to withhold American agricultural "necessaries"
from the Atlantic market and thereby force France and England to
cease preying on neutral commerce. This measure, as Madison outlined in the 1807 *National Intelligencer*, would rouse "the virtue of
the nation" and provide a happy alternative to both "disgraceful
submission and war."[53]

The embargo's failure—it apparently had little effect on the European belligerents while depriving and alienating America's commercial classes—caused Jefferson and Madison considerable disillusionment and bitterness. Under the pressure of events, these veteran
Republicans began to question the adequacy of commercial discrimi-
nation and nonviolent pressure and guidelines for international conduct. As early as 1806 Jefferson worried about the misconception that
"our government is entirely in Quaker principle" and concluded that
this "opinion must be corrected when just occasion arises, or we shall
become the plunder of all nations." By early 1812 he admitted that
"patience and love of peace is exhausted." After becoming President,
Madison too confessed that "peaceable coercion" seemed unworkable
and worried that continued American acquiescence would be "a dere-
liction of our National rights . . . not less ruinous than dishonor-
able."[54]

By 1810 such ambiguous and nervous attempts to sustain a "peaceful spirit" largely were giving way before a more exacting, vigorous
version of republican ideology. Many Jeffersonian Republicans—
especially younger ones—ceased worrying whether war would corrupt the republic. Rather, they grew convinced that it *must* absorb the
shock of violent conflict to prove its worth. They further insisted that
the republic held untapped sources of strength that adequately prepared it to meet this challenge. This "energized" republicanism of
young Jeffersonians drew nourishment from the values of enterprise,
ambition, productive growth, and self-made success endemic to liberalizing change in the early-nineteenth-century republic. As Virginia Congressman John Clopton told his constituents in 1812, the
growing strength of the young republic, not its delicate, pacific
tendencies, had excited British commercial attacks to begin with.

"The prospect of these immense [American] resources rapidly multi-plying, and under the auspices of a vigorous, active spirit of enter-prise pushed into operation," he wrote, "alarmed the pride and jeal-ousy of that [British] government."[55]

The tenor of energized republicanism appeared clearly in two 1811 documents. Charles G. Haines, in an oration given in Con-cord, Massachusetts, which was later published, contended that the republic's foreign affairs crisis was actually a fortunate occurrence. "Like the strong man, America has risen from her lethargy, and explored the strength of her own resources. It is only upon extraordi-nary occasions, that a nation can realize its own force, and call its physical powers into operation," Haines declared. "Happily for us, this spirit continues to grow in energy, and made daily advances toward the highest state of perfection." An 1811 editorial from the *National Intelligencer,* widely reprinted in other newspapers, stated flatly, "There is no nation on earth that so underrates its power and resources as the American people." The essay explained that after the Revolution "our people universally devoted themselves to the ad-vancement of their interest by industrious and enterprising habits." Consequently, they had been "more intent on the promotion of their own interest, or surrounding their families with comfort and plenty, than regardful of the quantum of power that would ensue from an aggregation of individual resources." Yet now the republic seemed poised for "advancing by the bold and virtuous development of its resources to great solid power."[56]

Thus while older figures like Jefferson and Madison only be-grudgingly abandoned a republican strategy of reason and economic coercion by 1810, substantial numbers of Republicans did so enthusi-astically. Although nurtured on republican principles, many younger Jeffersonians had drawn ideological nourishment from the liberaliz-ing changes transforming the United States since the Revolution. They began to demand a strategy of "energy" rather than "enlighten-ment" to guarantee the republic's survival. They envisioned war as a bracing exercise for a growing and vibrant republican society, as an opportunity for realizing its political potential. Prominent among these Republican activists were an eloquent Western legislator and a forceful journalist from Maryland.

In the spring of 1812 an angry Felix Grundy took the floor of the U.S. House of Representatives. Enraged over continued British violations of American commerce, and determined to prod the gov-ernment into a strong and aggressive response, this thirty-five-year-old lawyer from Tennessee faced the Speaker. He demanded that the Madison administration create a "Board of War" to replace the solitary secretary of war, arguing that such a body would channel more effectively the restless energy of the growing young republic. "Sir, we are changing from a state of peace to that of war. In a nation long accustomed to peaceful habits—a people divided in opinion—this operation is not easily effected," Grundy declared. "It requires time—it requires talent and perseverance; not the talents of one man only but of many." This theme—that the tranquil, pacific character of the republic needed to give way to an ethos of power and vitality— had preoccupied Grundy since his entry into Congress six months earlier. In this concern the young Republican was far from alone.[57]

Grundy had been born on September 11, 1777, in western Virginia. While he was an infant, one of his brothers was killed during one of the sporadic frontier clashes with Indian raiders. In 1780 the Grundy family migrated to Kentucky, and by 1793 two other brothers were dead from the Indian wars. Having begun to read law as an adolescent, young Felix was accepted to the Kentucky bar in 1795, where he gained a reputation for legal maneuver and oratorical skill that carried him into the Kentucky House of Representatives in 1800. Grundy quickly emerged as the principal rival of Henry Clay in the state assembly. Whereas Clay championed the older, wealthier "bluegrass" section of the state, into whose circles he had married and whose established economic interests he defended, Grundy led the forces assaulting this "monied aristocracy." In 1807 he was elected Chief Justice of the Kentucky Court of Appeals. But later that year Grundy suddenly resigned his judgship and moved his family to Nashville, Tennessee, perhaps seeking a more fertile field in which to cultivate his ambition. Elected to the U.S. Congress by his new constituents, he came to Washington, D.C., in late October 1811.[58]

Like many other young Republicans, Grundy had grown impatient with the "enlightened" approach of Jefferson's and Madison's foreign policy. While they stressed the importance of negotiation, commercial leverage, and the shielding of America's virtuous but delicate republican institutions, the Tennessean dispensed with such concerns. Having come of age in the post-1790 United States, Grundy was most impressed with the burgeoning strength of the young republic, not its frail virtue. Almost immediately after his appearance, he began to shake the walls of Congress with denunciations of America's fainthearted conduct in foreign affairs. Energetic American republicans, Grundy insisted, would not brook "doubt" and "manifestations of uneasiness" from representatives who "linger in this Hall." "No, sir, public opinion condemns delay; it condemns a halfway state of things; it calls for action; it demands a firm and determined course to be taken by the National Legislature," he asserted confidently. For Grundy, there was no question but that "the people will put forth their strength to support their rights."[59]

Behind this faith in America's republican strength lay an appreciation of the nation's dynamic economic development since the early 1790s. Shortly after entering Congress, Grundy announced, "The United States are already the second commercial nation in the world" and proudly acclaimed the "maritime greatness of this republic." But more than mere commerce, a high appraisal of America's growing, industrious domestic producers fueled Grundy's optimism. As he told his colleagues on December 9, 1812, he "should feel great unwillingness" to involve the republic in war over "the carrying trade," an endeavor "the enjoyment of which the community at large are not more deeply concerned." For Grundy, "the true question in controversy, is of a very different character; it involves the interest of the whole nation; it is the right of exporting the productions of our own soil and industry to foreign markets." And a few weeks earlier the Tennessean also had declared his support for legislative encouragement of "all the manufactures of the country," noting that America's foreign crisis was a favorable time "for adopting some measures to give our manufactures countenance and support." Thus Grundy's support for an aggressive foreign policy came not from a regard for America's commercial interests as such, but more from his esteem for the republic's hard-working producers—farmers and manufacturers—and the valuable commodities they brought forth.[60]

Yet Grundy's insistence on the republic's strength did not lead him to reject traditional republican ideology totally. He wished only to animate its spirit and tried to do so by turning republican tenets to new purposes. The Tennessean endorsed "virtue," for instance, but argued that sacrifice to the public good might best be demonstrated by a willingness for war "with a view to secure national independence, individual liberty, and a permanent security for property." Like senior Republicans, Grundy also distrusted "a heavy system of Internal taxes." He insisted, however, that "if the question of War plainly and distinctly put shall go in front," adoption of taxes also would be a question of virtuous self-sacrifice. As Grundy indicated in late 1811, he realized that he was reworking older, revered republican positions. Addressing a "particular portion of the members of this House—I mean, sir, the Republican members," he reminded them that Federalists always had been "charged with being friendly to standing armies in times of peace and favorable to expensive establishments." "If your minds are resolved on war, you are consistent, you are right, you are still Republicans," Grundy reassured his colleagues. But as he warned, each Republican had to face the suspicion that "you have abandoned your old principles, and trod in the paths of your [Federalist] predecessors."[61]

Felix Grundy's affirmation of the young republic's strength and his revamping of traditional republican commitments led him to reject the "old commercial restrictive system" of the enlightened Republicans. "I feel an entire aversion to such a system, with a view to coerce both or either of the belligerents to respect our rights," he admitted. "It has been tried; the experiment has failed. . . . We ought not longer to rely on it." Commercial restrictions, he insisted, not only failed to utilize American energy but actually dampened it. With such a policy, Americans could only conclude that "industry has not stimulus left, since their surplus products have not markets." For the Tennessean, "something must be done, or we shall lose our respectability abroad, and even cease to respect ourselves." With the overriding necessity of an energetic, republican foreign policy, the choice between war and submission was obvious. Grundy told Congress in 1811 that it must confront "the new test to which we are to put this government. We are about to ascertain by actual experiment how far our Republican institutions are calculated to stand the shock of war." For the forceful young congressman from the West, however, the success of this experiment was foreordained. He had unshakable faith that "the united energies of the people will be brought into action."[62]

While Felix Grundy was tongue-lashing timid colleagues in the national capital, the first issue of *Niles' Weekly Register* appeared. The September 7, 1811, initial number of this Baltimore newspaper promised to assay a broad variety of subjects: "Political, Historical, Geographical, Scientifical, Astronomical, Statistical and Biographical, Documents, Essays and Facts; together with notices of the Arts and Manufactures, and a Record of the Events of the Times." But for Hezekiah Niles, the paper's young founder and an ardent Republican, foreign affairs and political economy were of the utmost concern. The newspaper's opening essays revealed his preoccupation with the state of the American republic—and American republicanism—while also laying out a path of corrective action.

Niles' first editorial in this journalistic enterprise observed that in the present state of foreign affairs the United States had been deprived of "our accustomed commerce" and "our right to carry the productions of our own soil to the proper markets for them." These restrictions by the European belligerents made necessary a new direction for American industry. According to the editorial, "It is imperiously demanded of the American people that they should look to themselves, and in themselves, and from the inestimably valuable raw materials of their country's growth, make for themselves those items . . . it once suited them to obtain from the workshops of the old world." For Niles it was clear that the "internal trade of any country . . . is incalculably more important" than foreign commerce. Thus he rejoiced that in the American republic "the *home trade* is daily approaching its natural importance." This was particularly evident with the growth of "manufactories." "The prejudices which existed against manufactures have been dispelled," Niles explained, "and our country is now advancing with giant strides to a real independence by a proper application of the public labor to the public wants." Now the only problem was to shape an energetic foreign policy reflective of American economic vitality. Young Niles dedicated himself to the task, vowing of the *Weekly Register*, "Its politics shall be *American*—not passive, not lukewarm, but active and vigilant."[63]

Like Felix Grundy, Hezekiah Niles had been born in 1777, but his birth occurred in more harried circumstances. Fleeing their home in Wilmington, Delaware, in front of advancing British troops, his parents hid out in Chester County, Pennsylvania, where Hezekiah arrived. After the British raid subsided, the family returned to Wilmington. Young Niles' childhood unfolded quietly—both of his parents were of Quaker stock—until 1791, when his father was killed instantly by a falling signpost in a freak accident. Having completed his basic schooling, the boy was apprenticed to a Philadelphia printer. Working in the national capital, young Niles became attracted to political affairs. He wrote several essays in opposition to the Jay Treaty and gravitated toward the Jeffersonian Republicans. In 1797 he returned to Wilmington and established his own press printing calendars, assorted books, and local newspapers. Niles gradually established a reputation in the community, holding several local political offices and surviving several financial reverses. In 1806 he moved to Baltimore and became the editor of the *Evening Post*, a Republican paper. For the next six years he utilized the newspaper to defend Jeffersonian foreign policy and to promote the advancement of America's domestic manufactures. Then in 1811 he founded the famous *Niles' Weekly Register* in Baltimore. Unique in that it eschewed advertising and depended solely on subscribers' fees, Niles' newspaper increased its circulation by leaps and bounds within the first half-year of publication. It became one of America's leading journals of news and opinion for the next three decades. No small amount of the *Weekly Register*'s initial popularity came from Niles' constant agitation for an energetic, aggressive foreign policy in 1811–12.[64]

Niles had loyally supported the "enlightened" strategy of Jefferson and Madison in the half-decade after 1804. By 1810, however, his patience with "peaceable coercion" had evaporated. "Our love of peace is known to the world; nay, so powerful is the desire to preserve it, that it has been tauntingly said . . . that 'we cannot be kicked into war,'" he wrote disgustedly in the *Weekly Register*. "Every measure that Forbearance could devise, has been resorted to—and we have suffered injuries . . . which no *independent* nation ever submitted to." Niles continually reprimanded the Madison administration and Congress for enervating "the energy of the American government." Too much debate and pontification—"giant-words and colossal declamations"—had resulted in too little action. "The vacillations of the government have not only injured its character and politics," the editor insisted, "but have done more than anything else to keep down domestic manufactures." For Niles, the republic by 1812 had arrived at a "momentous crisis." He told his readers in March of that year, "The powers of reason, of truth and argument have failed—nothing remains but submission or resistance." For Niles, the time for enlightened republican tactics clearly had come to an end.[65]

The *Weekly Register*'s editorials in 1811 and 1812 held that a policy of energy meant war, or at least an aggressive foreign posture coiled for war. Yet, as Niles insisted to his readers, war would not rend the fabric of America's republican society. To the contrary, it would serve as a conduit for the surging energy of an expanding United States. Although no one desired war, argued the editor, it was not "the greatest of evils." "The political, as well as the natural atmosphere, may become turbid and unwholesome," Niles noted, and war like a violent thunderstorm "purges the atmosphere, gives a new tone, as it were, to listless nature, and promotes the common good." In another essay he switched metaphors, comparing war to the use of a "pruning knife," after which "the national tree, luxuriant in resources . . . shall flourish with renewed vigor." Regardless of the imagery, the pen of Hezekiah Niles depicted war as an expression of republican vigor, not a harbinger of republican declension.[66]

Much of Niles' confidence stemmed from his awareness of American economic growth since the Revolution. A foreign policy of energy and assertion, he believed, suited well the dynamism and growing self-reliance of the republic's economy. Niles frequently maintained that the foreign crisis had proved useful to the young nation by removing the temptation of foreign goods—"the fleshpots of Egypt" he liked to call them—and forcing entrepreneurial energy inward. He noted in November 1811 that the "astonishing" progress of American manufactures "would make a man suppose some mighty genii had been at work." This promising state of affairs "increases the *treasure at home*, and keeps the heart from wandering," and Niles saw an aggressive policy toward the European belligerents as reinforcing this happy economic process. Not only would it clinch the "weaning" of American citizens from foreign economic dependence, but it would subvert the influence of the American "trading class of society" with their vested interest in foreign commerce. War, the Baltimore journalist suggested, would serve a very useful purpose in political economy. "It will teach our citizens a most useful truth, which in the hurry and bustle of commerce too many did not recollect, that they have a country; and cause them to look to themselves, instead of extending their views across the Atlantic, for sources of happiness."[67]

In a larger sense, Niles anticipated an aggressive foreign policy as quickening and capturing American productive energies. He wrote in June 1812: "We are young and vigorous, in all the freshness of youth as to national resources. They require only to be called into action." In contrast to the corruption and decadence of English society, in the American republic the "road to competency is free to all, and the same perseverance, frugality, and industry that a poor Englishman exercises merely to exist at home, would make a man rich in the United States, in a few years." And if war indeed came, the young editor insisted, "there will be ample employment for all. Some part of the labor and capital of the United States, at present devoted tc commerce, will be directed to objects calculated to seal the independence of the country, in the establishment of a thousand works, needful to the supply of our wants. . . . Our agriculturalists will have a steady and better market at home." "Our country is rich. Our resources are great," he noted succinctly at another point. Niles proclaimed in July 1812, "Let us make the war a trial of skill, as well as a trial by battle."[68]

A few weeks after hostilities with Great Britain had begun, the *Weekly Register* presented to readers an editorial entitled "Energy in War." The piece aptly summarized Hezekiah Niles' rejection of traditional republican strategy and his endorsement of a forceful international stance more appropriate to the growing republic's strength. War, asserted the editor, involved "our national pride and individual feelings—our rank among the people of the earth with our self-esteem, and the glory of future safety of these states." War further demanded "the exertion of every energy, corporeal and mental." Niles' confidence in the republic's vitality was steadfast. "A new spirit appears to invigorate the government and the people," he wrote. "The torpor and indifference . . . are giving way to the impulses of patriotism; and narrow local prejudices are sacrificed on the shrine of the republic." Hezekiah Niles did not fear war's effect on a delicate, virtuous republic; he welcomed its catalyzing impact on a restless republican spirit. The editor concluded typically and confidently: "Our country is rich, and its resources inexhaustible. . . . We have everything to hope for, if united with energy."[69]

For many young Republicans, it seemed imperative that the United States present an energetic foreign policy to prove itself. Like Felix Grundy and Hezekiah Niles, they believed that facing up to an international clash of wills—and doing so with a willingness to go to war—was the only way to demonstrate the viability of the republican form of government. Moreover, in advocating an "energized" rather than an "enlightened" strategy, these men harnessed the powerful thrust toward domestic production and a home market in American political economy. Thus by 1812 a broad new ideological sensibility was gaining influence in the Jeffersonian circles that dominated national politics. In this atmosphere of ideological ferment and war crisis, articulate proponents of a revamped republic began to emerge from the shadows and step onto political center stage.

The Liberal Republicans: "A New Era in Our Politics"

The vast, multifaceted changes in post-Revolutionary America subtly transformed its republican society. In the process, as we have seen, citizens of the early republic experienced and participated in a reshaping of familiar notions of society, culture, economy, and personality. By 1810 these liberalizing tendencies were converging on and reshaping American political ideology. The subterranean agitation of such influences in the political world of the young nation—along with the overt pressures in foreign affairs—gradually forced to the surface a new breed of political men, especially within the Republican majority.

These insurgent Republicans—men like Henry Clay, Charles J. Ingersoll, Spencer H. Cone, Hezekiah Niles, and Felix Grundy— did not remain insurgent very long. Eloquent and forceful, they resolved to overcome the early-nineteenth-century "crisis of republicanism" by political innovation. These Liberal Republicans, as they accurately might be called, found political sustenance in the emerging values of a growing market society: self-made success, moral free-agency, decision of character and self-control, entrepreneurial production, the home market, an ethos of energy and assertion. Melding these values with traditional republican commitments, they surged to the forefront of American political discourse as opinion-shapers. They also pulled in their wake older, often more traditional, but ultimately receptive Republicans like Thomas Cooper, Philip Freneau, Benjamin Rush, Albert Gallatin, Hugh Henry Brackenridge, James Madison, and even John and John Quincy Adams.

In the hands of these Jeffersonians, eighteenth-century American republicanism thus shifted noticeably toward what would become nineteenth-century liberalism. This new ideological orientation took shape around several intellectual and moral convictions: that pursuit of many self-interests would result in the public good; that politics was the arena for sorting and settling the interests of self-controlled individuals; that energy in foreign affairs and a productive home market in political economy best promoted the expansive young republic; and finally, that progress and growth rather than decay and decline promised to color the future of the United States. And by 1812, war with Great Britain had become the catalyst for the formulation of a politics of the marketplace. Two figures in particular, Tench Coxe and John C. Calhoun, illustrated well the dynamics of this long-fermenting ideological process. An urbane political economist from Pennsylvania and a severely charismatic congressman from South Carolina offered two variations on how the liberalization of American society translated into the liberalization of American politics.

Tench Coxe had led a life of many ironies. A Tory during the American Revolution, after its conclusion he became one of the republic's strongest advocates of cultural and economic nationalism. A Federalist-turned-Republican, this Philadelphian managed to gain the respect and then alienate the friendship of both Alexander Hamilton and Thomas Jefferson. A prosperous merchant and calculating businessman in his early career, in middle age he veered close to bankruptcy in a frenzied burst of land speculation and spent much of his declining years in severe financial straits. Yet from the sum of these contradictory impulses emerged a coherent, even single-minded vision of the nature and future prospects of the young American nation. As much as any man of his time, Tench Coxe reflected politically the spirit of a dynamically liberalizing American society.

Coxe was fond of noting that while post-Revolutionary Americans retained a certain regard for the past, they radiated far more a self-reliant, forward-looking energy. He observed of his countrymen in an 1809 essay, "They have not suffered a blind veneration for antiquity, for custom or for names, to overrule the suggestions of their own good sense, the knowledge of their own situation, and the lessons of their own experience." This pragmatic instinct often took the form of productive enterprise, and since the early 1790s the citizens of a "plentiful and energetic America" had proved themselves to be "a people of intelligence and exertion," "spirit and resolution." Coxe wrote enthusiastically of "the energetic talents of our countrymen": "We have industriously traversed every sea; and in a few years, we have made new towns, districts, counties, and states out of our immense forests." He put it more succinctly in the same essay: "There is a great operation in the accumulation of wealth in the United States, peculiar, in its degree, to their affairs." This appreciation, and affirmation, of America's explosive post-Revolutionary growth made Coxe an ideological prophet among Liberal Republicans in the early nineteenth century.[70]

His career before 1812 had been a most interesting and varied one. Coxe was born in Philadelphia in 1755, the second of thirteen children, to one of the city's most prominent merchant families. Young Tench entered the College of Philadelphia in 1773, studied there for two years, and then joined the mercantile firm of his father. He gradually emerged as the active director of the family's commercial affairs. During the Revolution, Coxe like many others was forced to make an agonizing decision of loyalty. As an ambitious young man, he made a choice that was to haunt him for the next fifty years: Coxe became a Tory. He remained in Philadelphia during the British occupation, attempted to remain neutral, but eventually emerged as a willing associate of the British invaders. By the war's end Coxe had reintegrated himself into America's republican society, but he remained a person of suspicion to many Pennsylvania patriots.

Coxe continued his commercial activity in the 1780s while slowly becoming involved in politics. Serving as a member of the Continental Congress in 1788 and vigorously working for ratification of the new national Constitution, in 1790 Coxe moved into the highest circles of the new Washington administration. He took a position as assistant secretary of the treasury and worked closely with his superior, Alexander Hamilton, over the next several years. He especially took an interest in Hamilton's "Report on Manufactures"—apparently he wrote much of the document himself—and played a major role in the Society for Establishing Useful Manufactures.

At the same time, Coxe also began to work with Secretary of State Thomas Jefferson. Fully supporting the Virginian's belief in commercial reciprocity, the assistant secretary of the treasury helped Jefferson prepare the 1791 report to Congress recommending adoption of such a principle. By the mid-1790s Coxe had drifted toward the Jeffersonian Republicans and become suspicious of the "monarchical" tendencies of both Hamilton and John Adams. He emerged as a political leader of Pennsylvania Republicans, was dismissed from his Treasury post in 1797, and resumed his mercantile activities in the latter part of the decade. For much of the 1790s, Coxe also indulged in an orgy of land speculation—much of it in the state of North Carolina—that seriously drained his financial resources. In 1800 the Philadelphian worked tirelessly for Jefferson's election, after which he became such a nuisance in demanding high political office that the new President became extremely annoyed and suspicious of Coxe's motives. Jefferson had no personal communication with Coxe for the next six years, but in 1803 Coxe finally received an appointment—at the insistence of Albert Gallatin—as purveyor of the United States. He served in this office as purchasing agent for all supplies and provisions required by the national government until 1813. For the final ten years of his life, Coxe held several minor positions for the state of Pennsylvania. He died on July 16, 1824.[71]

Tench Coxe's first and lasting intellectual love was political economy, and the incessant stream of writing on this and related topics comprised the most distinguishing feature of his career. What set Coxe apart from many fellow Republicans, however, was his unambiguous insistence on prodding the American republic to a more "advanced" stage of society. While most Jeffersonians feared the effects of an urbanized, manufacturing, fully commercialized society—decadence, corruption, widespread poverty[72]—Coxe did not. He proceeded carefully, however, by acknowledging the dominance of "republican principles" in the young nation. He noted that "the citizens of this country . . . easily and quietly assimilate themselves in a prudent opposition to the power of a few, and in an open, legitimate maintenance of the rights of the whole of the members of the community." Coxe dutifully paid homage to certain republican pieties: religious liberty, the equal right to pursue happiness, the destruction of primogeniture statutes, a reliance on the militia and distrust of standing armies. Yet he contended that social and economic development need not destroy this republican structure. Coxe's singular talent, as one student of his career observed, lay in his ability to cast innovative aims "in the language of the prevailing ideology."[73]

The Philadelphian steadfastly held that to guarantee its survival the United States must move beyond a commercial-agricultural stage. For Coxe the key was to republicanize this process of growth. As he wrote in 1804, it seemed clear that "the republican system is equally adapted to every species of industry that the citizens can be honestly employed in." The pursuit of manufactures, for instance, did not have to be accompanied by the wretchedness of the poor that was evident in advanced societies like Great Britain's. To the contrary, as early as 1787 Coxe suggested that domestic manufactories on an extensive scale might acutally hold the key to America's republican future. He envisioned highly mechanized factories where machine-tending would comprise the normal labor, and with but few hands needed to maintain such institutions, people would not be removed from agriculture. Instead, work would be provided for the idle. Moreover, the attention of Americans would be turned away from "European luxuries" and toward the domestic manufacture of useful, practical necessities. As Coxe put the matter in 1804, an "enlightened Congress" had responsibility for moving these "confederated republics" to a "more advanced state of society."[74]

An integrated economy of agriculture, commerce, and manufactures comprised the main support for this vision of an "advanced" republican society. Sole reliance on agricultural production, Coxe explained, would lead the American republic into decay for several reasons. Agricultural dependence would create a significant class of wandering farmers as they wore out the soil in one area and migrated to another. Second, the productivity of American farmers would make large numbers of them unnecessary and likely drive many citizens into idleness. Finally, dependence on foreign countries for manufactured goods would subvert the young republic's independence while needlessly draining her economy of specie. Thus it seemed evident that an economy resting equally on the "three great branches of National Industry" would be far better. As Coxe argued in 1804, an integrated structure of farmers, merchants, and manufacturers would stabilize and secure the republic. Not only would population growth be secured and property become more valuable, but American dependence on foreign markets would decline, and hence the threat of foreign war as well.[75]

Yet Tench Coxe fully realized that an integrated American economy required two additional components. This political economist spent much of his career advocating, first, the encouragement of American manufactures. He recognized that American republicans harbored a "prejudice" against manufactures, a disposition that appeared both in public writing and in government policies. For Coxe this unfortunate, outdated view reflected America's colonial past rather than her national future. A system of domestic manufactures, he insisted over and over again, would help guarantee an integrated economy and hence the survival of America's republican way of life. It would generate jobs, productive enterprise, and economic security for virtuous republicans. A "Memorial of the Artists and Manufacturers of Philadelphia," which Coxe attached to his 1804 *Essay on the*

Manufacturing Interest, echoed his hopes in this regard. With the development of American manufactures,

> New sources will be laid open for the employment of capital in the interior. . . . The coasting trade and internal commerce will receive a new impulse. . . . Domestic industry will put to shame idleness and dissipation. . . . Foreign nations will lose their influence over our councils. . . . The fertile lands of America will rise to their just value, by bringing a market to the door of the farmer. . . . The riches with which nature has so bountifully blessed this country will be explored and brought into use.

These explicit advantages, Coxe argued, demanded a program of legislative protection. If moderately high duties were imposed on the import of foreign manufactured goods, industrious Americans increasingly would "manufacture for themselves, and their fellow citizens."[76]

A second component of Coxe's integrated economy also required special attention. If domestic manufactures were to gain an equal footing with agriculture and commerce, and hence American dependence on foreign goods was to decline, a greatly expanded home market appeared essential. Throughout the 1790s, and even more so in the early 1800s, Coxe forcefully presented the case for American reliance on domestic rather than foreign commerce. As the Philadelphian emphasized in 1810, because of its economic linkages the home market "has become a decisive consideration for the continuance of the federal union—a connexion *vital* to the general commerce of the American people." European attacks on American commerce after 1803 only strengthened Coxe's resolve on this point. Where was the advantage in exporting raw materials "to be plundered, rejected, restricted or excluded, according to their criminal will, by foreign markets?" The beneficial alternative, explained this innovative Republican, was "to provide a market at home, free from injury, insult, and vexation."[77]

An expansive vision of the young nation's future ultimately gave Coxe's program of political economy its synthetic quality. Like other Liberal Republicans of the early nineteenth century, he anticipated an unfolding story of republican progress rather than dreading a process of republican decline. The American Revolution had suggested to the Philadelphian the possibility of an American political millennium. He came to believe that its realization depended only on the fulfillment of the young republic's promise, and Coxe saw in post-Revolutionary liberalizing trends the beginnings of such a process. As he wrote in a series of 1809 essays on "The New World" of America, the typical republican was a person of "tenacious, firm and substantial materials." He was a subduer of nature dutifully engaged in "an habitual course of moralizing industry and economy." Collectively Americans had "carved their productive country out of the stupendous forest" and stood "under the favour of Heaven, the energetic and temporal creators of their own cities, towns, and villages." For Coxe, this "high independent personal spirit and resolution" of his countrymen had given the republic a special position in the world. He cast America's republican institutions in the form of a civil religion "under the favour of Divine Providence." As Coxe indicated in 1809, he had few fears for "our favoured land, unhurt, nay prospering, amidst the war of nations, the wreck of empire, and the fall of thrones."[78]

In the escalating foreign affairs crisis of the early nineteenth century, Coxe discovered a catalyst for his precocious formula of republican progress. By 1810 this Philadelphia Republican emerged as an ardent advocate of action against Great Britain, and he offered a two-layered rationale. War with England, Coxe argued first, would demonstrate the young republic's vitality and strength. In the words of Coxe's biographer, "Having for years urged his countrymen to fight rather than to acquiesce in British aggression, he viewed the War of 1812 as a means of vindicating the nation's honor and proving its military prowess." Coxe himself described the energetic republic and the conflict in 1812. War promised to sustain "public and individual rights," "liberty to our mariners," "commerce to our merchants," and "free sales of our produce . . . to our men of landed property." Coxe added another element to this argument that a vigorous republic required, and could sustain, a vigorous defense. While the Revolution had been successful thirty-five years before, chances for victory were even better in 1812, because the difference "is greater, in respect to the various manufactures necessary to defence, than it is in respect to any other matter, in the whole circle of its national industry."[79]

Yet more than just a confirmation of existing strength, war promised to Coxe an atmosphere conducive to *further* advancement of America's republican society. Here the possibilities for the growth of domestic manufactures most fired his imagination. "The belligerent powers have really placed our manufactures in a hot-bed," he wrote gleefully in 1810. "Capital has become abundant. . . . Employment in foreign trade is so much reduced, that men of the best business, habits and talents are at leisure to engage in manufactures." National defense presented a compelling new rationale for Coxe's vision of economic growth, and he leaped at the logic. With the likelihood of "a sudden and effectual exertion of the whole public force" in war, all domestic manufactures had become "incalculable in their value." Foreign attacks "are powerful considerations in favor of every proper attention to the internal walks of our national industry," the Philadelphian lectured. "Let us then turn our agriculture, our business, our capitals, and our minds, in timely anticipation, to the beneficial and necessary increase of manufactures requisite to comfort and defence."[80]

Thus, for Tench Coxe the War of 1812 marked a significant juncture in the development of American republicanism. The conflict affirmed the liberalizing growth of the young nation since the Revolution. It promised as well to accelerate the republic's progress to a more advanced and viable form, a process long advocated by this Republican enthusiast. Coxe shrewdly observed that peace might "restore our commerce, but nothing can deprive us of our established manufactures. They have passed the infantile stage. They are now adult."[81] Reacting with delight to America's foreign exigency, this forward-looking elderly Jeffersonian joined the Liberal Republicans in viewing war as opportunity, rather than disaster, for the maturing republic. Another younger Republican, however, did not just react to the crisis. Convinced that the hidden power of the growing republic needed only to be tapped ideologically, he moved decisively to the forefront of the Liberal Republican vanguard for war.

By all accounts, John C. Calhoun presented a striking appearance upon entering the House of Representatives in November 1811. Only twenty-nine years old, the South Carolinian was over six feet tall, slender, and blessed with severely handsome features. A shock of thick black hair, combed straight back, added an illusion of even greater height while emphasizing the large, dark, piercing eyes that were already becoming famous. Calhoun appeared as a dynamic, young version of—this wonderful phrase would later by used by Englishwoman Harriet Martineau—"the cast-iron man who looks as if he had never been born, and never would be extinguished."[82]

On November 29, 1811, the House Foreign Relations Committee presented its report on the tense situation with Great Britain. Only a few weeks in his seat, Calhoun had not yet spoken on the floor of Congress, but this report was largely his work. It carried the stamp of his vigorous writing and reflected his unbending confidence in the strength of the young republic:

> The occasion is now presented, when the national character, misunderstood and traduced for a time by foreign and domestic enemies, should be vindicated. . . . That proud spirit of liberty and indepen-

dence, which sustained our fathers in the successful assertions of their rights, against foreign oppression, is not yet sunk: The patriotic fire of the Revolution still burns in the American breast with a holy and unextinguishable flame, and will conduct this nation to those high destinies, which are not less the reward of dignified moderation, than of exalted valor.

Such forceful, eloquent language helped propel Calhoun to the head of those in Congress ready for confrontation with foreign enemies. But more important, the masterful way the young South Carolinian gathered the hopes and fears of liberalizing change into a ideological rationale for war made him an appropriate leader of the Liberal Republicans.[83]

Calhoun's meteoric rise to national political prominence in 1811 reflected the social fluidity of the early republic. He had been born in 1782 in the western South Carolina upcountry to comfortable gentry parents of Scotch-Irish background. A precocious youth, young Calhoun quickly exhausted the educational possibilities of various country schools in this environment. Upon his father's death in 1796, the fourteen-year-old boy retired to the family plantation to assist his mother. Over the next four years he took on increasing business responsibilities and emerged as the manager of the farm operation. Resuming his education at a local academy in 1800, two years later Calhoun journeyed northward to Yale College, from which he graduated in 1804 after an impressive academic career. The next several years were spent in legal study, both in South Carolina and at the famous law school of Judge Tapping Reeve in Litchfield, Connecticut. Calhoun was admitted to the South Carolina bar in 1808 and began a highly profitable law practice in his native upcountry. He was elected to the South Carolina legislature a few months later and to the U.S. Congress in 1811.[84]

Two interesting character traits stand out from the scant documentation on Calhoun's early personal life. Each reflected a larger dimension of liberal change in the early republic and would play a role in the young congressman's ideological reformulations. Calhoun's burning ambition was the first such characteristic. As early as 1803, writing to a friend from Yale College, he complained about the restrictions of college life. "That ambition must be small indeed, which can be gratified in college," he wrote impatiently. "Rather then rejoice, that you have passed through college; and that you are now engaged in the busy scenes of the 'scrambling world.' You are now your own master." Eager for "the temple of fame" and "popular renown," five years later Calhoun was complaining about being "chained" to the practice of law. He vowed in 1809 his determination "to forsake it as soon as I can make a decent independence; for I am not ambitious of great wealth." This disdain for monetary reward was at least partly genuine. Young Calhoun had long exhibited a deep interest in history and politics rather than material advancement, having prepared in 1804 a commencement address at Yale on "the qualifications necessary to constitute a perfect statesman." Disavowals of wealth, however, are not difficult for those who are rapidly attaining it. By 1809 Calhoun's legal brilliance was bringing such prosperity that shortly he would buy his own plantation. Moreover, he had begun assiduously to cultivate his older widowed cousin, Mrs. Floride Calhoun. Her wealth and high social standing in Tidewater South Carolina led to important connections in Savannah. Calhoun married Floride's sixteen-year-old daughter in 1811.[85]

However persistent Calhoun's ambition may have been, his rigid sense of self-control appeared even more so. Writing to a friend in 1805, the young lawyer observed typically, "It is laid down as a maxim of prudence by many philosophers, that we ought always to make our pleasure act in subordination to our duties and obligations." Calhoun's Calvinist upbringing undoubtedly had an influence here, and probably too his desire for worldly success. Alexander Bowie, a longtime friend, recalled many years later his early acquaintance with the self-controlled South Carolinian around 1810. On their frequent early morning three-mile walks, Calhoun would discuss how "he had early subjected his mind to such a course of rigid discipline, and he had persisted without faltering, until he had acquired a perfect control over it." It had become "his uniform habit," he told Bowie, "to select a subject for reflection, and . . . never suffered his attention to wander from it until he was satisfied with its examination."[86]

This obsession with self-command shaped in Calhoun a rather severe repression of sensuality and even a denial of emotion. At age twenty-seven he seemed shocked over his capacity to fall in love, admitting, "I formerly thought that it would be impossible for me to be strongly agitated in an affair of this kind." Around the same time, the young lawyer apparently attempted to write a poem to his fiancée, abandoning the effort after beginning every line with the word "Whereas." Calhoun's repression of emotion sometimes extended to extreme lengths. After the death of their infant daughter in 1815, he seemed unable to understand why his wife's grief had overwhelmed her reason. A perplexed Calhoun wrote to his mother-in-law, "So fixed in sorrow is her distressed mother, that every topic of consolation, which I attempt to offer but seems to grieve her the more. It is in vain that I tell her it is the lot of humanity. . . . She thinks only of her dear child; and recalls to her mind every thing that made her interesting, thus furnishing additional food for her grief."[87]

Such personal standards spilled over into a moral critique of society. In young manhood, for example, Calhoun often denounced the vivacious society of Charleston as "in everything . . . so extremely corrupt, and particularly so inattentive to every call of religion." He opined at another point—almost with relish—that an epidemic sweeping the city "may be considered as a curse for their intemperance and debaucheries." In 1811 the young lawyer happily reported that his wife had attended the theater with friends—without him, of course—but returned with "no inclination to renew her visit there." "I was pleased to see that her good sense prevented her from being dazzled by the glare of novelty." Calhoun previewed his social ethic of self-control in 1803. Studying at Yale College, he wrote of New Englanders: "They are certainly more penurious, more contracted in their sentiments, and less social than the Carolinians. But as to morality we must yield."[88]

Calhoun's political goals before entering Congress took shape far less clearly than his personal quest for success and self-control. The aspiring young statesman revealed few political inclinations beyond loyalty to the Republican party, a vague discontent with what he saw as a weak Jeffersonian foreign policy, and an equally inchoate but restless desire to harness politically the energy and productive power of the republic. Part of the reason lay in his youth and political inexperience. Yet the very impulsiveness of Calhoun's early politics was a significant fact, in addition to forming a connection to his personal qualities. It was the accelerating war crisis in the half-decade after 1807 that gave ideological form to what previously had been merely political instinct. Calhoun's intuitive appreciation of liberalizing change in the early republic fused inseparably with his desire for military confrontation. Thus it was no accident that he emerged as the most forceful Congressional advocate of war and the most articulate shaper of Liberal Republican ideology. Each impulse fed the other.

Calhoun first revealed this melding of war and congealing liberalism in an emerging critique of American republican traditions. In a speech made shortly after entering Congress, he granted that time-honored qualms made it necessary that "this country should never resort to war but for causes the most urgent and necessary. It is sufficient that, under a government like ours, none but such will justify it in the eye of the nation." Yet it was dangerous, he argued in the same speech, to conclude that "our Constitution is not calculated for war, and that it cannot stand its rude shock." Such a position would subject the republic to "the pity or contempt of other nations for our existence." In private correspondence, Calhoun also complained bitterly that President Madison was the prisoner of republican fears in his war policy. "Our President, tho' a man of amiable manners and great talents, has not I fear those commanding talents which are necessary. . . . He reluctantly gives up the system of peace."[89]

Such reluctance to face the strain of war ran across the grain of the young South Carolinian's experience in the early republic. "We are a people essentially active. I may say we are pre-eminently so," he declared to his colleagues in 1812. "Distance and difficulties are less to us than any people on earth. Our schemes and prospects extend everywhere and to everything. . . . [Americans are] in action superior to all others; in patience and endurance inferior to many." For Calhoun this liberalizing ethos of energy and ambition made many traditional republican verities irrelevant. "The difference is great between the passive and active state of the mind," he argued. Thus a policy of "commercial restriction . . . sinks the nation in its own estimation." It "leaves you poor, but even [when] successful dispirited, divided, discontented, with diminished patriotism and the manners of a considerable portion of your people corrupted." Military confrontation, on the other hand, would appeal to "that which makes men love to be a member of an extensive community—the love of greatness, the consciousness of strength." As Calhoun simply noted of war's effect in 1812, "The national character acquires energy."[90]

If war seemed for Calhoun a realization of the growing republic's vitality, it also promised to soothe his underlying fears about the consequences of liberalizing change. Although exhilarated by the resourcefulness and ambition of his countrymen, the young legislator was far from comfortable with accompanying values of individual profit and materialism. In his first major speech to Congress on December 12, 1811, he grew livid in attacking the argument that Americans would not suffer the tax burden of war. "Sir, I here enter my solemn protest against this low and 'calculating avarice' entering this hall of legislation," he proclaimed. "It is only fit for shops and counting houses." Calhoun explained in another speech that war would temper such selfishness because "the common danger unites all—strengthens the bonds of society, and feeds the flame of patriotism." While opponents of war might demonstrate their attachment to "profits and luxuries only," to "the love of present ease and enjoyment, the love of gain," war appealed to higher values. Calhoun described the task facing war Republicans: "It is theirs to support the distant but lasting interest of our country; it is theirs to elevate the minds of the people, and to call up all those qualities by which present sacrifices are made to secure a future good."[91]

In addition to an "energized" republicanism and "civism," the young congressman betrayed in his rhetoric even deeper compulsions to armed conflict. Like many other citizens of the early republic, his personal concern with self-control nourished a political justification of war. The first public expression of Calhoun's politics that we have revealed the influence of his character ethic. The "Resolutions on the Chesapeake-Leopard Affair" from his native town of Abbeville— written largely by the young legislator—examined the attack of a British frigate on an American ship within sight of the Virginia coast. A pacific and vacillating response, warned the author, "would disgrace our character abroad, and exhibit us as a degenerate and pusillanimous people." Equally dangerous, however, would be an unrestrained and "wanton desire of war." Borrowing the language of self-control, Calhoun listed the characteristics for a policy of firm national "character": a posture of "independence," "determination," "a joint exertion of strength," maintenance of a "united and indivisible" spirit. This emphasis on focusing the will for success—while avoiding both passion and sloth—suggests that war, at some level of consciousness, appeared to Calhoun as part of a larger American struggle for self-controlled character.[92]

The young man saw a final private specter rising in the early-nineteenth-century war crisis. As Calhoun often noted, he perceived the situation as "the war of the Revolution revived." No simple gesture of political piety, this was a highly emotional issue of self-substantiation for a parvenu in a fluid, liberalizing society. Calhoun joined many other Americans here in half-consciously comprehending war as a means for establishing personal identity and authority. He revealed this psychological impulse in almost anguished tones in 1812. The battles of the American Revolution had left glorious memories, Calhoun told his colleagues, "but what will history say of [commercial] restrictions? . . . What pride, what pleasure will our children find in the events of such times?" Due to the heroic Founding Fathers, the United States had formed "a mighty empire, with prouder prospects than any nation the sun ever shone on . . . risen in the West." Now only through war could the Sons prove themselves worthy in their own right. "This is the second struggle for our liberty," Calhoun proclaimed, "and if we but do justice to ourselves, it will be no less glorious and successful than the first."[93]

By early 1812, this gifted Republican scion had become exhilarated by the prospect of war. In public he declared to Congress, "What more favorable [result] could we desire than that the nation is, at last, roused from its lethargy and, that it has determined to vindicate its interest and honor." In private correspondence Calhoun felt free to cut to the heart of the matter. The present crisis, he wrote to a friend in Charleston, had brought the young republic to a crossroads in its history. In years past the republic's leaders had tried to resolve foreign difficulties "by a sort of political management," a tactic that "might suit an inconsiderable nation." But for the South Carolinian, "experience has proved it improper for us. . . . We have said we will change; we will defend ourselves by force. I hope Congress will stick to this salutary resolve." As he put it simply in the same letter, war had brought "the commencement of a new era in our politics."[94]

Calhoun echoed the sentiments of countless Republicans who were restlessly reshaping republican ideology even as they were changing the social, economic, and cultural landscape of the United States. The South Carolinian, of course, would continue his ascent over the next few years to become Congressional champion of the Republicans' war effort and promoter of economic policies that became known as the American System. In June 1812, however, he authored a report presented to Congress by the Foreign Relations Committee. Perhaps more than any other document of the period, it illuminated the broad path by which the Liberal Republicans ideologically led the transforming young nation into war.

The Liberal Impulse to War

With his election in 1810, Henry Clay became the youngest Speaker of the House of Representatives in American history. The dynamic Kentuckian, only thirty-three years old, defeated the venerable Jeffersonian stalwart from North Carolina, Nathaniel Macon. The election proved to be far-reaching. Symbolically, it marked the passing of a political baton between generations, because like a host of other fledgling congressmen, many of whom first came to Washington in 1810, Clay was an energetic Liberal Republican. While respectful of Jeffersonian maxims and contemptuous of Federalist social elitism and economic mercantilism, this youthful and talented group nonetheless displayed a new ideological sensibility. They were determined to rewrite the Republican agenda in accordance with imperatives of liberalizing change in the post-Revolutionary republic. In a practical sense, Clay's selection also made an immediate impact. "Harry of the West" wasted little time in packing key House committees with able and assertive Liberal Republicans.

The most important of those committees was that dealing with foreign affairs. Thanks to Clay's skillful manipulations, it emerged as a showcase for Liberal Republican talent. Peter B. Porter of New York became chairman, and he was supported by two freshman congressman soon to be noted for their oratory and legislative leadership: John C. Calhoun of South Carolina and Felix Grundy of Tennessee. The Foreign Relations Committee became the center around which the deliberations of the Twelfth Congress revolved. From the late fall of 1811 to the early summer of 1812, the reports and recommendations emanating from this small assemblage dominated the flow of Congressional discourse. The committee acted as the lever by which the Jeffersonian Republican machinery was inched slowly toward confrontation with Great Britain.[95]

On November 29, 1811, Chairman Porter submitted a report on American relations with the hostile European powers. It acknowledged that France had repealed her restrictive decrees against American commerce, and it castigated Great Britain's continuing transgressions at considerable length. The document concluded by appealing to the "patriotism and resources" of the country to support a program of military preparation. Subsequent proposals of the Foreign Relations Committee focused Congressional debate well into the spring of 1812. Questions of finance, taxes, commercial policy, strengthening of military forces, the degree of popular mobilization—all in the context of impending war—riveted the attention of most congressmen.

Exhaustive and exhausting discussions of these issues revealed an emerging pattern. Most Federalists gradually backed away from initial support of war preparation and began to emphasize the great dangers of conflict with the powerful Great Britain. A handful of traditional Republicans joined in this dissent, fearing that war would fatally undermine republican institutions. On the other hand, moderate administration Republicans steadily deserted the time-honored strategy of peaceful coercion to endorse a vigorous defense of American rights. From the smoke of this political battlefield the Liberal Republicans emerged in a strong position of leadership. Having pushed hard and steady for a military solution to the crisis, they succeeded in shaping a Republican consensus for war. By late spring, all the war preparations recommended by the Foreign Relations Committee had passed through Congress, although some survived only in diluted form.[96]

On April 1, 1812, decisive action began. On that day President Madison asked Congress for a sixty-day embargo on American shipping—the measure was understood as clearing the commercial decks for war—and it was passed and signed on April 6. Although more vigorous than many other of his Presidential messages, it still appeared to be a workmanlike document. It methodically listed those British affronts to America's position as "an independent and neutral nation": the plundering of American neutral commerce, impressment of American sailors, harassment of the American coastline, encouragement of Indian raids, and the "sweeping system of Blockades" by the British on the European continent. The failure of the embargo and diplomatic protest, Madison admitted, had exhausted the patience of the young republic. "We behold, in fine, on the side of Great Britain, a state of war against the United States, and on the side of the United States, a state of peace towards Great Britain." Perhaps as a reminder of his characteristic republican reluctance to take the nation into war, Madison made a point of ultimately placing this "solemn question" in the hands of Congress. "I am happy in the assurance," the President concluded warily, "that the decision will be worthy of the enlightened and patriotic councils of a virtuous, a free, and a powerful nation."[97]

Congressional Liberal Republicans displayed none of Madison's hesitance. In the absence of Peter Porter—who had already left Washington for military service—acting Chairman John C. Calhoun presented to the House on June 3 a bill to declare war on Great Britain. Before submitting the war measure, however, the brilliant young South Carolinian gave to Congress on behalf of the Foreign Relations Committee one of the most fascinating and suggestive documents in the history of the early republic. Largely the work of Calhoun—with Felix Grundy likely adding several rhetorical touches[98]—the "Report on the Causes and Reasons for War" revealed more than its authors probably intended or even knew. Although cast as a review of British-American relations since 1805, the passionate eloquence of the War Report overflowed its form. Superficially, it summed up the ideological impulses that fired the war demands of the Liberal Republicans. But at a deeper level it indicated how an emerging liberal ideology drew together the social, cultural, and psychological hopes and frustrations of a people experiencing massive changes in their lives and focused them in a national crusade. Pulsating with the nervous energy of a liberalizing society, the War Report exhibited the whole complex pattern of the Jeffersonian motivation to war in 1812. A close examination of its language reveals several layers of meaning—conscious beliefs, half-conscious fears, unconscious drives—amid the flashing rhetoric.[99]

"No people ever had stronger motives to cherish peace. . . . But the period has now arrived, when the United States must support their character and station among the nations of the earth, or submit to the most shameful degradation."[100] With this ringing declaration, the War Report launched its appeal for military confrontation with Great Britain from an ideological base. Calhoun and his Liberal Republican associates here clearly conveyed their belief that the peaceful instincts of republicanism had grown weary and that the time had come for an infusion of energy. They developed this point further in the text, cautiously referring to "the commercial restrictions to which the United States resorted as an evidence of their sensibility, and a mild retaliation of their wrongs." Although carefully avoiding direct attack on this policy of their Jeffersonian elders, the Liberal Republicans stressed that "the motive was mistaken, if their [Americans'] forbearance was imputed either to the want of a just sensibility to their wrongs, or a determination . . . to resent them." The point could not have been clearer: regarding traditional republican antiwar sentiment, "the time has now arrived when this system of reasoning must cease."[101]

The War Report further pressed the case for an energized political vision by asserting, first, the great need for a show of American vigor and strength in war. "The United States must act as an independent nation, and assert their rights, and avenge their wrongs, according to their own estimate of them," read the document. Second, the Liberal Republicans insisted that the republic be capable of meeting this challenge. Scornful of those who feared for the fragility of republican institutions and themselves bolstered by an appreciation of America's liberalizing growth since the Revolution, they showed little fear. The United States "have suffered no wrong, they have received no insults, however great, for which they cannot obtain redress," noted the text confidently.[102]

This spirit of ideological innovation was sustained by similar sentiments rising outside the halls of Congress. By mid-1812 most Republicans were convinced of the need to overcome republican prejudices against war-making. Scoffing at traditional republican qualms about "a standing army," the *Western Intelligencer* rejoiced in June 1812, "It will be a moving, fighting conquering army—and as soon as its duty is done, it will be disbanded." The *National Intelligencer*, seeing in 1812 the commencement of a "new era" for the United States, went so far as to suggest that only war could save "our present system of government." Lack of success would likely "diminish our confidence in republican principles." The *Richmond Enquirer* expressed even better this regenerative ideological impulse. Announcing the declaration of war in an editorial entitled "The New Era," the editors proclaimed, "The energies of the Republic are fast disclosing themselves; and may God desert those who now desert their country!"[103]

"The hostility of the British Government to these States has . . . made manifest that the United States are considered by it as the commercial rival of Great Britain, and that their prosperity and growth are incompatible with her welfare."[104] With these phrases the War Report disclosed a related, overt motivation to war. Unlike traditional republicans fearful of luxury and decay, young Jeffersonians like Calhoun and Grundy had observed and drawn confidence from America's economic "prosperity and growth" since the Revolution. However, the entrepreneurial energy of the liberalizing young republic demanded free market access. As the War Report explained elsewhere of overseas trade, Americans "with their usual industry and enterprise, had embarked in it, a vast proportion of their shipping, and of their capital." But the British had initiated "a system of hostility on the commerce of the United States." To the Liberal Republicans, this explicit denial of markets and implicit denial of entrepreneurialism could not be tolerated.[105]

Explicating the war's economic motivation in more detail, the Foreign Relations Committee unfolded an important additional argument. On the first page of the text, the War Report indicted British aggression against "an important branch of the American commerce, which affected every part of the United States, and involved many of their citizens in ruin." Here the authors referred not to the carrying or reexport trade, but to the sale of commodities actually produced in the American Republic. So while certain maritime groups opposed war to keep open the lanes of trade for commercial carriers, Liberal Republicans sympathetic to productive farming and manufacturing interests endorsed war to protect the American-produced commodities that filled many of those lanes. This distinction—and the 1812 conflict—put a line of demarcation between two stages in the economic development of the young republic: an older commercial capitalism and an expansive, entrepreneurial, producing capitalism.[106]

Another point in the War Report suggested a final overt motive in the economic rationale for military action. Near the end of a long discussion of commercial violations by both France and England, the report's authors inserted a significant statement: "An utter inability alone, to resist could justify a quiet surrender of our rights. . . . To

that condition the United States are not reduced nor do they fear it."
In the context of an economic discussion, and given the nature of
Liberal Republican rhetoric over the previous two-score months, the
statement's meaning was clear. In the eyes of many Republicans, the
rapid development of domestic manufactures and internal commerce
since 1790 had bolstered the republic's capacity for war. They could
endorse the conflict with confidence, believing that an expanding
home market would provide economic strength for survival. Moreover, support for an Anglo-American war would likely quicken the
shift toward a reliable home trade and wean America from a decadent
dependence on foreign commerce.[107]

The War Report's assurances of American economic vitality was
once more but the crest of a large public wave. By June 1812 Republican popular discourse was bursting with indignant claims from
American producers eager for war. For more than two years the
Richmond Enquirer had been insisting that it was "unwise to plunge
this country into war, to enrich a few merchants" engaged in "the
carrying trade." However, as the editors insisted just as often, "when
G.B. declares to us; 'you shall not export your *own* productions . . . you shall not send your own articles to their natural markets'; we ask, whether we are to submit to his proud pretension."
Congressman Jonathan Roberts of Pennsylvania agreed. Productive
Americans would not fight for "a speculative right or an empty
name" of the carrying trade, he argued, but they would defend "our
fair export trade." General Andrew Jackson utilized a similar appeal
in March 1812, calling for militia volunteers to help protect "free
trade" and "open a market for the productions of our soil." A July 4,
1812, resolution from two Virginia counties stated this argument for
war most succinctly: "The right . . . to seek unmolested a market for
the products of the labor of our hands forms another of those im-
prescriptible rights, appertaining to our national sovereignty, and
most essential interests."[108]

Avid Republican advocates of productivity and the home market
had created a receptive atmosphere for the economic arguments of the
War Report. By mid-1812 they were filling the air with excited
claims that war would hasten the happy economic development of the
republic. As an unknown contributor to the *National Intelligencer*
wrote on February 22, 1812, war could bring nothing better than
"the increase of useful manufactures. . . . With a policy of this kind,
the United States may bid defiance to the world; because by following
it, they will become truly independent." A July 31, 1812, article in
the *Western Intelligencer* followed a similar tack. War, promised the

author, would encourage "the manufacturing spirit" and serve for "promoting internal commerce, and lessening the necessity of importations." Hezekiah Niles lucidly explained this logic of economic self-sufficiency. "During the war there will be ample employment for all. Some part of the labor and capital of the United States, at present devoted to commerce, will be directed to objects calculated to seal the independence of the country, the establishment of a thousand [manufacturing] works, needful to the supply of our wants," he predicted on May 31, 1812. "Our agriculturalists will have a steady and better market at home."[109]

Thus, by declaring war in 1812 many Jeffersonians hoped that America's republican government would draw badly needed energy from her dynamically growing society and economy. Instead of merely guarding the commonweal or nurturing public and private virtue, the revitalized republic would assert itself in war to demonstrate productive prowess, social vitality, and civic strength. By this process, the Liberal Republicans accelerated the departure of ideology and political economy from traditional republican moorings.

"But one sentiment pervaded the whole American Nation. No local interests were regarded, no sordid motives felt. Without looking to the parts which suffered most, the invasion of our rights was considered a common cause, and from one extremity of our union to the other, was heard the voice of a united People."[110] With this rhetorical flourish the War Report brought to light another layer of war impulses lying just beneath the evident rationalizations of political economy and ideology. In this submerged realm of social relations and cultural values, desires and compulsions of doubt and guilt over rapidly liberalizing social change found partial resolution in war. As this passage indicated, the workings of "civism" comprised one such impulse. As we have seen, countless observers noted that the post-Revolutionary decades witnessed an unprecedented fragmentation of American society as a rapidly growing population, geographical mobility, and social aspiration created a society of people on the make. By the early nineteenth century, deference had declined. Moral restraints on wealth-making had withered. The traditional community context for individual action had faded. In this fragmenting context, Americans confronted problems of commitment beyond pure self-interest. In what form was loyalty to the commonweal possible? How could private and public virtue exist in a society increasingly devoted to the main chance? The War Report's clarion call indicated one attractive answer. Taking the battlefield against Great Britain would transcend mere self-regard by blending "the voice of a united people" in "one

sentiment," in "common cause." By providing such a compelling opportunity for civism, the War of 1812 comprised a ritual absolution of guilt for many American possessive individuals.[111]

"The mad ambition, the lust of power . . . of Great Britain. . . . [Facing this] degrading submission to the will of others . . . the United States have had to resist, with the firmness belonging to their character, the continued violation of their rights."[112] The text of Calhoun and Grundy here moved half-consciously to the terrain of cultural values. By juxtaposing the unrestrained craving of Great Britain with the firm "character" of the young republic, the War Report touched a cultural nerve. In the consolidating liberal society of the early republic, popular discourse had given new meaning to the word "character." Signifying "reputation" in the eighteenth century, by 1812 the term was also coming to designate one's inner moral structure. More specifically, it connoted the self-control of the self-made man. In one sense the character ethic referred to the shaping of one's own destiny through marshaling talent and ambition, and the 1812 war gave vent to that impulse. As depicted in the War Report, an aristocratic, mercantilist Great Britain was confining American entrepreneurialism by dominating the ocean and exercising "an unbounded and lawless tyranny." War thus materialized in part as a means for citizens of a hard-working liberal society to break artificial restrictions and to assert control over their destiny. As the War Report noted, the "high character of the American people" only required a proving ground. "Forbearance has ceased to be a virtue," wrote the authors in the language of self-control. "There is an alternative only, between the base surrender of their rights and a manly vindication of them."[113]

This affirmation of character, however, carried still another meaning: not just control over one's own destiny, but repression of one's instinctual and emotional appetites. The directives of an emerging capitalist culture—hard work, individual opportunity-seeking, calculating judgments—necessitated self-discipline as well as self-assertion, and that meant avoiding the temptations of avarice, immorality, and self-indulgence. War in 1812 provided a singular opportunity in the cultural struggle for repression. For years critics had railed against the manipulative, voluptuous materialism of the commercializing young republic, and now Great Britain became the target for the projection of such fears, and war a means of opposing them. As the War Report described, the "lust," "mad ambition," "commercial avarice," and "unbounded tyranny" of England demanded that Americans resist "with the firmness belonging to their character." Embodying "no sordid motives" but only moral purpose, and exploding the manipulative masks endemic to "Teagomania," war appeared in 1812 as a compelling exercise for repression of base instinct and elevation of self-disciplined character.[114]

"Happily for the United States, their destiny, under the aid of Heaven, is in their own hands."[115] As this War Report sentence related, many Republicans found but a short distance between self-control and a belief in divine assistance in their movement toward conflict in 1812. In other words, the war of 1812 served as a clarion call for American "civil religion." Heirs of a Protestant millennial tradition, Americans tended to see their society as an exemplary gathering of godly, industrious communities counterpoised between the heathen Indian and the decadent popery of Europe. As good republicans, they also envisioned the United States as a virtuous, enlightened, vigorous New World polity arrayed against the hoary, tyrannical oligarchies of the Old World. These two strands of national hubris first had intertwined during the American Revolution, and the nation's post-1790 socioeconomic growth only reinforced this sense of the republic's special mission. In 1812 war seemed to offer a rich historical moment for the fulfillment of America's divine destiny. With commingled Protestant hopes and republican dreams, the War Report assured Americans that they could join battle with Great Britain "confidently trusting the Lord of Hosts will go with us to Battle in a righteous cause."[116]

"We wish to call attention of the House to those injuries . . . as could not fail to deprive the United States of the principal advantages of their Revolution, if submitted to. . . . The proof which so complete and disgraceful a submission . . . would afford of our degeneracy, could not fail to inspire confidence, that there was no limit to which, our degradation, might not be carried."[117] With these curiously emotional sentiments, the War Report finally brought close to the surface a cluster of deeply submerged impulses to war. Bowing to the legacy of the Revolution and the Founding Fathers, the authors followed with familiar warnings about their own generation's "degeneracy." Like many other citizens of the young nation, these Liberal Republicans betrayed acute anxiety over their position and status in a congealing liberal society. Burdened with an image of the heroic and self-sacrificing Fathers, and guilty over the growing materialism and grasping competitiveness of the post-Revolutionary generation, these Sons had inflicted on themselves a crisis of authority. By sacrificing material pursuits and joining together in heroic enterprise against a threatening enemy, in 1812 they could prove themselves worthy heirs to the Founders. In war the Sons could authenticate the emerging spirit of capitalism and show liberal man to be as morally purposeful as republican man. In

war they could uphold and guarantee for Americans "the principal advantages of their Revolution."

"Our flag has given no protection . . . ; it has been unceasingly violated, and our vessels exposed to dangers by the loss of men taken from them. . . . An exemption of the citizens of the United States from this degrading oppression, and their flag from violation, is all that they have sought. . . . The United States must act, and avenge their wrongs."[118] If violent conflict in 1812 promised to resolve these Republican Sons' crisis of authority, the War Report revealed that war also addressed another psychological difficulty. Through this oblique use of imagery—ostensibly a discussion of impressment's horrors—Calhoun and Grundy half-consciously pictured war as a "return of the repressed." As Richard Sennett has argued, for the modern personality continually beset by repressions, conformities, and commercial banalities it is often the case that "to be aggressive is to be alive." The War Report suggested that in 1812 the Liberal Republicans had indeed tapped a hidden desire among their countrymen for cathartic, violent escape from repressive demands for self-control. The document angrily denounced—in highly sensual language—the "violation" of "exposed" Americans. It also bitterly complained of Great Britain's disregard for "obligations which have heretofore been held sacred by civilized nations." It indignantly denounced England's Indian allies for commencing "that system of savage warfare on our frontiers which has been at all times indiscriminate in its effects, on all ages, sexes, and conditions and so revolting to humanity." Sensing an acute libidinous appeal to repressed character-types, the Liberal Republican authors emotionally denounced such forbidden outrages. Yet they quickly turned to offer their *own* acceptable, organized, and civilized mode of violent release: war. By entering on an aggressive crusade to quash "savagery"—by mustering violence in the name of resisting violence—Americans could escape momentarily and legitimately the iron cage of repression. As the Liberal Republicans described in the War Report, in a psychologically explosive atmosphere struggling Americans were "calling on their Government to avenge their wrongs."[119]

"The attempts to dismember our Union, and overthrow our excellent constitution, by a secret mission [we denounce]. . . . It must be evident to the impartial world, that the contest which is now forced . . . is radically a contest for their sovereignty and independence."[120] With this rhetorical lightning flash, the Liberal Republicans fleetingly disclosed the visage of the "personae" as it anxiously moved toward war in 1812. Complaining here of a furtive British political mission in 1811 designed to foment division in the American republic,[121] the authors of

the War Report also unconsciously portrayed a hidden, knotty identity function of the conflict. They lashed out emotionally at an external enemy seeking by "a secret mission" to "dismember our Union, and overthrow our excellent constitution." This highly symbolic language objectified the pressures descending on the individual psyche in this era of liberalizing change, and suggested its subsequent tendency toward fragmentation. This imagery also indicated that the early-nineteenth-century "personae"—a diffuse personality structure lacking identity beneath the manipulative masks of liberal social relations—was drawn to the cohesive dynamic of war. As other phrases from the War Report suggested, the conflict offered a "total" pseudo-identity by paranoid definition. The authors extravagantly condemned the evil enemy for assailing American individuals: "Our citizens are wantonly snatched from their country, and their families; deprived of their liberty and doomed to an ignominious and slavish bondage." The Liberal Republicans darkly discerned a "system of hostile aggression, by the British government." What was even more outlandish was their perception of "full proof that there is no bound to the hostility of the British government . . . no act, however unjustifiable, which it would not commit." Thus Americans, by creating and fighting an evil foe bent on their destruction, could find psychological cohesion themselves. As Calhoun and Grundy wrote—probably with more significance than they realized for the "personae" of liberalizing Americans—the war was "radically a contest for their sovereignty and independence."[122]

The War Report of the Liberal Republicans, in the complexity and symbolism of its language, thus displayed the various threads of motivation leading to the war declaration in the summer of 1812. Its final paragraph, designed as a stirring call to arms by the young members of the Foreign Relations Committee, emotionally wove these threads into whole cloth:

Your committee, believing that the freeborn sons of America are worthy to enjoy to liberty which their Fathers purchased at the price of so much blood and treasure, and seeing in the measures adopted by Great Britain, a course commenced and persisted in, which must lead to a loss of National character & Independence, feel no hesitation in advising resistance by force—In which Americans of the present day will prove to the enemy and to the World, that we have not only inherited the liberty which our Fathers gave us, but also the will & power to maintain it. Relying on the patriotism of the Nation, and confidently trusting that the Lord of Hosts will go with us to Battle in a righteous cause, and crown our efforts with success, your Committee recommend an immediate appeal to Arms.[123]

Certain historians have suggested that in many ways the War Report resembled nothing so much as a second American "Declaration of Independence."[124] Its serial condemnation of a depraved Great Britain, its appeals for American resistance and assertion, and its defiant cadences of barely restrained emotion suggested an almost self-conscious duplication of the brave polemic of 1776. There is a germ of truth here, and it is easy to see the 1812 conflict as merely a second, pale "War for Independence," with Calhoun, Clay, and Grundy attempting to play the heroic roles of Jefferson, Adams, and Washington. However, a close, penetrating reading of the War Report reveals much more. Rather than simply a bellicose expression of growing nationalist sentiment, the demands in the document for a vigorous "independence" carried myriad deeper meanings. Its authors actually painted a miniature portrait of the liberal impulse to war in 1812 and its complex characteristics—an expansive entrepreneurial economy, an energized republican ideology, the desire for civism and self-control, reverence for American civil religion, and the personae's frantic search for authority, emotional release, and identity. Thus the War Report ultimately tells us much about the transforming forces at work in the early republic. It illustrates how the young Liberal Republicans captured politically many of the aspirations and deeper confusions accruing to consolidating liberal capitalism and projected them into a conflict with Great Britain.

As the passions aroused by war swept through the United States in 1812, the momentum of historical change began to increase. Over the next three years the War of 1812 would accelerate and finally sanction the liberalizing transformation that had begun in earnest in the late eighteenth century. But it would do so in ways both unexpected and predictable.

VI

The Republic Reordered
1812–1815

War—or at least modern war waged by a democratic republic
against a powerful enemy—seems to achieve
for a nation . . . the full realization
of that collective community in which each individual somehow
contains the virtue of the whole. . . . At war, the individual becomes
almost identical with his society. He achieves a superb self-assurance,
an intuition of the rightness of all his ideas and emotions,
so that in the suppression of opponents or heretics
he is invincibly strong; he feels behind him all the power
of the collective community.
The individual as social being in war
seems to have achieved almost his apotheosis.

RANDOLPH BOURNE
The State

War has always been the Nemesis of the liberal tradition in America.
From our earliest history as a nation there has been
a curiously persistent association between
democratic politics and nationalism, jingoism, and war.
Periodically war has written the last scene to some drama begun
by the popular side of the party struggle.

RICHARD HOFSTADTER
The Age of Reform

Once begun, the War of 1812 defied the expectations of nearly all Americans. Federalists had reacted to the declaration of hostilities with panic, pronouncing near-hysterical eulogies over the grave of the nation. War with powerful England, they believed, had doomed the infant republic to an early death. Most Jeffersonians had embraced the conflict as a bracing test for the restless and ambitious self-made citizens transforming the traditional republic. Yet war fulfilled neither Jeffersonian hopes of ecstatic regeneration nor Federalist fears of cataclysm. Instead, two and a half years of military confrontation took shape as an exercise in frustration, ineptness, and survival. Strategic victories and crushing defeats alike evaded American arms, and the 1815 Treaty of Ghent brought little practical recompense beyond peace. Indeed, the United States gained virtually nothing concrete from the conflict save a new national hero, Andrew Jackson—in front of whose barricaded soldiers at New Orleans the British graciously paraded several thousand troops to be mowed down—and an unsingable national anthem.[1]

Yet despite such infelicities, the second war with Great Britain had a profound impact on American life. As scholars have noticed since the nineteenth century, the end of the clash seemed to inaugurate a new phase in the brief history of the United States. Historians of Jeffersonian America traditionally have associated the "successful" English conflict with a post-1815 acceleration of economic development, government centralization, and nationalist fervor. As Henry Adams remarked over ninety years ago, for instance, the peace announcement turned attention from issues that had dominated the public agenda for a generation. "A people which had in 1787 been indifferent or hostile to roads, banks, funded debt, and nationality had become in 1815 habituated to ideas and machinery of that sort on a great scale," he wrote. "Monarchy or aristocracy no longer entered into the public mind as factors in future development."[2] More recently, students of early American political ideology have discerned a similar if rather differently defined aftermath to the war: the "second war for independence" may have assured the permanence of American republicanism, but that very process of assurance seemed to transform familiar republican meanings. One historian observed typically that while the 1815 peace agreement assured Americans "that their experiment in republican government was going to endure," it also marked the "point at which to write an end to the debate that traced back to the 18th century argument between the English Country and Court." For such scholars, the war's end brought a new ideological concern with "the needs of the future" and "the most appropriate means of national development."[3]

While perceptive, these older and newer historical judgments of the war's impact remain incomplete. Usually coming at the conclusion of earlier period studies or at the outset of later antebellum studies, they savor of intuition more than concentrated analysis. Two particular obscurities persist. First, general references to economic growth, nationalism, and a politics of "prosperity" tend to substitute vagueness for definitional rigor. Second, vital connections between economic change, transforming social values, developing political ideology, and the actual circumstances of the war have remained in the shadows. A clear focus on the experience and meaning of the War of 1812 reveals its consequences to be far more complex, integrated, and far-reaching than generally recognized.[4]

The "victory" of 1815 marked a watershed in the making of liberal America. While the 1812 declaration of hostilities had been a catalyst for liberalizing trends gathering force in Jeffersonian circles over the previous two decades, the conflict's remarkable resolution gave them a resounding affirmation. The emotional heat of 1815 melded these various trends and sanctioned a coherent liberal creed that would dominate nineteenth-century America. So the war not only prompted a quantitative growth of the young republic, but also shaped the *qualitative*, hegemonic mode in which that geographic, economic, and intellectual expansion would proceed. This sanctioning process first emerged amid the wartime travails of the United States.

The decision of Congress to fight the British in June 1812 triggered a landslide of problems that nearly overwhelmed the young American nation and its Republican leadership. Eager for violence but unprepared for war, the Jeffersonian majority appeared almost startled to find themselves facing the massive predicaments endemic to large-scale conflict. A sullen and uncooperative Federalist minority did not ease the task. Hopes for quick and glorious victory faded rather quickly before intractable military, logistical, and political obstacles. As events unfolded, three difficulties emerged to afflict American efforts in the War of 1812: financial support, military mobilization and organization, and impassioned domestic political dissent. The manner in which Jeffersonian Republicans moved to resolve such problems revealed, and eventually promoted, their reworking of republican categories into a liberal conceptualization of society and ideology.

Secretary of the Treasury Albert Gallatin formulated the original

Republican plan for financing the war. He proposed to meet regular government expenses from existing taxes and to defray the cost of war from special loans authorized by the national government. However, a series of factors intervened to wreck this proposition. The relatively small population and economic immaturity of the United States made for a small tax base and limited supply of capital to begin with. Americans' traditional republican hostility toward taxes also made for an unreceptive audience among the people. Thus the mounting cost of war rapidly outdistanced the limited revenue raised by Gallatin. Moreover, in different ways the two parties exacerbated the nation's financial distress. Reluctant to demolish older Jeffersonian principles and eager to stay in power, the bulk of Republicans remained reluctant to impose heavier internal taxes. The Federalists, on the other hand, largely refused to loan money to the national government. So in 1813 prowar forces took a desperate new tack, initiating a disastrous program of paper financing by issuing huge sums of Treasury certificates and authorizing large government loans. Thus by the fall of 1814 the national government was approaching bankruptcy. Public credit had virtually disappeared—Treasury notes were circulating at 20 percent of value and loan bonds at 70 percent—while a serious specie drain from banks throughout the nation, especially in the middle states and New England, had caused a suspension of much specie payment.[5]

Republican reactions to the financial crisis ranged from surprise to dismay to anger. "Our finances are in a deplorable state," wrote James Monroe to Thomas Jefferson during the war. "With a country consisting of the best materials in the world, whose people are patriotic & virtuous, & willing to support the war; whose resources are greater than those of any other country; & whose means have scarcely yet been touched, we have neither money in the treasury or credit." Younger Republicans like Charles J. Ingersoll grew even more frustrated. Criticizing in June 1813 his party's reluctance to tax, the Pennsylvania congressman insisted that war without financial backing was a mockery. It could not be "what it ought to be— an attitude of defiance and annoyance to the enemy, of protection and safeguard to us—unless it be erected on a well-founded Treasury capable of perpetual reproductiveness and never-failing replenishment." Such anxiety eventually forced Jeffersonians to an explicit revision of respected republican principles. In late 1814 Republicans began preparing an expanded program of internal taxation. In a report to the House Ways and Means Committee in October 1814, Secretary of the Treasury Alexander J. Dallas took another step by bluntly detailing the wartime financial crisis and proposing a remedy. A new national bank, he argued, would greatly assist in gathering and distributing public revenue and would provide a means to halt the flood of paper currency in the various states. War had forced Liberal Republicans into the open and had created followers even among reluctant colleagues. By 1814 the party of Thomas Jefferson had become the party of taxation and a revived United States Bank.[6]

Jeffersonian problems with raising wartime revenues paralleled those of raising and organizing a fighting force. In June 1812 the American peacetime army contained only seven thousand troops and suffered a severe shortage of experienced officers. A Republican Congress had passed several measures from November 1811 to June 1812 to enlarge the regular army, but they had borne little fruit by the early stages of the war. Frustrated letters from President Madison reflected the military incompetence of the United States. "The lapse of time and the unproductiveness of the laws contemplating a regular force, and volunteers for an entire year and under federal commissions, compel us to moderate some of our expectations," he complained to Henry Dearborn on August 9, 1812. A letter to William Wirt several months later gave a fuller account of military disarray: lack of recruits, low pay, a chaotic officer system, disorganization in the quartermaster's department. The "utter inexperience" of the American effort, Madison bemoaned, was probably inseparable "from a Country among whose blessings it is to have long intervals of peace, and to be without those large standing armies which even in peace are fitted for war." Events quickly reminded, however, that those "blessings" seemed about to fall prey to military disasters. A series of inept campaigns along the northern warfront—which included at one point a refusal of American militia to cross over into Canada—and the British invasion of the Chesapeake region in the late summer of 1814 highlighted the republic's precarious position.[7]

The Jeffersonian majority responded to this military plight by again reluctantly rethinking traditional assumptions. Cherished notions of the citizen-soldier and decentralized central government slowly lost legitimacy in face of wartime exigencies. By November 1812 President Madison was appealing to Congress for legislation to raise soldiers' pay, lengthen the period of enlistment, strengthen the structure of the officer corps, and revise militia laws "for the purpose of rendering them more systematic and better adapting them to emergencies of the war." In addition to consistently raising the size of the regular army and its wages during the first two years of the war, by the fall of 1814 Republicans were considering more extreme legislation: release from debt and land bounties for recruits, and mandatory troop quotas for the states that verged on a "conscription" system. War had shaped the party of Thomas Jefferson into the party of expanding military force and the draft.[8]

The final and perhaps most painful Republican travail came with Federalist subversion of the war effort. Sustained opposition intensified financial and military hardships and thereby threatened to destroy the republic from within. Dissenting congressmen did their part by voting against the vast majority of supportive wartime legislation and constantly ridiculed Republican maladroitness in prosecuting the conflict. War opposition also took more concrete and disruptive forms. First of all, Federalist political leaders, ministers, and partisan newspapers actively discouraged merchants and bankers from loaning money to the government. Their argument that such money would both support a war of foreign conquest and destroy commercial wealth found a receptive audience among wealthy Federalists. Second, Federalist governors of several New England states refused to release the militia for deployment outside state lines. This imbroglio seriously undermined administration war plans and also edged the nation toward a constitutional confrontation over national versus state power. Finally, mounting discontent in the same region, especially in Massachusetts, culminated in the 1814 commencement of the Hartford Convention. Dissatisfied with Republican sincerity in negotiating for peace, and convinced that the administration was manipulating the war to destroy New England, disaffected Federalist leaders gathered in the late fall of 1814. The threat of New England secession hung in the air and made the state of national affairs even more dire.[9]

Republican nerves wore thin under the Federalist challenge. Young Jeffersonian Felix Grundy raised a national uproar by accusing war opponents of "moral treason." "I accuse him who announces with joy the disasters of our arms, and sickens into melancholy when he hears of our success," the Tennessean thundered in Congress on June 18, 1813. "Is not that man then subserving the interests of the enemy, who, to the extent of his power, keeps money from our coffers and men from our armies?" Workaday Jeffersonians vented frustrations in less official ways, as some three days of prowar rioting in July 1812 in Baltimore illustrated. The town crier of Hartford, Connecticut, provided a sardonic twist on Republican annoyance when he paraded a company of U.S. soldiers around the Federalist convention hall playing "The Rogue's March," a melody usually reserved for criminals as they wound their way to the gallows. Even the mild temperament of James Madison eventually gave way to bitter denunciations of Federalist opposition. New England's conduct comprised "the source of our greatest difficulties in carrying on the war," he wrote angrily in April 1814. "The greater part of the people in that quarter have been brought by their leaders, aided by their priests, under a delusion scarcely exceeded by that recorded in the period of witchcraft; and the leaders are becoming daily more desperate in the use they make of it. Their object is power."[10]

This staggering array of difficulties created a mounting sense of crisis in the wartime republic. Even the astute, veteran Jeffersonian Albert Gallatin lamented to a French correspondent in April 1814 that the United States had been "placed in a more critical situation than ever they were since the first years of their Revolution." Thomas Cooper voiced the anguish of many Republicans in a gloomy survey of American affairs and the American character in August 1814. The Republic's post-Revolutionary prosperity, he noted with concern, may have fatally undermined its citizens' capacity for "habitual preserving energy." "You cannot excite the people to turn out even to defend their country for they are so happy and idle at home," Cooper despaired to Jefferson. "How can you fill our armies with men, who by an idle kind of labour at home, undergone when the fit takes them during 4 or 5 days in the week, can earn all that nature requires and whiskey enough for intoxication in the bargain?"[11]

Yet ironically, in many ways the crisis was less than it should have been. With military, financial, and political confusion reigning at home, the infant United States should have been crushed in a military contest with a major European power. But it was not. The bungled campaigns of 1812 and 1813 caused no immediate military threat. Even when the general European peace of 1814 brought an end to the Napoleonic Wars and released thousands of veteran troops for use in North America, the British invasions of northern New England and the Chesapeake pulled up short after mixed success. By the time peace negotiations began at Ghent in August 1814, America's survival seemed strangely secure. But more important in the long run, amid American wartime adversity several political, social, and cultural trends had coalesced. These less conspicuous but ultimately crucial developments suggested that the short-term disarray of war had encouraged a long-term reordering of the young republic.

The first portent of the war's lasting impact appeared in Republican responses to wartime exigencies. Their steady movement toward a legislative program of increased internal taxes, military conscription, and a national bank made explicit what prewar tendencies had only suggested: a liberal revision of Republican principles. As Hezekiah Niles observed during the darkest days of 1814, "the events of the war," however grim, were forcing traditional notions into new shapes. "The defects of our system, or the errors of our practice, shall be discovered by experience," he exhorted his countrymen, "and our strength, and the best way of applying it, shall be ascertained as our wants demand its exertion." The Jeffersonian willingness to reshape republican government also became manifest in a reconsideration of political economy. Logistical problems and economic shortages during the war years greatly intensified Republican commitments to internal improvements, manufactures, and the home market.[12]

Another omen of the postwar liberal future appeared with the decline of the Federalists, the party associated with a society of paternal authority, a politics of deference, and an economy of overseas trade and commercial wealth. While Federalist hostility to the war steadily grew after 1812, so too did their isolation from mainstream opinion. The stream of abuse leveled at the Republican war eventually began to ring a false note with many American citizens, as dissent seemed to cross a line into self-serving partisanship, if not disloyalty. Two events further backed Federalists into a corner. The British invasion of the United States in the summer of 1814 comprised the first. By this one stroke the English succeeded in making the war a justifiable defensive struggle and in kindling a new sense of domestic unity. Whatever the conflict may have been in 1812, by August 1814 it had become, in the words of the Federalist governor of Vermont, "a common and not a party concern" that deserved the support of all citizens. In the early fall of 1814 many Federalist leaders joined the American armed forces, while a caucus of Federalist congressmen and senators agreed that they would support moves to repel invasion. Second, adverse publicity surrounding the convocation of the Hartford Convention drove nails in the lid of the Federalist coffin. For the great majority of Americans outside New England, this gathering tainted Federalist politics with treason. To others, the Hartford meeting merely affirmed the foolishness and unrealism of the dissenting party. When asked to speculate on the likely product of the convention, even Federalist leader Josiah Quincy snorted, "A great pamphlet!" By late 1814, as Federalist opposition to the war fell increasingly into disrepute, their political principles tended to do likewise.[13]

News of the Treaty of Ghent and of Andrew Jackson's great victory at New Orleans arrived nearly simultaneously on the East Coast in mid-February 1815. At that moment the dark clouds of America's wartime tribulation dispersed to reveal the clear, bright outlines of the liberal republic. With explosions of patriotic exuberance lighting up the American landscape, it became clear that a process of affirmation had largely been fulfilled. Both public and private discourse revealed that the liberalizing instincts summoned in 1812—not just political, but social and cultural as well—had intensified and hardened in the crucible of war.

The Vindication of God's Republic

Celebrations of peace in February 1815 barely contained American exultation. With much of Washington, D.C., still in ashes from the British assault only six months before, and rumors of further invasions still circulating, the peace treaty offered cathartic relief to a highly agitated citizenry. In addition, the decisive triumph of western troops over British regulars at New Orleans added an unexpectedly glorious conclusion to what had been a rather ignominious war. As elation swept through the republic, Jeffersonian rhetoric soared.

Niles' Weekly Register marveled that "the war was finished in a blaze of glory, as though God had tested Americans and their government in a short contest to *secure* future peace and *establish* our mild and benevolent institutions." As the editorial concluded with a flourish, her people could be *"proud in the belief that America now stands in the first rank of nations."* Other Republican newspapers saw the hand of heaven at work and ran headlines proclaiming, "Praise Ye the Lord for the Avenging of Israel." A plethora of such sentiments suggested that the peace of 1815 brought home two immediate messages: first, that the war had established a new sense of energy and character for republican government, and, second, that it had demonstrated the special place of the United States in the eyes of God. These themes would dominate many Republican assessments of the struggle.[14]

From the outset Jeffersonians had endorsed the war in part to regenerate republican institutions. Troubled by years of European attacks on foreign commerce, and also by the seeming weakness and vacillation of the American response, they saw in war a chance to revitalize the strength and prove the efficacy of the young republic. During the actual hostilities, this instinct remained strong, if most of the time unfulfilled. As Vice-President Elbridge Gerry informed the Senate in May 1813, for example, the English war was a test "to determine, whether the republican system adopted by the people, is imbecile and transient, or whether it has force and duration worthy of the enterprise."[15]

The conflict's glorious termination, however, finally told frustrated Jeffersonian Republicans what they wanted to hear. The young nation had met the Atlantic world's strongest monarchy and somehow fought her to a stand-off. Private and public discussion affirmed the republic's hard-won new respect in the community of nations and self-respect at home. As Secretary of State James Monroe wrote to the Senate barely a week after the announcement of peace, the war had "made trial of the strength and efficiency of our government," with the result that "our Union has gained strength, our troops honor, and the nation character." Congressman Jonathan Roberts of Pennsylvania testified to this strengthening effect on the nation in a private letter. The conflict's successful termination, he wrote to his brother on February 17, 1815, demonstrated that military prowess was not restricted to monarchies. "It is the triumph of virtue over vice, of republican men and republican principles over the advocates and doctrines of Tyranny."[16]

Speaker of the House Henry Clay perhaps best represented the revitalizing effect of the War of 1812 on American republicanism. This young Liberal Republican had agitated for a declaration of war with just such hopes, and he managed to sustain them even through the darkest hours of the contest. With the 1815 peace, Clay was jubilant. "A great object of the war has been attained in the firm establishment of the national character," he wrote in a public letter in Washington. Back in Lexington, Kentucky, later in the year, the Speaker assured a banquet audience: "The immediate effects of the war were highly satisfactory. Abroad our character which at the time of its declaration was in the lowest state of degradation, was raised to the highest point of elevation." But it was not until a speech before Congress in January 1816 that Henry Clay offered a final assessment of the republic's new-found vigor:

> Have we gained nothing by the war? Let any man look at the degraded condition of the country before the war. The scorn of the universe, the contempt of ourselves; and tell me we have gained nothing by the war? What is our present situation? Respectability and character abroad— security and confidence at home. . . . Our character and constitution are placed on a solid basis never to be shaken.[17]

For many Jeffersonians, however, the war's confirmation of America transcended mere politics. By its very implausibility, the "victory" of 1815 seemed to substantiate what pious war advocates had been saying since 1812: resistance to Great Britain was the crusade of a righteous people enjoying God's special favor. Minister John Stevens, for example, conveyed this Republican message in a

widely reprinted April 1813 sermon. "Such a war God considers as
his own cause," he intoned, "and to help in such a cause is to come to
the help of the Lord." Thus Andrew Jackson's miraculous, almost
unbelievable triumph at New Orleans easily became a divinely ordained event. Congressman George Troup of Georgia explained on
February 16, 1815, "The God of Battles and Righteousness took part
with the defenders of their country and the foe was scattered as chaff
before the wind." The *Rutland Vermont Herald* reached a similar
conclusion about the conflict, noting simply that Americans had
conducted "a holy war, for the Lord has fought for us the battles, and
given us the victories." The religious jubilation of 1815 often carried
over into vengeful attacks on the numerous Federalist ministers who
had denounced the war. One pamphleteer savagely asserted that the
American victory had proved the false piety of divines like "Pope"
Timothy Dwight, who supposedly had prayed in wartime "Our
Mother, who art in Europe, adored be thy name. Thy kingdom
come, Thy will be done, in New England as it is done in Ireland and
its dependencies."[18]

Baptists in Nottingham-West, Maine, heard a particularly striking expression of the war's religious function on April 13, 1815.
Speaking on the national day of Thanksgiving, the Rev. Daniel
Merrill presented a sermon entitled "Balaam Disappointed." Merrill, a graduate of Dartmouth College and a former Congrega-
tionalist, had long maintained that the war was a holy endeavor. Now
in the aftermath of a glorious peace he relished the nature of God's
judgment. The conflict's resolution had shown Great Britain to be
"the prolific mother of abominations" and exposed New England's
standing religious order as a haven of "superstition and religious
tyranny." According to this Baptist leader and Republican, it also
confirmed the special godly mission of the American republic:

> The Lord hath planted us and settled us. The Lord hath given us liberty,
> both civil and religious. . . . He hath poured contempt on our foes, and
> blasted their expectations. . . . For no nation, save Israel of old, hath
> experienced such great salvations. None possessed such a rich abundance
> of pleasant, fertile, and well-watered lands. None understand their civil
> rights so well or possess them so fully, or enjoy them so generally, as our
> nation.

For Merrill and many others, the War of 1812 had demonstrated the
special spiritual nature of "Israel, our beloved country."[19]

This same belief—that the citizens of the American Israel were
God's people—also inspired a more complex Jeffersonian reading of
the War of 1812. Rather than simply a preordained triumph of the

righteous, the conflict appeared to many Republican supporters as a test of that righteousness. As the contest wore on, this notion took two forms. Some observers cast the confrontation in terms of a chastening ordeal for American civic morality and private piety alike. An 1814 "Proclamation" of the Republican governor of South Carolina—printed in *Niles' Weekly Register* under the heading "Religious State Papers"—expressed this notion well. Citizens of the republic, contended Governor Joseph Alston, should thank God for their blessings because in the rest of the world the Almighty had "permitted man formed after His own image, to live sunk in ignorance and enslaved by his fellows." Now with the war the American ability to maintain those providential blessings was at trial. A virtuous people could only look heavenward, Alston concluded, and supplicate God to inspire its leaders with "wisdom and energy" and "all classes of citizens with a spirit of harmony, union and liberal confidence in each other." By weathering the storm of war, Americans would emerge a morally regenerate people.[20]

More introspective war supporters dwelt on a second variation of this theme. As the Rev. Joshua Hartt suggested typically in January 1815, a nation's sin provoked God "to send his judgements upon a land or nation, in order to reform them, if they will be reformed." Hartt, a Methodist preacher and long-standing advocate of the Republican crusade, analyzed the war as God's punishment for his wayward children, but also as a means for purgation of sin. Like many pious Americans, he believed that the abundant resources, growing wealth, and increasing population of the United States made her "the most favored nation on the face of the whole earth." But prosperity and blessings had given rise to moral decay. "Pride and fullness of bread too often accompany each other," Hartt confessed. "This was the case with Jerusalem before the Babylonian captivity. . . . This has been and still is the case with these United States." The defeats for American arms and the burning of Washington thus comprised God's means to "humble" a sinful people. Yet by confessing their sins, both individually and as a nation, and returning to God, citizens of the republic would prevail. Abandon sinfulness, urged Hartt, and "prepare to war aginst God's enemies." He concluded even before peace was achieved, "It appears evident that God has been on our side. . . . If God be for us, who can stand before us?"[21]

Yet the significance of the wartime vindication of the republic went beyond nationalism and piety. It lay in the singular way Americans combined them. Drawing on a cultural habit formed during the American Revolution—its roots stretched even further back to the

Puritans' "city on a hill"—Jeffersonian celebrants of New Orleans and the Ghent treaty depicted the War of 1812 as a great sanction for American civil religion. In turn, this doctrine helped ease the rise of a liberal mentality by providing a transcendent counterpoint to the soulless pursuit of material self-interest. This wartime fusion of revitalized national strength, liberal individualism, and godly affirmation of the republic surfaced everywhere in peace commemorations by Republican enthusiasts. It appeared nowhere more clearly, however, than in an 1815 publication written by an eminent minister from New York City.

A Scriptural View of the Character, Causes, and Ends of the Present War rolled off the presses in January 1815. Its author, the Rev. Alexander McLeod, was a highly esteemed Reformed Presbyterian minister in New York and a man described as "the most prominent clerical champion of the War of 1812." Composed, preached, and published while the city remained under blockade by the British fleet, this forceful series of sermons exuded commingled moral righteousness and fierce national pride. It became such a favorite in prowar circles—which, of course, rapidly expanded in February of that year—that a second edition appeared just a few weeks later. *A Scriptural View of the War* stood unsurpassed as an expression of Jeffersonian war-tempered civil religion.[22]

Alexander McLeod had been born in Scotland in 1774 and was orphaned as a boy. He migrated to the United States in 1792, where he first held a job as a teacher of ancient languages before attending Union College. During the late 1790s young McLeod also became a communicant in the Reformed Presbyterian Church. Having aspired to the ministry as a student, upon graduation the Scottish immigrant became licensed to preach and was ordained in 1800. In 1801 he accepted the pastorate at the First Reformed Presbyterian Church in New York City, and he remained in that post until his death in 1833. During the early nineteenth century, McLeod fashioned a reputation as one of America's most eloquent pulpit orators and was active as well in the early antislavery movement and various evangelical enterprises. But it was the *Scriptural View of the War* that disclosed the minister's larger, self-defined mission. As McLeod wrote to a friend upon the book's release, "My object is to spread the knowledge of Reformation principles in matters civil and religious. The good of my country is the next object to the good of Zion."[23]

Shortly after his arrival the young Scotsman became a convert to Jeffersonian politics and, in the words of a fellow minister, "while he saw and lamented the ignorance, the weakness, and the vices which were abroad in the land, he had strong confidence in the existing intelligence and moral power of the community, under the benign providence of the Prince of the kings of the earth, as adequate to the saving of the country." McLeod quickly brought these principles to bear in his *Scriptural View of the War*. The opening sermon offered a ringing justification of speaking from the pulpit on political questions. While some Jeffersonian Republicans, outraged by the New England clergy's violent attacks on the war, had denied the relation between religion and politics, the New York minister not only accepted it but turned it to advantage. The actions of Jesus and the prophets had established the biblical guidelines for political involvement by men of God, he argued. The important role of ministers in the American Revolution had established a national precedent as well. Yet most important, McLeod insisted that Christianity bore a political message favorable to Jeffersonian principles and hostile to "arbitrary power" and "superstitious establishments." In his words, "political morality is essential to Christianity," and the War of 1812 presented American political morality with a life-and-death challenge.[24]

As every Christian acknowledged, war brought numerous evils—death, material destruction, human malevolence. Yet, McLeod pointed out, war in behalf of virtuous principles or in defense of one's society had received godly sanction in the Bible. America's clash with Great Britain, in both its inception and its conduct, met both these criteria for "lawful war" and thus demanded the support of all citizens. This Republican minister wrote heatedly, "They have grossly misrepresented Christianity, who have described it as a system subservient to the ambition of the few, and the reduction to servitude of the many." To prove that the war with England was politically and morally just, he launched an extended comparison of the characters of "the British monarchy and the American republic."[25]

For McLeod the contrast could not have been more stark. The British government, he argued, was a "despotic usurpation" combining "civil and ecclesiastical power." To keep themselves afloat in "immense opulence," a corrupt monarchy and aristocracy continually involved the nation at war. Moreover, English merchants—"men of princely fortune," McLeod called them—had influenced the government to pursue policies of "commercial monopoly" that were no better than the attacks of "a licensed robber" on innocent travelers. Of this immoral and rapacious polity, this prominent Presbyterian concluded, "Neither God, nor Godly men who understand it, can approve it."[26]

In the opposite light stood the Jeffersonian republic. In McLeod's simple but forceful words, "A REPRESENTATIVE DEMOCRACY IS THE

ORDINANCE OF GOD." As he explained in more detail, "America gave to the civilized world, the first specimen of a country, great and enterprising, capable of order and prosperity without kings, without nobles, without degrading the lower classes of the community into a state of servitude, and without making of religion and its ministers an engine of political power." So the war, especially given Great Britain's venomous hatred of "republican institutions," was more than a battle for commercial rights or even national survival. It comprised, in McLeod's eyes, "the Providence of God for extending the principles of representative democracy—the blessings of liberty, and the rights of self-government."[27]

When he composed *A Scriptural View of the War,* the conflict with Great Britain had not yet ended. Nevertheless, McLeod had already begun to see the felicitous impact of the war. As he shrewdly observed of the "trial of our republican institutions," even war opposition was "ultimately strengthening the American democracy" because "the societies which are formed, whether to support or to oppose the administration, are so many small democracies, which still tend to promote the principles of civil liberty." Looking ahead to the peace, McLeod envisioned further benefits coming from the war: increased piety, a greater sense of American "moral order" and social cohesion, validation of American character in the family of nations. He wrote optimistically in January 1815, "The present war appears destined by the God of heaven, to answer the purposes of a judgement—a trial—and, a benefit."[28]

In a matter of weeks, Republican prophecies like McLeod's appeared fulfilled with glorious tidings of Ghent and New Orleans. He concluded with satisfaction in a prefatory "Advertisement" to the second March edition of *A Scriptural View of the War* that the arm of heaven had guided America to victory.[29] For countless Jeffersonians the War of 1812 had proved to be a vindication of God's Republic.

The Triumph of Self-Made Men

In 1815 jubilant Jeffersonians paid homage to their regenerate nation. The young republic had suffered at the hands of a powerful foe, absolved itself of sin and weakness, drew strength from the ordeal, and emerged from the war worthy of God's special sanction. Yet satisfied citizens celebrated more than the renewal of their collective public identity. They acclaimed as well the ascendancy of a private ideal that had been taking shape in the decades since the Revolution: the American self-made man. The War of 1812 had provided an opportunity for enterprising, willful, self-controlled individuals to prove their mettle. After months of struggle, they had persevered to conquer both the enemy and themselves.

Numerous Republican declarations in 1815 extolled the resourceful ambition of Americans in the British conflict. Alexander McLeod, for instance, included in his paean to civil religion praise for the principle of self-made success. As he wrote in behalf of "honest enterprise" and "personal liberty," "every man should be permitted to pursue his lawful industry. . . . These are the principles for which this nation contends by the sword." Opposed to this social vision of opportunity, McLeod continued, Great Britain represented a society of painful restrictions where "the child is pinned down in the place of his nativity as in a prison, and unto its local authorities he is forever in thralldom." *Niles' Weekly Register* expressed this theme bluntly several months after peace, contending that the war had proved the resiliency and strength of a nation driven by "the almost universal ambition to get forward." Whereas in Europe opportunity for the average man scarcely existed, suggested the newspaper, in the postwar republic prosperous men were emerging in society who "were once common day laborers, or journeymen or otherwise very humble in their circumstances when they began the world." In other words, America's victory represented the superiority of liberalizing social values.[30]

According to Jeffersonian celebrants, the war's affirmation of American self-made men highlighted two of their special qualities. In one sense victory could be attributed to the singular youthfulness—and hence vitality—of the republic's defenders. "It is a most delightful truth," Mathew Carey wrote in March 1815, "that three-fourths of all our triumphs, by sea and land, have been achieved by heroes who were far below the meridian of life—some of them 24, 25, 26, or 27 years of age." But even more than a shot of youthful energy, the productivity of the striving American citizen had happily received a boost during the War of 1812. Two Republican reports of 1814 reflected this trend. The territorial government of Michigan wrote to Congress that the war had intensified "that spirit of enterprise which marks the American character." With the end of the war, it warned, that spirit "will soon turn a great portion of capital, both material and individual, to internal improvements. . . . It is a tide which is swelling and will soon burst over the mounds which restrain it." Near the war's end John C. Calhoun paid similar tribute to his productive fellow citizens in a speech before Congress. While they exhibited "a power and energy of character" in the face of wartime adversity, he argued, those very problems had provided Americans with new opportunities for material success. The Republicans' new national bank, the South Carolinian explained as an example, had arisen in response to the conflict's financial burden. Yet it also presented "the opportunity to every capitalist, however inconsiderable, to share in the capital of the bank, and to disseminate its benefits all over the country."[31]

An interesting piece of Republican legislation also subtly revealed this wartime sanctioning of the aspiring individual. Distressed by early military failures, the Jeffersonian majority moved in late 1812 to bolster the army with a group of bills. Among them stood a proposal to authorize the enlistment of young men ages 18–21 without permission of parent or master. The bill raised howls of protest from Federalist defenders of a traditional society. They argued that such a recruitment practice would undermine not only the family order but also the paternal authority of the master/apprentice relationship. So violent was the Federalist outcry that the bill died. In late 1814, however, Republicans resurrected the proposal and ramrodded it into law over Federalist objections. As one Jeffersonian congressman contended typically of young recruits, the "best blood of this nation runs in their veins." He "could not by his vote suffer the overfondness of a mother, the timidity of a father, or the avarice of a master to restrain them," but he favored "breaking their bonds and letting them loose." Along with other provisions to exempt recruits from punishment for debt while granting them several hundred acres of federal land, this package made the majority's object become clear. For Jeffersonians, military demands had accelerated a natural sympathy for the release of the self-made man.[32]

Praise for the wartime growth of individual ambition and productivity, however, did not neglect the other side of the self-made ideal: self-control. According to many Jeffersonian moralists, the contest with Great Britain forged in the crucible of war those qualities of the character ethic—restraint of passion, focusing of will—necessary to the channeling of energy and success.

With Republicans, attention fell particularly on the disciplining effects of military struggle. Critics like Mathew Carey noted that upon entering the war Americans had been "lost in the sordid pursuit of gain" and obsessed with gaining status at any cost. This "upstart pride" had been reflected in a "disorderly and irregular" militia system. But military defeats, Carey concluded, had shown Americans by war's end the necessity of subordination and discipline. John C. Calhoun concurred. Speaking to the House of Representatives in 1814, he belittled the pre-1812 attitude of his countrymen that had persisted in peace "because we wished to enjoy the blessings of peace; its ease, its comforts above all, its means of making money." The declaration of war, proclaimed the intense young Southerner, had brought forward a new maxim: "To do our duty is more important than to be rich." This hard-learned lesson in self-control had been further reinforced by the self-indulgent, avaricious war opposition of the Federalists. Calhoun believed that by 1814 most Americans were rejecting their dissenting complaints of interrupted profits. "Have we no self-command? Must we, like children yield to the impulse of present pleasure, however fatal?" he asked rhetorically. President Madison summed up much Republican sentiment in late 1813. The War of 1812, he told Congress, "by diffusing through the mass of the nation the elements of military discipline and instruction; by augmenting and distributing warlike preparations applicable to future use," had bolstered Americans' self-control and exhibited "proofs of the national character."[33]

Ironically, Federalists contributed unwittingly to this process. Fearing that war resistance might spill over into a dangerous release of the passions—and convinced anyway that liberalizing change had set the foundation for mayhem—certain Federalists began to caution restraint. Lyman Beecher, for instance, warned fellow Federalists in 1813 that protection of profit formed a poor basis for opposing the war. "Let us all cease from the inordinate desire of wealth, and that unhallowed enterprise which disregards every consideration, duty to God and to man, for its attainment," he counseled. Moreover, if America became a land where "the gospel does not restrain and civilize," political participation would become "a sword in the hand of a maniac, to make desolate around him, and finally to destroy himself." William Ellery Channing had voiced similar sentiments two years earlier. Speaking in Boston in July and August 1812, this Unitarian minister told a somber gathering of Federalists that "the moral influence of a war" must be bad because it encouraged "lawless pleasure" and "immoral pursuits." Thus it became imperative, warned Channing, for Federalist dissenters to "breathe nothing of insubordination, impatience of authority, or love of change." With a "feverish state of the public mind," "every man should feel the duty of speaking and writing with deliberation." Channing concluded decisively, "It is time to be *firm* without passion."[34]

So from Federalist fear as well as Republican hope, the British conflict helped implant the character ethic of self-control firmly in American cultural sensibility. When combined with qualities of ambition and energy, this ethic nourished the larger ideal of liberal individualism. A trio of Jeffersonian commentators—editor Hezekiah Niles, General Andrew Jackson, and the Rev. John Henry Hobart—illustrated the varied and fascinating ways in which the

War of 1812 took shape as a legitimizing ritual for self-made manhood.

In the months before June 1812, Hezekiah Niles had agitated for war in behalf of an energized republicanism and a political economy of domestic production and trade. During the course of the war, however, a new emphasis gradually crept into his commentary. While the Baltimore editor continued to address issues of political ideology and economic development, his commentary focused increasingly on the type of American emerging from the war to give these abstractions life. By 1815 Niles had become a self-conscious ideologue of productive, socially ambitious individualism.

This became evident in a front-page editorial in *Niles' Weekly Register* published a few days after news of peace had arrived on the East Coast. Entitled "Retrospect and Remarks," the piece proclaimed, "The last six months is the proudest period in the history of the republic," and extolled the American, "eagle-banner, sustained by the hand of God." It also gladly acknowledged that the conflict had established "our mild and benevolent institutions" and proven republican strength. But the editorial's closing sections disclosed a greater cause of Niles' elation. With the energizing of American character, citizens hardened by the conflict could work in peacetime to cement the "internal wealth and strength" created in wartime. The postwar republic, by collecting the sum of such efforts, would move to greatness "through her increased population and multiplied resources of wealth and power."[35]

During the war itself, Niles had not been so sanguine. He frequently complained that his countrymen lacked "energy in action" and could not muster their "power in resources." "At present we are semi-Englishmen," the Republican editor fumed at one point, "and have not a national character." Gradually, however, he came to believe that because of the challenges of war "the spirit of the nation is roused." By 1814, with Federalist opposition falling into disrepute because of the British invasion, their "pound, shilling, and pence patriotism" seemed to be declining in favor. Moreover, Niles argued, Americans were learning self-control due to wartime belt-tightening. With restricted trade and British blockades, "the many luxuries we rioted in" were no longer available.[36]

Yet most important for this young Republican, by turning inward during the war years to develop domestic trade and manufactures Americans were generating new productive energy. Niles' editorials noted with increasing frequency that "every person engaged in manufactures is rapidly adding to his wealth" and "the general stock of wealth." With this dawning of a "golden age," he described in late 1813, vast new opportunities had arisen for aspiring individuals: "The fact is resolved that the monied man cannot invest his capital to better advantage than in the manufacturing establishments . . . [and] there is enough employment, with liberal wages, for all."[37]

In 1815 Hezekiah Niles offered his readers a rich vision of the republic's future. The rich harvest of peace, he contended, had enhanced greatly Americans' capacity for enterprise and productivity and created a "NATIONAL CHARACTER." He reported, "Everywhere the sound of the axe is heard opening the forest to the sun. . . . Our cities grow and towns rise up by magic. . . . The busy hum of ten thousand wheels fills our seaports, and the sound of the spindle and the loom succeeds the yell of the savage or screech of the night owl in the late wilderness of the interior." As Niles summed up, in this war-enlarged arena for self-made success, "industry is rewarded, and enterprise walks forth unrestrained—*and the people are free.*"[38]

If Hezekiah Niles praised the spirit of productive enterprise enlarged by the War of 1812, Andrew Jackson both lauded and embodied another war-enhanced characteristic necessary to individual success: resolute focusing of the will. A self-made man of incredible energy and passion, Jackson had been born on the South Carolina frontier and migrated to Tennessee as a young man. Much of his early life comprised an anxious struggle for survival as an isolated individual. Orphaned by age fourteen, he spent most of his adolescence in gambling, horse-racing, and high living with other provincial youngbloods. Reading law in a small North Carolina town in his twenties, he finally began to prosper after crossing the mountains and settling in Nashville where he became a land speculator, merchant, and gentleman farmer, making and losing a fortune in mercantile transactions. Jackson eventually emerged as a prominent Tennessee politician and military figure, serving as a judge, congressman, senator, and general of the state militia. This frontier general distinguished himself in the War of 1812 leading several successful campaigns against the Creek Indians. Then in January 1815, commanding a loose contingent of Western volunteers, he achieved national fame by soundly defeating a much larger force of veteran British troops at New Orleans. With this unexpectedly glorious victory, Jackson became living proof for his countrymen of the possibilities of decisive action and willfulness.

From the outset of hostilities, the impetuous Tennessean intensely personalized the war with the British. Writing to a friend in 1813, he recalled the loss of his family and their fortune in the Revolution, but admitted, "I have been amply repaid by living under the mild administration of a republican government." Thus for Jackson, fighting in the second British war was in part "a duty I have ever owed to my country, to myself, and to posterity." But what is more significant, he often described the contest as a test for the "young men of America." "Unencumbered with families and free from the embarrassment of domestic concerns," he wrote in 1812, "they are ready at a moment's warning to march to any extremity of the republic." In armed confrontation, these youthful citizens could find ample opportunity to take "a firm and manly stand." As Jackson told the Tennessee militia on the verge of a campaign, he trusted that "they will not prove themselves a degenerate race."[39]

Events of the 1812 conflict, however, brought unexpected degradations. General Jackson complained bitterly and often about the demeaning wartime conduct of Americans: their "shrinking from the contest," their lack of "noble feelings," their "imbecility" and "general apathy," "this supineness, this negligence, this criminality, let me call it." However frustrating, these displays of impotence eventually became a source of stimulation for the Tennessean. He came to see them as challenges to individual character, as trials of private fortitude and will.[40]

For Andrew Jackson, the afflictions of the 1812 war tested whether he and his troops could "retrieve the fallen character of American prowess and discipline." Both his countrymen's weakness and the primordial confrontations with violence and death became demands for inner strength. Jackson exhorted his troops on the eve of the battle of New Orleans, "Soldiers, you want only the will. . . . But remember that without obedience, without order, without discipline all your efforts are in vain." This cultivation of disciplined will, argued the general, would lead the individual warrior to "self-possession." As he explained in more detail in 1814, not "boasting" but "resolution" would bring victory, and the ideal soldier should strive to be "silent, firm, obedient, and attentive to know and perform your duties." The results of this determined posture became manifest at New Orleans. As Jackson explained a few months later, such victories could be expected from brave soldiers who "will themselves to be free." Moreover, the ability to muster internal resources would serve them well after the war. Disbanding the militia after peace had been declared, the Tennessee leader cautioned that in private life they would encounter "the devices and intrigues of the turbulent, malicious, envious, and disappointed. . . . Let them preserve with solicitude the character they have won." In a letter to his nephew Jackson

warned that concentrated will had become a necessity for the individual in postwar American society:

> Independence of mind and action is the noblest attribute of man. He that
> possesses it, and practices upon it, may be said to possess the real courage
> of his creator. Without it, man becomes the real tool in the hands of
> others, and is wielded, like a mere automaton, sometimes, without know-
> ing it, to the worst of purposes.[41]

For many Jeffersonians, Jackson himself personified this strength
of character forged during the War of 1812. Typical of the widespread acclaim, Colonel Anthony Butler wrote to the New Orleans
hero and urged him to stand for President in 1816 as a man of
decisive action. The state of the world did not call for weak leaders
fitted only for "the calm of peace," he argued. Rather, it demanded
"that a man should be placed at the head of our government, whose
firmness and judgment in deciding on measures, and whose boldness
in execution, would unite the Nation around him. Every man in the
U.S. looks to you as this individual."[42]

Jackson's wartime fame as the self-driven, purposeful individual
received a considerable boost a few years later. In 1820 Samuel P.
Waldo's *Memoirs of Andrew Jackson*, a popular biography that presented the general as a model of the determined self-made man,
appeared. In the introduction, Waldo portrayed Americans in the
decades after the Revolution as a people mired in the "voluptuousness
and effeminacy" that attends "sudden wealth." But with the challenges of the War of 1812, "the character of the rising generation of
Americans developed itself," and Andrew Jackson led the way, according to the author, by virtue of his own "exalted character." As
Waldo described, Jackson had "entered the stage of life entirely
alone. With no intrinsic advantages to raise him into life, he sought
no aid out of himself, and he received no aid but what he commanded
by his own energy." In civilian life "unsatisfied with minor station,"
Jackson had climbed to prominence and prosperity. But the "clarion
call of war," the author contended, marked the time when his "military character suddenly developed itself." So for Samuel Waldo as for
countless other Americans, Andrew Jackson emerged as a shining
example of the powerful influence the War of 1812 had in fashioning
the resolute will of the individual.[43]

While Hezekiah Niles and Andrew Jackson charted the energetic
virtues of the self-made man, Jeffersonian sympathizers like the Rev.
John Henry Hobart saw the British conflict as staking out the boundaries of striving individualism. For this bishop of the Protestant

Episcopal Church, the war had been an object lesson in self-control. He had supported military action against England as a justifiable resort to arms and rejoiced at its positive outcome. But as the New York minister insisted in an April 1815 sermon entitled "The Security of a Nation," war had shown Americans beyond doubt the need to curb their appetites and passions.[44]

According to Hobart, the struggle with Great Britain had been a deserved application of "the rod of God's anger." But after desolating both the private enjoyment and the public prosperity of Americans, the Almighty had relented and granted victory. With this reprieve, the duty of chastened citizens appeared clearly to the New York bishop: Americans must at once acknowledge God's providence and hasten to embrace "Public Spirit" instead of "selfishness in all its various operations." Egoism and self-indulgence had first aroused God's wrath in 1812, and upon their removal hinged the return of divine favor.[45]

Hobart censured political division as one type of selfishness and passion. It was a disturbing sight, he argued, to see freemen abandoning the public good to stand "in hostility to each other, under the banners of faction." For this Episcopal minister, however, Americans' "selfishness in the pursuit of wealth" comprised a far more insidious trend. "There is no passion more debasing than the *selfish love of gain;* than the pursuit of it merely for its own sake, or on account of the personal advantages which it will bestow on its possessor," he insisted. "Where the selfish love of gain predominates, the national character is mean and sordid." Chaotic American affairs before and during the war, Hobart continued, had shown that "the pursuit of wealth should be regulated" away from "selfish gratification" and toward public projects "of science, of religion, of benevolence." However, as Hobart made clear, that regulation could come only from within.[46]

Self-control was the only way to happiness and virtue, and the bishop instructed his 1815 congregation to steer a middle course between "indolence" and "licentiousness." A zeal for enterprise should predominate—"No nation was ever flourishing or happy whose citizens were not distinguished by industry"—but the individual should not allow his zeal for prosperity to degenerate into avarice or luxury. "He who knows no idol but self, pursuing and employing wealth only for the gratification of his avarice or his sensual passions," warned the minister, would destroy the republic. So for Hobart as for many other Republicans, God's lifting of "war and revolutions" in 1815—"a most eventful period of the world," he described it—had given Americans a new chance to balance private prosperity and public good. But as the war had demonstrated, only self-controlled citizens could achieve that equipoise.[47]

The peace of 1815 brought more than one victor. The youthful United States had survived as a nation. The Godly Republic had suffered and renewed itself. But as Hezekiah Niles, Andrew Jackson, John Henry Hobart, and hosts of exuberant citizens attested, the War of 1812 also ensured the triumph of American self-made and self-controlled men.

The Victory of Liberalism

To participants in the extravagant celebrations of early 1815, the political impact of the war seemed obvious. Vindicated Jeffersonians announced that the successful British contest had proved the viability of a republican government by showing its ability to withstand the shock of war. Yet those very sounds of rhetorical affirmation barely masked a deeper reality: the meaning of republican principles had been subtly transformed. The military ordeal had in fact gathered, focused, and sanctioned post-1790 trends away from traditional republican ideology and political economy. By emotionally fusing a social creed of self-made success with changing civic beliefs and covering the whole with the mantle of civil religion, the war crisis of the early nineteenth century marked a definite passage for Americans into a new political world. In the hands of Jeffersonian ideologues who shaped much political discourse, older republican concepts became so altered in substance and sensibility by 1815 that they deserve a new nomenclature. The War of 1812 secured the consolidation of nineteenth-century American liberalism.

This process first became recognizable in a rough political consensus that took shape gradually and often painfully in the years after the war declaration. During the conflict, Republicans attempted to create domestic political unity through various patriotic appeals. The Rev. Elijah Robinson Sabin's message urging Americans to join hands against a common enemy was typical. In his Thanksgiving 1812 sermon, "A Discourse Chiefly on Political Unity; or, An Easy Scheme of Reconciliation for Honest Americans," he pleaded for political solidarity on the basis of shared values of republicanism and Christianity. Other Republicans like those in the U.S. Senate took a harder line. As they warned Massachusetts Federalists in a public proclamation of July 1812, opponents of the war were enemies of the republic. "The rightful authority has decreed. Opposition must cease. He that is not for his country is against it," they stated bluntly.[48]

The wartime forging of political solidarity, however, contained another element as well. The uncertain and self-destructive course of Federalist dissenters often reinforced Jeffersonians' pressure for national unity. Although opposed to the conflict in principle, many Federalists felt obliged to swallow their suspicions. The *New York Commercial Advertiser*, for instance, a leading Federalist newspaper, granted in July 1812, "We must submit." "The issue is now fairly before the public. Let it be fairly tried," the paper told its readers. "Federalists aim at nothing but the good of their country . . . and should the war eventuate in the restoration and security of our violated rights and in establishing and perpetuating our republican institutions, and our republican blessings, they would be the first to rejoice." Federalists who continued to oppose the conflict eventually were forced to confront accusations that they were in league with the republic's declared enemy. Like young Samuel Morse, many found this to be a treacherous, eventually impossible, balancing act. Living in England in 1811–12, this youthful Federalist gradually abandoned his antiwar stance as national pride exerted a stronger pull than ideological misgivings.[49]

With the British invasion of 1814, this already difficult Federalist position became obviously untenable. Federalists in large numbers came around to reluctant support for the war as a defensive struggle, while those who persisted in opposition increasingly appeared as self-serving extremists. By the time of the Hartford Convention, the body of dissenters had shrunk significantly and were faced with a barrage of accusations. A "Protest" from a strong minority in the Massachusetts House of Representatives dismissed the Hartford gathering as a "mad experiment" and called for unity to repel British attacks. At the same time, Republican journals like *Niles' Weekly Register* grew even more venomous in assailing the "New England Convention." They typically described it as a collection of "Boston jacobins" and prisoners of foreign commerce motivated by "ambition" and "avarice." With news of New Orleans and peace, the Federalist meeting became not only a disgrace but a laughingstock. Typical of the public mockery was the reply of the Pennsylvania Senate to the Hartford resolutions demanding a restriction on admission of new states to the union, a two-thirds majority for declarations of war, and prohibitions against reelecting a President or choosing consecutive Presidents from the same state. Such measures gave excessive power to an "obstructing minority," Nicholas Biddle, author of the Senate report, wrote contemptuously. Westward expansion had enhanced national wealth and power, as the war had demonstrated, and all citizens should have a full voice in governing "the fruit of their own industry."[50]

The precipitous decline of Federalism, however, signaled a development with significance far beyond the mere forging of wartime unity. It not only sounded the death knell of the American faction most suspicious of liberalizing change, but also ushered in a revised conception of "faction" itself. By the end of the War of 1812, political discussions among the Jeffersonian majority increasingly revealed a tentative new understanding of organized disagreement and competition in politics. After the peace of 1815, traditional republican categories of virtue vs. commerce, and monarchy vs. civic humanism, were generating less emotion and debate. Such terminology would survive, but the substance of political discourse increasingly turned on new assumptions of utility and opportunity, modes of economic and geographic growth, and election maneuvers. Organized, pluralist interest-group rivalry—a conceptualization alien to older republican ideals—emerged in nascent form from the republic's wartime difficulties. An older ideological vision of an American politics of "independent" producers and virtuous citizens had faded. By 1815 a new liberal politics of brokered "self-interest" and expansive growth was emerging in bright new colors to take hold of American civic life. It was hoped that unfortunate disputes between ideologically divided parties that had raged since the 1790s had finally given way to a political arrangement where social interests would negotiate in an atmosphere of prosperity.

Once again, Hezekiah Niles provided an illuminating glimpse of this Republican transformational impulse that gained considerable legitimacy during wartime. Presenting one of many wartime editorials against party agitation in July 1814, he insisted that a constitutional conflict demanded unified support from "reflecting men, republicans in principle of either party." The "will of the majority," he insisted, had decided upon war, and "violent party disputes" over ideological issues between Federalists and Jeffersonians had become subversive. Yet the postwar future would remove the need for ideological divisions, this young Republican editor believed. By vastly expanding the domestic arena for the pursuit of "profit" and "prosperity," the war would create "the political millennium of the United States." "Where the treasure is, the heart will be also," Niles contended, and the old disputes over principle would evaporate in the light of burgeoning economic opportunity. The growing production, manufacture, and exchange of goods would "slay the manyheaded

monster that has distracted the people and divided them into parties."
Niles concluded, "I know my disposition is sanguine; but I ap-
prehend the time is at hand, when the party designations of 'republicans' and 'federalists' will fall into disuse, and the people have
one proud American feeling."[51]

Two other figures, one a leading Federalist and the other a prominent administration Republican, corroborated this broad and subtle
movement toward a new political paradigm. Harrison Gray Otis, an
influential Massachusetts Federalist and member of the Hartford
Convention, led the bulk of his party into a postwar interest-group
politics. He urged Federalists to both vote for Republican Presidential candidates in 1816 and 1820 and support their national policies.
He argued in a public letter to his constituents in December 1818 that
old Federalist sympathizers would achieve more by avoiding ideological collisions and maneuvering for protection of their economic
interests. For Otis, *any* administration upholding the fisheries, rights
of navigation, and manufactures deserved endorsement. If Federalists took this position, he contended, they would effectively "baffle
the wiles of those who wish that collisions may be eternal, wear off the
edge of prejudices, and reconcile their opponents to the merit of their
claim."[52]

James Monroe arrived at a similar conclusion from a different
direction. This Republican stalwart from Virginia had served in a
variety of national positions since the 1790s—the last as Madison's
secretary of state—as a prelude to his nearly unopposed election as
President in late 1816. But even so, as he indicated in a December
1816 letter to General Andrew Jackson, the obliteration of old ideological distinctions stood high on his list of goals. "We have heretofore been divided into two great parties," wrote the President-elect,
but the achievement of "honorable peace" and the wreck of the
Hartford Convention had demolished Federalist strength. Since
Monroe believed that "the entire body of the federal party are republican," he concluded that his administration should isolate
Federalist leaders while moving to "bring the whole into the republican fold as quick as possible." The Virginian assured Jackson,
"The Chief Magistrate of the Country ought not to be the head of a
party, but of the nation itself." By adopting such a role, Monroe
hoped to "exterminate all party divisions in our country, and give
new strength and stability to our government."[53]

One of the most vivid illustrations of the wartime consolidation of
liberal politics occurred in late 1814. Worried by continued threats
of British invasion, incensed by the Hartford Convention, and distressed by the accumulated political bickering since 1812, Mathew

Carey, a longtime Republican journalist and critic, decided to act. In the fall of 1814 he began composing a long polemic that explicitly attempted to rework the venerable assumptions of American republican politics.

Carey had a most interesting background. Born in Ireland in 1760, this young Catholic and republican fled to the United States as a political and religious refugee. Arriving in Philadelphia, he set up a publishing establishment within a few years and made a reputation as a newspaper writer and pamphleteer. A supporter of the Jeffersonians, Carey concerned himself particularly with questions of politics and economic development. By the early nineteenth century, like other Liberal Republicans, he advocated development of a home market, internal improvements, domestic manufactures, a stronger banking system, free trade, and a general entrepreneurial ethos. In 1812 Carey supported the war against Great Britain as a necessary evil, but he grew increasingly disturbed by domestic political agitation in the wartime republic. Unhappy with the conduct of both Federalists and his own Republican colleagues, he presented in November 1814 *The Olive Branch; or, Faults on Both Sides, Federal and Democratic: A Serious Appeal on the Necessity of Mutual Forgiveness and Harmony.* This lengthy pamphlet sought to iron out political differences between the parties, but more important, it also moved to reconceptualize their role in public affairs.[54]

For Mathew Carey, the War of 1812 comprised a serious and possibly fatal crisis for the young United States. It was not that the conflict was unjust, because the Philadelphian believed that the republic had tried everything to avoid confrontation until "every species of outrage, insult, and depredation" had forced the issue. The problem, Carey argued, lay in the internal political disputes that were immobilizing the war effort and threatening the very existence of the United States. Political divisions had crippled military programs and pushed the national government to the edge of bankruptcy. But as this Republican journalist insisted, *both* political parties bore responsibility for the situation. In his words, "Whenever the interests of the nation and the interests of the party come in collision, the former had been too frequently sacrificed by both federalists and democrats to the latter." Consequently, the primary defect of American government —like other Liberal Republicans, he saw this as a want of "a due degree of energy"—had been exacerbated by wartime political wrangling. Such travails led Carey to define precisely his mission in *The Olive Branch*: "the restoration of harmony, and dissipation of party rage and rancour."[55]

He began by laying out in considerable detail the faults of his own

Republican colleagues, but the most striking aspect of Carey's critique here lay in its attack on those Jeffersonian positions most closely tied to traditional republican precepts. The Republicans' old "Country" obsession with public economy and frugality, he argued, suggested little more than "men of narrow minds carrying into public, the huckstering habits of private life." This attitude not only hamstrung war expenditures, but also in general "starves and smothers public undertakings, and public spirit." The traditional republican fear of taxes and central banks, Carey continued, also had led Jeffersonians during the war to depend on loans, "an error pregnant with baleful consequences to the finances and credit of the country." The long-standing Republican aversion to standing armies brought equally harmful consequences: a lack of military preparation in the prewar period and a disastrous reliance on the militia during the hostilities. For Carey, the Republican skepticism of government power had borne bitter fruit in the war with Great Britain as "the public anxiously, but in vain, expected remedies to be applied to the disorders of the state."[56]

The Federalists, however, fared even worse in *The Olive Branch*. Where the Jeffersonians were guilty of well-intentioned bumbling, their opponents deserved condemnation for willful disruption and petty selfishness. According to Carey, since their fall from power in 1800 the Federalists had engaged in a small-minded and partisan campaign of "virulent warfare" against Republicans. Friends of "order and good government" in the 1790s, they became mere "jacobins and disorganizers" in the early nineteenth century with few constructive proposals. For Carey, these sins had culminated in outrageous conduct during the War of 1812 when their "steady, systematical, and energetical opposition to the war" threatened "anarchy and civil war." Eager to regain political dominance by virtue of wartime chaos, "a few ambitious demagogues in Boston have been the guide of federalists throughout the union." Carey continued the attack by outlining Federalist maneuvers to subvert the credit of the national government and push it into bankruptcy. What made all of this worse, contended the Philadelphian, was the Federalist clamor for war against England in 1793 and 1805–6, against France in 1798, and Spain in 1803. Wrote Carey, "I must be pardoned for declaring that any man who was a partisan of war in the above cases, and reprobates the late war as unjust and unnecessary, betrays a most awful degree of inconsistency."[57]

This extensive list of Republican and Federalist faults ultimately prompted Carey to offer a program for the reform of American politics. He based it on one central fact. Prior to the War of 1812, the

Jeffersonian journalist insisted, America had been an economic "colony" of Great Britain even though politically independent. But with the successful issue of the military contest an increasing likelihood by late 1814, "a revolution, immense, striking, glorious, and delightful, has taken place in the affairs of our blessed nation. . . . Our prosperity is now fixed on a basis as firm as the rock of Gibraltar." By winning its economic independence, Carey believed, the United States had made it possible, indeed imperative, to turn attention to internal development. Rather than fighting among themselves for preeminence, as had happened in the decades before the war, the various economic interests in the republic—agriculture, manufactures, and commerce—needed to recognize their interdependence and strive together for economic growth. Carey trusted that this would happen, since the war had "emancipated us from our former slavish dependence on the looms, and the anvils of Great Britain."[58]

The Olive Branch also outlined the future implications of wartime experience for the structure of American politics. While domestic chaos during the war had illustrated the dangers of political faction, the promise of postwar prosperity showed the direction for reform to take. Carey argued that a new kind of politics, a politics based on the promotion of economic prosperity and a willingness to negotiate within that framework, was necessary. He pointed out, "Mere selfishness ought to prompt all men who have any interest in the welfare of the country" to support the government and cease petty haggling. Yet more was required. Self-interest required tempering upon entrance into political life, according to Carey. He urged both parties to "select calm, and dispassionate, and moderate candidates for public office." Moreover, he recommended that the Federalists restrain their thirst for power and become "a noble and dignified opposition party" that would "oppose all impolitic, injurious, or unjust measures" but "yield a cordial and hearty support to every one calculated to promote the public good." Finally, Carey advocated the end of deference and a move toward public opinion in the making of political decisions. Questioning the fairness of the high-level party "caucus," he proposed instead the creation of "committees of correspondence to ascertain the public sentiment." In Carey's new postwar politics of participation and prosperity, it was imperative to gauge fairly "the sense of the nation."[59]

An enthusiastic response greeted The Olive Branch in the United States. By December 1815 it had gone through seven editions, and by 1818 some ten editions and ten thousand copies had been sold. Harmonizing with the postwar messages of others like James Monroe, Harrison Gray Otis, and Hezekiah Niles, Mathew Carey struck a responsive chord with the public. His war-shaped agenda extolling moderate party competition, interest brokering, and public opinion helped focus Jeffersonian sentiment and move the young nation from a republican political world to a liberal one.

The War of 1812, however, played a crucial role in revising the substance, as well as the structure, of American politics. As events unfolded in the thirty months after June 1812, the war's lessons in political economy became steadily clearer to the Jeffersonian majority. Straining under heavy financial and logistical burdens, traditional republican tenets looked increasingly antiquated. A weak and frugal central government, low taxes, and a reliance on commercial agriculture and foreign markets appeared less and less efficacious to the growing cadres of Liberal Republicans. Consequently, they found themselves trying to establish during the war revisionist tendencies in political economy that had arisen in the early nineteenth century. For growing numbers of Republicans the home market, domestic manufactures, and a strong government financial structure seemed far better adapted to the demands of large-scale war. By the conflict's end, liberalizing trends and issues in political economy were setting the agenda of American civil discourse.

Problems with funding the war effort brought an initial shift in the direction of Liberal Republican sensibility. Reluctant to impose a heavier tax burden, Jeffersonians initially tried to support military operations through loans and public bonds. Implicitly, this plan depended on the republican virtue of citizens—their willingness to sacrifice voluntarily for the public good. But as early as the spring of 1812, certain hard-nosed Jeffersonians realized that a changing social atmosphere had undermined such possibilities. Ezekiel Bacon, for instance, a Massachusetts Republican and chairman of the House Ways and Means Committee, urged his colleagues to rid themselves of delusion. In the present state of society, he maintained, the success of public loans and war bonds depended not on virtue but on "the proportion between the interest which they bear, and the profit which can be made by investing individual capital in some private enterprise or employment." Bacon insisted, "The truth is, if we can make it for the interest of capitalists to lend us this money, we shall undoubtedly obtain it, even from our enemies; and on no other consideration should we flatter ourselves from obtaining a single cent from those whom we call our friends." The only appropriate program, asserted the Republican chairman, was a system of special war taxes. He concluded, "If the people will not bear the necessary taxes, it cannot with propriety be said that they will bear the contemplated war, and the sooner we know it the better."[60]

Jeffersonians' appreciation of a society of self-interest became more widespread as revenue from loans and bonds failed to materialize. Not only did their acceptance for higher taxes grow during the war years—a program of substantial war taxes finally cleared Congress in July 1814—but opinion favoring a central government bank did likewise. The First United States Bank had been allowed to die in 1811 by Jeffersonians, who regarded it as an instrument of Hamiltonian "Court" corruption. By 1814, however, growing numbers of Liberal Republicans, with the aid of a few sympathetic Federalits, began to lay the groundwork for a Second Bank of the United States. With the wartime ravaging of public credit, this institution began to seem critical to economic revival. Felix Grundy, for instance, observed of the wartime situation in April 1814, "I wish to see a bank established as a national object. . . . In point of time, [I think] the present situation of the country affords a cogent argument in favor of the measure." Although several versions of the bank bill fell to narrow defeat in 1814 and early 1815—this was due more to Republican bickering over details than to ideological opposition—the drift toward adoption was clear. In 1816 a unified Republican party spearheaded the charter of the Second Bank.[61]

No one better represented this liberalizing development in Jeffersonian financial thinking than Charles J. Ingersoll. Elected as a congressman from Philadelphia in late 1812, the young author of *Inchiquin's Letters* became a popular and eloquent Republican spokesmen in behalf of the war. This struggle, he proudly proclaimed on the House floor, was "the wisest and most fortunate act in the annals of America." For Ingersoll, the war's promise lay in its potential to reform and solidify a society that was growing excessively atomistic. It offered the opportunity for civism, "unanimity," and restraint to individuals preoccupied with self-interest. But like other Liberal Republicans, the Philadelphian also hoped that the war would inject badly needed vitality into tired republican traditions. One example of the "energetic and powerful measures which alone can save us," he believed, entailed abandonment of the militia system in favor of military conscription. Even more telling were Ingersoll's financial proposals.[62]

During his service in Congress from 1813 to 1815—he departed for a career in local politics after that—the youthful Jeffersonian emerged as an outspoken advocate of a national bank. Dismissing old Jeffersonian apprehensions about the virtue of such an institution as "procrastination and idle controversy," he insisted that wartime disarray demanded a central bank. "Any plan will answer my purposes that promises to restore public credit and create a circulating medium," Ingersoll announced. But more important in the long run for this Philadelphia Republican, a Second Bank of the United States would help systematize the scramble for wealth in the republic and thus attach to the government the ambitious, entrepreneurial, and successful "monied men of the community."[63]

Ingersoll grew even more insistent regarding another financial proposal. "I think, for my part, that the present will prove to be a blessed war, should it have no other effect than to give the United States a good system of permanent internal revenue," he proclaimed in June 1813. This system translated into one word: taxation. The British war, he believed, had stretched the tension between an expanding society and a government of virtue to the breaking point. He declared dramatically in 1813,

> Taxation is the last experiment of Republicanism. I do not use that term as a partisan, but in its general acceptance. If we can tax, Republicanism endures forever; if not, it is high time to be done with it. Without the power of waging war, Government is useless; and war cannot be waged without finances.

With a system of effective taxes for wartime revenue, Ingersoll concluded, America's republican government would be free of dependence on virtue. In his words, taxation would provide the republic both with a "well-funded Treasury, capable of perpetual reproductiveness" and with an energetic shot of "moral momentum."[64]

Although frequently pained by the struggles involved, the young congressman ultimately came to judge the war a splendid success. Like many other Liberal Republicans, he rejoiced at the elevation of "American national character" and the triumph of civism when "all hearts leap to the embrace of each other." Ultimately, however, Ingersoll found his greatest source of encouragement in the realm of finances and political economy. By 1815 the United States had become more productive and economically self-sufficient because of the war. Moreover, "Taxation, of which such apprehensions were indulged, seems to be submitted to without a murmur, without a sensation," he concluded gratefully. Thus for Charles J. Ingersoll as for many other Jeffersonians, the War of 1812 played a critical role in reshaping republican financial traditions to better suit a dynamic, liberalizing American society.[65]

The war also helped nail down other planks in the Liberal Republican platform of political economy. Ever since the Embargo of 1808–9, a growing contingent of Jeffersonians saw the foreign crisis as highlighting the need for greater reliance on the home market and domestic manufactures. Trust in the foreign trade since the Revolution, they argued, had put industrious republican producers at the mercy of avaricious European powers. In fact, many young Republicans had chosen to confront England in part to cut the tie of commercial dependence.[66] The course of the war did not disappoint them. Amid growing economic problems—specie drain, the drying up of overseas commerce, the government's crisis of credit—a turning point in political economy became clearly visible during the conflict. Not only was capital forced into domestic channels for investment, but the general wartime experience seemed to underline the point that domestic economic development held the key to national strength, and possibly survival.

By 1815 Liberal Republicans had grown euphoric at the wartime growth of American manufactures. Mathew Carey, for example, assessed the salutary effects of the conflict in a March 1815 "Appendix" to *The Olive Branch*. "It has accelerated the progress of our manufactures more in five or six years, than in the common course of events they would have been in thirty," he wrote. Hezekiah Niles acclaimed this same trend in numerous wartime editorials. In 1814, for instance, he praised the development of "manufacturing establishments" in the west, styling Pittsburgh the "Birmingham of America" and acknowledging that although in their infancy, "their infancy is like that of Hercules." Moreover, Niles carefully pointed out that the war had shown the necessity of not just household manufactures, but large, complex operations as well. He admitted in June 1813, "I was not, until lately, a warm friend of extensive manufacturing establishments. . . . But the present state of society presents only a choice of difficulties—we must manufacture for ourselves or be vexed with a foreign influence."[67]

A particularly prescient analysis of the war's hothouse effect on American manufactures came from the pen of Tench Coxe. In 1814 he published *A Statement of the Arts and Manufactures of the United States of America, for the Year 1810*. This innovative Republican initially had collected the data for this report while serving as purveyor of the United States in Madison's administration, a post he left in 1813. But his written report proved to be so long and bloated with unsolicited opinion that Treasury Secretary Albert Gallatin, Coxe's superior, found it unsuitable. So the author settled on a private printing some years later, and in the meantime integrated into a long introduction a number of observations concerning the impact of the War of 1812 on his 1810 findings. Coxe found those effects highly gratifying. Domestic manufactures had been rapidly growing in 1810, he reported, due both to interruptions of foreign commerce and to the profit potential of domestic production. Much of that

growth involved the adoption of "labor-saving machinery." The use
of these "modern processes and devices," Coxe noted, had increased
tremendously the volume and worth of American finished goods. But
with the commencement of hostilities in 1812, continued the report,
this trend received a dramatic boost. The "various manufactures
necessary for defense" provided a direct inducement to growth, while
indirect encouragement came from a thwarted foreign trade, which
freed badly needed capital for domestic investment. Ironically, it was
in New England—the commercial area that had been most overtly
hostile to domestic manufactures—where they seemed to be making
the most wartime progress. Coxe predicted, "The industry, abilities,
and capital of our seaports will be incessantly turned, by such commercial obstructions, towards manufacturing by machinery. . . .
The inhabitants of the maritime towns will not become farmers, but
will take large interests in great manufactories."[68]

Yet this wartime progress of manufactures was only part of a larger
Jeffersonian consolidation in political economy. As many Republicans were quick to see, the long battle with the British was cementing
the foundation for a true home market. Not only were domestically
produced goods seeking and finding internal markets, but military
problems of supply and logistics were demonstrating the crying need
for internal improvements. The wartime maneuvering of the Pennsylvania state government well illustrated the war's prompting of an
integrated domestic market. Republican Governor Simon Snyder set
the tone for discussion with his annual message to the legislature in
1813. "At no period of our history has the immense importance of
internal navigation been so strikingly exemplified as since the commencement of hostilities," he announced. Snyder went on to explain
that while "the watercraft of the enemy" had easily disrupted the
coastal trade between the states, "the clearing and improving our
rivers and creeks, and connecting them by canals would afford us a
safe, cheap, and expeditious mode of transportation, in defiance of
the thousand ships of our enemy." The legislature proved to be of a
similar mind, authorizing in the same year a company to begin
cutting a canal between the Delaware River and the Chesapeake Bay.
They justified the plan as a strategic means to "establish a perfectly
safe and rapid transportation of our armies and the munitions of war
through the interior of the country" *and* an economic means "to
operate as a cement to the union between the states." This commingling of military demands with civilian opportunity for productivity
and enterprise became steadily more pronounced among Pennsylvania Jeffersonians. In early 1814 the state legislature appealed to
Congress for a "great national road" connecting the republic from

"Maine to the Mississippi." Such a turnpike "would aid the civil or military measures of the national government." But in addition, they added carefully, the project would promote economic prosperity by rendering "the manufactures of the northern, the growers of the southern, and the raisers of consumable produce of the middle states mutually dependent upon, and serviceable to each other."[69]

By 1815 many Republican enthusiasts were flatly declaring the home market to be an unsurpassed achievement of the war. The "useful class of men" who had promoted manufactures and domestic commerce since the embargo, according to Mathew Carey's *Olive Branch*, "do more to establish the true independence of their country, than any other." Indeed, among Jeffersonians it became a commonplace that if the American Revolution had won political independence for the United States, the second British war had secured economic self-sufficiency, an equally important kind of independence. As a wartime editorial in *Niles' Weekly Register* put it rather simply, foreign trade was being supplanted by a "more profitable home commerce." This constituted "a revolution not less glorious than that of '76, but bloodless; and the United States will be, indeed, independent."[70]

The sanctioning of domestic manufactures, internal improvements, and the home market during the War of 1812 began to produce a rich harvest in its aftermath. President James Madison, an older but flexible Jeffersonian theorist, clearly reflected this new political atmosphere. During the war years, his "Annual Messages" to Congress had acknowledged the exasperating disarray of the national effort, but they also tried to find encouragement in an underlying strengthening of the economy. Madison comforted fellow Republicans in Congress with the fact that the military conflict had "cherished and multiplied our manufactures" which were creating "additional staples . . . durable in their value and necessary to our permanent safety." This development, he argued, in the long run promoted "our growing prosperity." With the peace of 1815, Madison extended and applied the wartime lesson in politics and economy. Experience had shown certain assumptions to be naive, the President asserted, one of those being the old republican fear of a strong, standing military establishment. In addition to calling for an enhanced peacetime defense force, Madison also sought to address "the activity which peace will introduce into all scenes of domestic enterprise and labor." In December 1815 he recommended to Congress a comprehensive set of economic recommendations: the charter of a new national bank to make uniform the national currency, government encouragement for building a network of roads and canals, and tariff protection for war-bred "manufacturing establishments, especially of the more complicated kinds." These provisions, he concluded, simultaneously comprised "undertakings conductive to the aggregate wealth and individual comfort of our citizens." Thus James Madison, an ideological shaper of Jeffersonian Republicanism for a quarter-century, summarized in his postwar program that party's mainstream shift toward a liberal political economy.[71]

America's wartime experience also helped prompt fresh theoretical justifications for a liberal political agenda. After several years of writing, Daniel Raymond published in 1820 his *Thoughts on Political Economy*, arguably the first comprehensive treatise on the subject written by an American. Of New England background, the author had moved to Baltimore in the early 1810s, began practicing law in 1814, and started to write on political and economic questions. In this volume Raymond presented a long blueprint for national economic development. Arguing that augmentation of national wealth was the paramount concern of public affairs, he spent the bulk of his energies explaining how to increase the productive energies of the nation. In keeping with the growing liberal commitment of the Republican coalition, Raymond urged several proposals: continued internal improvements, tariffs to assist enterprising entrepreneurs, encouragement of extensive manufactures with "labor-saving machinery," and pursuit of an integrated "home market." These economic measures, he believed, would provide a structure of opportunity and incentive for industrious, productive citizens. Such sentiments had become standard fare among Jeffersonians by this time, but an interesting aspect of Raymond's book was his explicit recognition of war's important impact on an American political economy of productive growth and economic nationalism.[72]

As this Marylander granted, war's terrible train of waste and destruction could hardly be ignored. But another of its functions also deserved recognition, as he argued in a section called "The Influence of War on National Industry." With the late War of 1812 obviously looming in the background, Raymond concluded, "War often operates as a powerful stimulant to national industry, and thereby promotes national wealth. . . . It will often infuse a degree of energy into the body politic, which will greatly promote its wealth and prosperity." As the theorist went on to explain, a military crisis often motivates the emotional and moral energies of the populace, which then translate into productive economic energy. Moreover, the needs of a wartime military establishment increase the demand of goods and thus provide even more market stimulus for labor and industry. In general, as the author noted, "war expenditures" served as a kind of pump-priming, exciting "an increased production" in the economy and augmenting "national wealth." So with Daniel Raymond, as with many others, the British contest's lessons in political economy had been absorbed into a larger ideological framework. War not only had helped move the nation into a new age of expansive market growth, but also had shown its potential for energizing and uniting productive, enterprising individuals.[73]

Many members of the Jeffersonian Republican majority exemplified certain aspects of the liberalizing impact of the War of 1812: Hezekiah Niles, Alexander McCleod, Mathew Carey, Henry Clay, John Henry Hobart, James Madison, Andrew Jackson, Daniel Raymond. Yet no one combined them quite so well as John C. Calhoun. As the brilliant and energetic wartime leader of Republicans in the House of Representatives, he earned the growing respect of political opponents and the open admiration of allies. Perhaps more forcefully than any other individual, this young congressman from South Carolina gave expression to the war-sanctioned qualities of liberal America.

As an outspoken proponent of military confrontation in the months before the declaration of hostilities, Calhoun faced no small task of justification when the war turned sour. In the House from 1812 to 1815, he frantically sought to bolster both official and popular support for the contest in the face of military bungling, collapsing government credit, and Federalist antagonism. Calhoun did so by steadfastly expounding the less obvious but more far-reaching consequences of an inauspicious conflict. This was not just a matter of public rhetorical strategy. He privately reassured a South Carolina correspondent, "I can only observe that as badly as our affairs have been managed in some respects, yet our situation is by no means so despondent as you have pictured it. There is an ultimate vigor in free government." A determined Calhoun stressed the point in another personal letter a few months later. "I by no means despair of the destiny of our nation or government," he wrote. "National greatness and perfection are of slow growth."[74]

In wartime speeches, this Liberal Republican champion pleaded with his countrymen for perserverance. Although the war was proving painful, he argued, forbearance and a steady course would bring ultimate success. Calhoun pointed to several trends that were "daily producing the most solid and lasting advantages to the community." If nothing else, he acclaimed in February 1814, the war "has already liberated us from that dread of British power, which was almost universal before the declaration of war." Moreover, even though American military success had been elusive, results had not been fatal:"If we have done little against our enemy, he has done still less against us." But perhaps most important in the long run, observed the South Carolinian, Americans were slowly overcoming the "repose" and "quiet industry" of peace to learn more forceful habits of conduct. They were acquiring "military skill and means, combined with the tone of thinking and feeling necessary to their use."[75]

In addition to this toughening of a flaccid "national character," a cluster of wartime political developments met the approving eyes of the young Republican. Calhoun looked first at the self-destructive conduct of the Federalists. Their disruption of the war effort had been a hindrance, he admitted, but ultimately it was undercutting their own legitimacy in the eyes of the people. Every day more citizens were concluding that Federalist war opposition was tending to "degenerate into a struggle for power and ascendancy, in which the attachment *to a party* becomes stronger than that *to the country*." As the war went on, he believed, Americans would refuse to be drawn into this "vortex of party rage." For Calhoun this situation was laying the groundwork for a calmer and less ideological spirit of politics. "Like the system of our state and general governments—within they are many; to the world but one. So it ought to be with parties; among ourselves we may divide, but in relation to other nations there ought to be only the American people." In the prospects for political economy, Calhoun beheld another wartime oasis. "I rejoice to behold the amazing growth of our manufacturing interests," he told his House colleagues in 1814. "Our internal strength and means of defence are by them greatly increased." For the South Carolina Republican this emerging economic self-sufficiency was a dramatic improvement over the prewar situation, "where the industry of the country is founded on commerce, and agriculture dependent on foreign markets."[76]

An especially intriguing dimension of Calhoun's wide-ranging and determined war support emerged indirectly in his rhetoric. In constructing metaphors and analogies to uphold the Republican crusade and discredit its Federalist opposition, he frequently seized on a telling social figure in the early-nineteenth-century republic: the aspiring individual and his need for self-control. The young statesman contemptuously described the typical war opponent as an addict to the "profits and luxuries" of commerce, as a weak victim of "the impulse of present pleasure, however fatal," as a dissipated disciple of peace's "ease, its comforts, above all, its means of making money." Calhoun also condemned war opponents as disobedient and licentious sons. "Suppose a father [is] to do some act, which in the opinion of a son, is not strictly just or prosper, by which he becomes involved in a contest with a stranger. Would the son be justified in taking part against him?" he asked. The young congressman concluded, "All the analogies of private life, as well as reason, forbid and condemn the conduct of our opponents." In other words, the opponent of war embodied the dark impulses that tempted the ambitious, self-made man, and everything that he should repress.[77]

On the other hand, Calhoun went to great lengths to praise the typical war supporter as a figure of sturdy self-control. He represented the loyal Republican citizen as the embodiment of "fortitude" and "self-command," willing to sacrifice "present and temporary interest" for "permanent advantage" and "lasting prosperity and greatness." In 1813, for example, he sharply contrasted the self-indulgent Federalist with the tenacious, willful individual who supported the war:

> The love of present ease and enjoyment, the love of gain, and party zeal were on their [the dissenters'] side. These constitute part of the weakness of our nature. We naturally lean that way without the arts of persuasion. Far more difficult is the task of the majority. It is theirs to support the distant but lasting interest of our country; it is theirs . . . to call up all of those qualities by which present sacrifices are made to secure a future good.

Thus, for Calhoun, the military contest had become in large part a shaper of social character. Commitment to the sacrifices of war, he believed, was tempering the pursuit of wealth and pleasure by inculcating self-control, focusing the will, and hardening the resolve of the individual.[78]

With the conclusion of the War of 1812, a grateful and vindicated Calhoun could only affirm that the United States had passed into an expansive new age. In a general sense, he believed that national pride had come to the young republic as a result of the "glory acquired in the late war, and the prosperity which had followed it." America's war-forged wealth and strength had been the will of God, Calhoun further insisted. "We are charged by Providence not only with the happiness of this great and rising people, but in a considerable degree with that of the human race," he told the House in early 1816. "We have a government of a new order. . . . If it succeed, as fondly hoped by its founders, it will be the commencement of a new era in human affairs."[79]

This bright new age would become a certainty, Calhoun asserted, if Americans adopted a new political sensibility for their dynamic postwar society. In the months after peace, he urged his colleagues to draw on "the experience of the last war" to reject "the old imbecile mode" of conducting public affairs. For his part, in 1816 and 1817 the South Carolinian proposed a sweeping set of reforms—most eventually were adopted in some form—that not only inculcated lessons of the war but thoroughly recast traditional Jeffersonian doctrine in the mold of Liberal Republicanism. First, he proposed a revision of the republic's military organization wherein the militia would be taught "discipline and subordination" and supplemented with a larger defense establishment. To this end Calhoun suggested the creation of several military academies that would muster the self-made ethic of aspiring young men in the "middle" and "lower" ranks of American society. "Rich men, being already at the top of the ladder, have no further motive to climb," he pointed out. "It is that class of the community who find it necessary to strive for elevation, that furnishes you with officers." In numerous speeches, Calhoun also demanded construction of "a good system of roads and canals" and tariff protection to encourage the continued growth of domestic manufactures. These measures would unite in a home market "every branch of national industry, Agricultural, Manufacturing, and Commercial." As this confident Jeffersonian concluded in his great "Speech on Internal Improvements" of February 4, 1817, with such proposals "the strength of the community will be augmented, and its political prosperity rendered more secure."[80]

Calhoun may have promoted an energetic new polity to encase a postwar American society of prosperity, growth, and social opportunity, yet true to form he also sounded a cautionary note of restraint. "The love of present ease and pleasure, indifference about the future" constituted the ruinous flaw in "individuals or nations," he reminded. Alluding to ancient mythology, the Southerner recalled the story of young Hercules being approached by two goddesses, one recommending a life of "ease and pleasure," the other a life of "labor and virtue." The hero adopted the latter and achieved fame and glory. "May this nation, the youthful Hercules, possessing his form and muscles, be inspired with similar sentiments and follow his example," Calhoun lectured his countrymen. For individual success and social stability, surging ambition required the tonic of self-control.[81]

The South Carolinian had once observed in the darkest period of the war that "prosperity has its weaknesses, adversity its strengths." With the conflict's successful issue, he believed, wealth and strength had been powerfully melded in the young nation. Calhoun enjoined Americans as he prepared to leave the House of Representatives in 1817, "We are great, and rapidly, I was about to say fearfully, growing. This is our pride and danger—our weakness and strength. . . . Let us then bind the Republic together. . . . Let us conquer space."[82]

Thus the War of 1812's strengthening of civil religion, self-made success, and self-control ultimately reinforced and intensified the fundamental reworking of American political life that had been under way since the beginning of the century. The same impatience with traditional republicanism that had led an emerging majority of Liberal Republicans initially to move toward a British confrontation before 1812 received a powerful legitimizing boost during the war years. Problems and demands of the conflict demonstrated conclusively for them the political need for an electorate of energetic self-made men, an agenda of domestic economic development, a spirit of expansive nationalism, and a framework of negotiating interest-groups. By 1815 the politics of virtue was quickly becoming a memory, while that of enlightened self-interest was becoming a fulfilled promise.

Into the Future

The gratifying denouement of the War of 1812 brought the history of the American early republic to a close. Victory—or perhaps more realistically, survival—in 1815 overwhelmed both dissent against liberalizing change and the past itself. Guided by energetic and innovative figures within the Jeffersonian Republican majority, the United States had ridden the vehicle of war to leave the world of eighteenth-century republicanism and enter that of nineteenth-century liberalism, and a new set of issues in public and private life, and a fresh array of problems, greeted them. More than thirty years later, venerable old Republicans like Charles J. Ingersoll still acknowledged and marveled at the war's influence. In an 1845 history of the conflict, he argued that its accomplishments—he described them as a boosting of "commerce, manufactures, navigation, agriculture, national character, the respect of nations, . . . and confidence in republican institutions"—had made it the equal of the Revolution in shaping the nation. The achievement of "moral, physical, and mental independence" was the lasting memorial of the 1812 ordeal, Ingersoll concluded.[83]

Yet such judgments were not restricted to hindsight. Even before the war ended, certain Jeffersonian commentators had begun to realize the extent of its transforming impact. For instance, Secretary of State James Monroe, writing in 1814 to American negotiators headed for Ghent, instructed them to brook no bullying from British ministers. The United States had been "roused by the causes and progress of the war," he argued, and "in every circumstance in which the war is felt, its pressure tends evidently to unite our people, to draw out our resources, to invigorate our means, and to make us more truly an independent nation." With the conflict's conclusion, this appreciation of wartime invigoration and change became pervasive. The "republican citizens of Baltimore" proclaimed in a public letter of April 1815:

> That struggle has revived, with added lustre, the renown which brightened the morning of our independence: it has called forth and organized the dormant resources of the empire: it has tried and vindicated our republican institutions: it has given us that moral strength, which consists in the well earned respect of the world, and in a just respect for ourselves. It has raised up and consolidated a national character, dear to the hearts of the people, as an object of honest pride and a pledge of future union, tranquility, and greatness.[84]

In this expansive postwar atmosphere, a dim awareness of ideological change gradually came to permeate the general sense of national renewal. In more than a few cases, perceptive observers explicitly noted the role of the Republican majority in spearheading America's advance into a new liberal age. Such was the case with two battle-scarred Republican veterans of early national political struggles. Albert Gallatin, writing to an associate in early 1816, praised the war's influence in strengthening nationalist sentiment and hence the permanency of the republic. But, in addition, he confirmed that "the war has laid the foundation of permanent taxes and military establishments, which [previously] the Republicans had deemed unfavorable to the happiness and free institutions of the country." And Thomas Jefferson himself noted that although the war had left the United States in debt, that was a small price to pay for the great advantages gained. The British contest had not only "harmonized intercourse and sweetened society" by discrediting Federalism, it had also revealed a necessary new path in political economy. At an earlier date, Jefferson admitted, he preferred reliance on a system that combined expanding American agriculture, British manufactures, and international free trade. But the foreign affairs crisis had ruined such prospects. As the War of 1812 had shown, the aging Republican chief concluded in 1816, placing "the manufacturer by the side of the agriculturalist" had become "as necessary to our independence as to our comfort."[85]

Perhaps the shrewdest surveyors of the wartime watershed were a young New Englander and a venerable Virginian. More than most, John Quincy Adams saw that the war with Great Britain had been a brush with disaster for the young republic. As one of the American negotiators at the Ghent conference, this Jeffersonian convert remained acutely sensitive to his country's internal divisions and his government's financial shakiness. Eager to end the conflict safely, he described the signing of the peace treaty as "the happiest day of my life." Yet as Adams noted in April 1815, he had become aware that the war had served "to bring forth energies" in the United States by bolstering "our national character," creating confidence in "our own vigor and resources," encouraging "our own domestic manufactures," and showing the need in government for a "vigorous and independent system of finance." Even more astutely, he sensed that the conflict had cleared the way for westward expansion of American energy on a gigantic scale. To preclude citizens from surging into the western territories—as the wary British sought to do by treaty—was impossible. As Adams saw clearly by war's end, any such attempt would be like "opposing a feather to a torrent."[86]

Like his more youthful Republican colleague from Massachusetts, James Madison also sensed that the postwar nation would be quite different from the prewar republic. In his last message to Congress in late 1816, the President paid tribute to the war's impact, pointing to an invigorated spirit of enterprise, a reconciliation of public strength with individual liberty, and the promise of territorial expansion. In the few years after peace, however, this elderly but still inquisitive Jeffersonian thinker probed into, and tried to come to terms with, the liberal society he had helped create. Madison recognized that self-interest had become the dominant social and economic fact of postwar America. He wrote in an 1817 letter, "I approve the policy of leaving to the sagacity of individuals, and to the impulse of private interest, the application of industry and capital." A few years later he similarly acknowledged, "I am a friend to the general principle of 'free industry,' as the basis of a sound system of political economy," arguing that in the nineteenth-century republic "profit being the object of each, as the profit of each is the wealth of the whole, each will make whatever change the state of the markets and prices may require."[87]

While Madison's pragmatic temperament always had led him to adapt his republican commitments to changing realities, this approval of postwar individualism was not without reservation. He foresaw several menacing difficulties. In the realm of government policy, the Virginian perceived the central problem of the future to be one of reconciling private interest with pressing public needs like national economic independence, the encouragement of domestic manufactures, and the creation of free trade in the world. In the arena

of American society, Madison predicted even more threatening difficulties. In 1819 he touched on a major theme, warning a correspondent that an obsession with pecuniary gain was leading too many
American citizens into excessive debt, extravagance, overextension of
resources, and addiction to "the monied means of gratifying his
present wishes." Two years later, the veteran Republican also pictured the likelihood of growing social inequality between "wealthy
capitalists and indigent labourers." He contended that "such being
the enterprise inspired by free Institutions, . . . great wealth in the
hands of individuals and associations, may not be infrequent." Hence
a situation of dependence and dangerous social resentment would
occur "between the great Capitalists in Manufacturers & Commerce
and the members employed by them," the former President concluded gravely.[88]

By 1819 Jeffersonian visions of a postwar liberal America like
those of Madison and the younger Adams were coming to life in
dramatic fashion. In that year three richly symbolic events captured
both the expansive vitality and new centrifugal predicaments of a
transformed society. First, the Transcontinental Treaty, negotiated
with Spain in that year, set the breathtaking pace for nineteenth-
century geographic growth by annexing the Florida territory and
extending American territorial claims clear to the Pacific Ocean.
Second, in the same year Missouri petitioned the national government for admission to the Union as a state, thereby setting off a
steadily accelerating and agonizing crisis over slavery in a society
ostensibly devoted to individual ambition and enterprise. Finally,
with the financial Panic of 1819, the problematic and unknown side
of postwar political economy was exposed to the shocked gaze of
American self-made men. This crippling depression—it was probably the first in American history attributable to the economic cycles of
modern capitalism—demonstrated not only the ascendancy of market
capitalism but also the economic and social divisions that accrued
to it.
Thus events of 1819 gave a glimpse of the future, revealing that
the decades after the War of 1812 would be dominated by the consequences of a complex and ironic historical development: the simultaneous solidification and segmentation of the liberal society promoted, often rather ambiguously, by innovative Jeffersonian Republicans since early in the century. Perhaps inevitably, given its
atomistic heart and its soul of self-interested ambition, this market
society began to fragment even at the moment of its consolidation.
Agreeing on fundamental principles but quarreling over tactics,
procedures, and tone—disagreement would focus on issues of access

to opportunity, limitations on individualism, appropriateness of labor systems, rate of westward expansion, government promotion and protection of economic endeavor—liberal Americans by the mid-1820s were already beginning an amoeba-like division into a variety of clashing interest-groups.

This splintering process became readily apparent in politics. The short-lived Jeffersonian Republican consensus split apart into rival camps peddling two versions of liberalism: a Jacksonian coalition agitating for expanding and equal opportunity for the individual, and a Whig coalition pushing a more orderly process of economic growth anchored by strong institutions and guided by social elites. More fundamentally divisive was the widening sectional division over slavery. In the context of rapid economic and geographic expansion, Southern ideologues would attempt to reconcile their slave society with their substantial market involvement by formulating racial and labor exploitation as the basis of a regional success ethic, while skeptical Northerners gradually but resolutely came to an unmoveable defense of "free labor" ideology. Foreshadowing a problem that would traumatize the republic by the late 1800s, the specter of class conflict also began to raise its head during the antebellum years. The development of a market economy was bringing the rapid growth of industrialization, a process that made more apparent certain inequalities of condition and opposition of interests based on social class.

The fragmentation of liberal America, however, would go far beyond the readily observable trends of politics and society; it also permeated the less tangible realm of values and perceptions. A central cultural division strained the cohesion of nineteenth-century market society. On the one hand, the great entrepreneurial middle class sought to overcome fundamental separations of liberal capitalist life—work from home, men from women, individual from individual, morality from ambition—by shaping an obsessive Victorian code of self-control and domesticity. On the other hand, many rural and urban working-class citizens resisted these rationalizing tendencies in the name of community, solidarity, and equality. And at an even deeper level of experience, pressures producing a fragmentation of self only intensified after 1819 and raised psychological ghosts that haunted the corridors of liberal individualism. Forced to mediate between conflicting demands for public self-interest and private virtue, fierce competitiveness and iron self-control, personal liberation and larger moral commitments, the solitary American would shoulder heavier and heavier burdens as the nineteenth century unfolded. The pressing weight created threatening stress fractures in the liberal psyche. Eventually this explosive combination of socioeconomic, political, cultural, and psychological factionalism would detonate in the greatest division of them all, the titanic clash of North and South in 1861. As the great crisis of American liberal society, this massive confrontation would bring survival and reaffirmation only through a massive blood sacrifice.[89]

So if the horrible grandeur of the Civil War has rightly come to dominate the historical imagination of liberal America, the crucial impact of an earlier process and a less dramatic conflict should not be forgotten. Under the auspices of Jeffersonian Republicanism, the War of 1812 served as the catalyst in the larger consolidation of American liberal capitalism. Serving as a vehicle for success-seeking individuals, the conflict had granted them soothing immersion in the commonweal and relieved anxieties about selfishness. Appealing to emerging imperatives of self-control, the war had promised to enhance character and will while also allowing release of repressed instinct. Tempting the inner rage of isolated, fragmented men on the make, it had offered them temporary psychological definition and cohesion. Appearing as a regenerative solution to the crisis of republicanism, the British contest boosted the fulfillment of an ideology of economic development and energized self-interest. Portions of the whole would be challenged by dissenting groups in future decades, but by 1815 the structure of nineteenth-century America—an economy of entrepreneurial capitalism, a society of self-made individualism, a bourgeois culture of self-control, and politics of liberalism—stood on a permanent footing.

Thus while the confrontation of 1812 played a critical role in the making of liberal America, it was no simple process. War did not simply cause nor result from liberalizing change, but instead reflected it, intensified it, and ultimately legitimized it. This suggests much about broader issues of the tremendous and complex power of violent conflict to shape the historical process, and in the case of the United States, about war's influence in the evolving hegemony of liberal capitalist imperatives. "War," as Edmund Burke once wrote, "never leaves where it found a nation." In this broad context, the War of 1812 might ultimately be judged on two counts: as an emotional catharsis for anxious, liberalizing Americans seeking both liberation and security, and as the crucial historical link between America's republican revolution and her industrial revolution.

Notes

Introduction

1. For older treatments of America's liberal "consensus," see Louis Hartz, *The Liberal Tradition in America: An Interpretation of American Political Thought Since the Revolution* (New York: Harcourt, Brace, & World, 1955), and Richard Hofstadter, *The American Political Tradition and the Men Who Made It* (New York: Alfred A. Knopf, 1948), the latter of which is far more critical of the American "democracy of cupidity." Newer studies that follow in this interpretive tradition include Carl Degler, *Out of Our Past* (New York: Harper & Row, 1958), and John P. Diggins, *The Lost Soul of American Politics: Virtue, Self-Interest, and the Foundations of Liberalism* (New York: Basic Books, 1984).

2. Examples of this "new" social and labor historiography from the pre-1900 period include Herbert G. Gutman, *Work, Culture, and Society in Industrializing America: Essays in American Working-Class and Social History* (New York: Vintage Books, 1976); Kenneth A. Lockridge, *A New England Town: The First Hundred Years* (New York: W. W. Norton & Co., 1970); James A. Henretta, *The Evolution of American Society, 1700–1815: An Interdisciplinary Analysis* (Lexington, Mass.: D. C. Heath & Co., 1973); Gary B. Nash, *The Urban Crucible: Social Change, Political Consciousness, and the Origins of the American Revolution* (Cambridge, Mass.: Harvard University Press, 1979); Sean Wilentz, *Chants Democratic: New York City and the Rise of the American Working Class, 1789–1850* (New York: Oxford University Press, 1984); and Steven Hahn, *The Roots of Southern Populism: Yeoman Farmers and the Transformation of the Georgia Upcountry, 1850–1890* (New York: Oxford University Press, 1983).

3. For a review of the literature of American "republicanism," see two essays by Robert E. Shalhope in the *William and Mary Quarterly*, 3rd ser., "Toward a Republican Synthesis: The Emergence of an Understanding of Republicanism in American Historiography," 29 (January 1972): 49–80; and "Republicanism and Early American Historiography," 39 (April 1982): 334–56.

4. Numerous recent studies reveal that liberal values had become dominant by the mid-1800s in American society, culture, and politics. See, for example, Daniel Walker Howe, ed., *Victorian America* (Philadelphia: University of Pennsylvania Press, 1975); Alan Dawley, *Class and Community: The Industrial Revolution in Lynn* (Cambridge, Mass.: Harvard University Press, 1976); Paul E. Johnson, *A Shopkeeper's Millennium: Society and Revivals in Rochester, New York, 1815–1837* (New York: Hill & Wang, 1978); and Eric Foner, *Free Soil, Free Labor, Free Men: The Ideology of the Republican Party Before the Civil War* (New York: Oxford University Press, 1970).

5. See Gordon S. Wood, *The Creation of the American Republic, 1776–1787* (Chapel Hill: University of North Carolina Press, 1969); Joyce Appleby, *Capitalism and a New Social Order: The Republican Vision of the 1790s* (New York: New York University Press, 1983); Joseph J. Ellis, *After the Revolution: Profiles of Early American Culture* (New York: W. W. Norton & Co., 1979); and Michael Paul Rogin, *Fathers and Children: Andrew Jackson and the Subjugation of the American Indian* (New York: Vintage Books, 1976).

6. See George M. Fredrickson, *The Inner Civil War: Northern Intellectuals and the Crisis of the Union* (New York: Harper & Row, 1965); Richard Slotkin, *Regeneration Through Violence: The Mythology of the American Frontier, 1600–1860* (Middletown, Conn.: Wesleyan University Press, 1973); and Richard Hofstadter, "Cuba, the Philippines, and Manifest Destiny," in his *Paranoid Style in American Politics* (New York: Vintage Press, 1967), 145–87.

7. Historians traditionally have focused on a number of factors in explaining the causes of the War of 1812—maritime issues like impressment and commercial violations, expansionist sentiment in the West and South, intolerable foreign affronts to national honor, and a breakdown in foreign relations between the United States and Great Britain. These studies include A. L. Burt, *The United States, Great Britain, and British North America* (New Haven: Yale University Press, 1940); Louis M. Hacker, "Western Land Hunger and the War of 1812," *Mississippi Valley Historical Review* 10 (March 1924): 365–95; Julius W. Pratt, *Expansionists of 1812* (New York: Macmillan Co., 1925), 36–50; George Rogers Taylor, "Agrarian Discontent in the Mississippi Valley Preceding the War of 1812," *Journal of Political Economy* 39 (1931): 471–505; Margaret K. Latimer, "South Carolina—A Protagonist of the War of 1812," *American Historical Review* 61 (1955–56): 914–29; Norman K. Risjord, "1812: Conservatives, War Hawks, and the Nation's Honor," *William and Mary Quarterly*, 3rd ser., 18 (April 1961): 196–210; Reginald Horseman, *The Causes of the War of 1812* (Philadelphia: University of Pennsylvania Press, 1962); and Bradford Perkins, *Prologue to War: England and the United States, 1805–1812* (Berkeley and Los Angeles: University of California Press, 1961). For a good historiographical essay on the coming of the war, see Warren H. Goodman, "The Origins of the War of 1812: A Survey of Changing

Interpretations," *Mississippi Valley Historical Review* 28 (1941): 171–86. More recent treatments of the war have stressed the influence of republican ideology, political economy, and political party formation. See Roger H. Brown, *The Republic in Peril: 1812* (New York: Columbia University Press, 1964); Richard Buel, Jr., *Securing the Revolution: Ideology in American Politics, 1789–1815* (Ithaca, N.Y.: Cornell University Press, 1972), 279–81; Drew R. McCoy, *The Elusive Republic: Political Economy in Jeffersonian America* (Chapel Hill: University of North Carolina Press, 1980), 233–38; Lance Banning, *The Jeffersonian Persuasion: Evolution of a Party Ideology* (Ithaca, N.Y.: Cornell University Press, 1978), 292–95; Ronald L. Hatzenbuehler, "Party Unity and the Decision for War in the House of Representatives, 1812," *William and Mary Quarterly*, 3rd ser., 29 (July 1972): 367–90; Rudolph M. Bell, "Mr. Madison's War and Long-Term Congressional Voting Behavior," *William and Mary Quarterly*, 3rd ser., 36 (July 1979): 373–95; J. C. A. Stagg, *Mr. Madison's War: Politics, Diplomacy, and Warfare in the Early American Republic, 1783–1830* (Princeton: Princeton University Press, 1983).

8. See Raymond Williams, "Base and Superstructure in Marxist Cultural Theory," *New Left Review* 82 (November–December 1973): 3–16; and T. J. Jackson Lears, "The Concept of Cultural Hegemony: Problems and Possibilities," *American Historical Review* 90 (June 1985): 567–93.

9. See Hofstadter, *American Political Tradition*, and Edmund Wilson, *Patriotic Gore: Studies in the Literature of the American Civil War* (New York: Farrar, Strauss, and Giroux, 1962). Gore Vidal discussed this genre in his book of essays, *The Second American Revolution and Other Essays (1976–1982)* (New York: Vintage Books, 1976), 212–13. David Brion Davis made this point in "Some Recent Directions in Cultural History," *American Historical Review* 73 (February 1968): 705.

10. For examples of books that treat in various ways the situations of less powerful social groups in the early republic, see Rogin, *Fathers and Children*; Wilentz, *Chants Democratic*; Ronald T. Takaki, *Iron Cages: Race and Culture in Nineteenth-Century America* (Seattle: University of Washington Press, 1982); Nancy F. Cott, *The Bonds of Womanhood: "Woman's Sphere" in New England, 1780–1835* (New Haven: Yale University Press, 1977); Howard B. Rock, *Artisans of the New Republic: The Tradesmen of New York City in the Age of Jefferson* (New York: New York University Press, 1979); and Bernard W. Sheehan, *Seeds of Extinction: Jeffersonian Philanthropy and the American Indian* (Chapel Hill: University of North Carolina Press, 1973). On the Federalists in particular, see James M. Banner, Jr., *To the Hartford Convention: The Federalists and the Origins of Party Politics in Massachusetts, 1789–1815* (New York: Alfred A. Knopf 1970); and Steven Watts, "The Republic Reborn: The War of 1812 and the Making of Liberal America" (Ph.D. diss., University of Missouri, 1984), esp. chap. 7, which analyzes the tortured and dissonant responses of Federalists to liberalizing social change in the early republic.

11. For provocative discussion of "the social history of ideas," see the

essays in John Higham and Paul K. Conkin, eds., *New Directions in American Intellectual History* (Baltimore: Johns Hopkins University Press, 1979).

Chapter 1: The Birth of the Liberal Republic, 1790–1820

1. John Melish, *Travels in the United States of America, in the Years 1806 and 1807, and 1809, 1810, and 1811*, 2 vols. (Philadelphia, 1812). Melish's conclusion appears in vol. 1, p. 399.
2. Ibid., 1:125–27, 172–75; 2:90.
3. Ibid., 2:55–60, 43–44, 150, 181, 231–35; 1:267.
4. Ibid., 1:399; 2:127–28, 241–42, 387–88, 401–2.
5. Ibid., 2:97–98, 188, 235, 356.
6. Ibid., 1:83, 101; 2:238.
7. Ibid., 1:44, 78; 2:324, 368–69.
8. Recent scholarship suggesting this thesis includes Gordon Wood, *The Creation of the American Republic, 1776–1787* (Chapel Hill: University of North Carolina Press, 1969); Michael Paul Rogin, *Fathers and Children: Andrew Jackson and the Subjugation of the American Indian* (New York: Vintage Books, 1975); Nancy F. Cott, *The Bonds of Womanhood: "Woman's Sphere" in New England, 1780–1835* (New Haven: Yale University Press, 1977); Drew R. McCoy, *The Elusive Republic: Political Economy in Jeffersonian America* (Chapel Hill: University of North Carolina Press, 1980); James A. Henretta, *The Evolution of American Society, 1700–1815: An Interdisciplinary Analysis* (Lexington, Mass.: D. C. Heath & Co., 1973), chaps. 4, 5, 6, and "Families and Farms: Mentalité in Pre-Industrial America," *William and Mary Quarterly*, 3rd ser., 35 (January 1978): 3–32; Joyce Appleby, *Capitalism and a New Social Order: The Republican Vision of the 1790s* (New York: New York University Press, 1984); Eric Foner, *Tom Paine and Revolutionary America* (New York: Oxford University Press, 1976); Paul E. Johnson, *A Shopkeeper's Millennium: Society and Revivals in Rochester, New York, 1815–1837* (New York: Hill & Wang, 1978); Henry F. May, *The Enlightenment in America* (New York: Oxford University Press, 1976), part 4; Joseph J. Ellis, *After the Revolution: Profiles of Early American Culture* (New York: W. W. Norton & Co., 1979); and Donald G. Mathews, "The Second Great Awakening as an Organizing Process, 1780–1830," *American Quarterly* 21 (Spring 1969): 23–43.
9. See Robert S. DuPlessis, "From Demesne to World-System: A Critical Review of the Literature on the Transition from Feudalism to Capitalism," *Radical History Review* 4 (Winter 1973): 3–40, and Eugene Genovese, *The World the Slaveholders Made: Two Essays in Interpretation* (New York: Vintage Books, 1971), 16. On colonial society, see Jack P. Greene, "Autonomy and Stability: New England and the British Colonial Experience in Early Modern America," *Journal of Social History* 7 (Winter 1974): 171–94; Michael Merrill, "Cash Is Good to Eat: Self-Sufficiency and Exchange in the Rural Economy of the United States," *Radical History*

Review 4 (Winter 1977): 42–71. J. E. Crowley, *This Sheba, Self: The Conceptualization of Economic Life in Eighteenth-Century America* (Baltimore: Johns Hopkins University Press. 1974); Rhys Isaac, *The Transformation of Virginia, 1740–1790* (Chapel Hill: University of North Carolina Press, 1982); and Henretta, "Families and Farms." The quotation comes from James Henretta, "Reply" to James Lemon, *William and Mary Quarterly*, 3rd ser., 37 (October 1980): 697.

10. On trends in early national agriculture, see Joyce Appleby, "Commercial Farming and the 'Agrarian Myth' in the Early Republic," *Journal of American History* 68 (March 1982): 833–49; Stuart Bruchey, ed., *Cotton and the Growth of the American Economy, 1790–1860* (New York: Harper & Row, 1966); and Henretta, "Families and Farms." On commercial and geographic expansion, see Douglas C. North, *The Economic Growth of the United States, 1790–1860* (New York: W. W. Norton & Co., 1966); McCoy, *Elusive Republic*, chap. 7; and Henretta, *Evolution of American Society*, chaps. 6 and 7.

11. See Diane Lindstrom, "American Economic Growth Before 1840: New Evidence and New Directions," *Journal of Economic History* 39 (March 1979): 289–301; Thomas C. Cochran, "The Business Revolution," *American Historical Review* 79 (December 1974): 1449–66; Alan Dawley, *Class and Community: The Industrial Revolution in Lynn* (Cambridge, Mass.: Harvard University Press, 1976), esp. 44–45; Howard B. Rock, *Artisans of the New Republic: The Tradesmen of New York City in the Age of Jefferson* (New York: New York University Press, 1979); and Sean Wilentz, *Chants Democratic: New York City and the Rise of the American Working Class, 1789–1850* (New York: Oxford University Press, 1984).

12. See Murray N. Rothbard, *The Panic of 1819: Reactions and Policies* (New York: Columbia University Press, 1962).

13. By "culture" I generally mean the broad values and thought patterns of a given society. As a practitioner of "the new intellectual history," I also have sought to ground ideas, expression, and world-views in their social context. See John Higham and Paul K. Conkin, eds., *New Directions in American Intellectual History* (Baltimore: Johns Hopkins University Press, 1979), part 1. Moreover, I have been influenced by Raymond Williams, who argues, first, that thought neither simply reflects nor determines social reality, but interacts dialectically with it, and second, that society and culture are not static "facts," but rather fluid "processes." Moreover, Williams modifies the fashionable but narrow "functionalist" view of culture by insisting that ideas and values are linked to class interests and divisions. See his "Base and Superstructure in Marxist Cultural History," *New Left Review* 82 (November–December 1973): 3–16. On the premodern character of colonial culture, see Isaac, *Transformation of Virginia;* Henretta, "Families and Farms" and *Evolution of American Society*, chaps. 1–4; Crowley, *This Sheba, Self;* Rock, *Artisans of the New Republic;* and Ellis, *After the Revolution*, part 1.

14. On early-nineteenth-century religious currents, see Mathews, "The Second Great Awakening as an Organizing Process"; Lois W. Banner,

"Religious Benevolence as Social Control: A Critique of an Interpretation,"*Journal of American History* 60 (June 1973): 23–41; Johnson, *Shopkeeper's Millennium;* John B. Boles, *The Great Revival, 1787–1805: The Origins of the Southern Evangelical Mind* (Lexington: University of Kentucky Press, 1972); and John F. Berens, *Providence and Patriotism in Early America, 1640–1815* (Charlottesville: University of Virginia Press, 1978). On transforming work culture, see Crowley, *This Sheba, Self;* Dawley, *Class and Community;* Johnson, *Shopkeeper's Millennium;* Rock, *Artisans of the New Republic;* and Gary Kulick, "Patterns of Resistance to Industrial Capitalism: Pawtucket Village and the Strike of 1824," in Milton Cantor, ed., *American Working Class Culture: Explorations in American Labor and Social History* (Westport, Conn.: Greenwood Press, 1979), 209–39. For discussions of the "Scottish common-sense" influence, see Henry May, "The Didactic Enlightenment" in part 4 of his *Enlightenment in America;* Donald H. Meyer, *The Instructed Conscience: The Shaping of an American National Ethic* (Philadelphia: University of Pennsylvania Press, 1972); Daniel Walker Howe, *The Unitarian Conscience: Harvard Moral Philosophy, 1805–61* (Cambridge. Mass.: Harvard University Press, 1970); and Gary Wills, *Explaining America: The Federalist* (New York: Random House, 1981).

15. On the emerging domestic ideal, see Cott, *Bonds of Womanhood;* Linda Kerber, *Women of the Republic: Intellect and Ideology in Revolutionary America* (Chapel Hill: University of North Carolina Press, 1980); and Mary P. Ryan, *Cradle of the Middle Class: The Family in Oneida County, New York, 1790–1865* (New York: Cambridge University Press, 1981). Discussions of developing success ideology can be found in Joseph F. Kett, *Rites of Passage: Adolescence in America, 1790 to the Present* (New York: Basic Books, 1977); John Cawelti, *Apostles of the Self-Made Man: Changing Concepts of Success in America* (Chicago: University of Chicago Press, 1965); and Irvin Wyllie, *The Self-Made Man in America: The Myth of Rags to Riches* (New Brunswick, N.J.: Rutgers University Press, 1954). The most suggestive treatments of consolidating bourgeois culture can be found in Ellis, *After the Revolution*, and Gordon S. Wood, "The End of the American Enlightenment," in Bernard Bailyn et al., *The Great Republic: A History of the American People* (Lexington, Mass.: D. C. Heath & Co., 1977), 389–419.

16. For surveys of the growing literature on American republicanism, see two articles by Robert Shalhope in *William and Mary Quarterly:* "Toward a Republican Synthesis: The Emergence of an Understanding of Republicanism in American Historiography," 3rd ser., 29 (January 1972): 49–80, and "Republicanism and Early American Historiography," 3rd ser., 39 (April 1982): 334–56. See also the collection of essays in a special issue of *American Quarterly*, Fall 1985, edited by Joyce Appleby and entitled "Republicanism in the History and Historiography of the United States." My understanding of republicanism has also been influenced in particular by J. G. A. Pocock, "Virtue and Commerce in the Eighteenth Century," *Journal of Interdisciplinary History* 3 (Summer 1972): 119–34; Gary B.

Nash, *The Urban Crucible: Social Change, Political Consciousness, and the Origins of the American Revolution* (Cambridge, Mass.: Harvard University Press, 1979); Dorothy Ross, "The Liberal Tradition Revisited and the Republican Tradition Addressed," in Higham and Conkin, *New Directions in American Intellectual History*, 116–29; Wood, *Creation of the American Republic;* and McCoy, *Elusive Republic.*

17. See Wood, *Creation of the American Republic,* and the "Introduction" to his edited volume *The Rising Glory of America, 1760–1820* (New York: Braziller, 1971); Richard Buel, Jr., *Securing the Revolution: Ideology in American Politics, 1789–1815* (Ithaca, N.Y.: Cornell University Press, 1972); and Ronald P. Formisano, "Deferential-Participant Politics: The Early Republic's Political Culture, 1789–1840," *American Political Science Review* 68 (June 1974): 474–87.

18. See Appleby, *Capitalism and a New Social Order;* Lance Banning, *The Jeffersonian Persuasion: Evolution of a Party Ideology* (Ithaca, N.Y.: Cornell University Press, 1978); David Hackett Fischer, *The Revolution of American Conservatism: The Federalist Party in the Era of Jeffersonian Democracy* (New York: Harper & Row, 1965); Richard Hofstadter, *The Idea of a Party System: The Rise of Legitimate Opposition in the United States, 1780–1840* (Berkeley and Los Angeles: University of California Press, 1969); Michael Wallace, "Changing Concepts of Party in the United States, 1815–1828," *American Historical Review* 74 (December 1968): 453–91; Ralph Lerner, "Commerce and Character: The Anglo-American as New-Model Man," *William and Mary Quarterly,* 3rd ser., 36 (January 1979): 3–26; and Rowland Berthoff, "Independence and Attachment, Virtue and Interest: From Republican Citizen to Free Enterpriser, 1787–1837," in Richard Bushman et al., eds., *Uprooted Americans: Essays to Honor Oscar Handlin* (Boston: Little, Brown & Co., 1979), 97–124.

19. My analysis of the Federalist persuasion has been derived and synthesized from a number of works. These include James M. Banner, Jr., *To the Hartford Convention: The Federalists and the Origins of Party Politics in Massachusetts, 1789–1815* (New York: Alfred A. Knopf, 1970); Linda Kerber, *Federalists in Dissent: Imagery and Ideology in Jeffersonian America* (Ithaca, N.Y.: Cornell University Press, 1970); Fischer, *Revolution of American Conservatism;* Buel, *Securing the Revolution;* McCoy, *The Elusive Republic.*

20. This view of the Jeffersonians requires an extensive historiographical explanation. My interpretation derives both from evaluating the primary sources and from wrestling with three recent and divergent scholarly treatments: Appleby's *Capitalism and a New Social Order,* McCoy's *Elusive Republic,* and Banning's *Jeffersonian Persuasion.* Banning argues that the Republicans embodied the "Country" tradition of Anglo-American dissenting politics and an even older heritage of republican "civic humanism," bringing both to bear against Federalists who were perceived as corrupt "Court" figures. At nearly the opposite end of the interpretive spectrum, Appleby contends that the Jeffersonians were in fact nascent liberals in the 1790s, while *both* "Court" and "Country" republican traditionalists gravi-

tated into the Federalist camp. McCoy takes something of a middle position, suggesting that while Jeffersonians were indeed influenced by classical republican ideas, they tried to "accommodate to modernity" and stave off decay by promoting westward expansion of agricultural production ("development across space") rather than the growth of an advanced commercial society ("development through time"). These evaluations are different, but not necessarily irreconcilable. I believe that a broader view focusing on three factors that might be a little shortchanged in these books—change over time, generational influence, the coalitional quality of the Jeffersonian movement—helps to clarify the situation. First of all, I am convinced that the Republican crusade initially coalescing in the early 1790s united various groups who opposed Federalism for various reasons: agrarians and domestic entrepreneurs who resented the wealth and power of urban merchants in the Atlantic trade, radical republicans who loathed tyranny under strong central government, old republicans who feared a loss of virtue with commercial development, and independent producers who bridled at the elite control and social restraints embodied in a paternalist social model. This coalition responded to the Jeffersonian vision of a virtuous republic where limited state power would allow the independent citizen to maintain political integrity and influence, where social freedom would permit the independent individual to exercise his talents, where a political economy based on expansive production and swelling territory would encourage the independent producer to utilize his industry and energy. But second, I am equally convinced that the Republican movement of the 1790s in behalf of the "independent" American slowly gathered powerful momentum to overwhelm the traditional republican restraints—and expectations—of many of its adherents. For Jeffersonians of the early 1800s, "independence" was no longer just a *means* to virtue; in many ways, and for complex reasons, it had *become* virtue. This older sense of individual integrity in Republicanism had slowly changed color, a shade at a time, into a liberal sense of self-interest. Finally, I believe that one must appreciate an important generational shift within the Republican movement shortly after its ascendancy. In the years following the great victory of 1800, the influence of older Republican warhorses like Thomas Jefferson and James Madison—such figures had come of political age in the intensely republican political culture of the Revolutionary age—slowly began to recede in the face of an emerging group of younger Republicans who had come to maturity in the transforming market society of the post-Revolutionary age. For men like Henry Clay, Mathew Carey, John C. Calhoun, Hezekiah Niles, John Quincy Adams, and Felix Grundy, the leap from "independent" republican to "self-interested" liberal was a far easier feat of ideological gymnastics. Thus what follows in this book is partly an attempt to describe and analyze the victorious and transforming Jeffersonian movement, and its ideas and inclinations in the early nineteenth century: the powerful appeals that propelled it to social and political dominance, the complex ways in which it gave rise to American liberalism, and the manner in which that emerging creed became entangled with war nearly at birth. I might also briefly note here the kinds of primary source material that have informed this picture of Jeffersonian Republicans moving—with varying degrees of awareness and enthusiasm—to shape a liberal creed in the early nineteenth century. For the years 1810 to 1815 I have consulted a wide array of representative Jeffersonian materials: some fifteen Republican newspapers and journals scattered throughout all sections of the country; all Congressional debates as recorded in the *Annals of Congress*; private papers, correspondence, and published works of leading Republican spokesmen; dozens of contemporary pamphlets, essays, and books presented in the microprint edition of *Early American Imprints: 1639–1800* (Worcester, Mass.: American Antiquarian Society, 1956–64) and *Early American Imprints, 2nd Series, 1801–1819* (Worcester, Mass.: American Antiquarian Society, 1964–), edited by Clifford K. Shipton and produced by the American Antiquarian Society. I have utilized these same materials for assessing the broader period from 1790 to 1820, only less comprehensively. In addition to the references given in the notes in this book, see the bibliography in Steven Watts, "The Republic Reborn: The War of 1812 and the Making of Liberal America" (Ph.D. diss., University of Missouri, 1984), for a full list of primary and secondary materials examined for this study.

21. See John Higham, *From Boundlessness to Consolidation: The Transformation of American Culture, 1848–1860* (Ann Arbor, Mich.: William L. Clements Library, 1969). For varied treatments of this "fragmentation and reordering" impulse, see Nancy Cott's discussion of culture in *Bonds of Womanhood*, Gordon Wood's treatment of politics in *Creation of the American Republic*, and Eric Foner's analysis of the "scientific system" of the market in *Tom Paine*, 154.

22. See Raymond Williams' discussion in "Base and Superstructure." Cathy N. Davidson, *Revolution and the Word: The Rise of the Novel in America* (New York: Oxford University Press, 1986), brilliantly explores fiction as an arena for cultural conflict between women and the lower class, who embraced the novel as an educational means to greater participation in the post-Revolutionary republic, and the traditional gentry, who derided this genre as potentially subversive. Other analyses of various patterns of residual dissent in the nineteenth century include Wilentz, *Chants Democratic*; Steven Hahn, *The Roots of Southern Populism: Yeoman Farmers and the Transformation of the Georgia Upcountry, 1850–1890* (New York: Oxford University Press, 1983); and Jackson Lears, *No Place of Grace: Antimodernism and the Transformation of American Culture, 1880–1920* (New York: Pantheon Books, 1981).

23. For three works that suggest this complicated picture of early national Americans "backing into the future," see McCoy's analysis of James Madison in *The Elusive Republic*, esp. pp. 128–32, 255–59; James Henretta on the complex motives behind rural commercialization in "Families and Farms"; and Robert F. Dalzell's analysis of traditional motives at work among early industrial entrepreneurs of the 1810s in "The Rise of the

Waltham-Lowell System and Some Thoughts on the Political Economy of Modernization in Antebellum Massachusetts," in *Perspectives in American History*, vol. 9 (Cambridge, Mass.: Harvard University Press, 1975).

24. A suggestive analysis of Taylor can be found in Wood, *Creation of the American Republic*, 587–92. Wood places Taylor in the context of a reworking of republican theory in late-eighteenth-century America, arguing that Taylor supported the new republican vision of functional checks and balances rather than a mixed government of social orders. Robert E. Shalhope's *John Taylor of Caroline: Pastoral Republican* (Columbia: University of South Carolina Press, 1980) is the most complete exploration of Taylor's career. Shalhope correctly approaches Taylor in terms of republican ideology and his attempts to uphold it in the face of massive social change in the early nineteenth century. However, the author does not adequately define either the nature and thrust of that change, or the way republican ideas fed it as well as blunted it.

25. See Shalhope, *Taylor*, for details of his life.

26. John Taylor, *An Inquiry into the Principles and Policy of the Government of the United States* (Fredericksburg, Md., 1814; reprint, New York: Bobbs-Merrill, 1969), 551, 485–86.

27. Ibid., 311–14, 98–99, 244–45, 285–86.

28. Ibid., 237; also 75, 230–38, esp. 233–35, and Taylor's *Arator; Being a Series of Agricultural Essays, Practical and Political, in Sixty-four Numbers* (Petersburg, Va., 1818; reprint, Indianapolis: Liberty Classics, 1977), 85.

29. See John Taylor, *An Inquiry into the Principles and Tendency of Certain Public Measures* (Philadelphia, 1794), 78–79; Taylor's *Defense of the Measures of the Administration of Thomas Jefferson* (Washington, D.C., 1804), 73–74; and Taylor, *Arator*, 102. This reformulation of the early national political economy has been suggested and explored to varying degrees by McCoy, *The Elusive Republic;* John R. Nelson, Jr., "Hamilton and Gallatin: Political Economy and Policy-Making in the New Nation, 1789–1812" (Ph.D. diss., Northern Illinois University, 1979); and Joyce Appleby. "What Is Still American in the Political Philosophy of Thomas Jefferson?" *William and Mary Quarterly*, 3rd ser., 39 (April 1982): 287–302.

30. See Taylor, *Inquiry*, 286, 499–501; and *Arator*, 379–80.

31. See J. G. A. Pocock, *The Machiavellian Moment: Florentine Political Thought and the Atlantic Republican Tradition* (Princeton: Princeton University Press, 1975), for the fullest treatment of traditional republicanism and civic humanism. The best examination of Adams, Taylor, and the reshaping of American republicanism can be found in Wood, *Creation of the American Republic*, 567–92.

32. Taylor, *Inquiry*, 140–41, 156, 373, 460–61, 355–56, and all of section 4.

33. Ibid., 3–4, 26. For discussion of emerging structures, institutions, and trends in early national market capitalism, see Cochran, "The Business Revolution"; North, *Economic Growth of the United States;* Appleby, "Com-

mercial Farming and the 'Agrarian Myth'"; and Lindstrom, "American Economic Growth Before 1840."

34. Taylor, *Inquiry*, 48–49, 3–4, 38.

35. Ibid., 311–13, 79–82; Taylor, *Arator*, 98–99, 111.

36. Taylor, *Inquiry*, 244–45, 255, 259, 292; Taylor, *Arator*, 338–89.

37. Taylor, *Arator*, 96, 183, 79–80; Taylor, *Inquiry*, 41, 46, 254.

38. Taylor, *Defense*, 73–74; Taylor, *Arator*, 86–87, 102, 95; Taylor, *Inquiry*, 271. For insightful analyses of Jeffersonian political economy and commercial agriculture, see McCoy, *The Elusive Republic*, and Appleby's "Commercial Farming" and "The Philosophy of Thomas Jefferson."

39. Taylor, *Inquiry*, 136–37, 486–87; Taylor, *Arator*, 380, 381.

40. Taylor, *Inquiry*, 289.

41. Page Smith, *John Adams*, 2 vols. (Garden City, N.Y.: Doubleday & Co., 1962), and Gilbert Chinard, *Honest John Adams* (Boston: Little, Brown & Co., 1933), offer perhaps the most complete accounts of Adams' life.

42. For the correspondence of the two men, see Lester J. Cappon, ed., *The Adams-Jefferson Letters* (Chapel Hill: University of North Carolina Press, 1959). For the writings and other letters of the New Englander, consult Charles Francis Adams, ed., *The Works of John Adams*, 10 vols. (Boston, 1856), the slowly emerging modern edition edited by Lyman C. Butterfield for the Harvard Press, or the microfilms of the Adams Papers at the Massachusetts Historical Society in Boston. For particular collections of Adams' correspondence, see John A. Schutz and Douglass Adair, eds., *The Spur to Fame: Dialogues of John Adams and Benjamin Rush, 1805–1813* (San Marino, Calif.: Huntington Library, 1966), and Worthington Chauncey Ford, ed., *Statesman and Friend: Correspondence of John Adams with Benjamin Waterhouse, 1784–1822* (Boston: Little, Brown & Co., 1927).

43. Peter Shaw, *The Character of John Adams* (Chapel Hill: University of North Carolina Press, 1976), viii, 24. For a broader discussion of fame and ambition in the Revolutionary generation, see Douglass Adair, *Fame and the Founding Fathers: Essays* (New York: W. W. Norton & Co., 1974).

44. See Wood, *Creation of the American Republic*, 567–92; Joyce Appleby, "The New Republican Synthesis and the Changing Political Ideas of John Adams," *American Quarterly* 25 (December 1973): 578–95; Zoltan Haratzi, *John Adams and the Prophets of Progress: A Study in the Intellectual and Political History of the Eighteenth Century* (1952; New York: Grosset & Dunlap, 1964); and John R. Howe, Jr., *The Changing Political Thought of John Adams* (Princeton: Princeton University Press, 1966).

45. See Haratzi, *Adams*, chaps. 2, 3, 9, 10, and Wood, *Creation of the American Republic*, 567–92.

46. Cappon, *Letters*, 506–7. For discussions of Adams' "Puritan" heritage, see Shaw, *Adams*, and Merrill D. Peterson, *Adams and Jefferson: A Revolutionary Dialogue* (New York: W. W. Norton & Co., 1976), 5–9.

47. Adams, ed., "Discourses on Davila. A Series of Papers on Political History," in *Works*, 6:232, 233.

48. Ibid., 239, 241.

49. Ibid., 237–38.

50. Ibid., 241, 234, 245. Much of Adams' explication was derived from Adam Smith's *Theory of Moral Sentiments*, as Zoltan Haratzi has made clear. See Haratzi, *Adams*, 169–71.

51. C. B. MacPherson, *The Political Theory of Possessive Individualism: Hobbes to Locke* (New York: Oxford University Press, 1964), 1–4, 263–64, 270–71.

52. For a discussion of "possessive individualism" in the antebellum United States, and northern and southern variations of it, see Eugene Genovese, *The World the Slaveholders Made: Two Essays in Interpretation* (New York: Vintage Books, 1971), 121–26.

53. Adams, "Davila," in *Works*, 6:79–80, 267–70; John Adams to Thomas Boylston Adams, March 18, 1794, Adams Papers, reel 377.

54. Adams to William B. Giles, December 22, 1812, Adams Papers, reel 121; Adams to John Quincy Adams, February 18, 1811, in Adams, *Works*, 9:633–34.

55. Adams, "Davila," in *Works*, 6:250–52, 274–76; Adams to Jefferson, November 15, 1813, in Cappon, *Letters*, 398–401.

56. Adams to Jefferson, December 21, 1819, in Cappon, *Letters*, 551; Adams, "Davilla," in *Works*, 6:270–71. See Adams' comments on Mary Wollstonecraft's *French Revolution* in Haratzi, *Adams*, 195.

57. Adams to John Taylor, 1814, in Adams, *Works*, 6:508; to Benjamin Rush, August 28, 1811, in *Works*, 9:638–39; to Jefferson, November 15, 1813, in Cappon, *Letters*, 401–2; to John Taylor, March 12, 1819, in Adams Papers, reel 123.

58. Adams to Benjamin Rush, September 27, 1808, in Adams, *Works*, 9:602; to Rush, August 28, 1811, in *Works*, 9:638–39; to Joseph Varnum, December 7, 1812, in Adams Papers, reel 121; Adams' comments on Mary Wollstonecraft in Haratzi, *Adams*, 188; to Benjamin Rush on June 20, 1808, and July 3, 1812, in Schutz and Adair, *Spur to Fame*, 110–11.

59. Adams' comments are transcribed in Haratzi, *Adams*, 18–19, 186–87, 240–41. Haratzi's entire book explores Adams' debate over "progress" with the *philosophes* of the Western Enlightenment.

60. Haratzi, *Adams*, 242, 258; Adams, "Davila," in *Works*, 6:279.

61. Adams, "Davila," in *Works*, 6:279–80, 272–73; Haratzi, *Adams*, 187.

62. Adams, "Davila," in *Works*, 6:280, 242–43; Adams to Thomas Boylston Adams, March 18, 1794, in *Adams Papers*, reel 377.

63. Adams to Richard Price, April 19, 1790, in Adams, *Works*, 9:564; "Davila," in *Works*, 6:233; to John Quincy Adams, February 12, 1808, in *Adams Papers*, reel 405; to Jefferson, November 15, 1813, in Cappon, *Letters*, 398.

64. Adams to Benjamin Rush, June 20, 1808, in Schutz and Adair, *Spur to Fame*, 110.

65. Joseph J. Ellis, *After the Revolution: Profiles of Early American Culture* (New York: W. W. Norton & Co., 1979), 92. Ellis' chapter, "Hugh Henry Brackenridge: The Novelist as Reluctant Democrat," is the

most penetrating cultural study of Brackenridge in existence. Ellis examines Brackenridge as a creative explorer of American cultural tension and as a critic of radical tendencies in emerging American "democracy." For older and more strictly literary treatments of the novelist, see Claude M. Newlin, *The Life and Writings of Hugh Henry Brackenridge* (Princeton: Princeton University Press, 1932); and Daniel Marder, *Hugh Henry Brackenridge* (New York: Twayne Publishers, 1967).

66. D. H. Lawrence, *Studies in Classical American Literature* (1923; New York: Penguin Books, 1978), 8.

67. Quoted in Newlin, *Life,* 57.

68. For general biographical information, see ibid., 44–57, 71–99, 213–14; Ellis, *After the Revolution,* chap. 4; and Henry Marie Brackenridge, "Biographical Notice of H. H. Brackenridge," *Southern Literary Messenger* 8 (1842): 1–19.

69. Hugh Henry Brackenridge, *Modern Chivalry* (reprint, New York: Hafner Publishing Co., 1962), 362. The volume was originally published in installments from 1792–1815.

70. See Hugh Henry Brackenridge, *Incidents of the Insurrection in Western Pennsylvania in the Year 1794,* ed. Daniel Marder (New Haven, 1972) for the Pennsylvania's personal memoir and analysis of the rebellion. Brackenridge explains his role on pp. 142, 195–96.

71. Ibid., 101, 130–31.

72. Ibid., 17. See Brackenridge, "Biographical Notice," p. 4, for an explanation of the Whiskey Rebellion's critical impact on Hugh Henry Brackenridge's thinking.

73. Brackenridge, *Modern Chivalry,* 20–22, 71, 196–97, 350–52, 382–83, 611, 629.

74. Ibid., 21–22. See McCoy, *The Elusive Republic,* 78–80, for an informed treatment of hard work, productivity, and republicanism.

75. Brackenridge, *Modern Chivalry,* 696, 221–22; Henry Marie Brackenridge, *Recollections of Persons and Places in the West* (1856), 51–52.

76. Brackenridge, *Modern Chivalry,* 480–81, 489.

77. Ibid., 6–8.

78. Ibid., 253–73, 608–9.

79. Ibid., 55–57.

80. Ibid., 105–6, 13–17, 18–19.

81. Ibid., 23–27. The entire novel chronicles the multifaceted career of Teague.

82. Ibid., 308–17, 228, 608–9, 30–34, and part 2, vol. 4.

83. Ibid., 391–92, 507, 53, 6.

84. Ibid., 38–40, 204–19, 148–51. For a discussion of self-control and Victorian cultural values, see Daniel Walker Howe, ed., *Victorian America* (Philadelphia: University of Pennsylvania Press, 1976).

85. See Erik H. Erickson, *Childhood and Society* (1950; reprint, New York: W. W. Norton & Co., 1963), 278–79, 193. For Freud's model of personality, see *The Interpretation of Dreams* (New York: W. W. Norton & Co., 1955), *The New Introductory Lectures on Psychoanalysis* (New York: W.

W. Norton & Co., 1964), and *An Outline of Psychoanalysis* (New York: W. W. Norton & Co., 1949). Brackenridge's comment appears in *Modern Chivalry*, 405.

86. See Newlin, *Life*, 277–78; Brackenridge, *Insurrection*, 193–94; Ellis, *After the Revolution*, 90–91.

87. See Newlin, *Life*, 107–11, 192–93.

88. See Sigmund Freud, *Wit and Its Relation to the Unconscious* (New York: Moffat and Yard, 1917), 138, 141, 149–50, 219; Newlin, *Life*, 107–11, 279.

89. Brackenridge, *Insurrection*, 56–57; Brackenridge, *Modern Chivalry*, 52; H. M. Brackenridge, "Biographical Notice," 4–5; Ellis, *After the Revolution*, 91.

90. For related discussion of the "personae," see Rogin, *Fathers and Children*, 8–9, 14–15, 48–74, and Richard D. Brown, *Modernization: The Transformation of American Life, 1600–1865* (New York: Hill & Wang, 1976), 94–121.

91. Brackenridge, *Modern Chivalry*, 605, 627, 804, 595–602, 804.

92. Taylor, *Inquiry*, 504–5; John Taylor to James Monroe, January 2, March 12, and May 10, of 1812, in William E. Dodd, ed., "Letters of John Taylor, of Caroline County, Virginia," in *John P. Branch Historical Papers of Randolph-Macon College*, vol. 2 (1905), 328–29, 337–38, 333–36.

93. Taylor, *Inquiry into Policy of the Government*, 247–48, 248–49, 504–5.

94. Adams, "Davila," in *Works*, 6:240; John Adams to Thomas Boylston Adams, March 18, 1794, Adams Papers, reel 377.

95. John Adams to Benjamin Rush, July 7, 1812, in Schutz and Adair, *Spur to Fame*, 228; Adams' comments on Mary Wollstonecraft are in Haratzi, *Adams*, 204; John Adams to John Quincy Adams, September 2, 1815, Adams Papers, reel 122.

96. John Adams to Benjamin Waterhouse, March 11, 1812, in Ford, *Statesman and Friend*, 76–77; Adams to Benjamin Rush. February 21, 1813, in Schutz and Adair, *Spur to Fame*, 275; Adams to James Madison, November 28, 1814, in *Works*, 10:106; Adams to John Adams Smith, December 14, 1808, in Adams Papers, reel 406; Adams to Benjamin Waterhouse, March 23, 1813, in Ford, *Statesman and Friend*, 95.

Chapter II: Ambition and Civism: War and Social Regeneration

1. Enos Hitchcock, *The Farmer's Friend; or, The History of Mr. Charles Worthy* . . . (Boston, 1793), 13–14, 14–15, 17, 42.

2. Ibid., 51, 124, 135, 205, 209, 254, 258.

3. See James A. Henretta, "Families and Farms: Mentalité in Pre-Industrial America," *William and Mary Quarterly*, 3rd ser., 35 (January 1978): 3–32; J. E. Crowley, *This Sheba, Self: The Conceptualization of Economic Life in Eighteenth-Century America* (Baltimore: Johns Hopkins University Press, 1974); Alan Dawley, *Class and Community: The Industrial*

Revolution in Lynn (Cambridge, Mass.: Harvard University Press, 1976), 17–19; Paul E. Johnson, *A Shopkeeper's Millennium: Society and Revivals in Rochester, New York, 1815–1817* (New York: Hill & Wang, 1978), 43–44; and Robert E. Shalhope, "Toward a Republican Synthesis: The Emergence of an Understanding of Republicanism in American Historiography," *William and Mary Quarterly*, 3rd ser., 29 (January 1972). The quotation is from Joseph F. Kett, *Rites of Passage: Adolescence in America, 1790 to the Present* (New York: Basic Books, 1977), 114.

4. Kett, *Rites of Passage*, 5, and James Henretta, "Reply" to James Lemon, *William and Mary Quarterly*, 3rd ser., 37 (1980): 696–700, both argue convincingly that the four decades after 1790 marked a cultural revolution in the secularization of success writing and in the placing of a new emphasis on the individual. On success ideology in the later nineteenth century, see John Cawelti, *Apostles of the Self-Made Man: Changing Concepts of Success in America* (Chicago: University of Chicago Press, 1965), and Irwin Wyllie, *The Self-Made Man in America: The Myth of Rags to Riches* (New Brunswick, N.J.: Rutgers University Press, 1954).

5. *The Youth's Guide to Wisdom . . . for the Rising Generation* (1812); *The New-England Almanack . . . for 1811* (New London, Conn., 1810); *Instructive History of Industry and Sloth . . .* (Windsor, Vt., 1810); *The Farmer's Almanack . . . for 1811* (Boston, 1810), "January" entry; *Moral and Prudential Maxims and Sayings . . .* (Philadelphia, 1810), nos. 22 and 6.

6. John Foster, *Essays in a Series of Letters to a Friend on . . . Decision of Character* (Hartford, Conn., 1807), 94–99, 102–4, 136; *Moral Sayings*, 5, 6, 10, 13, 27, 33.

7. *True Stories . . . to Inculcate Principles of Virtue and Piety . . .* (Philadelphia, 1811), 3–4, 9–10; *Moral Sayings*, 23.

8. Washington Irving, *Letters of Jonathan Oldstyle, Gent. and Salmagundi . . .*, ed. Bruce I. Granger and Martha Hartzog (1802–3; Boston: Twayne Publishers, 1977), October 15, 1807 entry; *New-England Almanack 1811*; George Beverstoc, *The Silver Key . . . Shewing the Benefit of Money, and the Contempt of the Poor . . .* (Boston, 1811).

9. "Gratitude to the Dead," *Richmond Enquirer*, December 7, 1811; *The Pullet; or, A Good Foundation for Riches and Honour . . .* (Philadelphia, 1810).

10. Thomas Gardner, *The Way to Grow Rich; or, Historical Memoirs of the Life of Tom Gardner . . .* (Frankfort, Penn., 1811).

11. David Humphreys, *The Miscellaneous Works of David Humphreys* (1804; reprint, Gainesville, Fla.: Scholars' Facsimilies and Reprints, 1968), 93–117; and a long letter from an anonymous correspondent urging the cultivation and processing of hemp, in *Houghton's Genuine Almanac . . . for 1811* (Keene, N.H., 1810).

12. "Oration by Lemuel Sawyer," *Kentucky Gazette*, October 23, 1810; "The American Academy," *Richmond Enquirer*, June 11, 1811; "To the Editor" by "T," *National Intelligencer*, October 31, 1811.

13. "To the Editor—No. II" by "Solon," *National Intelligencer*, May

9, 1811, and "For Nat'l Intelligencer—No. III" by "Solon," ibid., May 16, 1811.

14. Speeches by Mitchell and Clay, *Annals of the Congress of the United States* (Washington, D.C., 1853), 23:870, 918; *Cincinnati Western Spy*, October 6, 1810, and October 19, 1811; *National Intelligencer*, May 2, 1812; *Richmond Enquirer*, December 12, 1811.

15. George Fowler, *The Wandering Philanthropist; or, Letters from a Chinese* (Philadelphia, 1810), 138–39, 148–49.

16. James Kirke Paulding, *The Diverting History of John Bull and Brother Jonathan* (Philadelphia, 1812).

17. Ibid., 14–27, 61–63, 84, 85–92, 67–69.

18. For another literary satire, see Irving, *Salmagundi*, May 16, 1807 entry.

19. Winthrop Sargent, "The National Maxim," in Lewis P. Simpson, ed., *The Federalist Literary Mind: Selections from the Monthly Anthology and Boston Review, 1803–1811* (Baton Rouge: Louisiana State University Press, 1962), 68; Conrad Speece, *A Sermon, Delivered . . . August 20, 1812* (Richmond, Va., 1812), 9–10.

20. James B. Finley, *Autobiography of the Rev. James B. Finley . . .* (Cincinnati, 1853), 99–100, 107, 274; Speech of Governor Daniel Tompkins, *Niles' Weekly Register*, February 8, 1812; G. J. Clark, ed., *Memoirs of Jeremiah Mason* (Boston, 1917), 48.

21. "A Miser," *National Intelligencer*, May 5, 1812; "Desultory Remarks," *Niles' Weekly Register*, August 1, 1812.

22. "To the People" by "Lucius," *Richmond Enquirer*, March 2, 1810, and "For the Enquirer," February 13, 1810; Joseph Richardson, *The Christian Patriot Encouraged . . .* (Boston, 1813), 20; Bernard Mayo, *Henry Clay: Spokesman of the New West* (Boston: Houghton Mifflin Co., 1937), 523, n. 1 noting a diary entry of the Rev. William Bentley of Salem, Massachusetts; Editorial, *Philadelphia Aurora*, June 4, 1812.

23. An article by "Y," *Kentucky Gazette*, October 30, 1810.

24. Solomon Aiken, *The Rise and Progress of the Political Dissension in the United States . . .* (Haverhill, Mass., 1811), 19–20. See John R. Howe, Jr., "Republican Thought and the Political Violence of the 1790s," *American Quarterly* 14 (1967): 143–65; and Marshall Smelser, "The Federalist Period as an Age of Passion," *American Quarterly* 10 (1958): 391–419, on the intense factionalism of the 1790s.

25. Irving, *Salmagundi*, April 4, 1807 entry; "To the American People" by "Sallust," *Philadelphia Aurora*, February 28, 1811.

26. William Winder's July 4, 1812, oration, transcribed in *Niles' Weekly Register*, July 11, 1812; John T. Kirkland, "The Anthology: Objects and Principles," in Simpson, *Federalist Literary Mind*, 144.

27. "The Old Bachelor," no. 26, *Richmond Enquirer*, December 12, 1811; editorial on foreign affairs, ibid., July 20, 1810.

28. "The Stranger" essays by "Gregory Grindstone," *Kentucky Gazette*, February 18 and 24, 1812; Richard M. Johnson's speech of December 20, 1809, ibid., February 6, 1810.

29. "An Oration by Jesse Bledsoe," *Kentucky Gazette*, July 9, 1811.

30. "On Luxury and Commerce," *The Time Piece* (New York), November 17, 1797; Philip Freneau, *A Collection of Poems on American Affairs* . . . (1815; reprint, Delmar, N.Y.: Scholars Facsimilies and Reprints, 1976), Freneau quoted in the introduction by Lewis Leary.

31. Standard works on Freneau's life include Lewis G. Leary, *That Rascal Freneau: A Study in Literary Failure* (New Brunswick, N.J.: Rutgers University Press, 1941); Jacob Axelrod, *Philip Freneau: Champion of Democracy* (Austin: University of Texas Press, 1967); and Philip Marsh, *Philip Freneau: Poet and Journalist* (Minneapolis: University of Minnesota Press, 1968).

32. "For the Aurora" by "Nathan," *Philadelphia Aurora*, November 13, 1809. It should be noted that Philip M. Marsh, ed., *The Prose of Philip Freneau* (New Brunswick, N.J.: Rutgers University Press, 1955) includes an exhaustive listing of Freneau's scattered newspaper writings as well as his numerous pseudonyms. It also includes numerous selections from his writings.

33. "The Pilgrim, No. XII," February 13, 1782, in Marsh, *Prose of Freneau*, 58–60.

34. "A Midnight Soliloquy in the Market House of Philadelphia," in ibid., 72–73.

35. "Rules and Directions How to Avoid Creditors . . . ," ibid., 112–18.

36. "The Man Out of Business" and "The Man in Business," ibid, 110–12.

37. Philip Freneau, "The Projectors," in *Poems Written Between the Years 1768 & 1794* (1795; reprint, Delmar, N.Y.: Scholars Facsimilies and Reprints, 1976), 224; "Plan for a Nobility in the United States," *National Gazette*, May 7, 1792.

38. "For the Aurora" by "Atticus," *Philadelphia Aurora*, February 16, 1802; "The Bank Distemper" by "Sangrado," ibid., January 18, 1809, January 22 and 28, 1911, and February 14, 1811.

39. "The Old Soldier," *Philadelphia Aurora*, December 14 and 30, 1808; "For the Nat'l Gazette," *National Gazette*, April 20, 1793; "The Philosopher of the Forest, No. XI," "The Irrationality of War," "Tomo Cheeki the Creek Indian in Philadelphia, No. III," and "Man's Love of Warfare," in Marsh, *Prose of Freneau*, 230–33, 335–37.

40. "For the Aurora" by "An Old Soldier," *Philadelphia Aurora*, March 22, 1809; "To the People of the U.S." by "Mentor," ibid., November 28 and December 12, 1809.

41. "To the Members of the Eleventh Congress" by "Mentor," ibid., November 28 and December 12, 1809; "For the Aurora" by "An Old Soldier," ibid., March 22, 1809.

42. "The American," ibid., January 24, 1809; "To the People of the U.S." by "Mentor," ibid., August 1, 1809; "To the Federalists" by "An American," ibid., September 27, 1809; "To the Members of the Eleventh Congress" by "Mentor," ibid., November 28, 1809.

43. "To the Representatives of the People in Congress" by "Charles," ibid., June 22, 24, and 27, 1809; "To the People of the United States" by "Mentor," ibid., August 1, 1809.

44. "The American," ibid., January 24 and February 2, 1809; "To the Representatives of the People in Congress" by "Charles," ibid., June 23, 1809; "To the Federalists" by "An American," ibid., September 28, 1809.

45. "The American," ibid., February 2, 1809; "For the Aurora" by "An Old Soldier," ibid., October 21, 1812; "To the People of the United States" by "Mentor," ibid., August 1, 1809.

46. Henry Clay, "Speech on Increase in the Naval Establishment," in James F. Hopkins, ed., *Papers of Henry Clay* (Lexington: University of Kentucky Press, 1959), 1:621, 622–23, 624, 627.

47. The standard biographies of Clay are Clement Eaton, *Henry Clay and the Art of American Politics* (Boston: Little, Brown & Co., 1957); and Glyndon G. Van Deusen, *The Life of Henry Clay* (Boston: Little, Brown & Co., 1937). Fuller treatments of Clay's early career can be found in Mayo, *Clay*, and Margaret Ruth Morley, "The Edge of Empire: Henry Clay's American System and the Formulation of American Foreign Policy, 1810–1835" (Ph.D. diss., University of Wisconsin, 1972).

48. Quoted in Mayo, *Clay*, 114.

49. "Speech on Naval Establishment," in Hopkins, *Papers of Clay*, 1:619; "Speech on Domestic Manufactures," in ibid., 460, 461.

50. "Speech on Proposed Repeal of the Non-Intercourse Act," ibid., 449, 450.

51. "Speech on Domestic Manufactures," ibid., 459, 460, 461, 462.

52. Ibid., 462; quoted in Mayo, *Clay*, 120–21, 328.

53. "To Caesar A. Rodney," December 29, 1812, in Hopkins, *Papers of Clay*, 1:750; "Newspaper Editorial," April 14, 1812, ibid., 645, 646, 647; "Speech on Bill to Raise an Additional Military Force," December 31, 1811, ibid., 605, 604; "Speech Supporting Bill to Raise Volunteers," January 11, 1812, ibid., 613; "Answer to Boston Repertory," July 2, 1812, ibid., 693.

54. "Speech Urging Passage of the Embargo Bill," April 1, 1812, ibid., 641, 641–42; "Newspaper Editorial," April 14, 1812, ibid., 645; "Speech on the Bill to Raise an Additional Military Force," December 31, 1811, ibid., 606; "Speech on the Occupation of West Florida," December 28, 1810, ibid., 515–16.

55. "Speech on Repeal of the Non-Intercourse Act," February 22, 1810, ibid., 450; "Speech on an Increase in the Naval Establishment," January 22, 1812, ibid., 620.

56. "Speech on Bill to Raise an Additional Military Force," January 9, 1813, ibid., 758–59, 763, 773; "Speech on Bill to Raise an Additional Military Force," December 31, 1811, ibid.; "To William W. Worsley," February 9, 1812, ibid., 630.

57. "Speech on Proposed Repeal of the Non-Intercourse Act," February 22, 1810; ibid., 449; "Speech on Bill to Raise an Additional Military

Force," January 8–9, 1813, ibid., 765; "Letter to Thomas Bodley," May 12, 1812, ibid., 653.

58. Charles Jared Ingersoll, *Inchiquin, the Jesuit's Letters, During a Late Residence in the United States of America* . . . (New York, 1810).

59. The only biography of the Pennsylvanian is William K. Meigs, *The Life of Charles Jared Ingersoll* (Philadelphia, 1897), a work that contains significant extracts from his private letters. A brief sketch can also be found in Allen Johnson and Dumas Malone, eds., *The Dictionary of American Biography* (New York, 1930).

60. "Philadelphia Speech by Charles J. Ingersoll," *National Intelligencer*, May 26, 1812; *An Oration, Delivered at Mr. Harvey's Spring Garden . . . July 4, 1812* (Philadelphia, 1812), 4; Charles J. Ingersoll, *View of the Rights and Wrongs, Power and Policy of the United States of America* (Philadelphia, 1808), 4–6.

61. Ingersoll, *Inchiquin's Letters*, 122.

62. Ibid., 120, 141–42; Ingersoll's speech of December 9, 1814, *Annals of Congress* 28:818; Ingersoll, *Rights and Wrongs*, 6.

63. "Philadelphia Speech," *National Intelligencer*, May 26, 1812; Ingersoll, *Oration, July 4, 1812*, 7, 5; Ingersoll, *Rights and Wrongs*, 28.

64. See Ingersoll, *Inchiquin's Letters*, 113–17, 139, 146–47, 149–51, 123–24, 112–13.

65. The letters to Rufus King are quoted in Meigs, *Ingersoll*, 56–58, 59–60. See also "Letter to His Constituents by Charles J. Ingersoll," *National Intelligencer*, July 30 and 31, 1813; "To James Madison," November 26, 1808, James Madison Papers, Library of Congress, microfilm; "Philadelphia Speech," *National Intelligencer*, May 26, 1812.

66. "To James Madison," January 10 and February 26, 1811, Madison Papers.

67. Ingersoll, *Inchiquin's Letters*, 19, 33, 5–6.

68. Ibid., 112–13, 102, 106–10.

69. Ibid., 132–33, 134–37, 124–27, 128–29, 104–5, 100–101, 155–56, 152–53, 156, 121n.

70. Ibid., 110, 110–12.

71. Ibid., 158–59, 148–49, 153.

72. Speech of Mr. Ingersoll, *Annals of Congress* 26:353, 1406–32. "To Alexander J. Dallas," December 18, 1813, transcribed in Meigs, *Ingersoll*, 89–90.

73. Speech of Mr. Ingersoll, December 9, 1814, *Annals of Congress* 28:810, 811; Ingersoll, *Oration, July 4, 1812*, 3; "To George M. Dallas," June 23, 1812, quoted in Meigs, *Ingersoll*, 65–66.

74. Ingersoll, *Oration, July 4, 1812*, 7–8, 3–4; "Philadelphia Speech," *National Intelligencer*, May 26, 1812; "Letter to Constituents," *National Intelligencer*, July 30 and 31, 1813.

75. Ingersoll, *Oration, July 4, 1812*, 5, 8; "Letter to Constituents," *National Intelligencer*, July 30 and 31, 1813; "To Rufus King," October 8, 1809, in Meigs, *Ingersoll*, 56–58.

76. Resolutions of Baltimore citizens, *Niles' Weekly Register*, May 30, 1812; Editorial, *Western Intelligencer, (Worthington, Ohio),* January 31, 1812; Richard Rush, *An Oration, Delivered in the . . . House of Representatives . . . July 4, 1812* (Washington, D.C., 1812), 22; Editorial, *Niles' Weekly Register*, January 11, 1812; "To the Members of Congress," *Richmond Enquirer*, March 27, 1812, and "Spirit of Opposition," ibid., May 19, 1812.

77. Michael Walzer, "Socialism and Self-Restraint," in *Radical Principles: Reflections of an Unreconstructed Democrat* (New York: Basic Books, 1980), 291–99.

78. Governor Plumer's speech, *National Intelligencer*, June 20, 1812; Editorial, ibid., May 14, 1812.

79. Governor Smith's address, *Niles' Weekly Register*, December 14, 1811; Governor Gerry's speech, *New York Commercial Advertiser*, January 14, 1812; Editorial, *Kentucky Gazette*, July 14, 1812; Editorial, *Niles' Weekly Register*, April 18, 1812. For similar arguments, see Charles G. Haines, *An Oration, Pronounced at the Request of the Republican Citizens of Concord* (Concord, Mass., 1811); "Volunteers to Arms!" *Richmond Enquirer*, November 29, 1811.

80. *Niles' Weekly Register*, May 30, 1812; Editorial, May 5, 1812, *National Intelligencer;* "Indian War," June 6, 1812, ibid., and "From the Public Advertiser," July 4, 1812, ibid.

81. "To the Peoples of America" by "Americanus." *National Intelligencer*, May 19, 1812.

82. Speech of Mr. Widgery, January 4, 1812, *Annals of Congress* 23:658; "Be Just and Fear Not," *Richmond Enquirer*, January 25, 1812; letter from Jonathan Roberts, *Kentucky Gazette*, May 5, 1812.

83. "Editorial," *Niles' Weekly Register*, October 3, 1812; "Oration" by William Hendricks, *Cincinnati Western Spy*, July 18, 1812; "William O. Allen to Andrew Jackson," January 10, 1810, in John Spencer Bassett, ed., *Correspondence of Andrew Jackson*, vol. 1 (Washington, D.C., 1927), 197–98.

84. Richardson, *Christian Patriot*, 11–12.

85. "How the Wind Blows," *Richmond Enquirer*, April 10, 1812; "The American," *Western Intelligencer*, (Worthington, Ohio), September 4, 1812; Mr. Harper's speech, January 4, 1812, *Annals of Congress* 23:653–54; "Signs of the Times," *Kentucky Gazette*, January 15, 1810, and December 31, 1811; Editorial, December 3, 1811, and the address of Governor James Barbour on April 17, 1812, in the *Richmond Enquirer;* "Resolutions of the Ohio Assembly," *Cincinnati Western Spy*, January 18, 1812.

86. "An American," *Kentucky Gazette*, September 4, 1810; Governor Griswold's speech, *National Intelligencer*, June 15, 1811; editorials in *Niles' Weekly Register*, April 18 and May 30, 1812.

87. Mitchell's speech, June 17, 1812, *Annals of Congress* 24:1507–8; "Washington City," *National Intelligencer*, October 17, 1811.

88. Extract from the *New Hampshire Patriot*, quoted in *National Intelligencer*, June 2, 1812; "Domestic," *Richmond Enquirer*, October 4, 1811.

89. "Energy and War," *Niles' Weekly Register*, October 3, 1812; "Voice of Warning" by "Quintus," *Philadelphia Aurora*, July 20, 1812; "The Old Bachelor," *Richmond Enquirer*, January 10, 1811.

Chapter III: Religion and Repression: War and Early Capitalist Culture

1. Benjamin Franklin, "The Way to Wealth," in L. Jesse Lemisch, ed., *Benjamin Franklin: The Autobiography and Other Writings* (New York: New American Library, 1961), 188–97.

2. W. P. Strickland, ed., *Autobiography of the Rev. James B. Finley . . .* (Cincinnati, 1853), 99–100; Charles Francis Adams, ed., *Memoirs of John Quincy Adams . . .* (Philadelphia, 1874), 1:131; Charles Brockden Brown, *Arthur Mervyn; or, Memoirs of the Year 1793* (Philadelphia, 1799); Robert Brier, *The Georgia and South Carolina Almanack . . . for 1811* (Augusta, Ga., 1810).

3. Solomon Aiken, *The Rise and Progress of the Political Dissension in the United States . . .* (Haverhill, Mass., 1811), 12. For discussion of the "con man" later in the nineteenth century, see Karen Haltunnen, *Confidence Men and Painted Women: A Study of Middle Class Culture in America, 1830–1870* (New Haven: Yale University Press, 1982).

4. See "To the Public," *National Intelligencer*, October 8, 1811, and "Beware of Misrepresentation," ibid., April 14, 1812.

5. Washington Irving, and James K. Paulding, *Letters of Jonathan Oldstyle, Gent. and Salmagundi . . .*, ed. Bruce I. Granger and Martha Hartzog (1802–3; Boston: Twayne Publishers, 1977).

6. Caleb Bingham, *American Preceptor* (New York, 1810), 146–48; Peter Buel Porter, *Mr. P. B. Porter's Speech on Internal Improvements . . .* (Washington, D.C., 1810), 4; Brier, *Georgia and South Carolina Almanack for . . . 1811.*

7. Mason Locke Weems, *God's Revenge Against Gambling . . .* (Philadelphia, 1811 [1810]), 10; Emily Ellsworth Ford Skeel, *Mason Locke Weems: His Works and Ways* (New York: Plimpton Press, 1929), 3:71; Charles Brockden Brown, *Ormond; or, The Secret Witness* (1799; reprint, New York: Hafner Publishing Co., 1967).

8. David Riesman, *The Lonely Crowd: A Study of the Changing American Character* (1950; New Haven: Yale University Press, 1969), 14–16. For discussions of emerging new character demands in nineteenth-century America, see Richard D. Brown, *Modernization: The Transformation of American Life, 1600–1865* (New York: Hill & Wang, 1976), chap. 5; Joseph F. Kett, *Rites of Passage: Adolescence in America, 1790 to the Present* (New York: Basic Books, 1977), 102–7; and Daniel Walker Howe, "Victorian Culture in America," in Howe, ed., *Victorian America* (Philadelphia: University of Pennsylvania Press, 1976).

9. George Burder, *The Closet Companion; or, An Help to Serious Persons, in Self-Examination* (Hartford, Conn., 1810), 10.

10. Richard Johnson, *Blossoms of Morality Intended for the Amusement and Instruction of Young Ladies and Gentlemen . . .* (Philadelphia, 1810), 199, 154.

11. Bingham, *Preceptor*, 223–24; Enos Hitchcock, *The Farmer's Friend; or, The History of Mr. Charles Worthy* . . . (Boston, 1793), 16.

12. *The Youth's Guide to Wisdom* . . . (Boston, 1812), 3; Bingham, *Preceptor*, 19, 20.

13. Bingham, *Preceptor*, the introductory "advertisement"; Andrew Law, *Thoughts of Instinctive Impulses* . . . (Philadelphia, 1810), 9, 15, 57, 72, 81.

14. *Moral and Prudential Maxims and Sayings* . . . (Philadelphia, 1810), 7, 8; Johnson, *Blossoms of Morality*, 156–57; Bingham, *Preceptor*, 225.

15. John Foster, *Essays in a Series of Letters to a Friend* . . . , 1st American printing of 3rd London ed. (Hartford, Conn., 1807), 11. See Kett, *Rites of Passage*, 105, 288, n. 79 on the influence of Foster in America. He notes, for example, that Foster's essay went through nine editions in 1830.

16. Foster, *Essays*, 29, 30–34, 34–35, 18.

17. Ibid., 35–36, 89, 139, 161, 94–95, 102–4, 126–28.

18. Ibid., 86–87, 88–89.

19. Donald Mathews, "The Second Great Awakening as an Organizing Process, 1780–1830," *American Quarterly* 21 (Spring 1969): 27; William Burkitt, *The Poor Man's Help* . . . , 1st American ed. (Newburgh, N.Y., 1811); Foster, *Essays*, 2:3; "To Religion," *National Intelligencer*, July 9, 1811.

20. *Youth's Guide to Wisdom*; Bingham, *Preceptor*, 23; *The Reward of Avarice* . . . (Windsor, Vt., 1810), 23–29; *The Virginia & North Carolina Almanack for* . . . *1813* (Richmond, 1812); *Kentucky Almanack for* . . . *1813*; *The New England Almanack for* . . . *1813* (New London, Conn., 1812).

21. Bingham, *Preceptor*, 172–73, 21, 171, 173.

22. See Barbara M. Cross, ed., *The Autobiography of Lyman Beecher*, 2 vols. (Cambridge, Mass.: Harvard University Press, 1961).

23. Lyman Beecher, "A Reformation of Morals Practicable and Indispensable," *Sermons Delivered on Various Occasions* (Boston, 1852), 2:100–101, 77–79, 83.

24. Ibid., 78, 95.

25. Tench Coxe, "America," *The American Edition of the New Edinburgh Encyclopedia*, vol. 1, part 2 (Philadelphia, 1814), 656–57, 652, 670, 667, 668.

26. Ibid., 670, 661, 667, 655, 666, 660, 652.

27. Ibid., 667, 660.

28. Information on Cone's life can be found in Edward W. Cone, *Some Account of the Life of Spencer Houghton Cone, a Baptist Preacher in America* (New York, 1856), a volume that contains many of Spencer Cone's letters; "Spencer Houghton Cone, D.D." in William B. Sprague, *Annals of the American Pulpit* (reprint ed., New York: Garrett Press, 1969), vol. 6 on "Baptists," 642–56; and "Spencer Houghton Cone," in Allen Johnson and Dumas Malone, eds., *The Dictionary of American Biography* (New York, 1930), 3:342.

29. *Annals of the American Pulpit,* 642–43; Cone, *Life of Cone,* 15–31, 33–39.

30. Cone, *Life of Cone,* 34–46; *Annals of the American Pulpit,* 643.

31. Cone, *Life of Cone,* 48–51; *Annals of the American Pulpit,* 643–44.

32. Cone, *Life of Cone,* 47–48, 38.

33. Ibid., 47–48, 66–67, 53.

34. Ibid., 58, 66–67, 72–74.

35. Ibid., 53–56, 80–81, 58.

36. Ibid., 67.

37. Ibid., 61–62.

38. Ibid., 65, 59–60, 70–71.

39. Ibid., 71–72, 74–75, 82–83.

40. Ibid., 104–5, 74, 84. Cone even supported vehemently the prowar Baltimore riots in the summer of 1812 (pp. 77–80).

41. Ibid., 81–82, 63, 84–89.

42. Ibid., 108–30.

43. Ibid., 107, 90, 89–90, 134.

44. Ibid., 135, 131–33.

45. Ibid., 53.

46. Benjamin Rush, "A Plan of a Peace Office for the United States," in idem, *Essays, Literary, Moral, and Philosophical* (Philadelphia, 1798), 183–88; Rush to John Adams, June 17, 1812, in John A. Schutz and Douglass Adair, eds., *The Spur to Fame: Dialogues of John Adams and Benjamin Rush, 1805–1813* (San Marino, Calif.: Huntington Library, 1966), 227.

47. Standard biographies of Rush are Nathan G. Goodman, *Benjamin Rush: Physician and Citizen, 1746–1813* (Philadelphia: University of Pennsylvania Press, 1934), and David Freeman Hawke, *Benjamin Rush: Revolutionary Gadfly* (New York: Bobbs-Merrill, 1971). The best analytical treatments of Rush can be found in Daniel Boorstin, *The Lost World of Thomas Jefferson* (Boston: Beacon Press, 1948), and Ronald T. Takaki, *Iron Cages: Race and Culture in Nineteenth-Century America* (Seattle: University of Washington Press, 1982), 16–35. Takaki's treatment parallels mine in its emphasis on Rush as an ideologue of self-control, but he is concerned primarily with Rush's impact on racial thinking in the United States.

48. George W. Corner, ed., *The Autobiography of Benjamin Rush: His "Travels Through Life" Together with His "Commonplace Book for 1789–1813"* (Princeton: Princeton University Press, 1948), 46, 113–14; Benjamin Rush, "An Address to the People of the United States," quoted in Goodman, *Rush,* 300.

49. Corner, *Autobiography,* 55–56; Rush, "Thoughts upon the Mode of Education Proper in a Republic," in Frederick Rudolph, ed., *Essays on Education in the Early Republic* (Cambridge, Mass.: Harvard University Press, 1965), 10–11; Rush to Thomas Jefferson, August 1800, in Lyman H. Butterfield, ed., *Letters of Benjamin Rush* (Princeton: Princeton University Press, 1951), 2:820–21.

50. Benjamin Rush, "An Enquiry into the Influence of Physical Causes

upon the Moral Faculty" (1786), in his *Two Essays on the Mind* (reprint, New York: Bruner-Mazell Publishers, 1972), 20–21; Rush, *An Account of the Life and Character of Christopher Ludwick* . . . (Philadelphia, 1801), quoted in Goodman, *Rush*, 295.

51. Rush, "Education in a Republic," in Rudolph, *Essays*, 14–15; Rush to Thomas Jefferson, March 12, 1801, in *Letters of Rush*, 2:831–32; see also Rush in "Commonplace Book," 1791, in *Autobiography*; Rush, "Education in a Republic," in Rudolph, *Essays*, 19.

52. *Letters of Rush*, 1:454; Rush's quote from *Medical Inquiries and Observations* is taken from Boorstin, *Lost World*, 182.

53. Rush, "Commonplace Book," in *Autobiography*, 217–19, 200, 247.

54. See Goodman, *Rush*, 107–27, 192–93, 214–22.

55. Ibid., 301–6; Hawke, *Rush*, 41; Rush, *Autobiography*, 164.

56. Rush, *Essays*, 63; Rush, *Autobiography*, 28–33, 38–39, 83–84, 90–91.

57. Rush to Enos Hitchcock, April 24, 1789, in *Letters of Rush*, 1:511–12; Rush, "Commonplace Book," in *Autobiography*, 280–81; Rush, "Physical Causes Upon the Moral Faculty," in *Two Essays*, 1, 15, 40.

58. Rush, "Physical Causes," 13, 28–29, 68–70; Rush, "Education in a Republic," in Rudolph, *Essays*, 16; Rush, "An Inquiry into the Effects of Public Punishments upon Criminals and upon Society," in his *Essays*, 149–50.

59. Rush, "Physical Causes upon the Moral Faculty," in his *Two Essays*, 36–37; Rush, *Medical Inquiries and Observations upon the Diseases of the Mind* (1812; reprint, New York: Hafner Publishing Co., 1962), 98–134, 174–213, 26–29.

60. Ibid., 347–55.

61. Ibid., 181–82; Rush to Thomas Jefferson, March 15, 1813, in *Letters of Rush*, 1186–89.

62. Rush, "On the Influence of Physical Causes in Promoting an Increase of the Strength and Activity of the Intellectual Faculties of Man," in his *Two Essays*, 109, 117; *Letters of Rush*, 2:860; Rush, *Essays*, 59–60; Rush, "Commonplace Book," in *Autobiography*, 334; Rush, *An Inquiry into the Effects of Ardent Spirits upon the Human Body and Mind* . . . (New York, 1811).

63. Rush, "Commonplace Book," in *Autobiography*, 198; Rush, *Autobiography*, 71–73; Rush, "Address to Ministers of the Gospel," in his *Essays*, 114–15, 122; *Letters of Rush*, 1:412–13; Rush, *Essays*, 122.

64. Rush, *Letters of Rush*, 2:787, 871; Rush, "Commonplace Book," in *Autobiography*, 193.

65. Rush to John Adams, July 18, 1812, in *Spur to Fame*, 233; Rush to John Adams, December 21, 1810, in *Letters of Rush*, 2:1072–73; Rush, *Diseases of the Mind*, 70–71, 68–69, 65–66.

66. Rush to John Adams, August 8, 1812, and to Thomas Jefferson, March 15, 1813, in *Letters of Rush*, 2:1158–59, 1186–89.

67. Rush to John Adams, July 8, 1812, in ibid., 1148; Rush, *Diseases of the Mind*, 355; *Letters of Rush*, 2:1147–48.

68. *Letters of Rush,* 9:315–16; Rush, *Diseases of the Mind,* 263–69; *Letters of Rush,* 2:1189; Rush, "Education in a Republic" in Rudolph, *Essays,* 17–18; *Letters of Rush,* 2:1092.

69. Skeel, *Weems,* 1:47; Mason Locke Weems, *The Life of Washington,* ed. Marcus Cunliffe (Cambridge, Mass.: Harvard University Press, 1962; reprint of 9th ed., 1908), 172; Harold Kellock, *Parson Weems of the Cherry-Tree* . . . (New York, 1928), 104–5. The Skeel volumes are comprised largely of Weems' correspondence.

70. See Daniel Boorstin, *The Americans: The National Experience* (New York: Random House, 1964), 344–45; George B. Forgie, *Patricide in the House Divided: A Psychological Interpretation of Lincoln and His Age* (New York: W. W. Norton & Co., 1979), 35–49, 205–8; Marcus Cunliffe, "Introduction," in Weems, *Life of Washington,* ix, lxii.

71. The standard treatments of Weems are mentioned in the two preceding notes. See also two articles by William A. Bryan: "The Genesis of Weems' 'Life of Washington,' " *Americana* 36, no. 2 (1942): 142–56; and "Three Unpublished Letters of Parson Weems," *William and Mary Quarterly,* 2nd ser., 23 (July 1943): 121–41.

72. Skeel, *Works and Ways,* 3:411–13, 418, 393; 2:267; 2:132; and Cunliffe, "Introduction," lv.

73. Skeel, *Works and Ways,* 2:48, 3:23.

74. Mason Locke Weems, *The True Patriot; or An Oration on the Beauties and Beatitudes of a Republic* . . . (Philadelphia, 1802), 24; Skeel, *Works and Ways,* 3:122, 249, 74; 1:8; and 3:58.

75. Weems, *Life of Washington,* 24, 203, 211, 215, 210, 203–4, 203.

76. Ibid., 175–80, 204; Mason Locke Weems, "God's Revenge Against Adultery," in his *Three Discourses: Hymen's Recruiting Sergeant, The Drunkard's Looking Glass, God's Revenge Against Adultery,* ed. Emily Skeel (New York, 1929), 166.

77. In addition to his *Three Discourses,* see these other pamphlets written by Weems: *God's Revenge Against Murder* (Philadelphia, 1823; 1st ed., 1807) and *God's Revenge Against Duelling* (Philadelphia, 1821; 1st ed., 1820). The quote is from Weems, "Drunkard's Looking Glass," in *Three Discourses,* 122.

78. Weems, *God's Revenge Against Gambling,* 12, 18, 25, 26, 38–39.

79. Ibid., 32; Skeel, *Works and Ways,* 2:172, 277, 32, 350, 426, 290, 174–75.

80. Ibid., 2:270, 90, 428–29, 200, 362; 3:26. Cunliffe, "Introduction," discusses Weems' fabrication of his status.

81. Weems, *Life of Washington,* 4, 191, 116–27.

82. Ibid., 52, 204–5, 194–95, 186.

83. Ibid., 9–19, 187, 206.

84. Mason Locke Weems, *The Life of Benjamin Franklin* (Philadelphia, 1815), 87, 12–13; "God's Revenge Against Adultery," in *Three Discourses,* 146; *God's Revenge Against Murder,* 7.

85. Weems, "Drunkard's Looking Glass," in *Three Discourses,* 119;

Weems, *Duelling*, 22; Weems, "Hymen's Recruiting Sergeant," in *Three Discourses*, 22; Weems, "Drunkard's Looking Glass," in ibid., 127.

86. Weems, *Life of Washington*, 219; Weems, *The True Patriot*, 55–56.

87. *The True Patriot*, 5, 13, 55–56; Mason Locke Weems, *The Philanthropist; or, Political Peace-Maker Between All Honest Men of Both Parties* . . . (Philadelphia, 1809; 1st ed., 1799), 6, 18, 34, 37–38; Skeel, *Works and Ways*, 2:202.

88. Weems, "Hymen's Recruiting Sergeant," in *Three Discourses*, unnumbered page immediately following the title page; Weems, *Philanthropist*, 36–37; Mason Locke Weems, *The Life of General Francis Marion* (Philadelphia, 1814; 1st ed., 1810), 29.

89. Weems, *Life of Washington*, 27–28, 165, 216–17, 218.

90. Skeel, *Works and Ways*, 3:81, 68–75, 112–13, 68; Weems, *Duelling*, 44.

91. Weems, *Life of Washington*, 174–75; Skeel, *Works and Ways*, 3:117.

92. "An Oration, Pronounced by Ephraim M. Ewing, a Student in the Transylvania University," *Kentucky Gazette*, November 13, 1810.

93. "To the Parents of Youth . . . " by "Anti-Royalist," *National Intelligencer*, January 28, 1812. Governor Harrison's speech to the Indiana legislature can be found in the *National Intelligencer*, January 10, 1811.

94. Philip Mathews, *An Oration, Delivered on the 5th of July, 1813* (Charleston, S.C., 1813), 17–18; Conrad Speece, *A Sermon, Delivered . . . August 20, 1812* (Richmond, Va. 1812), 14.

95. "Supposes" by "Trim," *Richmond Enquirer*, October 16, 1810; "Speech of Mr. Lowndes from South Carolina," January 23, 1812, ibid.; "Extract, to the Editor," May 1, 1812, ibid.

96. "From the Boston Patriot," *National Intelligencer*, June 13, 1812.

97. Samuel Knox, *A Discourse, Delivered . . . the 20th of August, 1812* (Baltimore, 1812).

98. Gaillard Hunt, ed., *The Writings of James Madison* (New York, 1900–1910), 8:168–72; "Ministerial Confessions," *Richmond Enquirer*, April 17, 1812.

99. Joseph Richardson, *The Christian Patriot Encouraged* . . . (Boston, 1813), 8; John H. Stevens, *The Duty of the Union in a Just War* . . . (Boston, 1813), 14.

100. Knox, *Discourse*, 28–29; Mathews, *Oration*, 18.

101. Charles Ingersoll, "Letter to His Constituents," *National Intelligencer*, July 30 and 31, 1812; *Niles' Weekly Register*, 3:189, November 21, 1812.

102. Stevens, *Duty of the Union*, 17. See Robert N. Bellah, "Civil Religion in America," *Daedalus* 96 (1967): 1–21.

103. Knox, *Discourse*, 22; Peter Van Pelt, *The Goodness of God* . . . (New York, 1812), 20–21, 14; Richardson, *Christian Patriot*, 5, 15; John Giles, *Discourses Delivered to the Second Presbyterian Society in Newburyport* . . . (Haverhill, Mass., 1812), 8; Stevens, *Duty of the Union*, 18–19.

104. Stevens, *Duty of the Union*, 5–18; Speece, *Sermon*, 5–10; Aiken, *Rise and Progress*, 21; Stevens, *Duty of the Union*, 4–5; Speece, *Sermon*, 3–4, 11. See also Knox, *Discourse*, 6–7, 22–27.

105. Speece, *Sermon*, 11–12; Thomas Watson, *The Christian Soldier* . . . (New York, 1810), v, 8, 15, viii.

106. W. P. Strickland, ed., *Autobiography of Peter Cartwright* . . . (Cincinnati, 1856), 133; Jacob Young, *Autobiography of a Pioneer* . . . (Cincinnati, 1857), 292–94; Strickland, *Autobiography of the Rev. James B. Finley*, 258.

107. Peter Van Pelt, *The Goodness of God: A Discourse* (New York, 1912), 7–11, 18–19; "Circular" from John Clopton, *Richmond Enquirer*, June 30, 1812.

108. Joshua Lacy Wilson, *War, the Work of the Lord and the Coward Cursed* . . . (Boston, 1813), 3–4, 7, 8, 12, 4. For a similar effort, see William Parkinson, *A Sermon Preached* . . . *August 20, 1812* (New York, 1812).

109. Ibid., 9–10, 10–11, 15.

Chapter IV: Founding Fathers and Wandering Sons:
War and the Masks of the Personae

1. Richard Rush, *An Oration, Delivered in the* . . . *House of Representatives* . . . *July 4, 1812* (Washington, D.C., 1812). See Allen Johnson and Dumas Malone, eds., *The Dictionary of American Biography* (New York, 1930), 16:231–32, 34, for a brief sketch of Rush's life. Roger H. Brown, *The Republic in Peril: 1812* (New York: W. W. Norton & Co., 1964), 83–84, sketches Rush's relationship with President Madison.

2. Rush, *Oration*, 21–22, 3, 20, 19.

3. Ibid., 11, 22.

4. See above, Chapters II and III.

5. On Fourth of July rhetoric, see George Fowler, *The Wandering Philanthropist* . . . (Philadelphia, 1810), 271, 275–76; "Fourth of July," *National Intelligencer*, July 6, 1811; Philip Mathews, *An Oration, Delivered on the 5th of July, 1813* (Charlestown, S.C., 1813), 11–12, 26. For quotations, see Thomas Rodney, quoted in Bradford Perkins, *Prologue to War: England and the United States, 1805–1812* (Berkeley and Los Angeles: University of California Press, 1961), page facing p. 1; John Roane, "The Freeholders of the Congressional District," *Richmond Enquirer*, May 18, 1810; Samuel Knox, *A Discourse Delivered* . . . *the 20th of August, 1812* (Baltimore, 1812), 15–17; Francis Preston, "Revolutionary Fete!" *Richmond Enquirer*, November 6, 1810; "The National Standard" by "Vindex," ibid., January 25, 1810.

6. Peter Porter, December 6, 1811, *Annals of the Congress of the United States* (Washington, D.C., 1853), 23:415; James Kirke Paulding, *The Diverting History of John Bull and Brother Jonathan* (Philadelphia, 1812), 6–7, 13–14; Philip Freneau, "The Old Soldier," *Philadelphia Aurora*, December 30, 1808.

7. Philip Rieff, *The Triumph of the Therapeutic: Uses of Faith After Freud* (New York: Harper & Row, 1966), 2–3.

8. Fred Weinstein and Gerald M Platt, *The Wish to Be Free: Society, Psyche, and Value Change* (Berkeley and Los Angeles: University of California Press, 1969), 222. On changes in family life, see Edwin G. Burrows and Michael Wallace, "The American Revolution: The Ideology and Psychology of National Liberation," *Perspectives in American History* 6 (1972): 168–306; James A. Henretta, "Families and Farms: Mentalité in Pre-Industrial America," *William and Mary Quarterly*, 3rd ser., 35 (January 1978): 3–32; Nancy F. Cott, *The Bonds of Womanhood: "Woman's Sphere" in New England, 1780–1835* (New Haven: Yale University Press, 1977); Joseph F. Kett, *Rites of Passage: Adolescence in America, 1790 to the Present* (New York: Basic Books, 1977); Mary P. Ryan, *Cradle of the Middle Class: The Family in Oneida County, New York, 1790–1865* (New York: Cambridge University Press, 1981); and Michael Paul Rogin, *Fathers and Children: Andrew Jackson and the Subjugation of the American Indian* (New York: Vintage Books, 1975). For broader treatments, see Phillippe Aries, *Centuries of Childhood: A Social History of Family Life*, trans. Robert Baldick (New York: Vintage Books, 1962); Edward Shorter, *The Making of the Modern Family* (New York: Basic Books, 1975); and Christopher Lasch, *Haven in a Heartless World: The Family Beseiged* (New York: Basic Books, 1977). For a superb cultural and intellectual study of declining paternalism in late-eighteenth-century America, see Jay Fliegelman, *Prodigals and Pilgrims: The American Revolution Against Patriarchal Authority, 1750–1800* (New York: Cambridge University Press, 1982).

9. On changes in work life in this period, see Henretta, "Families and Farms"; Cott, *Bonds of Womanhood;* Christopher Clark, "Household Economy, Market Exchange, and the Rise of Capitalism in the Connecticut Valley, 1800–1860," *Journal of Social History* 13 (Winter 1979): 169–89; and Howard B. Rock, *Artisans of the New Republic: The Tradesmen of New York City in the Age of Jefferson* (New York: New York University Press, 1979).

10. David Riesman, *The Lonely Crowd: A Study of the Changing American Character* (New Haven: Yale University Press, 1969), 44–45. For treatments of a "modern" American personality, see Richard Brown, *Modernization: The Transformation of American Life, 1600–1865* (New York: Hill & Wang, 1976); Weinstein and Platt, *Wish to Be Free;* and Kett, *Rites of Passage*. Studies that emphasize the pressures descending on the liberal individual include Rogin, *Fathers and Children;* Lasch, *Haven;* and Ronald T. Takai, *Iron Cages: Race and Culture in Nineteenth-Century America* (Seattle: University of Washington Press, 1982).

11. Max Weber, *The Protestant Ethic and the Spirit of Capitalism* (New York: Charles Scribner's Sons, 1958), 119; Sigmund Freud, *Civilization and Its Discontents* (New York: W. W. Norton & Co., 1962), 62; Karl Marx, *The Economic and Philosophic Manuscripts of 1844* in Robert C. Tucker, ed., *The Marx-Engels Reader*, 2nd ed. (New York: W. W. Norton & Co., 1978), 95–96.

12. "A Virginia Soldier," February 25, 1812, *Richmond Enquirer;* and Editorial, January 11, 1810, ibid.

13. See Benjamin Rush, *The Autobiography of Benjamin Rush . . . Together with His "Commonplace Book for 1789–1813,"* ed. George W. Corner (Princeton, 1948), 357–60, for his narrative of this dream.

14. Weinstein and Platt, *Wish to Be Free,* 195–226, esp. 197–98, 214, 219. See also the discussion in Elizabeth Fox-Genovese, "Psychohistory versus Psychodeterminism: The Case of Rogin's Jackson," *Reviews in American History* 3 (December 1975): 407–18.

15. "Honor Calls for War" by "Quintus," *Philadelphia Aurora,* June 19, 1812.

16. Emily Ellsworth Ford Skeel, *Mason Locke Weems: His Works and Ways* (New York: Plimpton Press, 1929), 2:389; Mason Locke Weems, *The Life of Washington . . . ,* ed. Marcus Cunliffe, 9th ed. (1908; Cambridge, Mass.: Harvard University Press, 1962), 216–17; idem, *The True Patriot . . .* (Philadelphia, 1802), 55–56; idem, *Washington,* 213–14. See also the discussion of Weems in George B. Forgie, *Patricide in the House Divided: A Psychological Interpretation of Lincoln and His Age* (New York: W. W. Norton & Co., 1979), 42–48.

17. Erik H. Erikson, *Childhood and Society* (New York: W. W. Norton & Co., 1963), 278–79; idem, *Identity and the Life Cycle* (New York: W. W. Norton & Co., 1980), 102; Max Horkheimer, "The Lessons of Fascism," in Hadley Cantril, ed., *Tensions That Cause Wars* (Urbana: University of Illinois Press, 1950).

18. Weems, *Washington,* 1–2; Editorial, January 11, 1810, *Richmond Enquirer;* "The National Standard" by "Vindex," January 25, 1810, ibid.; Rush, *Oration,* 22.

19. "Mr. Selden's Oration Delivered on the Fourth of July," *Richmond Enquirer,* July 12, 1811.

20. A special note should be made concerning the Jeffersonian affiliation of these three dramatis personae. Brunson's political position was clear, but those of the other two were more tangled. In early life, John Quincy Adams considered himself a Federalist, partly out of loyalty to his father. But by around 1810 both the elder and the younger Adams had abandoned that party and had begun to drift into the Jeffersonian camp. Brown's explicit political loyalty in early life was vague, but his Quaker background and well-known attraction to the English political radicalism of William Godwin and Mary Wollstonecraft would have placed him in the spirit of Jeffersonian politics. After 1800 he apparently drifted toward a moderate Federalist position, but like many Republicans he continued to advocate westward expansion and free-trade policies.

21. John Bernard, *Retrospections of America, 1797–1811* (New York, 1887), 252.

22. See Paul Allen, *The Life of Charles Brockden Brown* (Delmar, N.Y.: Scholars Facsimilies and Reprints, 1975), 16; William Dunlap, *The Life of Charles Brockden Brown: Together with Selections from the Rarest of His*

Printed Works, from His Original Letters, and from His Manuscripts Before Unpublished (Philadelphia, 1815), 1:16.

23. See, for example, Norman S. Grabo, *The Coincidental Art of Charles Brockden Brown* (Chapel Hill: University of North Carolina Press, 1981), and Alan Axelrod, *Charles Brockden Brown: An American Tale* (Austin: University of Texas Press, 1983).

24. Biographical information on Brown can be found in Dunlap, *Life of Brown;* Barry R. Warfel, *Charles Brockden Brown: American Gothic Novelist* (Gainesville, Fla.: University of Florida Press, 1949); and David Lee Clark, *Charles Brockden Brown: Pioneer Voice of America* (Durham, N.C.: Duke University Press, 1952).

25. Brown's comments on the law are quoted in Warfel, *Brown*, 29; Brown to William Woods Wilkins, November 1792, in Clark, *Brown*, 32; Charles Brockden Brown, *The Rhapsodist and Other Uncollected Writings*, ed. Harry R. Warfel (Delmar, N.Y.: Scholars Facsimiles and Reprints, 1943), 4.

26. Brown, *Rhapsodist*, 1, 5, 6, 16, 7.

27. See Dunlap, *Life of Brown*, 40–43, 53–54.

28. See Brown-Wilkins letters in Allen, *Brown*, 50–55, and the letters in Clark, *Brown*, 23–40. Paul Allen originally was authorized by Mrs. Charles Brockden Brown to write a life of the deceased author, but Mrs. Brown disapproved of the work, and William Dunlap ended up finishing the biography in 1815. The Allen manuscript later was discovered in the twentieth century and reprinted.

29. Brown to Wilkins, quoted in Warfel, *Brown*, 51; Brown to Wilkins, January 22, 1793, in Clark, *Brown*, 34; Brown to Henrietta G., in ibid., 101; Brown to Wilkins, in Allen, *Brown*, 53; Brown to William Dunlap, in Warfel, *Brown*, 86–88.

30. Brown to Wilkins, in Clark, *Brown*, 26; Brown to Wilkins, in Allen, *Brown*, 52–53; Charles E. Bennet in the "Introduction," to ibid., xiv; Elihu Hubbard Smith in his diary, quoted in Axelrod, *Brown*, 171.

31. Allen, *Brown*, 12–13; Elihu Hubbard Smith, diary entry, quoted in Axelrod, *Brown*, 171; Brown to Wilkins, in Clark, *Brown*, 35; Allen, *Brown*, 56.

32. See Charles Brockden Brown, *Alcuin: A Dialogue* (New York, 1798); Brown, "The Man at Home" (1798) in Warfel, *The Rhapsodist*, 27–98. For a discussion of *Sky-Walk*, see Clark, *Brown*, 157–60, and Warfel, *Brown*, 88–91.

33. See the following novels by Charles Brockden Brown: *Wieland; or, The Transformation: An American Tale*, and *Memoirs of Carwin the Biloquist* (Kent, Ohio: Kent State University Press, 1977); *Ormond; or, the Secret Witness* (New York: Hafner Publishing Co., 1937); *Arthur Mervyn; or, Memoirs of the Year 1793* (New York: Holt, Rinehart & Winston, 1962); and *Edgar Huntly; or, Memoirs of a Sleep-Walker* (Port Washington, N.Y.: Kennikat Press, 1963).

34. Brown, *Edgar Huntly*, 147, and Brown, "Preface" in *American Review and Literary Journal for the Year 1801*, quoted in Robert Spiller,

ed., *The American Literary Revolution, 1783–1837* (Garden City, N.Y.: Anchor Books, 1967), 32.

35. See Brown, *Wieland*, 37–38; *Ormond*, 6; *Arthur Mervyn*, 8–9, 19. See also Brown, *Ormond*, 195–96.

36. Ibid., 3–4, 69, 147, 93; and Brown, *Arthur Mervyn*, 377, 280.

37. Brown, *Arthur Mervyn*, 309, 208.

38. Ibid., 90, 84; Brown, *Ormond*, 7–14, 81–82; *Wieland*, 93–95, 190, 244.

39. Brown, *Arthur Mervyn*, 377, 280.

40. Ibid., 218, 66, 80; Brown, *Ormond*, 94–96; *Arthur Mervyn*, 218.

41. Brown to Frenchwoman Miss DeMoure, quoted in Warfel, *Brown*, 94–95.

42. Brown, *Edgar Huntly*, 165–66.

43. Brown, *Wieland*, 35; *Carwin the Biloquist*, 248; *Arthur Mervyn*, 16–17, 413, 420–21.

44. Brown, *Wieland*, 90–91.

45. Ibid., 224–25.

46. Brown, *Arthur Mervyn*, 31–40, 102–7; *Ormond*, 222; *Wieland*, 89–96.

47. Brown, *Edgar Huntly*, 43–45, 124, 134.

48. Ibid., 111, 213.

49. Leslie Fiedler, *Love and Death in the American Novel* (New York: Stein & Day, 1975), 145; Brown, *Edgar Huntly*, 84, 156, 213, 194, 267.

50. Brown, *Edgar Huntly*, 173.

51. Brown to James Brown, April 1800, in Clark, *Brown*, 195; Brown to unknown correspondent, September 1, 1800, in Warfel, *Brown*, 187; Brown to Joseph Armitt, December 1799, in ibid., 166; "The Poet's Prayer" in the *Port Folio*, May 2, 1801, in ibid., 201; "Editor's Preface to the Public," *Literary Magazine*, October 1803, in Axelrod, *Brown*, 126.

52. "On Classical Learning," *Literary Magazine and American Regr*, April 1805, in Clark, *Brown*, 22–23; editor's preface to the 1803 *Literary Magazine* in Dunlap, *Brown*, 2:60–62, 228–29; Brown to Dunlap, 1805, quoted in ibid., 113.

53. Charles Brockden Brown, "Annal of Europe and America," *American Register* 1 (1806–7), in Clark, *Brown*, 284–85: idem, *An Address to the Government of the United States on the Cession of Louisiana* (Philadelphia, 1803), 64–65.

54. Charles Brockden Brown, *Monroe's Embassy; or The Conduct of the Government in Relation to Our Claims to the Navigation of the Mississippi* (Philadelphia, 1803), 35; Brown, "Preface," *American Register* 2 (1807), in Clark, *Brown*, 284–85; Brown, *Monroe's Embassy*, 27, 27–28; Brown, *Cession of Louisiana*, 16–17.

55. Brown, *Cession of Louisiana*, 70, 77–78, 80–81, 92.

56. Charles Brockden Brown, *An Address to the Congress of the United States on the Utility and Justice of Restriction upon Foreign Commerce* (Philadelphia, 1809), 74–75.

57. Dunlap, *Brown*, 2:94–95; Allen, *Brown*, 16; "Advertisement" to *Sky-Walk*, in Clark, *Brown*, 160; Brown to Wilkins, in ibid., 38–39.

58. Alfred Brunson, *A Western Pioneer; or, Incidents of the Life and Times of Reverend Alfred Brunson* . . . (Cincinnati and New York, 1872).

59. Ibid., 18–30.

60. Ibid., 31–35.

61. Ibid., 36–38, 40–42.

62. Ibid., 30–31, 35–37, 40, 43–45.

63. Ibid., 45–50.

64. Ibid., 52–53.

65. Ibid., 52–53, 55–56.

66. Ibid., 58–61.

67. Ibid., 61–62, 72–73.

68. Ibid., 66–69, 77, 97–99, 100.

69. Ibid., 107–8.

70. Ibid., 151–52, 107–8.

71. Ibid., 108–45, 113–14.

72. Ibid., 151–52.

73. Ibid., 152, 154–55.

74. Ibid., 72–73, 40.

75. The events surrounding the suicide are described in Samuel Flagg Bemis, *John Quincy Adams and the Union* (New York: Alfred A. Knopf, 1956), 177–84.

76. John Quincy Adams, "Diary," Adams Family Papers, Microfilm, Massachusetts Historical Society, Boston, reel 39, entries for May 3, 4, 5, 6, 7, 14, 16, 20, and 26, 1829. For parental relations with George Washington Adams, see Bemis, *Adams and the Union*, 115–18.

77. Aside from the Adams Papers the primary sources of information on John Quincy Adams' life are Charles Francis Adams, ed., *Memoirs of John Quincy Adams* (Philadelphia, 1874–77); David Grayson Allen et al., eds., *Diary of John Quincy Adams* (Cambridge, Mass.: Harvard University Press, 1981); Worthington Chauncey Ford, ed., *The Writings of John Quincy Adams* (New York: Macmillan Co., 1913–17). Hereafter these works will be referred to as *Memoirs*, *Diary*, and *Writings*.

78. See Samuel Flagg Bemis, *John Quincy Adams and the Foundations of American Foreign Policy* (New York: Alfred A. Knopf, 1949), 4–18. Bemis' two-volume biography is the only full-scale treatment of Adams' entire life. Other biographical efforts include George A. Lipsky, *John Quincy Adams: His Theory and Ideas* (New York: Thomas Y. Crowell, 1950), a thematic exploration of his intellect; Robert A. East, *John Quincy Adams, the Critical Years: 1785–1794* (New York: Bookman Associates, 1962), a study of his life in late adolescence and early manhood; and Paul C. Nagel, *Descent from Glory: Four Generations of the John Adams Family* (New York: Oxford University Press, 1983).

79. See John Quincy Adams (hereafter JQA), March 11, 1785, *Diary*, 1:233, and noted under the portrait of Thomas Jefferson, xiii; Elizabeth Shaw to Abigail Adams, November 6, 1785, Adams Papers, reel 366;

Abigail Adams to JQA, January 17, 1780, Adams Papers, reel 97; JQA, April 26, 1785, *Diary*, 1:256–57.

80. See Bemis, *Adams and Foreign Policy*, 19–26; East, *Adams' Critical Years*, cháps. 1–4. The graduation speech can be found in the *Diary*, 2:258–63.

81. JQA, *Diary*, 1:335, 374; 2:104–5; 1:330–31; 2:402–3, 346–49. For discussions of JQA's literary aspirations, see East, *Adams' Critical Years*, 18, 99, 173–201.

82. JQA, *Diary*, 2:55–56, 320.

83. Ibid., 1:350; JQA, Adams Papers, reel 223, second poem at the end of the reel. For a general discussion of JQA's amorous difficulties, see East, *Adams' Critical Years*, chaps. 2, 5, 6.

84. JQA, *Diary*, 2:343, 47–49; 1:398; 2:243; 1:380–81; 2:334.

85. JQA, *Writings*, 1:26, 34, n.1; *Diary*, 2:427–28; J's diary entry on December 24, 1787, Adams Papers, reel 15.

86. JQA transcribed this address in his diary on September 5, 1788. See *Diary*, 2:447–52.

87. JQA, *Memoirs*, 1:169. Another example of JQA's determination to lead a "life of application" appears in *Memoirs*, 1:170.

88. JQA to Abigail Adams, November 7, 1795, Adams Papers, reel 380; "Columbus" essays, No. II, *Writings*, 1:151 and "Publicola," No. I, *Writings*, 1:67–69; *Writings*, 2:464–65; *Writings*, 1:177; "Barneveld" essays, 1793, quoted in East, *Adams' Critical Years*, 189.

89. JQA to Abigail Adams, *Memoirs*, 1:194–95; *Writings*, 1:125–26; *Writings*, 2:453, 451.

90. See Bemis, *Adams and Foreign Policy*, chaps. 6 and 7.

91. JQA, *Memoirs*, 1:276, 326–27, 343; *Writings*, 3:150; *Memoirs*, 1:370–71, 249, 398, 282, 283.

92. JQA, *Memoirs*, 1:454–57; *Writings*, 2:105–6; *Memoirs*, 1:550; *Writings*, 3:319.

93. JQA, *Writings*, 3:171–72; *Memoirs*, 1:536–37; *Writings*, 3:244–45; *Memoirs*, 1:542–43.

94. JQA, *Memoirs*, 1:488–89, 502, 504.

95. JQA, *Writings*, 4:162, 262, 427.

96. Ibid., 4:160, 302, 305; 5:7–8; 4:436–37, 358; 5:150–51, 140–41.

97. Ibid., 4:376; 5:105; 4:461.

98. Ibid., 4:120–21, 267; 2:499–500; 3:234; 4:505.

99. John Quincy Adams, *An Oration Pronounced July 4, 1793, at the Request of the Inhabitants of the Town of Boston* (Boston, 1793), 12, 14–15; JQA, *Memoirs*, 1:188.

100. Asa Aiken, *An Oration, Pronounced Before the Republican Citizens of Windsor . . .* (Windsor, Vt., 1812), 1.

101. "War with England," *Niles' Weekly Register*, June 27, 1812.

102. "Fauquier and Prince William," *National Intelligencer*, July 14, 1812.

103. "Provision for the Officers and Soldiers Wounded . . . ," in Wal-

ter Lowrie and Walter S. Franklin, eds., *American State Papers, Military Affairs* (Washington, D.C., 1834), 1:312; "To the Freemen of Kentucky," *Kentucky Gazette,* May 12, 1812; "Public Sentiment," *Richmond Enquirer,* December 3, 1811; from the *Kentucky Argus* in the *Western Intelligencer,* December 4, 1811.

104. *Niles' Weekly Register,* September 28, 1811; "Communication" by "Juvenis," *National Intelligencer,* July 11, 1812.

105. Paulding, *Diverting History,* 15, 134; Editorial, *National Intelligencer,* July 2, 1812; John Giles, *Discourses Delivered to the Second Presbyterian Society in Newburyport, August 20, 1812 . . .* (Haverhill, Mass., 1812), 16. George B. Forgie made a similar argument regarding the Civil War generation. I would modify his contention by noting that the Founding Fathers complex appeared much earlier and that the Civil War may be part of a larger psychological pattern in nineteenth-century America.

106. *Western Intelligencer,* January 31, 1812.

107. Skeel, *Weems,* 3:112–13; Peter Van Pelt, *The Goodness of God . . .* (New York, 1812), 22.

108. New York, *Commercial Advertiser,* December 4, 1811; Robert Wright, December 23, 1811, *Annals of Congress,* 23:469; "From the National Aegis," quoted in the *National Intelligencer,* November 26, 1811. For Freud's analysis of the symbolic significance of fire, see Freud, *Civilization and Its Discontents,* 37, n.1.

109. "Anglo-Saxon War," *National Intelligencer,* June 4, 1812; *Philadelphia Aurora,* October 14, 1812; Skeel, *Weems,* 3:112–13; General Hull's proclamation, *Western Intelligencer,* July 24, 1812.

110. See Rogin, *Fathers and Children;* Takaki, *Iron Cages;* and Freud, *Civilization and Its Discontents.*

111. "The National Standard," *Richmond Enquirer,* January 25, 1810; "The Day," *National Intelligencer,* July 4, 1811.

112. Solomon Aiken, *Oration,* 8; "Oration," by William Hendricks, *Cincinnati Western Spy,* July 18, 1812; Editorial, *Niles' Weekly Register,* May 30, 1812; Governor James Barbour's address, *Richmond Enquirer,* April 17, 1812; "Ministerial Concessions," ibid., May 2, 1812; ibid., September 7, 1810; *National Intelligencer,* May 7, 1812; *Richmond Enquirer,* December 3, 1811.

113. See Erik Erikson, "Wholeness and Totality," in Leon Bramson and George W. Goethals, eds., *War: Studies from Psychology, Sociology, Anthropology* (New York: Basic Books, 1968), 119–31.

114. "For the National Intelligencer," *National Intelligencer,* March 21, 1812; Giles, *Discourses,* 8; Gaillard Hunt, ed., *The Writings of James Madison* (New York: G. P. Putnam's Sons, 1900–1910), 8:407–8.

115. Mathews, *An Oration . . . 1813,* 18; *Niles' Weekly Register,* November 21, 1812; Giles, *Discourses,* 8; Charles Ingersoll's letter to *Niles' Weekly Register,* February 8, 1812; James F. Hopkins, ed., *Papers of Henry Clay* (Lexington, Ky., 1959), 1:715; *Niles' Weekly Register,* May 9, 1812.

116. Van Pelt, *Goodness of God,* 20–21; D. H. Lawrence, *Studies in*

Classical American Literature (New York: Vintage Books, 1978), 89–90.

Chapter V: Politics and Productivity: War and the Emergence of Liberalism

1. Joel Barlow, "Oration Delivered at Washington, July 4, 1809 . . . ," in William K. Bottorff and Arthur L. Ford, eds., *The Works of Joel Barlow* (reprint, Gainesville, Fla.: University of Florida Press, 1970), 1:526. On Barlow's life, see James Woodress, *A Yankee's Odyssey: The Life of Joel Barlow* (Philadelphia: Lippincott, 1958), and Arthur L. Ford, *Joel Barlow* (New York: Twayne Publishers, 1971).

2. Barlow, "Oration," 525, 526, 530, 535, 527, 529.

3. Ibid., 527, 529, 530, 533, 535–36.

4. See the discussion in Chapter III, above.

5. See Gordon S. Wood, *The Creation of the American Republic, 1776–1787* (Chapel Hill: University of North Carolina Press, 1969).

6. *Richmond Enquirer*, June 12, 1810; *Mr. P. B. Porter's Speech on Internal Improvements . . . February 8, 1810* (Washington, D.C., 1810), 2–3.

7. William Winder, July 4th oration, *Niles' Weekly Register*, July 11, 1812; "To the American People" by "Sallust," *Philadelphia Aurora*, February 28, 1811; Washington Irving, *Letters of Jonathan Oldstyle, Gent. and Salmagundi . . .* , ed. Bruce I. Granger and Martha Hartzog (Boston, 1977), March 7, 1807.

8. See, for example, Joyce Appleby, "Commercial Farming and the 'Agrarian Myth' in the Early Republic," *Journal of American History* 68 (March 1982): 833–49; and Ralph Lerner, "Commerce and Character: The Anglo-American as New Model Man," *William and Mary Quarterly*, 3rd ser., 36 (January 1979): 3–26.

9. See Lance Banning, *The Jeffersonian Persuasion: Evolution of a Party Ideology* (Ithaca, N.Y.: Cornell University Press, 1978); Trevor Colbourn, *The Lamp of Experience: Whig History and the Intellectual Origins of the American Revolution* (Chapel Hill: University of North Carolina Press, 1965); and James M. Banner, Jr., *To the Hartford Convention: The Federalists and the Origins of Party Politics in Massachusetts, 1789–1815* (New York: Alfred A. Knopf, 1970).

10. See Drew R. McCoy, *The Elusive Republic: Political Economy in Jeffersonian America* (Chapel Hill: University of North Carolina Press, 1979).

11. Samuel Mitchell's speech, *Western Intelligencer*, March 6, 1812; *Richmond Enquirer*, July 6, 1810; "Mr Selden's Oration," ibid., July 12, 1811; Daniel Waldo Lincon's oration, ibid., August 10, 1810.

12. "From the New Hampshire *Patriot*," *National Intelligencer*, June 4, 1811; Richard M. Johnson's speech, *Kentucky Gazette*, March 27, 1810; "Mr. Selden's Oration," *Richmond Enquirer*, July 12, 1811; Daniel Waldo Lincoln's oration, ibid., August 10, 1810; "From the *National Intelligencer*," *Western Intelligencer*, November 6, 1811.

13. *National Intelligencer,* April 9, 1812; "Spirit of Opposition," *Richmond Enquirer,* May 19, 1812; "To the Members of Congress," ibid., March 27, 1812; *Philadelphia Aurora,* June 17, 1812; "To the Peoples of America" by "Americanus," *National Intelligencer,* May 19, 1812.

14. George Fowler, *The Wandering Philanthropist; or, Letters from a Chinese* (Philadelphia, 1810), 50–55; Irving, *Salmagundi,* August 14, 1807; "The Crisis," *Richmond Enquirer,* February 22, 1811.

15. Roger H. Brown, *The Republic in Peril: 1812* (New York: W. W. Norton & Co., 1964).

16. McCoy (*The Elusive Republic,* 166–84) discusses the emergence of the Republican critique of commerce in the 1790s.

17. See James Madison, "Embargo," *National Intelligencer,* December 25, 1807; Governor John Tyler's speech, *Richmond Enquirer,* December 6, 1810; Asa Aiken, *An Oration, Pronounced Before the Citizens of Windsor . . .* (Windsor, Vt., 1812), 6–7.

18. John Taylor, *An Inquiry into the Principles and Tendency of Certain Public Measures . . .* (Philadelphia, 1794), 78–79; Governor John Tyler's speech, *Richmond Enquirer,* December 6, 1810; "For the National Intelligencer" by "Solon," *National Intelligencer,* May 16, 1811.

19. Information on Cooper's life can be found in Dumas Malone, *The Public Life of Thomas Cooper, 1783–1839* (New Haven: Yale University Press, 1926).

20. *Emporium of Arts and Sciences,* 1:12–13, 161, 8, 4; 2:136–37n; 1:8.

21. Ibid., 1:173–74; 2:151n; Thomas Cooper to Thomas Jefferson, March 16, 1806, quoted in Malone, *Life of Cooper,* 191.

22. *Emporium of Arts and Sciences,* 2:130n; 1:165; 2:123–24.

23. Information on Gallatin's life can be found in Raymond Walters, Jr., *Albert Gallatin: Jeffersonian Financier and Diplomat* (Pittsburgh: University of Pittsburgh Press, 1957). See Edwin G. Burrows, "Albert Gallatin and the Political Economy of Republicanism, 1761–1800" (Ph.D. diss., Columbia University, 1974), for treatment of his career up to 1800. The latter study stresses the Genevan's character as a small entrepreneur of limited intellectual scope.

24. Gallatin's *A Sketch of the Finances of the United States* (1796) can be found in Henry Adams, ed., *The Writings of Albert Gallatin* (Philadelphia, 1879), 2:69–206. On the influence of this volume in Republican circles, see Walters, *Gallatin,* 93–94.

25. Gallatin, "Sketch," in Adams, ed., *Writings of Gallatin,* 3:143–49, 154, 161.

26. *Annals of Congress of the United States* (Washington, D.C., 1853), 3:2861–65 contains Gallatin's speech in the House of Representatives on February 11, 1799.

27. Ibid., 2862–67.

28. Gallatin to Jefferson on August 10, 1801, August 11, 1803, and November 8, 1809, in Adams, ed., *Writings of Gallatin,* 1:33, 135, 465–66.

29. See Gallatin's remarks on January 14, 1799 in *Annals of Congress,*

3:2649–50. See also Gallatin's "Report on Manufactures" (1810), in Walter Lowrie and Walter S. Franklin, eds. *American State Papers, Finance* (Washington, D.C., 1834), 2:430.

30. William Bibb's remarks, *Annals of the Congress of the United States* (Washington, D.C., 1853), 23:985, 977; "Our Manufactures," *National Intelligencer*, June 22, 1811.

31. "For the Aurora," *Philadelphia Aurora*, July 12, 1812; "To the People of Maryland," *National Intelligencer*, August 10, 1811; *Western Intelligencer*, July 17, 1811.

32. *Niles' Weekly Register*, November 14, 1812; "One of the People," *Kentucky Gazette*, April 3, 1810; "Manufactures," *Richmond Enquirer*, June 26, 1810.

33. "Dorothy Distaff," *Kentucky Gazette*, April 10, 1810; "Manufactures," *Richmond Enquirer*, January 4, 1810.

34. Oration by Lemuel Sawyer, *Kentucky Gazette*, October 23, 1810.

35. Ibid.

36. "External Commerce," *Richmond Enquirer*, September 10, 1811.

37. Editorial, *Kentucky Gazette*, September 18, 1810; Philip Freneau, "On the Morality of Commerce," in *A Collection of Poems on American Affairs* . . . (1815; reprint, Delmar, N.Y.: Scholars Facsimiles and Reprints, 1976); "Real Independence," *Kentucky Gazette*, February 18, 1810.

38. "For the National Intelligencer" by "Americanus," *National Intelligencer*, May 25, 1811; "Honesty Is the Best Policy" by "Common Sense," *National Intelligencer*, June 2, 1812; "Mr. Lincoln's Oration," *Kentucky Gazette*, August 28, 1810; "Real Independence," ibid., February 18, 1810.

39. *Letters on Internal Improvements in the State of Pennsylvania, New York, etc.* (Philadelphia, 1810), 11–12, 107; *Cincinnati Western Spy*, February 1, 1812; Peter Buel Porter, *Mr. P. B. Porter's Speech on Internal Improvements* (Washington, D.C., 1810), 2.

40. "To the Editor of the Aurora" by "Atticus" (Philip Freneau), *Philadelphia Aurora*, November 17, 1808; Porter, *Internal Improvements*, 2–3.

41. Cooper's remarks in his *Political Essays* (1800) are quoted in Malone, *Life of Cooper*, 100; *Emporium of Arts and Sciences*, 2:140n.

42. Cooper, *Political Essays* (1800), quoted in Malone, *Life of Cooper*, 100; Cooper to Jefferson, December 4, 1808, quoted in Malone, *Life of Cooper*, 193; *Emporium of Arts and Sciences*, 2:126–27n.

43. *Emporium of Arts and Sciences*, 1:4–9. Drew McCoy has discussed Cooper in *The Elusive Republic* in two contexts. He describes Cooper first as a Republican critic of "speculative" commerce and the carrying trade in the 1790s. McCoy later describes the expatriate political economist as an exemplary proponent of trends in Republican political economy during and after the War of 1812: a dynamic economy of manufacturing and the home market that would not succumb to mercantilist corruption. I would amend McCoy's interpretation by emphasizing not only the connection between the critique of commerce and the subsequent argument for a home market, but also, and more important, that Cooper's stress on the home market—like

that of many other Republicans—seemed quite evident *before* the War of 1812 and indeed played an important role in shaping an atmosphere conducive to that conflict.

44. Gallatin's "Report on Roads and Canals," in Walter Lowrie and Walter S. Franklin, eds., *American State Papers* (Washington, D.C., 1834), 1:724–25.

45. Ibid., 917–21, 725.

46. Gallatin's "Report on the Bank of the United States" (1809), in ibid., 2:351–53.

47. Gallatin's "Report on Manufactures" (1810), in ibid., 430–31. My understanding of Gallatin's political economy has profited from the analysis of John R. Nelson, Jr., "Hamilton and Gallatin: Political Economy and Policy-Making in the New Nation, 1789—1812" (Ph.D. diss., Northern Illinois University, 1979).

48. Informative and succinct discussions of the embargo and subsequent nonintercourse legislation can be found in Brown, *Republic in Peril*, 16–23, and McCoy, *The Elusive Republic*, 216–19.

49. See Banning, *Jeffersonian Persuasion*, 259–64, for a good discussion of the traditional republican distrust of war.

50. For treatments of the Enlightenment influence on republican thinking about war, see Felix Gilbert, *To the Farewell Address: Ideas of Early American Foreign Policy* (Princeton: Princeton University Press, 1961), and Gerald Stourzh, *Alexander Hamilton and the Idea of Republican Government* (Stanford, Calif.: Stanford University Press, 1970).

51. John Rhea's remarks, January 4, 1812, *Annals of Congress*, 23:638–39; "For the Enquirer" by "A Republican," *Richmond Enquirer*, December 21, 1811.

52. My reading of Jefferson and Madison has been influenced in various ways by McCoy, *The Elusive Republic*; Joyce Appleby, *Capitalism and a New Social Order: The Republican Vision of the 1790s* (New York: New York University Press, 1984); and Banning, *Jeffersonian Persuasion*.

53. See Jefferson's comments in Andrew A. Lipscomb and Albert E. Bergh, eds., *The Writings of Thomas Jefferson* (Washington, D.C.: Thomas Jefferson Memorial Assoc., 1905), 7:461 and 13:41–42; and in Paul Leicester Ford, ed., *The Writings of Thomas Jefferson* (New York, 1892–99), 7:328. For an earlier expression of these views, see Jefferson's *Notes on the State of Virginia*, ed. William H. Peden (Chapel Hill: University of North Carolina Press, 1955), 174. Madison's comments appear in Robert A. Rutland et al., eds., *The Papers of James Madison* (Chicago: University of Chicago Press, 1962–), 10:443, 284; Gaillard Hunt, ed., *The Writings of James Madison* (New York: G. P. Putnam's Sons, 1900–1910), 6:174–75; James Madison, *Letters and Other Writings of James Madison* (Philadelphia, 1865), 4:491–92. For a useful discussion of these attitudes, see Reginald C. Stuart, *The Half-Way Pacifist: Thomas Jefferson's View of War* (Toronto: University of Toronto Press, 1978). The following works offer penetrating analyses of the two Virginians' evolving commercial strategy: Merrill Peterson, "Thomas Jefferson and Commercial Policy, 1783–1793," *William*

and Mary Quarterly, 3rd ser. 31 (1974): 633–46; and Burton Spivak, *Jefferson's English Crisis: Commerce, Embargo, and the Republican Revolution* (Charlottesville: University of Virginia Press, 1979).

54. Jefferson "to Judge Cooper," February 18, 1806, Thomas Jefferson Papers, Library of Congress (microfilm); Jefferson to Charles Pinckney, February 2, 1812, cited in Bradford Perkins, *Prologue to War: England and the United States, 1805–1812* (Berkeley and Los Angeles: University of California Press, 1961), 42. Madison's commentary appears in Hunt, ed., *Writings*, 8:129, 174.

55. John Clopton's "Circular" to his constituents, *Richmond Enquirer*, June 30, 1812.

56. Charles G. Haines, *An Oration, Pronounced . . . on the Fourth of July, 1811* (Concord, Mass., 1811): "From the National Intelligencer," *Cincinnati Western Intelligencer*, November 6, 1811.

57. Grundy's remarks, *Annals of Congress*, 24:1355–56.

58. Available information on Grundy's early life can be found in his only scholarly biography: Joseph H. Parks, *Felix Grundy: Champion of Democracy* (Baton Rouge: Louisiana State University Press, 1940), chaps. 1–4.

59. Grundy, *Annals of Congress*, 24:1407–8.

60. Ibid., 23:425, 25:357, 23:424, 351.

61. Ibid., 24:1412; Grundy to Andrew Jackson, February 12, 1812, in John Spencer Bassett, ed., *Correspondence of Andrew Jackson* (Washington, D.C.: Carnegie Institution of Washington, 1927), 1:215–16; Grundy, *Annals of Congress*, 23:424.

62. Grundy, *Annals of Congress*, 24:1409–10, 23:426, 423, 24:1410.

63. See the "Prospectus" and Niles' essay on "Domestic Manufactures" in *Niles' Weekly Register*, September 7, 1811.

64. Information on Niles' life can be found in the only biography: Richard G. Stone, *Hezekiah Niles as an Economist*, Johns Hopkins University Studies in History and Political Science, 51, no. 5 (Baltimore: Johns Hopkins University Press, 1933), esp. chap. 2, pp. 33–56.

65. *Niles' Weekly Register*, May 30, March 7, and March 14, 1812.

66. Ibid., May 30 and April 18, 1812.

67. Ibid., November 21, 1811; July 18, 1812.

68. Ibid., June 27, 1812; May 30, 1812; July 18, 1812.

69. Ibid., October 3, 1812.

70. Tench Coxe, "America," in *The American Edition of the New Edinburgh Encyclopedia* (Philadelphia, 1813), 1:655, 633–34, 654. This essay originally had been serialized and printed in the 1809 *Philadelphia Democratic Press*.

71. The details of Coxe's life can be found in Jacob E. Cooke, *Tench Coxe and the Early Republic* (Chapel Hill: University of North Carolina Press, 1978). Also useful is Harold Hutcheson, *Tench Coxe: A Study in American Economic Development* (Baltimore: Johns Hopkins University Press, 1938).

72. See McCoy, *The Elusive Republic*, for an analysis of the Republicans' advocacy of a "middle state" of economic development.

73. Coxe, "America," 668, 652–57, 657–59, 662, 659; Leo Marx, *The Machine in the Garden: Technology and the Pastoral Ideal in America* (New York: Oxford University Press, 1959), 188.

74. Tench Coxe, *An Essay on the Manufacturing Interest of the United States . . .* (Philadelphia, 1804), 31–32; Tench Coxe, *An Address to an Assembly of Friends of American Manufactures . . .* (Philadelphia, 1787); Coxe, *Manufacturing Interest*, 25–26.

75. Coxe, *Manufacturing Interest*, 5–10, 11–14.

76. Ibid., 7–8, 14–17, 23, xi.

77. Tench Coxe, *A Statement of the Arts and Manufactures of the United States of America, for the Year 1810* (Philadelphia, 1814), xxi; Coxe using the pseudonym "Juriscola," "To the Cultivators, the Capitalists, and the Manufacturers of the United States," *National Intelligencer*, August 6, 1810.

78. Coxe, "America," 670, 656, 661, 660, 665.

79. See Cooke, *Tench Coxe*, 484; Coxe writing as "Juriscola," "To the Wise and Good of All Parties and Places Throughout the United States," *National Intelligencer*, August 6, 1812; Coxe, *Statement of the Manufactures*, xxiii.

80. Coxe as "Juriscola," *National Intelligencer*, August 3 and 20, July 27, August 3, 1810.

81. Ibid., August 10, 1810.

82. Harriet Martineau, *Retrospect of Western Travel* (London, 1838), 1:243.

83. "Report on Relations with Great Britain," in Robert L. Meriwether et al., *The Papers of John C. Calhoun* (Columbia: University of South Carolina Press, 1959), 1:67. For a discussion of Calhoun's large role in writing the Report, see p. 69, n. 46.

84. Information on Calhoun's early life can be found in the standard biography, Charles M. Wiltse, *John C. Calhoun, Nationalist, 1782–1828* (New York: Bobbs-Merrill, 1944), and in the more provocative study by Gerald M. Capers, *John C. Calhoun—Opportunist: A Reappraisal* (Gainesville: University of Florida Press, 1960). Also useful is the "anonymous" campaign biography *Life of John C. Calhoun . . .* (New York, 1843). Wiltse believes that this document was approved by Calhoun but not written by him. Capers, along with Gaillard Hunt, argues that it is essentially a "political autobiography." See Wiltse, *Calhoun*, 401–2, and Capers, *Opportunist*, 255–56.

85. Meriwether, *Papers of Calhoun*, 1:8, 41; *Life of Calhoun* (1843).

86. Meriwether, *Papers of Calhoun*, 1:1, n. 2.

87. Ibid., 1:44, 283; Capers, *Opportunist*, 20.

88. Meriwether, *Papers of Calhoun*, 1:28, 60, 10.

89. Ibid., 76, 82, 99–100.

90. Ibid., 131–32, 144–45, 132–33.

91. Ibid., 79, 133, 159–60.

92. Ibid., 34–35.

93. Ibid., 254–59, 133, 82–83, 107.

94. Ibid., 107, 90–91.

95. See *Annals of Congress*, 23:330–43, for details on Clay's election as speaker and the subsequent process of committee selection.

96. Ibid., vols. 23 and 24, contains the official record of Congressional action and debate between November 1811 and June 1812. Useful discussion of this session can also be found in Brown, *Republic in Peril*, chaps. 3–8, and Norman K. Risjord, *The Old Republicans: Southern Conservatism in the Age of Jefferson* (New York: Columbia University Press, 1965), 96–145.

97. Madison's war message can be found in Hunt, *Writings of Madison*, 8:192–200.

98. Robert L. Meriwether makes a convincing case for Calhoun's primary authorship with Grundy as contributor. See Meriwether, *Papers of Calhoun*, 1:122–24.

99. The "War Report" is in *Annals of Congress*, 24:1546–54.

100. Ibid., 1547.

101. Ibid., 1553.

102. Ibid., 1547.

103. Adams, *Writings of Gallatin*, 1:517; *Western Intelligencer*, June 19, 1812; Letter from "Cato," *National Intelligencer*, July 21, 1812; "The New Era," *Richmond Enquirer*, June 23, 1812.

104. *Annals of Congress*, 24:1553–54.

105. Ibid., 1548, 1550.

106. Ibid., 1547.

107. Ibid., 1553.

108. *Richmond Enquirer*, February 10, 1810, and December 21, 1811; Jonathan Robert's remarks, December 13, 1811, *Annals of Congress*, 23:503; Bassett, *Correspondence of Jackson*, 1:220–23; *National Intelligencer*, July 4, 1812.

109. *National Intelligencer*, February 22, 1812; *Western Intelligencer*, July 31, 1812, *Niles' Weekly Register*, May 30, 1812.

110. *Annals of Congress*, 24:1549.

111. See Chapter II for a more detailed discussion of civism and the social impulse to war in 1812.

112. *Annals of Congress*, 24:1547, 1553.

113. Ibid., 1553, 1547.

114. Ibid., 1547, 1553.

115. Ibid., 1547.

116. Ibid., 1554. See Chapter III for a more in-depth analysis of character, civil religion, and the cultural compulsion to war in 1812.

117. *Annals of Congress*, 24:1554.

118. Ibid., 1551, 1553.

119. Richard Sennett, "Surrender of the Will," *New York Review of Books*, April 18, 1974; *Annals of Congress*, 24:1549, 1551.

120. *Annals of Congress*, 24:1551–52, 1554.

121. John Henry, an Irishman residing in the United States, traveled to New England in 1811 as an agent for Canadian-British authorities. Perceiv-

ing the great political discontent in New England over Jeffersonian commercial restrictions and the likelihood of war, he wrote a number of letters to British authorities suggesting the possibility of secession. When these letters came into the hands of leading Republicans and were turned over to Congress by President Madison, they caused a public uproar concerning both British "spying" and Federalist "disloyalty."

122. *Annals of Congress*, 24:1551–52, 1554. For a more complete discussion of the various psychological impulses to war—the crisis of authority, the return of the repressed, the attempt at "total" identity—see Chapter IV.

123. *Annals of Congress*, 24:1554.

124. See, for instance, Robert L. Meriwether's comments in his *Papers of Calhoun*, 1:122.

Chapter VI: The Republic Reordered, 1812–1815

1. J. C. A. Stagg, *Mr. Madison's War: Politics, Diplomacy, and Warfare in the Early American Republic, 1783–1830* (Princeton: Princeton University Press, 1983), offers the best account of the military, administrative, and legislative aspects of the war. A less scholarly but highly readable account can be found in Glenn Tucker, *Poltroons and Patriots: A Popular Account of the War of 1812* (New York: Bobbs-Merrill, 1954).

2. Henry Adams, *History of the United States During the Administrations of Jefferson and Madison* (New York, 1889–1896), 9:80, 195. For similar assessments, see Paul C. Nagel, *One Nation Indivisible: The Union in American Thought, 1776–1861* (New York: Oxford University Press, 1964); George Dangerfield, *The Awakening of American Nationalism, 1815–1828* (New York: Harper & Row, 1965); and George Rogers Taylor, *The Transportation Revolution, 1815–1860* (New York: Rinehart & Co., 1951).

3. Lance Banning, *The Jeffersonian Persuasion: Evolution of a Party Ideology* (Ithaca, N.Y.: Cornell University Press, 1978), 295–96, 301–2. See also Roger H. Brown, *The Republic in Peril: 1812* (New York: W. W. Norton & Co., 1964) and Richard Buel, Jr., *Securing the Revolution: Ideology in American Politics, 1789–1815* (Ithaca, N.Y.: Cornell University Press, 1972).

4. See Gordon Wood, "The End of the American Enlightenment," in Bernard Bailyn et al., *The Great Republic: A History of the American People* (Lexington, Mass.: D.C. Heath & Co., 1977), esp. 389–419, and Drew R. McCoy, *The Elusive Republic: Political Economy in Jeffersonian America* (Chapel Hill: University of North Carolina Press, 1979), 235–48, for essays that start to go beyond these difficulties.

5. See Stagg, *Madison's War*, chaps. 6–10, for a thorough analysis of Republican wartime financial maneuvering, and Donald R. Hickey, "The Federalists and the War of 1812" (Ph.D. diss., University of Illinois, 1972), 162–96, for a survey of these matters from the Federalist perspective. Also useful is William R. Barlow, "Congress During the War of 1812" (Ph.D. diss., Ohio State University, 1961), 135–85.

6. Monroe to Thomas Jefferson, December 21, 1814, in Stanislaus M. Hamilton, ed., *The Writings of James Monroe* (New York: G. P. Putnam's Sons, 1903), 5:305; remarks of Ingersoll, June 29, 1813, *Annals of the Congress of the United States* (Washington, D.C., 1853), 26:352; "Treasury Report" from Treasury Secretary Alexander J. Dallas, printed in *Niles' Weekly Register*, October 27, 1814.

7. Gaillard Hunt, ed., *The Writings of James Madison* (New York: G. P. Putnam's Sons, 1900–1910), 8:205–8, 261–65. See Stagg, *Madison's War*, chaps. 3–5; Hickey, "Federalists and the War," 126–61; Barlow, "Congress During the War," 95–134, 186–243.

8. Madison's "Fourth Annual Message," November 4, 1812, in Hunt, *Writings of Madison*, 8:228; Stagg, *Madison's War*, chaps. 6 and 10; Hickey, "Federalists and the War," 126–53.

9. See Hickey, "Federalists and the War," 163, 282–87, 302–22 and Stagg, *Madison's War*, chap. 11. On the political revolt in New England, see James Banner, *To the Hartford Convention: The Federalists and the Origins of Party Politics in Massachusetts, 1789–1815* (New York: Alfred A. Knopf, 1970), and Samuel Eliot Morison, *The Life and Letters of Harrison Gray Otis, Federalist, 1765–1848* (Boston: Houghton Mifflin Co., 1913).

10. Remarks of Grundy, June 18, 1813, in *Annals*, 26:225–26; Hickey, "Federalists and the War," 321; Madison to Wilson Cary Nichols, November 26, 1814, in Hunt, *Writings of Madison*, 8:319.

11. Gallatin to LaFayette, April 21, 1814, in Henry Adams, ed., *The Writings of Albert Gallatin* (Philadelphia, 1879), 2:605–6; Thomas Cooper to Thomas Jefferson, August 17, 1814, Thomas Jefferson Papers, Library of Congress (microfilm).

12. "Editorial Address," *Niles' Weekly Register*, September 10, 1814.

13. See "Proclamation" by the governor of Vermont, ibid., October 15, 1814; Governor William Pennington's Address to the New Jersey Legislature, ibid., November 19, 1814; Hickey, "Federalists and the War," 136–37; Barlow, "Congress During the War," 188; Edmund Quincy, *The Life of Josiah Quincy* (Boston, 1867), 358.

14. "Retrospect and Remarks," *Niles' Weekly Register*, March 4, 1815; extracts from the *Richmond Enquirer*, *New York National Advocate*, and *Albany Argus*, quoted in John William Ward, *Andrew Jackson: Symbol for an Age* (New York: Oxford University Press, 1975 [1955]), 106–7.

15. "Vice-President's Speech to the Senate," *Niles' Weekly Register*, May 29, 1813.

16. James Monroe, "To the Military Committee of the Senate," February 22, 1815, in Hamilton, *Writings of Monroe*, 5:321–22; Jonathan Roberts to Mathew Roberts, February 7, 1815, quoted in Brown, *Republic in Peril*, 190–91.

17. James F. Hopkins, ed., *Papers of Henry Clay* (Lexington, Ky.: University of Kentucky Press, 1959) 1:754–73, and 2:63, 70, 149.

18. John Stevens, *The Duty of Union in a Just War* . . . (Boston, 1813), 3; Congressman George Troup's speech, printed in the *National Intelligencer*, February 17, 1815; *Rutland* (Vt.) *Herald*, August 23, 1815, and

Hector Benevolus, *The Hartford Convention in an Uproar*, quoted in William Gribbin, *The Churches Militant: The War of 1812 and American Religion* (New Haven: Yale University Press, 1973), 133–34.

19. Daniel Merrill, *Balaam Disappointed: A Thanksgiving Sermon . . . April 13, 1815* . . . (Danville, Vt., 1815), 7, 10–12, 18, 28. For a brief biographical discussion, see Gribbin, *Churches Militant*, 87.

20. "Religious State Paper," *Niles' Weekly Register*, April 23, 1814.

21. Joshua Hartt, *A Sermon, Prepared for the General Fast . . . January 12, 1815* (Brooklyn, N.Y., 1815), 5, 6, 27–29, 10–11, 30, 26.

22. Alexander McLeod, *A Scriptural View of the Character, Causes, and Ends of the Present War* (New York, 1815). For the description of McLeod, see Gribbin, *Churches Militant*, 111–12.

23. Information on McLeod's life can be found in Dumas Malone, ed., *Dictionary of American Biography* (New York: Charles Scribner's Sons, 1933), 12:131–32, and William B. Sprague, ed., *Annals of the American Pulpit* (1857–69; reprint, New York: Arno Press, 1969), 9:9–25.

24. Recollection of the Rev. Gilber McMaster, a close friend of McLeod, in Sprague, *Annals*, 9:17; McLeod, *Scriptural View*, 13, 42, vii, 47, 36.

25. McLeod, *Scriptural View*, 105–6, 150–51, 103, 105–20, 127, 146–47, 118, 51.

26. Ibid., 60, 96, 95–96.

27. Ibid., 61, 213–14, 162, 220.

28. Ibid., 211–14, 220–21, 214, 209.

29. Ibid., vi–vii.

30. Ibid., 196, 175–76; *Niles' Weekly Register*, December 2, 1815.

31. Mathew Carey, *The Olive Branch: or, Faults on Both Sides* . . . (Philadelphia, 1815), 464–65; the Michigan government's "Reports on Canals," *Niles' Weekly Register*, April 30, 1814; John C. Calhoun's "Speech on the Results of the War," February 27, 1815, and his "Remarks on the Form of Subscription to the Bank," November 21, 1814, both in Robert L. Meriwether, ed., *The Papers of John C. Calhoun* (Columbia, S.C., 1959), 1:280, 269–70.

32. Quoted in Barlow, "Congress During the War," 124. See discussion of this bill in Hickey, "Federalists and the War," 128–31, 140–41.

33. Carey, *Olive Branch*, 64, 391, 443–44; Calhoun, "Speech on the Loan Bill," February 25, 1814, in Meriwether, *Papers of Calhoun*, 1:219, 227; James Madison's "Fifth Annual Message," December 7, 1813, in Hunt, *Writings of Madison*, 8:274.

34. Lyman Beecher, *Sermon Delivered in Hartford*, 19; Lyman Beecher, *An Address of the Charitable Society for the Education of Indigent Young Men* (New Haven, 1814), 19–20; William Ellery Channing, *A Sermon, Preached in Boston, July 23, 1812* . . . (Boston, 1812), 11–12; idem, *A Sermon, Preached in Boston, August 20, 1812* . . . (Boston, 1812), 4–5, 13.

35. "Retrospect and Remarks," *Niles' Weekly Register*, March 4, 1815.

36. Ibid., June 23, 1814; Editorial, September 10, 1814, ibid.; "At-

tachments and Antipathies," June 19, 1813, ibid.; "Monopoly," January 8, 1814, ibid.

37. "To Independence," November 20, 1813, ibid.; "The Prospect Before Us," September 2, 1815, ibid.; "Reasons Against the War," October 30, 1813, ibid.; "This Leads to Independence," July 3, 1813, ibid.

38. "The Prospect Before Us," September 2, 1814, ibid.; "To Mr. Cobbett," December 2, 1815, ibid.

39. See Jackson's comments in John Spencer Bassett, ed., *Correspondence of Andrew Jackson* (Washington, D.C.: Carnegie Institution of Washington, 1926–33), 1:254–55, 251, 209–10, 241–42.

40. Ibid., 1:410, 2:64, 130.

41. Ibid., 1:486–88, 2:135–36, 229, 188.

42. Ibid., 2:440–42, 220–21.

43. Samuel P. Waldo, *Memoirs of Andrew Jackson* . . . (Hartford, Conn., 1820), 12, 17, 334, 335.

44. See John Henry Hobart, *The Security of a Nation: A Sermon . . . April 13, 1815* (New York, 1815). On Hobart, see Gribbin, *Churches Militant*, 116–17.

45. Hobart, *Security of a Nation*, 6–8.

46. Ibid., 10–11, 8–9, 9–10.

47. Ibid., 11, 12, 18, 20–21.

48. Elijah Robinson Sabin, *A Discourse, Chiefly on Political Unity; or, An Easy Scheme of Reconciliation for Honest Americans* . . . (Castine, Me., 1812); "Address of the U.S. Senate to the People of Massachusetts," printed in the *Western Intelligencer* (Worthington, Ohio), July 31, 1812.

49. Extract from the *Vermont Washingtonian*, printed in the *New York Commercial Advertiser*, July 2, 1812; Edward L. Morse, "Letters of Samuel Morse, 1812," *North American Review* 195 and 196 (1912).

50. "Protest" from the Massachusetts House minority, in *Niles' Weekly Register*, November 12, 1814; "New England Convention," November 26, 1814, and January 21 and 28, 1815, ibid.; reply of the Senate of Pennsylvania, ibid., April 1, 1815.

51. "Hints to Patriots," ibid., July 9, 1814; "Domestic Manufactures," October 2, 1813, ibid.; "War Prospects," ibid., October 23, 1813.

52. Harrison Gray Otis' public letter to his constituents, originally published in the *Boston Columbia Centinel*, December 26, 1818, has been quoted in Morison, *Life of Otis*, 2:202.

53. Monroe to Andrew Jackson, December 14, 1816, in Hamilton, *Writings of Monroe*, 5:343–49.

54. Mathew Carey, *The Olive Branch* . . . , 7th ed. (Philadelphia, 1815). For information on Carey, see Kenneth W. Rose, *Mathew Carey: A Study in American Economic Development* (Baltimore: Johns Hopkins University Press, 1933); and Edward C. Carter, "Mathew Carey and 'The Olive Branch,' 1814–1818," *Pennsylvania Magazine of History and Biography* 84 (1965): 399–415.

55. Carey, *The Olive Branch*. 244, 22–23, 48, 11–12, 9.

56. Ibid., 51–52, 85, 62–64, 68–72, 73.

57. Ibid., 86–90, 328–29, 243, 315–18, 301, 308, 245, 250.

58. Ibid., 351, 22, 444, 275–83, 295, 377, 362.

59. Ibid., 11–12, 342, 437–38, 467–75, 477.

60. Speech of Mr. Bacon, February 25, 1812, *Annals*, 23:1096, 1097, 1102.

61. Remarks of Mr. Grundy, April 2, 1814, ibid., 27:1944. For a detailed discussion of the Republican drift toward higher taxes and a Second Bank, see Stagg, *Madison's War*, 314–16, 438–53.

62. See Ingersoll's speech on December 9, 1814, *Annals*, 28:810, 819, 814.

63. Ingersoll's speech of November 17, 1814, ibid., 612, 604, 609, 608.

64. Ingersoll's speech of June 29, 1813, ibid., 26:355, 370, 357–58, 352.

65. See Ingersoll's speeches of February 16, 1815 and February 14–15, 1814, ibid., 28:1159–61, 27:1431.

66. See Chapter V.

67. Carey, *The Olive Branch*, 362; "Resources and Improvements," *Niles' Weekly Register*, May 28, 1814; "Attachments and Antipathies," ibid., June 19, 1813.

68. Tench Coxe, *A Statement of the Arts and Manufactures of the United States of America for the Year 1810* (Philadelphia, 1814), lvi, xxiv, xxiii, liv, lv.

69. "Governor's Message to the Legislature of Pennsylvania," *Niles' Weekly Register*, December 18, 1813; "Law of Pennsylvania," ibid., April 3, 1813; "Resolutions of the Pennsylvania Legislature," ibid., February 5, 1814.

70. Carey, *The Olive Branch*, 444; "Attachments and Antipathies," *Niles' Weekly Register*, June 19, 1813; Tench Coxe, *Statement of Arts and Manufactures*, xxi.

71. See Hunt, *Writings of Madison*, 8:273–74, 311, 324, 325, 339, 341–42, 344.

72. In studying Raymond, I have used the second edition of his book. See Daniel Raymond, *The Elements of Political Economy, in Two Parts* (1823; reprint, New York: A. M. Kelley, 1964). For additional information on Raymond, see Joseph Dorfman, *The Economic Mind in American Civilization* (New York: Viking Press, 1949–59), 2:566–74.

73. Raymond, *Elements of Political Economy*, 2:91–95.

74. Calhoun to Dr. James Macbride, February 2, 1813, and June 23, 1813, in Meriwether, *Papers of Calhoun*, 1:162, 177–78.

75. Calhoun's speech of February 25, 1814, ibid., 1:237.

76. Calhoun's speeches of January 14, 1813, and February 25, 1814, in ibid., 1:237, 238, 236, 161, 234, 238.

77. Ibid., 155, 227, 219, 232.

78. Ibid., 227, 160.

79. Calhoun's speeches of January 2 and January 31, 1816, in ibid., 288, 329.

80. See Calhoun's speeches of January 2, 20, and 31, 1816, and February 4, 1817, in ibid., 314–15, 324–25, 287, 398–99, 406–7.

81. Ibid., 330.

82. Ibid., 225, 401.

83. Charles J. Ingersoll, *Historical Sketch of the Second War Between the United States and Great Britain* (Philadelphia, 1845), 1:14, 15.

84. Monroe's instructions are printed in *Niles' Weekly Register*, October 22, 1814; "Address to the President" by "republican citizens of Baltimore," ibid., April 10, 1815.

85. Adams, *Writings of Gallatin* (Philadelphia, 1879), 700–701; Andrew A. Lipscomb and Albert E. Bergh, eds., *The Writings of Thomas Jefferson* (Washington, D.C.: Thomas Jefferson Memorial Assoc., 1905), 15:114–18, and 14:387–93.

86. See Charles Francis Adams, ed., *Memoirs of John Quincy Adams* (Philadelphia, 1874–77), 3:114; Worthington Chauncey Ford, ed., *The Writings of John Quincy Adams* (New York: Macmillan Co., 1913–17), 5:256, 314; Adams, *Memoirs*, 3:28.

87. Hunt, *Writings of Madison*, 8:385, 392–93; Saul K. Padover, *The Complete Madison* (New York, 1953), 272–73.

88. Hunt, *Writings of Madison*, 8:171–81, and 9:15–20; Marvin Meyers, ed., *The Mind of the Founder: Sources of the Political Thought of James Madison* (Indianapolis: Bobbs-Merrill, 1973), 504–5.

89. The development of liberal society in antebellum America—especially in terms of its internally fragmenting tendencies that eventually culminated in the Civil War—is the subject of a forthcoming book-length study by the present author, entitled *Desolations of Solitude: The Consolidation and Crisis of Liberal America, 1820–1861* (forthcoming, Johns Hopkins University Press).

Index